PENGUIN

ROUNDHEAD

Blair Worden is Professor of Early Modern History at the University of Sussex and is Emeritus Fellow of St Edmund Hall, Oxford. His publications include *The Rump Parliament 1648–1653* and *The Sound of Virtue: Philip Sidney's 'Arcadia' and Elizabethan Politics*.

He has been Literary Director of the Royal Historical Society and is currently British Academy Research Professor.

BLAIR WORDEN

Roundhead Reputations

THE ENGLISH CIVIL WARS AND THE PASSIONS OF POSTERITY

PENGUIN BOOKS

PENGUIN BOOKS

Published by the Penguin Group
Penguin Books Ltd, 80 Strand, London WC2R 0RL, England
Penguin Putnam Inc., 375 Hudson Street, New York, New York 10014, USA
Penguin Books Australia Ltd, 250 Camberwell Road, Camberwell, Victoria 3124, Australia
Penguin Books Canada Ltd, 10 Alcorn Avenue, Toronto, Ontario, Canada M4V 3B2
Penguin Books India (P) Ltd, 11, Community Centre, Panchsheel Park, New Delhi – 110 017, India
Penguin Books (NZ) Ltd, Cnr Rosedale and Airborne Roads, Albany, Auckland, New Zealand
Penguin Books (South Africa) (Pty) Ltd, 24 Sturdee Avenue, Rosebank 2196, South Africa

Penguin Books Ltd, Registered Offices: 80 Strand, London WC2R 0RL, England

www.penguin.com

First published by Allen Lane The Penguin Press 2001
Published in Penguin Books 2002
1

Printed in England by Clays Ltd, St Ives plc

For Jenny, Gina and Natalie Skilbeck

Contents

	List of Illustrations	ix
	Preface	xi
	Prologue	1
1	Edmund Ludlow: the Civil Wars and After	21
2	Ludlow the Puritan	39
3	Ludlow the Whig	65
4	Ludlow's Editor	86
5	Algernon Sidney the Republican	122
6	Sidney the Whig	147
7	The Patriots	181
8	Oliver Cromwell: from Villain to Hero	215
9	Victorian Cromwell	243
10	Carlyle's Cromwell	264
11	The Cromwell Statue	296
12	The Levellers and the Left	316
	Epilogue	339
	Bibliographical Survey	345
	General Index	361
	Index of Modern Historians and Editors	385

List of Illustrations

Illustrations listed by page number
(Photographic Acknowledgements in parentheses)

22. Edmund Ludlow. Engraving (1689) by R. White from the *Memoirs of Edmund Ludlow*, 1698

40. Title-page of volume 1, *Memoirs of Edmund Ludlow*

72. Preface to volume 3, *Memoirs of Edmund Ludlow*, 1699

120. Ludlow's note of 1674, from 'A Voyce from the Watch Tower' (photo © Bodleian Library, Oxford)

123. Algernon Sidney, portrait after Justus van Egmont. (Reproduced by kind permission of Viscount De L'Isle, from his private collection at Penshurst Place)

160. Algernon Sidney. Engraving from his *Discourses*, 1763 edition

171. *Top:* The Temple of British Worthies at Stowe (photo: National Trust Photographic Library/Andrew Butler). *Bottom:* Busts of John Milton, John Hampden and Alexander Pope (photo: National Trust/Thames & Chiltern Regional Office)

186. Robert Blake. Engraving from Frederic Hervey, *The Naval History of Great Britain*, 1779

199. Sir Henry Vane. Engraving from George Sykes, *The Life and Death of Sir Henry Vane, Kt.*, 1662

239. Cromwell visits Milton. Illustration by Daniel Neal in *The Graphic*, 21 November 1885 (photo: Illustrated London News Picture Library)

245. Benjamin West, *Oliver Cromwell Dissolving the Long Parliament*, 1783, oil on canvas. (Museum purchase; Members Acquisition Fund, 1960.5. The Montclair Art Museum, Montclair, New Jersey)

255. Augustus Leopold Egg, *The Night before Naseby*, 1859, oil on canvas (© Royal Academy of Arts, London)

265. Thomas Carlyle. Photograph by Julia Margaret Cameron (National Museum of Film & Photography, Bradford/Heritage Images)

297. Statue of Cromwell by Hamo Thornycroft, 1899, the Palace of Westminster. (Reproduced by permission of the Palace of Westminster)

300. *Top:* Charles West Cope, *Charles I erecting his Standard at Nottingham in 1642*, 1861, waterglass, Peers' Corridor, House of Lords. *Bottom:* Charles West Cope, *The Setting Out of the Train Bands from London in 1643*, 1865, waterglass, Peers' Corridor, House of Lords. (Both reproduced by permission of the Palace of Westminster)

303. John Bell, *Lucius Cary, 2nd Viscount Falkland*, commissioned 1845, marble, St Stephen's Hall, House of Commons. (Reproduced by permission of the Palace of Westminster)

305. The unveiling of the statue at St Ives (Cromwell Museum, Huntingdon)

307. Stained glass window, 1908, showing Cromwell, Vane and Hampden, Mansfield College, Oxford. (Reproduced by permission of Mansfield College, Oxford)

341. Samuel R. Gardiner (College Archives, King's College London)

Preface

I hope to interest readers of two kinds, which perhaps will overlap. First there are those who care to know about the civil wars of the mid-seventeenth century and about their place in English memory and culture. Secondly there are those who are drawn to the history of historical thinking and ask how successive generations come to form their perspectives on the past.

Some preliminary remarks about the scope, vocabulary and conventions of the book may aid the cause of clarity. I am concerned mostly with opinions expressed in England, only occasionally with views voiced in Scotland or Ireland or elsewhere in the world. Outside England, interpretations of the country's mid-seventeenth-century conflict have largely distinctive traditions and are subjects in themselves. By the term 'the civil wars' I mean the period of upheaval from the meeting of the Long Parliament in 1640, which heralded the collapse of King Charles I's regime, to the Restoration of the monarchy in 1660: 'the civil war' means the military conflict between Crown and parliament of 1642–6. The reader wishing to be informed or reminded of the general course of events in the civil wars will find assistance in Chapter 1. 'The later Stuarts' refers to Charles II and James II (and not to James's daughters Mary and Anne). 'The Revolution' refers to the replacement of James II by William III and Mary in 1688–9 and the constitutional changes that accompanied it. In a study which has so much to say about the anachronisms of others, I should acknowledge the anachronistic character of my own uses, for purposes of shorthand, of the word 'radical', whose meanings, while varying according to their contexts, will I hope be broadly evident within them. Also for shorthand I use two terms which originated as, and long remained, pejorative epithets, but which time has neutralized: 'the regicide', which means the execution of Charles I in 1649, and 'the regicides', which means the judges who condemned him. 'Historiography', a word which has sustained more than one definition over time, here means the history of historical writing and thinking. Except on a handful of occasions, which will announce themselves, I modernize spelling and punctuation in quotations.

Although most of the book rests on original research, substantial debts to the publications of others lie behind my text. The direct ones are indicated in the Bibliographical Survey, where I also acknowledge the permission of publishers to reproduce material from specialized publications of mine. There too I point the specialist towards the sources on which my arguments draw. I was greatly helped by the characteristic generosity of the late Colin Matthew, who lent me his copy of the 'Nineteenth-Century Cromwell' archive together with invaluable notes for his own contribution to it. For assistance on particular points I am indebted to the kindness of Jeremy Cater, Justin Champion, Stephen Daniel, John Goldsmith, Frances Henderson, Elaine Kaye, Paulina Kewes, Mark Knights, Anne McGowan, Stephen Porter, Roland Quinault, Isabel Rivers, Ian Roy, Paul Seaward, Nicholas Tyacke, John Walsh and Abigail Williams; to Claudia Engler of the Stadt- und Universitäts Bibliothek, Bern; and to the Keeper of Rare Books in the Bodleian Library, Clive Hurst. I have drawn heavily on the time and attentiveness of three friends who read a draft of the book, Nicholas von Maltzahn, Susan Wormell and Brian Young. I am most grateful to them, and to Simon Winder of Penguin UK, for their criticisms and suggestions, and no less for their encouragement. Publishing with Penguin has been a pleasure.

Prologue

The civil wars have been, from that time to this, the most controversial episode in English history. They broke its rules. A country which has been uniquely characterized by institutional continuity and constitutional evolution experienced a sudden break from them. In 1649 Charles I, the defeated king, was tried for treason and executed; monarchy and the House of Lords were abolished; England was declared a 'Commonwealth and Free State'. The Church of England succumbed to the conflict too. Bishops and the Prayer Book were removed, to be replaced by a diversity of religious belief and practice perhaps never matched before or since.

The wars, which tore the nation apart, have been fought again in the heart of posterity. The clash of Cavalier and Roundhead has never gone away. For some the wars have been what they were for the historian the Earl of Clarendon, adviser to Charles I and to his son and heir Charles II: a 'rebellion', a wilful and sinful assault on institutions of which the worst that could fairly be said was that they had been temporarily mismanaged. To others the conflict has mattered because tyranny and persecution were challenged and the way pointed for later struggles for liberty. The enduring conflict between royalist and parliamentarian perspectives is not our principal concern. The hostilities we shall trace are of subtler and to my mind greater interest. They lie mainly within the parliamentarian or Roundhead tradition. During the wars, supporters of the parliamentarian cause often contended as intently or angrily against each other as against their common enemy. So have they ever since. Even so the enduring contest between Roundhead and Cavalier interpretations is the essential background to our story, and we must first meet it.

The experiences and images on which it has thrived derive from the wars themselves. The notion that king and parliament (of which the monarch was, with the Lords and Commons, one of the three estates) could be opposed to each other, let alone go to war with each other, shocked contemporary sensibilities, though that was but the first of the surprises brought by the wars to a nation that had taken the forms and the unitive capacity of its ancient constitution for granted. Labels of allegiance – 'royalist', 'parliamentarian', 'Cavalier', 'Roundhead' – were pejorative, cast on men who were accused of wantonly splitting the nation. In December 1641, when the parties that would go to war eight months later were beginning to emerge, sympathizers with the king's cause gave the term 'Roundheads' to groups of London apprentices who were demonstrating on the parliamentary side. The epithet played derisively on the regulation which obliged apprentices to keep their hair cropped. In retaliation those of the king's supporters who, around the same time, tried to raise armed forces for him were called *Caballeros*, after the Spanish troopers whose cruelty had been visited on the Protestant Netherlands in the later sixteenth century. *Caballeros* soon became 'Cavaliers'.

By the summer of 1642 'Roundheads' was being applied to the supporters of the parliamentarian cause as a whole. In the civil war severe penalties awaited those parliamentary soldiers who, less earnest in their cause than their fellows, teasingly called them Roundheads. Meanwhile parliamentarians assailed 'that bloody and butcherly generation', 'that heap of scum and dross and garbage of the land', 'known by the name of Cavaliers'. 'Cavalier' gave less pain than 'Roundhead', for it could be suggestive of gentility and honour and horsemanship. Charles I encouraged his followers to adopt the term, and after the battle of Marston Moor in 1644 a supporter of parliament acknowledged the 'brave chivalry' of the royalist left wing, which 'gave such a Cavalier-like assault'. Yet the word, no less than 'Roundhead', belonged to the process by which the opposing sides learned to caricature one another. Posterity has sometimes been deceived by the caricatures. The notions, promoted in Victorian paintings, that the two parties were distinguished by the length of their hair, and that the royalists dressed more colourfully or elegantly than their rivals, are refuted by descriptions and portraits of the time.

Polarization there none the less was. It could not be escaped, for the whole community was sucked into the war. Informed speculation – it can be no more – has suggested that one in every four or five adult English males was enlisted into an army at some point between 1642 and 1646. Over the course of the wars in England, it is estimated, at least 150 towns suffered serious destruction of property; around 11,000 houses were burnt or demolished and 55,000 people made homeless; nearly four per cent of the population died in fighting or from war-related disease, a much higher figure than that in the First World War. Beside the big battles there were frequent sieges and skirmishes, in which civilians were killed or wounded alongside soldiers. Sieges, which could be terrifying experiences, produced large-scale levelling of property, not only by the assailants but for purposes of defence. Between military engagements the hungry soldiers of roaming armies pillaged and plundered, quartered themselves on hapless households, threatened fire and sword to extract money from civilian communities. Houses and churches were stripped of wood and lead; horses were commandeered, cattle slaughtered; legal processes broke down; trade routes were interrupted, supplies of water and fuel cut off. Victors in battle and occupiers of territory appropriated, sometimes by ruthless means, the property of the vanquished. There were endless opportunities for the settling of old local scores and the creation of new ones. Friends divided against each other, families against themselves.

It was the defeated royalists who suffered most. When they kept their property it was often at the cost of crippling fines set by parliament. Excluded from political life, they despaired at the destruction of their religion. With impotent fury they watched the desecration of churches, the changes made by the Puritans in religious organization and observance, the ejection of loyal clergy from their livings. After the return of the monarchy and Church under Charles II in 1660 the roles were reversed. Now it was Roundheads who lost their power and estates, parliamentarian clergymen who were evicted from livings. If there is a single force which perpetuated the divisions of the civil wars it is the religious settlement of the Restoration, which excluded hard-line Puritans from the Church and made Puritan Nonconformity, or Dissent, into a lasting alternative culture.

In the later seventeenth century the divisions of the civil wars persisted. The polarization of the nation is, perhaps, the largest and longest legacy of the conflict. In 1679–81 it seemed, in the common phrase of the time, that '[sixteen-]forty-one is come again'. Those were the years of the 'exclusion crisis', when, against a background of fierce parliamentary and public agitation, the Crown's critics tried to restrict the royal prerogative and exclude the Catholic James Duke of York, Charles II's brother and heir, from the succession. Men understood the crisis in the light of the previous one. Documents from the civil wars were collected and reprinted, some to illustrate Charles I's case, some that of his opponents. It was now that the terms 'Whig' and 'Tory', which to begin with were likewise pejorative, came into being. 'Whig' succeeded to 'Roundhead', 'Tory' to 'Cavalier'. Whigs inherited the Dissenting allegiance, Tories the Anglican one.

Charles II weathered the storm, but in 1688, after the three-year reign of his brother, the Stuart dynasty was toppled for a second time. In cause and character the revolts of 1642 and 1688 were continuous. Like Charles I, James II tried to impose absolute monarchy. Like him he was accused of 'popery'. Interpretations of the civil wars have, as we shall find, been intimately bound up with assessments of the second upheaval, the 'Glorious Revolution' as it came to be called. In the quarter-century after its occurrence, during what seemed the precarious reigns of James II's successor William III and William's successor Anne, the memory of the Revolution was profoundly divisive. The rage of conflict between Whig and Tory kept the earlier animosities alive. 'This too much divided nation', complained the pamphlet *A New Test of the Church of England's Loyalty* in 1702, 'has always been comprised of two contrary parties . . . distinguished by names of contempt.' Though the labels had 'often changed' – 'Cavaliers and Roundheads, Royalists and Rebels, Malignants and Fanatics, Tories and Whigs' – the substance of conflict, the pamphlet maintained, had been consistent.

The wounds were slow to heal, and many strove to keep them open. The gradual stabilization of the post-Revolutionary order after the accession of the Hanoverian dynasty in 1714 did not diminish the partisanship of historical writing on the civil wars. Most eighteenth-century narratives of the conflict were factual bombardments in a party cause. In 1726 the prominent Whig historian John Oldmixon complained that Laurence Echard, his still more prominent Tory adversary, had summoned 'two armies of epithets', which represented the royalists as

> gallant, courageous, famous, punctual, modest, brave, honest, valiant, fearless, intrepid, wise, industrious, active, rich, invincible, undaunted, witty, judicious, polite, learned, sober, pious, devout, faultless, excellent, virtuous, inviolable, reputable, studious, opulent, . . . incomparable, . . . sweet-tempered, lovely etc.

and the parliamentarians as

> infamous, villainous, hypocritical, inveterate, seditious, swinish, furious, inconsiderable, unreasonable, cowardly, . . . insolent, . . . mad, raving, . . . ill-dressed, wretched, heretical, unjust, irregular, obscene, proud, subtle, blasphemous . . .

In April 1737 the journal *Common Sense* observed that if an aspiring poet were to take the civil wars as his subject he would inevitably make himself 'liable to a capital objection . . . viz. the imputation of writing for a party'. In September 1741 Dr Johnson's friend Richard Savage published in *The Gentleman's Magazine* a satirical poem which placed both Echard and Oldmixon in the lists of 'false historians', and which noticed how, from the 'ashes dead' of 'party libels', 'A monster, misnamed history, lifts its head.'

The divisions of the wars endured outside the history books too. A statute of 1660 stipulated that 30 January, the date of the regicide, and 29 May, that of Charles II's Restoration, be 'grand solemnities' in the liturgical calendar of the Church. The anniversary of the regicide was the more intensively commemorated of the two. Vigilantly observed in the later seventeenth century, it produced a succession of provocative sermons and publications in the eighteenth. Royalist and Tory agitation was the stronger, first under the later Stuarts, when friends of the monarchy held the ascendancy, and then under the Whig supremacy of the earlier Hanoverians, when seventeenth-century memories offered a consolation for defeat. Parliamentary election campaigns of the eighteenth century were punctuated by Tory cries of

'Down with the Rump!', the appellation by which the government that replaced Charles I after his execution in 1649 was known. Roundhead memory survived too. In the 1750s Henry Fielding, a magistrate as well as a novelist, described rival factions among the 'loose and disorderly youth' of London, who were distinguished by their hats: those who wore them 'fiercely cocked' were 'Cavaliers and Tory Rory Ranter Boys'; those who had 'the brim flapping over their eyes' were 'Wags, Round-heads, Shake-boys, Old-Nolls [Oliver Cromwells]'. Six decades later, in 1813, the poet Robert Southey remarked that the passions of the civil wars had 'continued to this day'.

Yet eighteenth-century readers of seventeenth-century history were often less zealous in their allegiances than its writers. In society at large, naked partisanship, though it persisted, lost its dominance. There were a number of reasons for this. Party rivalries became more fluid and complex, the Tory–Whig divide less clear-cut; the enmity of Anglican and Nonconformist was to an extent defused; the prospect that the exiled Stuarts might regain the throne receded, and with it the inflammatory theory of royal absolutism; the clash of Cavalier and Roundhead now belonged to a more distant past and so could be viewed with a measure of detachment. It became easier to be interested in the civil wars, or to be drawn into the drama of them or seek lessons from them, without taking either the royalist or the parliamentary side, or at least without finding merit on only one side. In 1764 Horace Walpole explained that when he thought about the wars he felt no instinctive preference for either Charles I or Oliver Cromwell. 'If I sometimes commend, sometimes blame them, it is not from being inconsistent, but from considering them' from varying perspectives. We shall see how events and individuals of the civil wars could look, to a single viewer, hideous from one angle, praiseworthy from another.

So partisanship had lost its early ferocity. It has never quite regained it. Yet ardour persisted. In the nineteenth century it received a series of fresh stimuli. In the first place the Romantic and post-Romantic eras brought a new energy to the imaginative recovery of the past. Secondly there were the battles over parliamentary and social reform. Whigs, and their successors the Liberals, saw the Roundheads as the forerunners of their own progressive cause, while Tories identified with the royalists' aversion to innovation and disorder. Class conflict intensified the debate. On one side the Roundheads (or some of them) were viewed as friends of the oppressed, the Cavaliers as their enemies: on the other, royalists were admired for embodying the aristocratic and chivalric values that were succumbing to the social dislocation and coarse materialism of the present. Finally the nineteenth-century religious revival, which revitalized both Anglicanism and Nonconformity, gave a new relevance to the quarrel between the high churchmanship of Charles I's Archbishop of Canterbury, William Laud, and the Puritans, whom he had assailed and whose heirs the Nonconformists were proud to be.

'We are Cavaliers or Roundheads,' declared the historian W. E. H. Lecky in 1892, 'before we are Conservatives or Liberals.' 'I judge a man by one thing,' Isaac Foot, the Liberal and Nonconformist politician of the earlier twentieth century, used to say: 'Which side would he have liked his ancestors to fight on at Marston Moor?' If Liberalism and Nonconformity, those invigorating forces of nineteenth-century Roundhead allegiance, were in decline by Foot's time, the conflicts of class which also inspired it were more enduring. The self-conscious division of the modern nation into 'them' and 'us' has drawn, however distantly, on civil-war memories and civil-war stereotypes. That delicate barometer of English social attitudes, the game of cricket, testifies to their perseverance. They can be glimpsed in the categorization, which lasted into the second half of the twentieth century, of amateur players as 'gentlemen' and professionals as 'players'. When, towards that century's end, reporters portrayed the rivals for the England captaincy, the dashing David Gower and the pertinacious Graham Gooch, as the Cavalier and the Roundhead, their readers knew what they meant.

Down the centuries Roundhead sympathizers – Whigs, Nonconformists, Liberals, socialists – have united against their Cavalier opponents but have divided against themselves. Historians, looking for a term to cover what they take to have been the parliamentarian orthodoxy in ages before their own, now write breezily about 'the Whig interpretation of history', as if it has been static and uniform. In reality it has been fluctuating and fractious. We can simplify, but not distort, by saying that over the course of the existence of the Whig party, from the later Stuart period to the earlier Victorian one, there were essentially two Whig approaches to seventeenth-century history, one moderate, the other radical. As a rule the first was favoured by the party's leadership, the second by critics of it. Of the two mid-seventeenth-century upheavals, moderates preferred the Revolution of 1688, radicals the civil wars. Moderate Whigs thought of the Revolution as the foundation of civil and religious liberty. The Roundhead cause, they knew, had produced bloodshed, destruction, political and religious anarchy. It had destroyed the ancient English constitution. The swift and successful Revolution of 1688, by contrast, had preserved it. The Stuarts' endeavour to subvert the constitution, and to impose absolutism and non-parliamentary rule in its place, had survived the first upheaval but succumbed to the second. So had the alliance between the Crown and popery. Whereas the Roundhead challenge to Stuart religious policy had produced sectarian chaos and extremism and provoked the intolerant Anglican – or, as Whigs said, popish – reaction of the Restoration, the Revolution separated popery from the Crown. It also secured freedom of worship for the Dissenters, even if they remained excluded from public office and the universities.

Until the late eighteenth century, perhaps even for longer, most moderate Whigs were embarrassed by the memory of the civil wars. Before 1688, when the Whig party was one of opposition, royalists and Tories derided the Roundhead cause and crowed over its defeat. The Revolution made the Whigs a party of power. They held office, or at least shared it with Tories, for the greater part of the period between William III's accession and the death of Queen Anne in 1714, and then secured a virtual monopoly of it under the first two Georges. The post-Revolutionary Whig leaders wanted to draw a line under the Stuart era. They presented themselves as the friends of the present and Tories as obstinate adherents to bygone principles. They would have liked to convince the nation that 1688 had made the old enmities redundant.

It could not be done. In the historical and antiquarian writing of the post-Revolutionary era a powerful anti-Whig tradition lived on. Jacobites (the supporters of the exiled Stuart family) and Tories (whose acceptance of the Revolution was at best qualified and tenuous) dwelt insistently on the evils of the civil wars. The regicide, Tories maintained, showed where Whig principles – the accountability of monarchs, government by consent, liberty of conscience – inevitably led, and where, if those principles prevailed, they could be expected to lead now. Charles I had been executed in the name of the people's representatives in parliament. Yet it was armed force, not the nation's consent, which achieved that coup and which sustained the long period of republican rule from 1649 to 1660. By what criteria could the governments of those years – the Commonwealth from 1649 to 1653, the Cromwellian protectorate of 1653–9, the restored Commonwealth of 1659–60 – be deemed less tyrannical than that of Charles I?

The case had to be answered. In the earlier eighteenth century the moderate Whig view of the civil wars was spelt out, with varying emphases, in histories by Gilbert Burnet, White Kennett, Paul de Rapin Thoyras, John Oldmixon, Daniel Neal. All those works insisted on the Whigs' commitment to constitutional rule. All of them renounced the regicide and the republican regime that had followed it. Only with respect to its early phase was the Roundhead cause represented in moderate Whig writing in favourable terms, and even on that subject a minority was guardedly neutral. Most moderate Whigs were ready to suggest that the Long Parliament, which met in November 1640, had been right, in the first year of its life, to dismantle the apparatus of tyranny. Even though there might have been failings both of policy and of motive, they reasoned, it had been necessary to abolish the prerogative courts of Star Chamber and High Commission which Charles I had made instruments of despotism and to legislate for the regular summoning of parliaments. A smaller majority was prepared to indicate that the parliamentarians had been justified in taking up arms in 1642: that if MPs had been driven, in self-defence and in the face of an extreme peril to liberty, to use unconstitutional means, it had been to a constitutional end. What happened after the king's defeat, explained the moderates, was not an enactment of Whig principles but a perversion of them. Yet it was hard to identify a point at which the Roundhead momentum, once started, might have been stopped. The Tories clung to their claim: at heart, they alleged, the Whigs were friends to regicide and republicanism.

Some of them were. The moderate Whig interpretation of the civil wars was a repudiation not only of the Tory case but, more discreetly yet no less firmly, of a radical Whig one. A principal subject of this book is the conduct, and its impact on posterity, of a dissident Whig minority in the reign of William III, which rejoiced to remember the overthrow of Charles I. For those men 1688, and the settlement of 1689 which confirmed and defined the Revolution, were but half a victory. About the evils of the regime which the Revolution dethroned, radicals and moderates could agree. It was common ground of Whig history, from the seventeenth century to the nineteenth, that the post-Restoration period had been one of harsh and degenerate reaction against the forces of civil and religious liberty. The evils of Charles II and James II were a less contentious subject than those of their father. But if Whigs were at one in reviling later Stuart rule, they were at odds over the regime that had replaced it. In the radicals' eyes the Revolution had gone not nearly far enough. James II might have been deposed, popery thwarted, but the prerogatives of the Crown remained largely intact. The blame was laid on the Whig leaders, who during and after the Revolution, it was alleged, had sold principles for power. The radicals themselves had been sidelined in and from 1688–9. They thought of themselves as 'old Whigs' or 'true Whigs' or 'real Whigs', whose cause had been betrayed by the new, untrue, unreal ones. To identify the cause's principles they looked, not to 1688, but to 1649. It was not the resort to armed force in order to bring Charles I to justice that pleased them. Like all Whigs they believed in government by consent, a principle they accused the leadership of betraying. But they did rejoice in the knowledge that the tyrant Charles had been brought to justice, and they did admire the achievements of the Commonwealth which ruled in his place.

For essentially the radical cause was a republican cause. Republicanism was the voice of a small minority. The leaders and most supporters of the Revolution of 1688, Whig as well as Tory, were as firmly opposed to it as to absolutism. There is a certain simplification in using the term 'republican', for the radicals would often have settled for the strict limitation of kingship rather than its abolition. A republic, or at least something close to one, was none the less their ideal. The recovery of the neglected tradition of republicanism in English historical writing will be one aim of this book.

*

It was the radical Whigs who produced the first of the three decisive moments on which the book turns. In 1698–1700 they published what would be described in the eighteenth century, and become known in the twentieth, as a 'canon' of historical literature. All subsequent interpretation of the civil wars has been directly or indirectly influenced by it. By skilful editing and marketing, the radical Whigs made the lives and prose of four republicans of the civil wars, Algernon Sidney, the poet John Milton, James Harrington and Henry Neville, a central element of the seventeenth century's political legacy. Enterprising as that achievement was, their main triumph was still more so. In 1698–9 they published a work that has always been one of the main sources for the civil wars: the *Memoirs* of Edmund Ludlow, a parliamentary commander and MP who had been one of the signatories of Charles I's death-warrant.

Ludlow's *Memoirs* were a forgery; or rather a semi-forgery, for they were based on a text by Ludlow, which was fundamentally rewritten to serve the political aims of the radical Whigs. The rewriting was an achievement of genius. The pretence of authenticity survived from the late seventeenth century to the late twentieth, when the discovery of a part of Ludlow's own text exposed it. Both in its brilliance and in its endurance the fabrication of the *Memoirs* is a feat without parallel in English historical literature. There have been other civil-war fabrications, most famously the letters relating to Oliver Cromwell which took in Thomas Carlyle in the 1840s, but they were altogether less ambitious and enduring. From one generation to the next, historians happily quoted Ludlow's *Memoirs* and endorsed their authority. When one of the greatest of the historians of the civil wars, C. H. Firth, edited them in 1894 he pronounced them genuine. In the twentieth century the authenticity of the text was unquestioningly accepted by large numbers of university teachers and students in courses in which the *Memoirs* were a principal text for analysis.

The identification of the perpetrators of the deception will need detective work, which will take us into the undergrowth of late seventeenth-century publishing and polemic. We shall also seek to establish the publishers' political purpose, for without an understanding of it the inspiration and guiding thread of the *Memoirs* will elude us. The work gave Ludlow, a figure from a past age, characteristics of the present one. A civil-war Puritan was turned into a radical Whig. Thus revised, he became a figure for present emulation. The transformation of the personality we meet in his own manuscript into the ostensible author of the *Memoirs* was profound. For if the political and religious issues of the 1640s remained alive in the 1690s they flourished within an altered mental framework, which his text was adjusted to meet.

Religious mentality had changed above all. Ludlow's Puritanism, which was intense, was at the centre of his life and writing. Had it been revealed by his publishers in the 1690s it would have seemed laughably dated. The England of the scientific revolution and of the incipient Enlightenment had turned its back on its Puritan past. Although Whiggism would remain permanently allied to Dissent, and would stand with it against the political and religious pretensions of the Church of England and against 'popish' tendencies within Anglicanism, the thrust of Whig writing, both moderate and radical, was as antagonistic to the 'fanaticism' of Puritanism as to the 'superstition' of Catholicism and high Anglicanism. The rewriter – or editor, as for convenience I shall call him – of the *Memoirs* virtually eliminated Ludlow's religion. His strategy had enduring consequences for the interpretation of the civil wars. For though the *Memoirs* have been by no means the only autobiographical source for the period, none of the others has offered, to so many generations, so rounded and compelling an image of a Roundhead mind. The editor's treatment of Ludlow's religion was persuasive because it conformed to the perspectives of readers of post-Puritan generations. There have been times when historians have acknowledged the size of the religious dimension of the civil wars, but only rarely have they been at ease with it. Mostly they have either represented it as an extension of the political struggle or been puzzled to know how to connect the two. In Ludlow's mind the two were inseparable. His Puritanism was nowhere more consuming than in his thinking about the climax of the civil wars, the execution of the king. To recover Ludlow's beliefs is to locate at that moment, the most revolutionary of English history, a religious fundamentalism of overwhelming force, about which posterity has preferred not to know. It is also to realize how heavily our understanding of the past is conditioned by the editorial treatment of documents.

From Ludlow we shall turn to his fellow-republican Algernon

Sidney, and to Sidney's posthumous reputation. Little known since the mid-nineteenth century, he was famous and revered in the eighteenth. Like Ludlow he had fought in the Roundhead cause and then joined the government of the Commonwealth. The men who published Ludlow's *Memoirs* also produced, at the same time, Sidney's *Discourses concerning Government*. His character, too, was revised by his publishers. Forgery again played its part, though this time on a smaller scale. The radical Whigs resurrected the republicanism of Ludlow and Sidney in the service of their republican aspirations, which the Revolutionary settlement of 1689 had dashed. But they needed to proceed subtly. They knew that republicanism was too isolated and unpopular a creed to win much support on its own. So in projecting images of Ludlow and Sidney they blended the republicanism of the two men, or diluted it, with safer sentiments, which corresponded more closely to general public anxieties of the 1690s than to the views of the men themselves. Perhaps in the long term that tactic was all too successful, for the republicanism of Ludlow and Sidney, in the minds of their eighteenth-century admirers, was not so much merged with more conventionally approved virtues as subordinated to them.

Sidney in particular met the eighteenth century's need for a certain kind of historical hero. In the seventeenth century the primary target of political dissent had been tyrannical or arbitrary or absolute government. Now it was corruption. The government was still judged all too capable of enslaving its subjects, but the instruments available to it had changed. Fears of non-parliamentary rule, and of illegal taxation or imprisonment, had yielded to anxieties about the regime's capacity, through its expanding resources of patronage and bribery, to weaken the independence of MPs and abate their moral and constitutional vigilance. Like late republican Rome, on whose political literature commentators amply drew, England seemed too sunk in luxury and venality to contend for its liberties. The historiography of England's seventeenth-century troubles adjusted to that new perspective. The evolution of Sidney's reputation is the most telling register of the shift. To the eighteenth century he was a forerunner of those present-day 'patriots' and 'independent country gentlemen' who saw the post-Revolutionary regime as a corrupt oligarchy. They bemoaned their age's want of principle and blamed it on the party system and on the 'mercenary' instincts which sustained it. Only from 'disinterested' figures, who resisted the baits of power and fortune, could the country hope for salvation. Those sentiments, fed as they were by the resentments of backbenchers on both sides of the Commons and by wide public disaffection, produced a cross-party view of seventeenth-century history which has been little noticed, but which may tell us at least as much about the eighteenth century's public values as can the increasingly repetitive and predictable productions of straightforward Whig and Tory history. To men who subscribed to it, Sidney and Ludlow became attractive less for their republican principles than for the impregnable integrity with which, in the face of 'mercenary' inducements, they clung to them. Similar patterns of fastidiousness and uprightness, we shall find, won eighteenth-century applause for other mid-seventeenth-century figures, both republican and non-republican.

Our second decisive moment is the publication in 1845 of another work of literary genius, Thomas Carlyle's edition of *Oliver Cromwell's Letters and Speeches*. Like the radical Whigs of the 1690s before him, Carlyle wrought an enduring historiographical change by editing texts and bringing them to a wide audience. Where the radicals had deliberately distorted the documentary legacy of the civil wars, he strove to be faithful to it. Yet his work is coloured no less than theirs by the character and values of the editor.

Carlyle did not know about the editorial exertions of the radical Whigs a century and a half earlier, but he did something to reverse their achievement. He hated the religious scepticism of all post-Puritan ages, hated their readiness to brand earnestness or zeal of faith with the pejorative terms 'enthusiasm' and 'fanaticism'. Puritanism, which the radical Whigs had banished to the historiographical wings, was restored by Carlyle and his followers to centre-stage. Yet the achievement was a partial one, for the Puritanism which Carlyle's Victorian readers admired was closer to nineteenth-century Nonconformity than to the original; and when, around the end of the century, Nonconformity began to wither, the nation's interest in seventeenth-century Puritanism dwindled too.

Carlyle, who vilified the eighteenth century's godlessness, scorned that age on a further count. He repudiated the 'patriot' conception of heroism which had then flourished, and substituted another. Eighteenth-century patriots saw themselves, and their seventeenth-century predecessors, as rising above the evils of political action. To Carlyle such levitation was an evasion of duty. If the seventeenth and then the eighteenth century had turned against the temptations and abuses of power – absolutism in the first era, corruption in the second – the nineteenth warmed to the responsible exercise of it. Sidney and Ludlow had both been politicians; both had exercised power; but it was not for their political involvement that the eighteenth century preserved the memory of their conduct, rather for their stands against the political practices of others. In the nineteenth century, when the virtue of incorruptibility lost its charisma, the following of the two heroes fell away. Ludlow's *Memoirs* retained their importance as a historical source, but not as an incitement to upright conduct. Carlyle's hero was Cromwell, who took on the world.

When, in the 1730s, an English version was compiled of the great *General and Historical Dictionary* of the philosopher Pierre Bayle, only three men who had fought in the parliamentary cause in England were awarded entries in it: Ludlow, Sidney and Cromwell. They are the three Roundheads to whose reputations we shall give most attention. Cromwell's reputation, the principal focus of the later part of this book, rose as those of the other two declined. Ludlow and Sidney had come to revile him. Their antagonism, which the eighteenth century had approved, counted against them in the nineteenth. Before Carlyle, published commentary on Cromwell was mainly hostile. The hatred of him by royalists was matched, even exceeded, by the detestation of republicans. To them he was the destroyer of the Commonwealth, the man who, by making himself Lord Protector through armed force in 1653, sacrificed the cause of virtue to his own ambition. From the Restoration onwards his religious zeal was widely regarded as either fraudulent or fanatical, if not both. Carlyle's commentary on Cromwell's letters and speeches recovered the sincerity of Cromwell's religion and located the key to his life in it. After Carlyle's book Cromwell would never seem the same. The Victorians turned him from a villain into a hero. His apotheosis came in 1899, the year of the tercentenary of his birth and of the erection of a statue to him outside the Houses of Parliament.

Revolutionary as Carlyle's achievement was, it was less single-handed than he and his admirers liked to think. New attitudes to Cromwell, to heroism, to Puritanism were emerging anyway in Carlyle's time. We shall explore the movements of society that made the impact of Carlyle's book possible. For like the fame of Ludlow and Sidney, Cromwell's was created and shaped by readers as well as writers. As in the late seventeenth century, so in the mid-nineteenth, a lasting historical interpretation was created not solely by editorial labour, not solely by the values of the age that produced the editing, but by the interaction of the two. In common with the radical Whigs, Carlyle reached an audience with opinions far removed from, and mostly much less extreme than, his own. If Ludlow's *Memoirs* and Sidney's *Discourses* were absorbed by eighteenth-century patriotism, Carlyle's *Cromwell* was assimilated and softened by Victorian liberalism.

The third moment is longer than the first two, for it extends from the mid-1880s into the first decade of the twentieth century. It is also the product of a wider range of publications. Essentially it is the achievement of the historian S. R. Gardiner, whose career was devoted to the chronicling of the politics of early and mid-seventeenth-century England, and of his protégé C. H. Firth, who carried on Gardiner's work. Though Gardiner had only peripheral contact with the academic world, it is with him that what is often called the professionalization of seventeenth-century studies begins. Gardiner adopted the form of historical writing favoured by his predecessors, narrative on a large scale. Yet in the depth and scrupulousness of his scholarship his work is far different from theirs. Frederic York Powell, who became Regius Professor of Modern History at Oxford in 1894 after Gardiner had declined the post (and whom Firth would succeed in it ten years later), remarked that Gardiner 'found the story of the first two Stuarts legend and has left it history'. The exaggeration is intelligible, for Gardiner's work stands like a mountain range between the modern historiographical landscape and the territory of the previous two centuries. His precedessors were often scholars of diligence and judgement; often they wrote better than he and were quite as intelligent; but they used a limited range of sources and often read them in what to a post-Gardiner age seems an uncritical spirit.

Those sources, it is true, did expand in the eighteenth century and through the earlier and mid-nineteenth. Over that long period many publications brought documents from the civil wars into print. In the nineteenth century the opening and ordering of a number of archives also made its mark. Yet while those developments did something to enlarge and refine the documentary basis of the historiography of the civil wars, they brought no basic alteration to it. Historians continued to rely heavily, sometimes exclusively, on their predecessors. If they sometimes differed from them in their arguments, they rarely departed from their methods. Gardiner revolutionized those methods. In doing so he brought a novel momentum to scholarly pursuit and gave it a new excitement. To the other passions which we shall watch shaping posterity's perceptions of the civil wars – republicanism, hatred of political tyranny and corruption, hostility to religious fanaticism, before 1800: Nonconformity, hero-worship, liberalism and socialism after it – we must add, from Gardiner's time, the passion of scholarly inquiry.

When Gardiner wrote, public hostility to the Roundhead cause was far on the wane. Espousal of the Cavalier cause had become little more than a fringe impulse. Since Carlyle, disputes within the Roundhead tradition have overshadowed the wider conflict between parliamentarian and royalist. The old tension between radical and moderate Whiggism has taken new forms. The Victorian assimilation of Carlyle's account of Cromwell by conventional liberalism is, from one perspective, a victory of the moderate tradition over its radical counterpart. While liberals succeeded to the moderate Whig position, socialists and Marxists took over the radical one. The rival claims, on which earlier interpretative conflict had turned, of the two upheavals of the seventeenth century, those of 1640–60 and 1688–9, persisted into the twentieth. The moderate view was now that, whereas Continental countries had in modern times been damaged by sudden and violent breaks with the past, England, thanks largely to 1688 and the settlement that followed it, had benefited from prudent evolutionary progress. The Left was irritated by that assumption. England, it wished to show, was as capable of bloody revolution, and had been as profoundly shaped by it, as its neighbours. In 1939, the two hundred and fiftieth anniversary of the settlement of 1689, G. M. Trevelyan, the twentieth century's most influential inheritor of the moderate Whig tradition, published his book *The English Revolution 1688–9*. The following year, the three hundredth anniversary of the meeting of the Long Parliament, the young Marxist historian Christopher Hill replied with *The English Revolution 1640*.

The rise of socialism gave a novel aspect, too, to divisions among supporters of the Roundhead cause. In our last chapter, which takes us into the twentieth century, we move from Cromwell to the Levellers, who provided a new focus of radical sympathy. Where Victorian Nonconformists found an ancestral hero in the Lord Protector, twentieth-century socialists looked back to the movement of social and political protest that threatened his control of his army. The mid-nineteenth century had turned away from the criticism of Cromwell voiced by the republican tradition, whose originators he had suppressed: the late nineteenth and the twentieth century found in the Levellers, another group he suppressed, a fresh angle of objection to him. Marxist and socialist judgements on the seventeenth century had all the boldness and vigour, all the transparent partisanship, of Whig and Tory ones in earlier times. They were formulated, none the less, within the transformed methodological framework built by Gardiner and his followers. At the end of the book we touch on the effects, and the limits, of the transformation.

Our path is but one of a number which might be taken through the historiography of one episode in one country. Yet the story which follows has, I hope, a broader significance. This is a book about the dialogue of past and present: about the power of the past to speak to the present, and about the present's habit of indicating what it wants to hear. Every age understands itself in relation to a history whose legacy it cannot alter or escape, but on which it imposes shapes that suit its own needs. In modern times the complexity of that process has been hidden by two opposing ideas, which will be the Scylla and Charybdis of our voyage. First there has been the pursuit of 'scientific' or 'objective' history, an ideal which credits historians with the capacity to transcend the perspectives of their time and of their personalities. That ambition, which emerged during the nineteenth century, has subsequently lost much of its authority, so much so that the enduring insight on which it rested, the value of disciplined and independent scholarship, has become obscured. The second and more recent idea, favoured by saluters of postmodernism, is that the past exists only in the present's head, and that the writing of history is the same as the writing of fiction. But fiction is that which can be neither proved nor disproved. If, in a novel, one character kills another, the question whether the death is truthful can be answered only as an aesthetic or moral one. If a historian were to write that only seventeen people were killed at the battle of the Somme, a different criterion of truthfulness would be brought into court. The distinction is elementary, yet often overlooked. Historical writing is a striving for proof, conducted with evidence which may sometimes be manipulated, abused, even fabricated, but only within a boundary of testable and obstinate fact.

It is none the less true that historians, like novelists, are makers of order. The making of historical order, by successive generations, will be our theme. The process has been sometimes conscious, sometimes not, sometimes sophisticated, sometimes not. Sometimes it has been comfortable and soothing. More often it has been troubled and contentious. Historians are used to being asked what 'history will decide' about a particular episode or individual. It will decide little. It may be able to resolve disputes of evidence or chronology, but rarely does it come together on larger interpretative questions. Even if it does it will change its mind, as one generation's experiences yield to those of the next and as the mirror of the past turns to catch them. We now move to the unfolding of the generations which have seen their reflections in the civil wars.

I

Edmund Ludlow: the Civil Wars and After

If we leave aside Oliver Cromwell and John Hampden, probably no one who fought on the Roundhead side has been more familiar to posterity than Edmund Ludlow. His reputation is not owed primarily to his deeds in the Roundhead cause. Though they made him a conspicuous personality at the time, perhaps one of the fifty or a hundred best-known figures of the civil wars, he was not a prime mover of events. It was his *Memoirs* that immortalized him. Published posthumously at the end of the seventeenth century, the book was the first autobiography to centre on the military and political conflicts of his time. Its vivid narrative, and its easy and polished prose, brought the period alive for a generation of readers fascinated by the civil wars but not old enough to remember them. In the four decades since the Restoration of monarchy in 1660 there had been histories and biographies and documentary compilations, some dull, some transported by animus, but none of them atmospherically compelling. Ludlow's *Memoirs* supplied that need.

In 1702, four years after their publication, a royalist rival appeared, likewise posthumously. This was the first portion of the great *History of the Rebellion* by Edward Hyde, Earl of Clarendon, who had been a prominent participant in the conflict. The publication would be completed in 1704. Among royalist sympathizers Clarendon's *History* has been revered. Many of them would have concurred with Robert Southey's remark in 1821 that 'there is no historian, ancient or modern, with whose writings it so behoves an Englishman to be thoroughly familiar as Lord Clarendon's'. Ludlow's *Memoirs* cannot compete with the eloquence or depth or subtlety of Clarendon's narrative, and they have not earned a comparable veneration. People whose

From the first edition of the *Memoirs of Edmund Ludlow* (1698).
Engraving by R. White, 1689.

Roundhead sympathies have taken a moderate form have found much in them from which to dissent. The work has none the less held readers of many persuasions, has attracted their sympathy and permeated their perceptions. Though other sources for the period have been as frequently consulted, Ludlow and Clarendon are the ones to have been most often read.

In Clarendon's *History* Ludlow makes only fleeting and colourless appearances. A more noticeable part is given to his father, Sir Henry. The Ludlows (or Ludlowes, to use Edmund's own spelling), whose estates lay in and around Maiden Bradley in Wiltshire, were among the leading gentry of the shire. Sir Henry's wife Elizabeth was first cousin to that prominent critic of royal policies in the 1620s, Sir Robert Phelips of Montacute in Somerset. His own criticisms would be bolder. Even within a generation so largely angered and alienated by the policies of Charles I in Church and state, Sir Henry's reaction to them was extreme. Only as the civil war approached, however, did his views become conspicuous. Before we come to them we must recall the events that shaped them.

From early in his reign, which began in 1625, Charles attempted to shift the balance of power between monarch and subject. The Crown's right to tax without parliamentary consent, and the subject's duty to yield unconditional obedience to royal commands, were strenuously asserted. The central government alarmed the nobility and gentry by encroaching on the semi-autonomy they enjoyed in the running of the regions. In religion it seemed that the Reformation might be undone. Under the influence of Archbishop Laud the Calvinist credentials of the Church of England were undermined. Laud strove to heighten the dignity of church services and of the clergy by an emphasis on ceremony and formality which was interpreted by zealous Protestants as a return towards popery. The large degree of control over the parishes which the nobility and gentry had secured at the Reformation was threatened. If Protestantism was imperilled at home, so was it abroad. Charles, like his father James before him, distressed Englishmen of Protestant ardour by keeping the nation out of the Thirty Years' War, which ravaged the Continent from 1618 to 1648. In the later 1620s, when the Catholic armies threatened to push the Protestant ones back to the northern seaboard, the English gave only the most fleeting and inept succour to their beleaguered co-religionists.

During the four years following Charles's accession there were three stormy parliaments. Thereafter he resolved on non-parliamentary rule. Until the late 1630s the policy was successful. His parliamentary opponents of the later 1620s were scattered and powerless. Through the test case of 1637–8 in which John Hampden was successfully prosecuted for refusing to pay the non-parliamentary tax of ship money, the Crown strengthened its prospects of financial independence. That ambition might have been fulfilled had Charles's innovative aims been confined to England. Instead his regime provoked first Scotland (an independent nation, but ruled, like England, by the Stuart dynasty) and then Ireland to revolt. The Scots rose in 1639–40 against Charles's attempt to impose the English Prayer Book upon them. His efforts to crush the rebellion commanded little enthusiasm in England and ended in military humiliation and financial exhaustion. He was obliged to call a parliament in April 1640 and another in November.

The second parliament, the Long Parliament as it would come to be known, sat for thirteen years. In its first nine months it secured the execution of the Earl of Strafford, the king's most powerful and dangerous minister, confined Laud to prison, swept away the prerogative courts, outlawed ship money and provided for the regular holding of parliaments. Those measures, extensive as they were, could not cure men's mistrust of the king. In the autumn of 1641 a rebellion in Ireland raised the political temperature still higher. Massacres of Protestants by Irish Catholics, exaggerated in the reporting, strengthened the already fierce anti-papist feeling at Westminster and through much of England. The king himself, whose own Protestantism seemed infirm, was suspected, together with his Catholic queen Henrietta Maria, of complicity in the rising. In November 1641 the mood in parliament reached a new intensity when the Commons passed its 'Grand Remonstrance', a polemical account of the evils of the reign. In January 1642 Charles took an armed guard to Westminster and entered the Commons with the aim of arresting five of its leading members, only to discover that they had slipped away into the city of London, where mass demonstrations and the arming of citizens were heralding the coming of war.

By now the parliamentary leadership's resort to popular agitation, and its refusal to compromise with the king, were producing their own reaction. Edward Hyde, the future Earl of Clarendon, was one of the many MPs who had supported the parliament's initial reforms but who, now believing the institutions of Church and state to be in peril, rallied round the king in 1641–2. It was one thing to overturn royal policies and topple royal advisers, another to take up arms against an anointed sovereign. After the escape of the five members Charles withdrew from the capital to rally support in the wider nation. Henceforth Crown and parliament alike prepared for war, though it was not until August, when the king raised his standard at Nottingham, that it began.

Sir Henry Ludlow sat in the Long Parliament as one of the two members for the county seat of Wiltshire. He seems not to have been a natural parliamentarian, and it was only in December 1641, as the Commons polarized, that his presence began to be felt. In January 1642 he demanded that the publication of a pamphlet attacking the five members be declared 'a traitorous conspiracy' and that men who had offered armed support to the king be punished. Soon he was criticizing not merely Charles's advisers but the monarch himself. Most MPs avoided that course. Eager as they were to present the parliament's aims as moderate and constitutional, they told themselves, and the nation, that they were contending not against the king but against the advisers who had led him astray. Sir Henry was more forthright. Clarendon recalls his remark to the Commons in May 1642 that Charles was not fit to be King of England, a statement on which royalist polemicists swooped at the time as evidence of parliament's treasonous aims. Seven years later, when Edmund Ludlow signed the king's death-warrant, such assertions could pass with impunity. In 1642 they were explosive. Not only was Sir Henry placed on a list of parliamentary traitors published by the king. He was rebuked by the Speaker of the Commons, who told him that his speeches ought to be 'accompanied with that duty which is due from a loyal subject to so gracious a sovereign'. Early in 1643, the last year of his life, Sir Henry's political radicalism became blunter still. He told his fellow MPs that 'the king is derivative from the parliament, and not the parliament from the king, and if he govern not by parliament then he govern by force and abuseth the law'. Again Sir Henry was well ahead of the

Commons, which would not openly propound claims for the constitutional supremacy of Westminster for nearly six years. Royalists were shocked by his statement. They were appalled too by comparable observations by another MP, Henry Marten, with whom Sir Henry Ludlow collaborated and who later in 1643 was sent to the Tower by the Commons for voicing republican or semi-republican sentiments.

Marten, who was released in 1646, thereafter became an ally of Edmund Ludlow, who inherited Sir Henry Ludlow's political standpoint. Edmund was born in 1616 or 1617, and so was in his mid-twenties when the war began. His upbringing followed a conventional path for a gentleman's son: two years at Oxford, followed by admission to the Middle Temple. At the start of the civil war he immediately enlisted, with other young members of the Inns of Court, in the bodyguard of the parliament's Lord General, the Earl of Essex, with which he fought at the first set battle of the war, at Edgehill in October 1642. In the years ahead a high proportion of his fellow radicals would be older men, whose outlooks had been formed by the dark political experience of the 1620s. Edmund's perspective on the earlier part of Charles's reign seems to have been shaped by Sir Henry, whose work, after the father's death, the son resolved to carry on.

Most of the civil war Edmund spent in Wiltshire, first as captain of a troop of horse, then as colonel of his own cavalry regiment, though he did take part in battles and skirmishes elsewhere and was briefly a prisoner at the royalist headquarters at Oxford. He came to national attention in the summer of 1643 through his tenacious defence of Wardour Castle in Wiltshire during a three-month siege. In that year the Roundheads' military fortunes were at their lowest ebb. In desperation parliament formed an alliance with the Scots, whose army, when it arrived in England, was sometimes as much disliked in Roundhead circles as in Cavalier ones. Even after the famous parliamentary victory at Marston Moor outside York in 1644 the war remained evenly balanced. It was not until 1645, after the reorganization of the Roundhead command and the formation of the New Model Army under Thomas Fairfax and his second-in-command Oliver Cromwell, that parliament gained the upper hand. The battles of Naseby in June and Langport in July were decisive, although only in May 1646 did Charles give himself up. He surrendered to the Scottish army, which handed him over to the English parliament in January 1647 before returning home.

In the month of Charles's surrender a by-election enabled Ludlow to succeed to his father's county seat. For the time being his military service was over. Politics engaged him instead. The parliamentarian cause, always an uneasy coalition of moderates and radicals, fell apart after the king's defeat. Ludlow thought – or at any rate would come to believe that he had thought – that Charles should be brought to justice immediately. Like his father's, Ludlow's radicalism placed him in a small minority. Most MPs wanted to restore the king to the throne, though they were divided over the terms of his readmission.

By 1647 the New Model Army, now dominated by Cromwell, was ready to assert itself as a political force. Like Ludlow, Cromwell had been uncompromising in his zeal for victory. But after the war was won he came to seem, to his more forward supporters, not zealous enough. A profoundly inspirational figure, he was no less a profoundly mistrusted one. Not least was he mistrusted in his own army. His readiness to negotiate, on generous terms, with the king, and the limits of his enthusiasm for constitutional and social reform, provoked suspicion and resentment among the junior officers and the rank and file. In November there was mutiny in the ranks, though it was soon crushed. Ludlow's sympathies were with the mutineers. By the spring of 1648, however, when a new royalist menace imperilled the Roundhead cause, he and other radicals had rallied behind Cromwell, who in turn had renounced the policies which had offended them the previous year. By now the national support for parliament was fading rapidly. An institution traditionally expected merely to cooperate with and advise the king, or to secure the redress of grievances, had in effect become the government. In fighting the war it had acquired powers of taxation and local control beside which Charles I's resources in the 1630s paled. Its new character might have been warrantable during the emergency of the civil war but was hard to vindicate thereafter. Parliament's army, the massively expensive New Model, which had thwarted the attempts of its political masters to disband it, was quartered on an increasingly resentful population. That was the background against which the second civil war began in March 1648. It was a much briefer contest than the first but a still more bitter one.

The resurgence of royalist sentiment prompted a series of uprisings which found backing among former Roundheads as well as from defeated Cavaliers. In July the danger was heightened by the invasion of a royalist army from Scotland.

By the autumn the war was over, thanks mainly to Cromwell's spectacular campaigns in Wales and the north of England. The war intensified the radicalism of the victorious soldiers and gave them a new political steel. So long as Charles remained alive, the army concluded, there could be no lasting basis of peace or justice. In parliament, by contrast, a majority continued to seek a negotiated settlement with him, which would leave the army isolated. In December, to forestall that now imminent danger, the army marched on London. In the operation known as Pride's Purge (after Colonel Thomas Pride, who carried it out) it forcibly excluded its enemies from the Commons. Only a minority, the Rump, continued to sit.

Now came the climax of the civil wars. In January the Rump set up a High Court of Justice to bring Charles to trial for treasonably levying war on his subjects and shedding their blood. He was convicted and was executed on 30 January. The next four months produced the constitutional revolution that ended monarchy and the House of Lords, made England a Commonwealth, and awarded sovereignty to the people's representatives in the House of Commons. Ludlow was in the thick of those changes, first as one of the king's judges and a signatory of his death-warrant, then as one of the five MPs chosen to nominate members of the Council of State, the Commonwealth's executive arm, and finally as a significant figure on the council itself.

It was not in parliament, however, that his main contribution to the Commonwealth's cause would be made. The regicide had been a high risk. Not only did it provoke hostility, even revulsion, across England. Like the events of 1688–9 exactly forty years later, it made powerful enemies among rulers on the European continent and provoked fury in Ireland and Scotland, countries now deprived of their lawful king. To meet those dangers the English army had to be expanded, the navy overhauled, huge sums raised by taxation and by the confiscation and sale of royalists' lands. Ireland had been in disorder since the rebellion of 1641. In August 1649 Cromwell led a large army there. Over the next nine months his ruthless methods cowed the Irish resistance. They did not end it. On his return he persuaded Ludlow to become one of parliament's civil and military commissioners at Dublin. He was in Ireland from 1650 to 1655. From 1651 to 1652 he was commander-in-chief, crushing the remains of the native resistance in an arduous campaign.

Cromwell, on his return from Ireland, addressed the now larger military threat from Scotland. Until this point, though he had long been the leading personality of the New Model, he was second-in-command to Thomas Fairfax. In the summer of 1650 he replaced him as Lord General and marched into Scotland. His campaign, the last and most demanding of his life, culminated triumphantly in his pursuit of the Scottish army into England and its defeat at Worcester in September 1651. The royalists had finally been beaten. Yet victory turned sour. The Commonwealth, which to its surprise had defeated its external enemies, succumbed to its own army. Following Cromwell's return to Westminster after Worcester, old tensions between parliament and army resurfaced. The army was frustrated by parliament's seeming indifference to the programme of constitutional and social reform which the soldiers were demanding as a return for their services. Parliament resented the army's continuing claims to a political voice. It had its own ambitious programme. It strove for the heightening of English sea-power, for the expansion of the nation's overseas and domestic trade, for the incorporation of newly conquered Ireland and Scotland into the English Commonwealth. From the summer of 1652 to the beginning of 1654 the navy, which had already provided critical support for Cromwell's Irish and Scottish campaigns, was engaged in an epic war with the Dutch for control of the neighbouring seas and of the maritime carrying-trade. Cromwell was unsympathetic to the war. More profoundly he was exasperated by parliament's indifference to the army's reform programme. On the morning of 20 April 1653 he suddenly led a troop of musketeers into the Commons. After an intemperate harangue he ordered his troops to clear the chamber and declared the parliament dissolved. 'Thus,' reflected the MP Bulstrode Whitelocke who was present at the coup, 'was this great parliament, which had done so great things', 'this assembly famous through the world for its actions, undertakings and successes, wholly at this time routed'.

The dissolution took the Roundhead cause into new territory. Until then, amid all the constitutional convulsions and violations of the previous thirteen years, the existence of the Long Parliament had supplied a thread of continuity. What would the army do now? Since the abolition of monarchy and Lords in 1649, the remnant of the Commons had held undivided constitutional power. So did the assembly which Cromwell summoned in July to replace it, the 'Nominated Parliament', or 'Barebone's Parliament' as its enemies derisively called it, for its members included a leatherseller with the mockable Puritan name Praisegod Barebone. Instead of the remains of a bad parliament, decided the army officers, there would now be a good parliament. In time, Cromwell hoped, the nation would be ready to choose a good parliament for itself. As it could not yet be trusted to do so, the army officers chose one for it. Yet Barebone's, no less than the Rump, fell out with its military creators. Where the Rump had obstructed the reform of the Church, of the law, of society, Barebone's launched into it with what seemed to Cromwell alarming rashness. In December there came another military coup, which sent Barebone's the way of the Rump.

Within days there followed, in Ludlow's eyes, the fatal moment of the civil wars. Cromwell had lost patience with parliamentary sovereignty. He made himself Lord Protector under a new constitution, the Instrument of Government, devised under the guidance of the prominent army officer John Lambert. There would be elected parliaments, but of limited powers and duration. In September 1654 the first of them was called. It refused to ratify the Instrument and was angrily dissolved by the protector in January. Now Cromwell resorted to open military rule. England was divided into eleven regions, each presided over by a Major-General. Yet he yearned for constitutional legitimacy. In 1656 he called another parliament, which the following year, desperate for a return to stability and civilian rule, persuaded him to accept a new constitution, the Humble Petition and Advice. It contained many features of the Instrument, but gave them a new civilian sanction. The rule of the Major-Generals lapsed.

In 1653, when Lambert presented him with the Instrument, and again in 1657, when parliament submitted the Humble Petition, Cromwell was at first offered the title of king rather than protector. He refused on both occasions. Yet to Ludlow and many other supporters of the Commonwealth his usurpation was a return to kingship in all but name. The coup of December 1653 outraged Ludlow. He resigned his civilian office in Ireland, though not his military one, which he perhaps hoped to find a way of using against the new regime. In 1655 he was discovered to be circulating pamphlets against Cromwell's rule. He came to England, was briefly imprisoned, and was twice summoned before the protector, who eventually allowed him to live quietly with relations in Essex.

Cromwell's death in 1658 offered Ludlow new hope. Early in 1659 he was elected to the parliament of the new protector, Oliver's son Richard, whose authority he strove, with other republicans or 'commonwealthmen', to undermine. In May there came, as it seemed, the moment of deliverance. The army turned against Richard, deposed him, and restored the parliament of the Commonwealth. Ludlow at once became a leading figure in the revived regime. He was appointed to its Committee of Safety and its Council of State and given command of an English regiment. In June he was put in charge of the army in Ireland, where he spent the summer. Yet what had seemed the new dawn of the commonwealthmen's cause proved to be its dusk. On his return to England in October Ludlow found that the parliament had once more been forcibly expelled. Over the next six months the Roundhead cause disintegrated amid a succession of coups and constitutional reversals. While army and parliament quarrelled with each other and among themselves, the tide of public feeling ran ever more swiftly for the return of the Stuart monarchy. Ludlow, who vainly urged the civilian and the military leaders to overcome their differences, earned the displeasure and distrust of both sides for his pains.

In February 1660 Pride's Purge was undone. The Long Parliament, which had been prevented by the purge from restoring Charles I in 1648, resumed power and prepared to restore the exiled Charles II. In desperation, and in vain, Ludlow tried to organize a rising of republican soldiers. In April the parliament made way for the elected 'Convention' that would bring the king back the next month. Shortly before Charles's return the Convention began proceedings against his father's surviving judges. Over the next three months, while the restored court and the Convention debated how to punish them, Ludlow looked on anxiously. For a time he went into hiding. In August, deciding that his life was in danger, he slipped out of the capital. Like Richard Cromwell a few weeks earlier – and like Charles II after the battle of Worcester – he made his way secretly to the Sussex coast. A sailor's garments and the growth of a beard enabled him to escape detection, though there were close calls. Eventually he found a boat to take him to France, the sailors covering him with their coats as it left the harbour.

Once ashore Ludlow resolved to make for Switzerland, where he went first to Geneva. Within a fortnight he learned of the executions, carried out in brutal fashion, of four of his fellow regicides, among them his intimate friend John Cook, who had been the prosecuting Solicitor at the king's trial. Further executions would soon follow. To Ludlow, whose outlook was profoundly marked by the deaths, they seemed inhuman acts of revenge.

In 1662 he settled in Vevey on Lake Geneva, where his wife visited him from England in 1663 and came to live four or five years later. The marriage, which had taken place in or around 1649, was an affectionate though childless one. Vevey would be their home for the rest of his life. A small colony of fugitives grew up around the Ludlows. The exiles were accorded protection by the Council of Bern, a generous act and, in view of the close contacts between the government of England and that of Bern's mighty neighbour France, a courageous one. In succeeding generations it would often be applauded by admirers of Ludlow in both England and America. But it was no proof against the assassins who, with backers in the English and French courts, stalked the exiles. Though Ludlow himself survived, in 1664 his fellow-regicide and colleague in the Commonwealth regime John Lisle was shot dead on his way to church in Lausanne.

The pursuit of Ludlow was not motivated solely by revenge. In the early 1660s his name acquired what in successive forms it would retain through his life and far beyond it, a symbolic significance. Plotters against the restored monarchy, some of them in England, some in exile, looked to him to return to England in order to head an uprising and win the nation's deliverance. What they hoped, the government, nervous of Puritan insurrection, feared. Time and again Ludlow was reported to be in England (or sometimes Ireland), raising or leading troops. In reality, though he was in regular correspondence with radicals in England, he thought the plotters among them misguided. During the Anglo-Dutch war of 1664–7 some English commonwealthmen urged the republican party in the United Provinces (the Dutch confederation) to unite with them to destroy the English monarchy. Ludlow exasperated them by holding back. Hopes of him did not vanish. In 1684, when the plans for the Duke of Monmouth's rebellion were being laid, two of Monmouth's supporters visited Switzerland, where they stayed with the Ludlows for some months and tried to persuade Edmund to head a rising in the West Country. Now in his later sixties, he told them that his work in the world was done.

So it seemed. Then, in 1688–9, deliverance from Stuart rule arrived. The Dutch leader William of Orange, whom republicans had long regarded as the ally of the evil Stuart dynasty, turned against it. He invaded England and, with his wife Mary, replaced her father James II, who had fled the realm, on the throne. In July 1689, deciding that William was a 'Gideon' (the Old Testament deliverer), Ludlow bade farewell to the magistrates of Vevey and made his way to England. He may have hoped to lend assistance to the new king, perhaps in the campaign in Ireland on which William would embark the following year. Or he may have hoped, with other commonwealthmen, to steer the Revolution in a republican direction. Tories alleged that during the few months he spent in England 'his house was crowded' with 'old rebels and republicans', with the kind of men who 'in Cromwell's time had laboured to introduce a commonwealth'. If he did have republican hopes they were sadly disappointed. In most circles the word 'commonwealth' still aroused fearful memories. In November 1689, reportedly because of the seditious company he was keeping, the House of Commons recalled that Ludlow 'stands attainted of high treason by act of parliament for the murder of King Charles I', and persuaded the king to offer a reward for his arrest. For the second time in his life he slipped abroad, this time to Holland, whence he made what must have been a melancholy journey back to Vevey. He died there in the autumn of 1692.

His visit to England, failure as it was, proved not to have been fruitless. It kept the symbolic property of his name alive. In 1691–3 four pamphlets were published which purported to be 'Letters' written by

Ludlow to Tories and high churchmen in England. As the last of the tracts admitted, they were plainly not his. Like many other pamphlets of the 1690s they dwelt on the reign of Charles I. Their theme is his tyranny and the valour and wisdom of the Long Parliament in challenging it.

The Ludlow pamphlets were Whig pamphlets, but their Whiggism was of a particular kind. Like the parliamentarians and royalists to whose causes they succeeded, the Whig and Tory parties were coalitions, often drawn together by immediate political pressures but easily divisible when those pressures subsided. The Revolution of 1688 split the Tories of James II's reign between those who accepted the new Williamite order and those who adhered to the Jacobite cause, though many hedged their bets. It split the Whigs too. William III took the English throne for purposes of Dutch foreign policy. He wanted to bring England into the war against France. He was not interested in English constitutional liberties. On the contrary he was determined to uphold the Crown's prerogatives as far as possible. The Whigs had come into being as enemies of prerogative powers. How were they to respond to William's stand?

There were arguments, which the more moderate and pragmatic Whigs found persuasive, for straining their principles in supporting it. William had rescued England from Stuart tyranny. He had also delivered it from popery, which under Charles II and James II had come to seem inseparable from tyranny. The exiled Stuarts were backed by the mighty power of the later seventeenth century, the France of Louis XIV, with which England was now engaged in a war that had to be financed and organized on an enormous scale. Within England there was extensive, if mainly latent, support for the Jacobites. If the new regime's enemies, abroad and at home, were to be overcome, the executive needed to be not weak but strong. Besides, if the Whigs did not mobilize parliamentary support for William, there was the danger that the Tories would. The Whigs, as the party which had stood up to the dynasty he had now deposed, were his natural allies, but a late seventeenth-century king did not need to choose between the two parties. He could select his ministers from either side. Early in his reign William alarmed Whigs by bringing into his administration men who had guided the later Stuarts. Their championship of the Crown's prerogatives and their intolerant high churchmanship were anathema to Whig principles. If the Whigs were to steer William in their own direction, the moderates among them told themselves, they needed first to convince him that he could rely on their support.

The radical Whig position was very different. It lay behind the publication of Ludlow's 'Letters', as later it would inspire that of the *Memoirs*. The Whigs had been divided before. In the later years of Charles II's reign the more restrained of them had been content to pursue a single objective. They aimed to exclude the king's Catholic brother from the succession. Bolder spirits of that time urged a revision of the constitution that would prevent any king, whatever his character or religion, from invading his subjects' liberties. Thwarted in that hope in 1679–83, the radicals returned to it in 1688–9. In their eyes the Revolution was a golden chance to impose fundamental restrictions on the powers of the Crown. Again they were thwarted. Their own political ambitions were denied too. Though some radical Whigs gained office and favour at the outset of William's reign, they soon lost them. Through the 1690s the radicals sustained a sense of betrayal and resentment.

The Ludlow pamphlets revived memories of the civil wars. That achievement suited radical Whigs, not moderate ones. Moderates emphasized the differences between the two seventeenth-century upheavals: radicals dwelt on the similarities and continuities. Moderates recognized the revulsion still felt by so large a portion of the nation at the turmoil of mid-century: at the blasphemy of the regicide and at the republican anarchy that followed it. Every 30 January, that 'general madding-day' as the Ludlow pamphlets called it, Tories used press and pulpit to portray Whigs as the heirs of the men who had killed the 'sacred martyr'. It was the radicals whose publications met that challenge. The Tories' uses of the 'madding-day', argued radical Whigs, showed that the pernicious doctrines of tyranny remained alive and that only constitutional changes more profound than those of 1688–9 could make the nation safe from them. On both sides controversialists dressed their present aims, which it would have been over-hazardous to express nakedly, in statements about the mid-century past. Those who regarded the deposition of James II as unlawful dwelt on the horror of Charles I's: those who wanted James's overthrow to be declared a vindication of the people's sovereignty recalled the invocation of that principle in 1649. The sponsors of the Ludlow pamphlets did not openly argue for republicanism, but they did make it clear that Charles I had merited his trial and execution. If James II had stood his ground at the time of William's invasion, they implied, the same fate would properly have attended him.

Just as, in 1679–81, the radicals had broken with those Whigs who were only willing to press for the exclusion of James II from the succession, so now, in the same spirit, they insisted that the crisis of 1688 should be blamed not on James alone but on the system of government that had permitted his tyranny. The conflicts of his reign, in their view, were continuous with the earlier seventeenth-century struggles between tyranny and liberty. As a pamphlet of 1698, *A Defence of the Parliament of 1640*, published by the men who put out Ludlow's *Memoirs*, remarked, 'the controversy between the advocates for Charles the First, and his wicked favourites, and the friends of the parliament and people', had 'been spun out into above forty years'. The Ludlow pamphlets compared 'the oppressive government of King Charles I in the first four years of his reign with that of the four years of the reign of King James II'. To the sponsors of the pamphlets, the long seventeenth-century contention against the Stuarts was the 'good old cause', a term that had been claimed by the opponents of Cromwellian rule in the 1650s and used by radicals ever since. Ludlow's journey to England in 1689 had illustrated his steadfastness to that cause. 'Though I am decrepit,' declared the third of his 'Letters', 'this *good old Cause*, I rest assured, will abide firm and unshaken' against all royalist and Tory 'assailants'. Tories alleged that 'great numbers' of readers, having 'sucked up the venomous poison' of the Ludlow pamphlets, had been turned against monarchy by them and were hailing the 'good old cause'.

Ludlow was not the cause's only hero. There was Algernon Sidney, who like him had gone into exile at the Restoration, though he had been allowed to return in 1677. His execution in 1683, after a treason trial presided over by the infamously partial judge George Jeffreys, made him a martyr. A pamphlet of 1689, *Sidney Redivivus*, produced by the circle in which Ludlow is likely to have moved during his stay in England in that year, exploited and confirmed that status. Then there was the poet John Milton. In the wake of the Revolution, tracts in which Milton had vindicated the regicide were republished. His prose writings on behalf of the Commonwealth had raised a storm on the Continent in the 1650s. In 1660 the blind poet was selected, along with signatories of the king's death-warrant, for exemplary punishment. *Paradise Lost* recalls his plight that summer, 'In darkness, and with dangers compassed round'. Like Ludlow he went into hiding in London, though in the end his life was spared and he was allowed to live quietly. In the 1690s Milton's and Sidney's names were closely associated by radicals – as by Tories – with Ludlow's.

It was in the first and the last third or so of William's thirteen-year reign that the radicals were assiduous in fostering civil-war memories. The momentum of radical publishing that gathered from 1689 fell away after 1693, the year of the last of the Ludlow pamphlets. For in 1694 the political scene altered. The Whigs in William's administration, who had hitherto battled with the Tories for political ascendancy, decisively gained the upper hand. They held it for the next three years, with a majority in the Commons behind them. The radicals remained excluded from power. In their eyes the 'junto Whigs', as the leaders who now dominated the government were called, had deserted 'old Whig' principles for the rewards of office. Chief among them was John Somers, who had been a key figure among the brave spirits of Whig opposition in the early 1680s and who had now abandoned his former friends. Instead of curbing the royal prerogative the 'junto' was using it – so the radicals alleged – to its own ends. The patronage dispensed by the junto had its inevitable effect, the dwindling of the radicals' following. In any case it was difficult for radicals to mount an open attack on a ministry guided by the leaders of their own party, particularly while the nation remained at war.

In 1697 the tide turned again. The Peace of Ryswick brought the war to an end and reduced the junto's unity and authority. It also provoked a crisis that overshadowed English politics for two years. William resolved, with the junto's support, to keep up his army in peacetime. It was a massive force, far larger than those of Cromwell or the later Stuarts and a vivid presence in the society and economy of England. In tense moments during the 1660s, the 1670s, the 1680s, MPs had warned urgently against the menace posed by a standing army to the nation's liberties. The gathering of James II's army on Hounslow Heath in 1686 to awe the nation had concentrated fears of despotism. Now the spectre rose again. Men supposed that William might turn his forces, as Charles I had done in the 1640s, against his subjects, or that at the least he might use them to cow his critics. In terms of foreign policy the case for a standing army, kept in permanent training and readiness, was overwhelming. The only alternative, the amateur county militias, offered no basis for national security. But in the winter of 1697–8, and again in that of 1698–9, feelings against the army reached feverish levels. It was against that background that the momentum of the publishing activity of the radical Whigs was resumed. Early in 1698 there appeared the greatest of their literary achievements: the *Memoirs of Edmund Ludlow*.

2

Ludlow the Puritan

Ludlow's *Memoirs* were published, at the first of the two peaks of the standing army controversy, early in 1698, probably in February although possibly in January. Printed in two volumes, the book covered the period from the accession of Charles I in 1625 to the Restoration in 1660. It made a sensation – *un grand bruit*, as an ambassador in London wrote – and was soon in heavy demand. In the light of its success a third volume, covering the years 1660 to 1672, was brought out in the spring of 1699. The *Memoirs* launched a genre of civil-war autobiographies. In 1699 there appeared the *Memoirs of Denzil Holles* (a leading parliamentarian of the 1640s), the *Memoirs of Sir John Berkeley* (a royalist negotiator with Cromwell's army in 1647) and the *Short Memorials of Thomas Lord Fairfax* (parliament's Lord General). Like Ludlow's *Memoirs*, those were Whig publications. In 1700 the Tory writer William Baron, chaplain to the heir of Edward Hyde, Earl of Clarendon, mocked 'that *à la mode* way of Memoirs'. But in 1701 a Tory counter-attack began. The *Memoirs* of the royalist Sir Philip Warwick appeared in that year. They were followed in 1702 by the first volume of Clarendon's (partly autobiographical) *History of the Rebellion* and by the *Memoirs* of another royalist, Sir Thomas Herbert.

Baron's jibe was made in the second of two substantial pamphlets which he wrote against the *Memoirs*. One of his allegations was that the publishers had been unfaithful to Ludlow's text. The *Memoirs* were 'but an abridgement of many more reams', which Ludlow's 'party, and printer, thought fit to lick into something of form, contract, and perhaps alter too, as might best serve the present design of promoting the Good Old Cause'. They had 'cut off the superfluities of that fanciful Swiss dress' in which the text had reached them. Though

MEMOIRS

OF

Edmund Ludlow *Esq*;

Lieutenant General of the Horse, Commander in Chief of the Forces in *Ireland*, One of the Council of State, and a Member of the Parliament which began on *November* 3, 1640.

In Two Volumes.

VOL. I.

Switzerland,
Printed at *Vivay* in the Canton of *Bern*,
MDCXCVIII.

Ludlow had 'provided the ingredients' it was the publishers who had 'composed the dish, from a confused heap'.

Similar charges were made at various moments of the eighteenth century. A dinner party at Lambeth Palace in 1705 discussed the question whether the *Memoirs* were 'an impudent forgery'. In 1728 the Jacobite antiquary Richard Rawlinson reported having heard that they were 'drawn up in England, under the mask of Ludlow, by one who was a favourer and defender of his principles'. In the years 1777–80 'suspicions' were voiced 'against the authenticity of Ludlow's *Memoirs*', which were said to have been 'fabricated' or 'compiled' from 'a heap of Ludlow's papers'.

By the nineteenth century those doubts had disappeared. In 1859 they were fleetingly revived. The writer W. D. Christie discovered that the philosopher and political thinker John Locke had copied a series of passages from the manuscript, written by Ludlow, on which the *Memoirs* were based. All of them contained hostile accounts of Locke's patron Anthony Ashley Cooper, first Earl of Shaftesbury, who had been a Cromwellian in the 1650s and the leader of the Whigs during the exclusion crisis. None of the passages appear in the *Memoirs*. Christie wondered whether other passages had been suppressed.

His question made little impression. In 1894 C. H. Firth produced a new edition of the *Memoirs* which made them more accessible and easier to use. The edition of 1698–9 (printed cheaply in small volumes) had been reprinted in 1720–22, and there were handsome folio editions in 1751 and 1771, but the *Memoirs* had received no close scholarly appraisal or commentary. Firth, with his senior colleague S. R. Gardiner, brought new and formidable standards of scholarship to the study of seventeenth-century England. There has probably never been a shrewder or more clear-headed historian of the period than he. His edition of Ludlow, which carries a long biographical introduction as well as substantial appendices which relate the *Memoirs* to their historical background, is a masterly achievement in every respect except a single essential one. He made a fundamental misjudgement. He noticed the earlier tradition of scepticism about the authenticity of the *Memoirs*, only to dismiss it. The *Memoirs*, he ruled, 'have every internal sign of genuineness, and stand every test which can be applied to their contents'. It now seems a surprising conclusion. Firth's appendices reproduced letters and other documents which survive in Ludlow's hand and which differ strikingly, in both language and emphasis, from the *Memoirs*. (Firth did incorporate the passages discovered by Christie, but did not notice the discrepancies discernible between them and the remainder of the work.) His judgement was accepted, almost without demur, for eighty years.

In 1970 the Bodleian Library at Oxford bought a manuscript from Sotheby's which had recently emerged from Warwick Castle. Its title is 'A Voice from the Watch Tower', and its author is Edmund Ludlow. It is a portion of the text on which the *Memoirs* were based. Alas, it is only a portion. It is the second of three sections of 'A Voice from the Watch Tower'. It begins in late February 1660 (a little more than two months before the chronological point, in early May 1660, at which the two volumes of the *Memoirs* published in 1698 finished). It ends in 1677. The third section (as we can tell from a table of its contents bound into the Bodleian manuscript) ended in 1685.

The missing portions are unlikely to reappear. The signs are that the text now in the Bodleian had become separated from the other sections of 'A Voice from the Watch Tower' by the time the publication of the *Memoirs* was complete (perhaps between the appearance of the first two volumes and that of the third). The loss of the last portion of the manuscript, relating events of 1677–85, does not merit grave regret, for by the end of the section in the Bodleian much of the vigour and interest has gone out of Ludlow's text, and the table of contents for those years, which refers chiefly to familiar events of international conflict, is not appetizing. It is the disappearance of the first portion, which covered the years down to 1660, that has had greatest effect on the study of the civil wars. Most of the Bodleian manuscript is devoted to Ludlow's time in Switzerland. It is in the account given by the *Memoirs* of the long period when Ludlow was at or near the centre of events in England that the principal interest of the published version has always lain.

The Bodleian manuscript is none the less revolutionary enough by itself for our understanding of the politics of the civil wars. It shows that the eighteenth-century observers who questioned the authenticity of the *Memoirs* were right and that Firth was wrong. In the first place the *Memoirs* were indeed 'an abridgement of many more reams'. From the pagination of the Bodleian manuscript, which happily for us is continuous with that of the first portion, and from the table of the contents of the third portion, we can calculate that 'A Voice from the Watch Tower' must have been nearly a million words long, four times the length of the *Memoirs*. In preparing the third volume (the one which begins in 1660) the publishers became increasingly ruthless. The Bodleian manuscript is more than five times the length of the corresponding portion of the *Memoirs*. Ending in 1672, the *Memoirs* omit Ludlow's account of the years 1672–85, which must have been around 70,000 words.

Not merely was Ludlow's manuscript heavily abbreviated. It was no less heavily rewritten. There are profound differences of emphasis and tone and style. There is also fabrication. In the third volume of the *Memoirs*, the one for which we have the corresponding portion of the manuscript, Ludlow is made to say things that have in some cases little basis in the manuscript, in others none. It is by tracing the rewriting of the Bodleian manuscript that the aims of the publishers, and the influence of their intentions on subsequent interpretations of the civil wars, can be assessed. But what of the first two volumes, for which (except near the end of the second of them) we do not have the corresponding manuscript material, and which we therefore cannot compare with Ludlow's own words?

It is of course impossible to reconstruct his text. But there are many things about it that we can deduce. In the pre-1660 portion of the *Memoirs*, the presence of the techniques and the verbal formulae which were used in the abbreviation and revision of the Bodleian manuscript is often recognizable. Behind them there lay a political purpose. Once we have recovered it, as we shall find later on, the tactics of editorial revision which shaped the first two volumes of the *Memoirs* can be easy enough to identify. The further the publishers move from the original the more transparent their intervention becomes.

We also have more particular clues. To register them we need to pause for a moment on points of textual analysis. First, remarks of Ludlow in the Bodleian manuscript tell us something about the previous section. Sometimes he alludes to material in it. He also looks back frequently to events of the civil wars, especially those that matter most to him, and passes judgements on them. The judgements are unlikely to have differed markedly from the ones we would find in the earlier portion. The two sets of opinions were mostly expressed close to each other in time, for Ludlow, who evidently began to write 'A Voice from the Watch Tower' in the early 1660s, had written most of the fuller and more revealing of the retrospective passages of the Bodleian manuscript by around the middle of that decade. Secondly, John Locke's copy of the passages concerning the first Earl of Shaftesbury records the page numbers of the manuscript from which he took them. The passages are tantalizingly brief. Taken together with the page numbers, however, they enable us to infer that Ludlow's account of those years must have been broadly similar, in its literary character and proportions, to his narrative of the period from 1660, and that it must have received broadly similar treatment from the publishers.

The passages Locke copied all belong to the 1650s. Nothing survives of Ludlow's account of the years before that decade. That account evidently gave the publishers a problem. The retrospective passages of the Bodleian manuscript reveal that, while his memories of personal experiences of his youth remained reasonably alert after the Restoration, his recollection of public events during the earlier part of his life had become frail. The publishers met the problem by inserting into the *Memoirs* passages which we can see to have been stitched together from narratives and documentary compendia of the civil wars published earlier, especially the *Memorials of Bulstrode Whitelocke*, which had appeared in 1681–2. The result is an account of the misgovernment of Charles I that probably owes little to Ludlow. Its emphases resemble those of the descriptions of Charles's reign in the Ludlow pamphlets of the early 1690s.

Much of the revision and abbreviation of Ludlow's manuscript can be explained by the publishers' need to produce a coherent text of readable length. The most significant changes, however, at least in their impact on subsequent interpretations of the civil war, are of another kind. They lie in adjustments made to Ludlow's character and beliefs. Above all they lie in the publishers' treatment of his religious convictions.

A reader of the *Memoirs* – as of the Ludlow pamphlets of 1691–3 – could be forgiven for wondering whether Ludlow had religious convictions. As an eighteenth-century historian of religion observed, the Ludlow we meet in the *Memoirs* is 'a man of Roman rather than Christian virtue'. The nineteenth-century French statesman and historian François Guizot remarked, after reading the *Memoirs*, that Ludlow 'made war like a gentleman, not like a sectary'. When in the *Memoirs* men profess religious zeal or motive, that stance is usually represented by the narrator as a cover for 'ambition'. Not least is that true of the clergy, whose 'corrupt interest' it is to flatter evil rulers and encourage them to rule by 'arbitrary' means, and who are the 'principal authors and abettors' of the crisis that leads to the civil war. It is true too of Cromwell and his toadies, who are shown to cloak their sinister purposes behind appeals to the will of divine providence.

The Ludlow of the *Memoirs* does, it is true, express his own views on religious questions. He dislikes 'formality' in worship and the 'new ceremonies and superstitions' introduced by Archbishop Laud in the 1630s. He is shown conversing knowledgeably (as readers would have expected a self-respecting seventeenth-century gentleman to be able and ready to do) about the meaning of scriptural texts, though his customary purpose in doing so is to dissuade others from applying them to harmful political ends. He recognizes the presence of 'sober and virtuous' men among the pre-war clergy, whom Charles I 'discouraged'. From time to time 'God' appears as a guiding influence on events, even if normally one operating from a distance. Occasionally Ludlow's cause is described as 'the cause of God'. God's cause is, however, indistinguishable from that of Ludlow's 'country' and of its civil 'liberties'. It has no discernible doctrinal content. The great issues of religious aspiration and debate on the Roundhead side – the government of the Church, the liturgy, the quality and status and financial maintenance of the clergy, the spreading or 'propagation' of Gospel truths, liberty of conscience, the ceremony of baptism – are either ignored or mentioned only passingly. The Ludlow of the *Memoirs* is a secular figure.

The Ludlow of the Bodleian manuscript could not be more different. He is a Puritan of the most fundamental conviction. His title – which echoes verses of Isaiah (21.5–12) and Habakkuk (2.1), where prophets stand on watch towers in God's service – is intimation enough of the intensity of his faith. He writes in witness of the God who intervenes continually and continuously in the world he has made, and whose purposes his servants are enjoined by their maker to discover. If Ludlow ever doubted the purposes God held for him, they were confirmed during his escape from England in 1660, when the Lord 'hid me in the hollow of his hand. O that I might be so affected as to sacrifice the remainder of my life to his praise and service.' 'A Voice from the Watch Tower' is written in that 'praise and service'.

In Puritan thinking the civil wars were a critical moment in the divine scheme of history, perhaps a prelude to the Second Coming. For Ludlow political events are the workings of the God who 'shakes nations', 'levels mountains', 'overturns, overturns', and prepares for the destruction of the Beast. The manuscript is swamped with references to biblical texts, which he expounds with urgent and swelling fervour. 'A Voice from the Watch Tower' surprises the reader of the *Memoirs* not only by its religious intensity but by its religious radicalism. Among Puritan gentry and MPs, Ludlow was on an extreme wing. All Puritans were repelled by the high churchmanship of the Laudian regime, and many of them rejoiced in the abolition of episcopacy (the government of the Church by bishops) in the 1640s. But most of them – or at least of the movement's political and ecclesiastical leaders – wanted to preserve the bond between Church and state and to maintain the parochial structure through which the Church was administered and held together. Though some favoured a degree of liberty of conscience, a greater number were at least as committed to the principle of uniformity of worship as the Anglican hierarchy had been before them. Ludlow, by contrast, believes in the almost total separation of Church and state. In the early times of Christianity, he observes, the Church was a purely voluntary organization. It 'consisted only of the willing', as it still should. With the conversion of the Emperor Constantine, when the Church 'came to be countenanced by worldly authority', 'Antichrist began to prevail'. Persecution for faith's sake is a challenge to God's spirit, that 'wind which bloweth where it listeth'. All insistence on outward forms in religion is a remnant of the Jewish law, from which the Gospel has set us free.

The Gospel itself, Ludlow argues, should have been liberated from its worldly chains by the Reformation. Instead Henry VIII, 'that monster of mankind', appropriated the Church for his own marital and political purposes. In Switzerland too Ludlow found that the Reformation, instead of 'making progress', had 'rather gone backward, and brought forth sour grapes'. With his fellow-exiles he refused to take communion among Swiss congregations, a decision that caused problems for his protectors in the Bernese government, who had to explain, before their colleagues, that affront to civility. In the English civil wars the refusal of self-styled 'godly' parishioners to share the communion service with ungodly neighbours had fissured the parishes. Among the Bernese, Ludlow explains, 'we had not a freedom to communicate in that holy ordinance of the Lord's Supper, of whom we had not a particular satisfaction of a work of grace in their hearts'. For 'by communicating with such who in our judgement eat and drink unworthily, we should contribute to their sin and consequently to their punishment, such eating and drinking their own damnation'. As usual Ludlow had Scripture in mind, for Paul had said, 'he that eateth and drinketh unworthily, eateth and drinketh damnation to himself, not discerning the Lord's body' (I Corinthians 11.29).

A position still more contentious during the civil wars was the belief that baptism should be reserved for adulthood, when believers are equipped to consent to it. Ludlow scorns the orthodoxy of infant baptism, which he thinks a remnant, like so much else in the post-Reformation Church, of popery. There is 'nothing more express in Scripture than that none but believers were subjects of water baptism'. In the 1640s Baptists were perhaps the most influential sect in England, partly because of their following within Cromwell's army and of his readiness to protect them. In the 1650s they were rivalled by the new movement of the Quakers, a militantly disruptive group very different from the pacific denomination known to later generations. Though Ludlow was probably not a Quaker himself, he viewed the movement's sufferings under the Restoration with close sympathy. On his journey through France to Switzerland in 1660 he was asked by some German travellers 'whether I were a Lutheran or a Calvinist; I telling them I was for both as far as they agreed with the word of God, but for neither any further'. One of the Germans 'cried out, He is a Quaker, a Quaker; to whom I replied, I was one who desired to tremble at God's word'.

There are some matters on which Ludlow maintains a strict Puritan orthodoxy. Like so many Puritans he watched with horror the spread, across Europe and across England, of a corrosive scepticism that subjected matters of faith to the scrutiny of human reason. Two developments were especially alarming to him. The first was the undermining of the Calvinist doctrine of predestination, which acknowledges the worthless depravity of mankind and the miracle of divine mercy that rescues God's chosen ones from hellfire. God separates, by eternal decree, the saved from the damned, the 'precious' from the 'vile'. Ludlow was horrified by 'the growth of that opinion touching universal grace, or Christ's dying for all', a doctrine 'which would have man's salvation depend on the sandy foundation of his own merits'. Secondly there was Socinianism, that intellectually assured doctrine which, to Ludlow's dismay, 'struck at the mystery of the Trinity'. On other fronts too he was appalled to observe the human mind usurping the claims of God's spirit. It was even preferring pagan and classical authorities to it. Men were arguing 'that we are to take the history of the holy Scriptures as those of Titus Livius or Polybius; that to interpret them, there is nothing needful but the knowledge of words; that reason ought to be the judge of the Scripture'.

From exile Ludlow watched the afflictions of those Nonconformists or Dissenters who would not subscribe to the restored Church of England and who suffered deprivation in consequence. As government agents were aware, he kept closely in touch with them through letters and messages. 'A Voice from the Watch Tower' was written with a Nonconformist audience in mind, which Ludlow hoped to counsel and fortify in its adversity. The persecution of the 'godly' after 1660, that 'rage of Satan and his instruments' in Ludlow's words, was the shaping experience of English Nonconformist culture. The godly sometimes exaggerated their hardships. The Conventicle Act of 1664, which proscribed, under severe penalties, all religious gatherings outside the Church, and the Five Mile Act of the following year, which forbade Dissenting preachers and teachers from coming within five miles of a corporate town, were harsh on paper but often mitigated or ignored by local authorities. Even so there were enough prosecutions, imprisonments and sufferings for Dissenters, reared as they were (and as the nation had been since Elizabeth's reign) on *Foxe's Book of Martyrs*, to interpret those experiences as part of a universal pattern of oppression.

It was not merely with their punishment at human hands, however, that Puritans had to come to terms. It was the apparent withdrawal of God's favour. In the civil war his blessings had been miraculous. The godly had been delivered from the oppression of the 1630s, the Laudian years. They had been vouchsafed astonishing victories, which had been won, as they knew, not through human capacities but by God's outstretched arm. To comprehend the size and meaning of those mercies they turned to the Old Testament, which they knew so intimately and where they found the figurative models, the 'parallels', that determined their interpretations of public events. The godly were, it seemed, the Israelites of the new dispensation. They had passed out of the Egypt of Laudian bondage, through the Red Sea of civil-war blood, towards a promised land. Yet in 1660, as Ludlow writes, 'all things ran contrary to what the providences of the Lord had led to for twenty years'. The cause to which God's servants had given the heart of their lives was, Ludlow observed, 'seemingly dead and buried'. In overthrowing the Puritans and restoring the Stuarts the Lord was pleased 'to make them the tail who before were the head'. Under 'Pharoah', as Ludlow calls Charles II, the godly returned to servitude. The king and his fellow-'vipers' and 'confederates of hell' are 'hunters of the lives and liberties of mankind, Gen. 10.9, feeding on the blood of the saints, Rev. 17.6'.

How was that reversal to be understood and borne? The triumphant royalists and Anglicans, who in the wars had often taken their own afflictions to be providentially ordained, now taunted the defeated Puritans. 'The court of heaven', remarked an Anglican clergyman in 1660, 'hath been solicited these many years *pro* and *con*, and now let the world judge whose prayers have been heard.' Ludlow knew better. The Lord had indeed 'lifted up' the godly's enemies, but only 'for a season'. When their fall came it would be fathomless. God's purpose was not to favour the Philistines, rather to make them 'rods to scourge us'. To his servants – his 'saints' as, following their biblical models, they liked to call themselves – the Lord had given the wondrous opportunity and the immeasurable responsibility to build a godly commonwealth. They had failed, not through conquest by their enemies but from their own sins and divisions. Now their punishment was upon them. Yet their sufferings, no less than their previous ascendancy, belonged to a larger providential design which, once understood, could bring them consolation, fortitude, hope. Their punishment, explained Ludlow, was a 'furnace of affliction' which would 'purge and purify' them. God's 'poor people', so wretchedly divided, would be 'melted into one lamp' and 'come forth as refined gold'. Once God has 'humbled' his servants and 'fitted them for himself, making them willing to be abused for him, he will certainly lift them up and bring them to honour'. A sequence of cosmic providences – comets, violent storms, hailstones 'as big as peas', plagues, fires, ghost armies fighting in the sky, huge whales washed up on beaches – portends the destruction of Charles II's Antichristian tyranny. Sometimes Ludlow thinks that 'the reign of Satan is to be but short', that 'the hour of the Lord's judgement is near at hand, Rev. 14.7', that 'the time is even at the door' when his enemies shall be scattered. Even so God's servants must grasp that they cannot force the pace. To militants and conspirators who are eager to topple the regime before their own sins have been expiated, Ludlow warns that 'the Lord's time is not yet come', that 'there is more of the bitter cup behind for his people to drink of', that 'this is the day of the patience of the Lord and his saints', that the strength of God's people 'sometimes consists in quietness and confidence, Isaiah 30.15'.

Ludlow's counsel of caution infuriated those fellow-exiles who, during the Anglo-Dutch war of the mid-1660s ('this fire between the houses of Abimalech and Shechem' as he likes to call it), wanted to work with the Dutch republicans for the overthrow of the English monarchy. He had one overriding objection. In 1661 three of the regicides who had fled to the United Provinces at the Restoration, John Barkstead, Miles Corbet and John Okey, were captured with the connivance of the Dutch government and brought back to England, there to be tried and executed the following year. Ludlow could never forgive that act of treachery, so 'contrary' as it was to a whole series of 'express texts of Scripture'. The Dutch 'have drawn innocent blood upon their heads', which 'cries out for vengeance' and which only repentance can hope to cleanse. For Ludlow was 'clear in my conscience that the blood of one person unavenged pollutes a whole land'. Bloodguilt was a main theme of Ludlow's thinking. 'Whoso sheddeth man's blood,' he knew from Genesis 9.6, 'by man shall his blood be shed.'

The execution of Charles I met that unanswerable biblical injunction, the king having 'the blood of thousands lying at his door'. Cromwell too contracted the blood of those slain in the civil wars, 'by betraying the cause and trust reposed in him, and sacrificing it to his own lusts'.

In 1672 more blood was spilled in Holland, when the republican leaders, the brothers John and Cornelis de Witt, were murdered by a mob. Ludlow blamed the outrage on the House of Orange, whose leader, the future William III of England, it brought to power in the United Provinces. His 'usurpation', ruled Ludlow, was founded in the blood of 'innocent souls'. In 1688 William would be hailed as England's deliverer from Stuart tyranny, but under Charles II the Orange and Stuart families, tied to each other as they were by marriage and by their hostility to republicanism, seemed to Ludlow and his allies partners in wickedness. If William was the ally of Charles he was also the Dutch equivalent of Cromwell, England's bloodguilty 'usurper'. Like him he had suppressed his country's liberties by acquiring the substance, yet not the title, of kingship. The parallel prompts this reflection in Ludlow:

> And when the nations shall have fully experienced the cruelty and justice of those kings who give power to the Beast, and are of one mind to make war with the Lamb and his followers, they shall hate the Whore and make her desolate, and shall eat her flesh and burn her with fire, Rev. 17.16, who hath made the kings of the earth and inhabitants drunk with the cup of their fornications, verse 2, and shall desire the righteous and peaceable sceptre of Jesus Christ to be set up, Hagg. 2.7 . . .

It is above all the innocent blood of the regicides, barbarously slain after rigged trials in 1660 and 1662, that torments Ludlow's memory. At times it almost seems to run from his pages. Charles I's execution was the central moment in the life of Ludlow, as of others of the king's judges. However reviled it might be by 'this generation of men', which 'hates the light', the execution of justice on the king 'will endure the light when the mouth of all wickedness shall be stopped, and those who have appeared in opposition to it, without serious and timely repentance, be cast into outer darkness'. Of all the iniquities of Restoration England, none seemed wickeder to the saints than the revenge taken on the regicides, that select band who at the crisis of the civil wars had steeled themselves to impose, through that 'eminent act of justice', God's implacable sentence. The fate of those of the king's judges whose mutilated, unburied bodies were exposed to the elements is described by Milton's *Samson Agonistes*, a poem that recalls the destruction of the faithful in language repeatedly close to Ludlow's: victims of 'the unjust tribunals, under change of times,' 'their carcases' are left 'To dogs and fowls a prey'.

In the slaying of the regicides, 'those poor innocent lambs of Christ', Ludlow found the key to a prophecy in the Book of Revelation that had long exercised Protestant interpreters of the Bible. The regicides, he concluded, corresponded to the two 'witnesses' who were 'slain for the word of God, and for the testimony which they held', and who 'cried out with a loud voice, saying, How long, O Lord, holy and true, doest thou not judge and avenge our blood on them that dwell on the earth?' For had not regicides, like their biblical type, been denied burial? Were not their corpses too an omen of impending cataclysm? It was in accordance with the timetable prefigured in Revelation, Ludlow noticed, that about three and a half years after the executions of 1660 there began a series of afflictions – among them the Anglo-Dutch war and the Great Plague – that seemed to announce the ascent of the Beast from the bottomless pit.

On no subject is the fate of Ludlow's religion at the hands of the publishers of the *Memoirs* more starkly illustrated than in the rewriting of his accounts of the regicides' trials and deaths in 1660–62. Describing the execution of Miles Corbet, Ludlow's manuscript recalls that in 1649, 'having many temptations upon him', Corbet 'forbore to appear' as a judge in the king's trial

> till the day the sentence was pronounced, at which time that word in Revelation 21.8, viz. the fearful and unbelieving shall have their part in the lake that burns with fire and brimstone, being set upon his heart by the Lord, did so work upon him and powerfully prevail with him that he durst not any longer absent himself, but made haste to come and sit amongst them, lest the threatened punishment of the fearful should be his portion.

In the *Memoirs* the passage becomes:

he appeared not among the judges by reason of some scruples he had entertained, till the day the sentence was pronounced. But upon more mature deliberation finding them to be of no weight, he durst no longer absent himself, coming early on that day into the court, that he might give a public testimony of his satisfaction and concurrence with those proceedings.

Corbet's character, like Ludlow's own, is transformed in the *Memoirs*. A surviving autobiographical fragment by him recalls the preoccupations and the religious intensity of Ludlow's manuscript. 'A Voice from the Watch Tower' itself recalls that Corbet was 'bred up to the law' at Lincoln's Inn,

yet not neglecting to search after the knowledge of the law of God, and to conform his own life thereto. And to that end, with several other gentlemen of the Inns of Court whose hearts the Lord had wrought upon by the power of his spirit, he frequented the ministry and company of Dr [John] Preston, that famous instrument in the Lord's hand.

The *Memoirs* tell us only that Corbet 'applied himself with diligence to the study of the laws of England in the society of Lincoln's Inn'.

Others of the king's judges are transformed too. In the manuscript Ludlow reports the execution of the regicide John Barkstead:

When the Lord called him forth to witness to the justice of that act [the regicide] for which he suffered, he did it with much cheerfulness and satisfaction, declaring himself ready and willing to be offered up, as being very clear in his conscience that what he was accused of and condemned for was done by him in obedience to the call of God, and the authority of the nation; and was often heard to say, and particularly the day before his execution to an eminent minister, that his great burden then was that he ever lifted up a finger against any of the people of God who were of a contrary opinion to him; and desired them to love the spirit of God wheresoever they found it.

We turn to the corresponding passage of the *Memoirs*:

When he was brought forth to confirm with the testimony of his blood that cause for which he had fought, he performed that part with cheerfulness and courage, no way derogating from the character of a soldier and a true Englishman.

Ludlow's long description of the spiritual exclamations with which two other convicted regicides, John Jones and Adrian Scrope, prepared for death is reduced in the *Memoirs* to the statement that 'the gravity and graceful mien of these ancient gentlemen' was 'accompanied with visible marks of fortitude and internal satisfaction'.

At every point the religious priorities of the Ludlow of the Bodleian manuscript were turned into secular ones. The same must have been true of the Ludlow of the pre-1660 portion, now missing, of his text. The *Memoirs* turned Ludlow from a saint into a patriot. The Bodleian manuscript does affirm his loyalty to his country, but the sentiment is far subordinate to his loyalty to God. In the *Memoirs* that priority is reversed. The main preface to the *Memoirs* (written by the publishers) places Ludlow among those virtuous men who 'make the service of their country the principal care of their lives', and reveals that when he returned to England in 1689 it was 'in an ecstasy to serve his country anywhere'. In the text of the *Memoirs* 'the cause of my country' is 'dearer to me than my life'. The 'love' and 'service' of one's 'country' are presented as the guiding ideal not only of Ludlow but of his allies. Aligned with patriotism is the readiness, with which the Ludlow of the *Memoirs* is amply blessed, to put 'the public good' or 'common good' before the selfish claims of 'faction' and of private 'interest'. In the Bodleian manuscript, too, the 'public good' exerts its own claims. In that as in most matters the publishers more often distort than invent. 'The public good' and 'common good' had been invoked often enough by participants in the civil wars, as had the ideal of 'service' to one's 'country'. The distortion is none the less severe. In the manuscript the political self-seeking that opposes the public good is merely the symptom of a deeper evil: of the 'carnal' – that is, the non-spiritual – sway of 'self' that fights God's spirit for mastery of the soul.

The Ludlow of the *Memoirs* is alert to another patriotic obligation:

the vigilant protection of those civil liberties upon which the nation's well-being rests. The main preface emphasizes that Ludlow's father (about whose religion next to nothing is known) 'strenuously asserted the rights and liberties of the people against the invasions made upon them by the pretended prerogatives of the Crown'. The text presents the son in the same light. Edmund contends for 'the laws and liberties of the nation', for 'our just rights and liberties'. His career is a constant struggle against 'arbitrary' government. There is the 'tyranny' first of Charles I, then of Cromwell. In exile the Ludlow of the *Memoirs* regards the 'arbitrary' power of Charles II, and his aim 'to render the monarchy absolute and uncontrolled', as the principal evil of the Restoration era. Again that picture has a basis in the manuscript, but again it involves a radical adjustment of it. 'A Voice from the Watch Tower' does attack political 'tyranny'. It also alludes, passingly, to 'civil rights'. But the essential evil of tyranny is shown to lie not in the violation of those rights but in the spiritual wickedness that inspires it and in its consequences for God's true worshippers. When the manuscript refers to 'civil and spiritual liberties', the civil ones count for much less than the spiritual. In the *Memoirs* the phrase becomes 'the liberties of the nation'.

The Ludlow of the *Memoirs* repeatedly distinguishes between 'civil' rule, which is virtuous, and 'military' government, which is wicked. He 'always endeavoured to assert the authority of the civil magistrate in opposition to the tyranny of the sword', and 'always declared it to be my opinion, that the military sword ought to be subject to the civil power'. Cromwell's protectorate is a military tyranny, rule 'by the sword'. Those sentiments, which are exactly attuned to the hostility to standing armies that prompted the publication of the *Memoirs*, are not those of the Ludlow of the manuscript. 'A Voice from the Watch Tower', it is true, does complain that Cromwell 'trampled the civil authority under foot'. But 'government by the sword' is mainly objectionable to Ludlow not on grounds of constitutional or civil liberty but because

it's against the whole series of God's word and promises, which declares that in the latter days violence shall no more be heard in the land, that there shall be no need to learn war any more, that the lamb shall lie down by the lion, and the leopard by the kid.

The *Memoirs* present a contradiction in Ludlow's responses to military intervention in politics. He is outraged by Cromwell's coups of 1653. Yet five years earlier he endorses, indeed takes part in, Pride's Purge, the military coup that paves the way for the regicide. The stickler for constitutional propriety is its violator – as, in the early eighteenth century, the criticisms passed on the *Memoirs* in the orthodox Whig histories of Burnet and Rapin would point out. In the manuscript there is no such contradiction, for 'the privilege of parliament', Ludlow there observes, is 'so far only to be made use of as a means tending to the advancement of God and the good of the nation'. In 1648–9 the army leaders saw it to be 'their duty rather to violate the privilege of parliament than to suffer the cause of God to be destroyed'. The regicides bore the sword, not of tyranny, but of justice. 'Looking upon a good cause and a good sword to be a good authority,' explains Ludlow, they 'judged it their duty not to bear the sword in vain, but to employ it for the terror of evil doers, and to the praise of them that do well, as the Lord commands, I Pet. 2.14.' Charles must die because 'he that killeth by the sword shall be killed by the sword, Rev. 13'.

Ludlow's attitude to Cromwell's coups of 1653, when the sword was put not to godly uses but to ungodly ones, is likewise distorted by the *Memoirs*. There he is made to eulogize the Long Parliament, and especially its Rump. His paean plainly owes something, and may owe a great deal, to his publishers, who, like the sponsors of the Ludlow pamphlets of the early 1690s, held up the Long Parliament for emulation in the present. Again the publishers' tactics make an aspect of Ludlow's conduct hard to understand. If Ludlow was so appalled by the coup of April 1653, why did he not protest against it, and why did he remain in his civilian and military posts in Ireland? For in 1653 it was not the expulsion of the Rump in April that devastated him and drove him into opposition to Cromwell. It was Oliver's seizure of personal power eight months later, after the dissolution of Barebone's Parliament, an assembly which had no basis of legitimacy in the civil or constitutional rights on which the *Memoirs* dwell. Only spiritual convictions can explain Ludlow's reaction to its fall from power. Barebone's had pressed ahead, all too rapidly for Cromwell's comfort, with measures of godly reformation of a kind which the Ludlow of the manuscript would have welcomed and which in his eyes had been frustrated in the Rump.

From a document signed by Ludlow at the time, we know that when he and the other Irish commissioners, men of religious persuasions close to his, received news of the fall of Barebone's, they exhorted their 'Christian friends' to meet in faith 'at the throne of grace by effectual fervent prayer' and to 'turn from every evil way, to the healing of our backsliding and the settlement of these poor nations'. Their attitude to Cromwell's usurpation parallels Ludlow's response to the Restoration seven years later. In both cases the 'backsliding' of the godly is to blame for political disaster. In both cases the price is the elevation of a sinful ruler. It is not Cromwell's use of the sword that distresses Ludlow but the triumph of his 'carnal interest', of his 'self', over the spirit of godliness. In the *Memoirs*, it is true, Cromwell's selfishness is likewise to blame: 'The perfidious Cromwell having forgot his most solemn professions and former vows, as well as the blood and treasure that had been spent in this contest, thought it high time to take off the mask, and resolved to sacrifice all our victories and deliverances to his pride and ambition.' But the crime is now a civil, not a spiritual one. Whereas the *Memoirs* have much to say about the political 'ambition' of Cromwell and other politicians, the manuscript talks of their 'lust', that prompter of a 'carnal' spirit. It seems to have been the inherent tendency of monarchical rule to promote that 'lust', not the concern for civil liberties underlined by the *Memoirs*, that made Ludlow a republican.

In a letter of 1662 to his friends in England, Ludlow reflected on the fate of the godly cause to which he and they had committed their lives. He recalled its marvellous epoch of prosperity:

> The Lord hath appeared in our days to do great things, such as our fathers had not seen, nor ears scarce heard of. He raised up the poor, foolish, unexperienced and weak ones of the earth, to confound the rich, the wise, and the mighty thereof, speaking clearly . . . that his design is to advance himself and the riches of his grace in his son, and to give him the necks of all his enemies who would not that he should reign over them.

Here, surely, was a decisive and momentous era in the world's history, when the saints were to be God's appointed instruments of deliverance. 'As, in all ages', the Lord 'hath been making way for this glorious reign of his, so did the wheel hasten to that end in our days'. The saints confronted massive obstacles, but God was 'so merciful that he made those mountains plain before him, and put a prize into our hands which, had we wisdom, we might have made a wonderful improvement of'.

It was Cromwell who destroyed that prospect. 'The lust of power and domination prevailing, much art was used' by the protector and his adherents 'for the drawing in of many zealous, well-meaning and pious Christians (who earnestly desired to see those good things which the Lord had promised, and their souls thirsted after, accomplished)', and who hoped that Cromwell would use his power to further those ends. Those deluded souls soon found themselves 'trodden under foot, and such only promoted to ride in the chariot with Jehu who with Jehonadab had their hearts right with his heart, who were for him and his interest, which was to make his will the rule of obedience in Church and state'. After the 'horrid and detestable impiety' of his usurpation there was soon, among the godly congregations, 'scarce anything of the power of godliness remaining, that principally consisting in a faithful witness to the work the Lord had upon the wheel in that our day'. In the *Memoirs* Cromwell usurps the rule of the people's representatives in parliament. In the manuscript he usurps the reign of Christ's spirit.

In the 1670s Ludlow's thoughts returned again to Cromwell's elevation. He saw it now as a turning-point not only in England but across Europe. From then there had arisen a fresh spirit of persecution, which first revealed itself in the 'storm of blood that fell upon the poor [Protestants] of Piedmont' in 1655. In the same year, Ludlow remembered, the protector's troops were humiliatingly routed on the Spanish island of Hispaniola (Haiti). How striking was the contrast between their successes in earlier days, when men 'engaged in a good cause succeeded almost to admiration', and the catastrophe incurred now that 'the hand of the Lord was against them'. The *Memoirs* replace Ludlow's spiritual explanation of the fiasco with a secular one: soldiers who had 'performed wonders' when 'they fought for the liberties of their country' lost their fighting qualities once they had 'engaged to support the late erected tyranny'.

There are comparable adjustments throughout. In the *Memoirs* the war aim of the parliamentarians is 'to remove the obstructions that were in the way of the civil government'. In the manuscript the word 'obstructions' is used to describe impediments to the reign of Christ. Again, Ludlow tells us that after his escape from England he was glad to find refuge in Switzerland, partly because he liked 'the air of a commonwealth' but 'above all' because he hoped to enjoy, in that Protestant community, God's 'ordinances' and the company of God's 'servants'. The publishers omit that devotional aspiration and in its place invent a tribute to William Tell and the origins of Swiss republicanism.

When we assess the significance of the Bodleian manuscript for the study of the civil wars, one obvious question presents itself. How reliable is the manuscript, written as it was after the wars, as a guide to Ludlow's Puritanism during them? Exile besets its victims with hazards of introspection and with temptations to embittered self-righteousness. Perhaps in Ludlow's case – as in that of the English Protestants who had fled to Switzerland from persecution under Queen Mary in the 1550s – it produced a heightening of spiritual radicalism and intensity. We should notice too his dependence, in his accounts of events in Restoration England, on sources supplied and slanted by his Nonconformist friends there. He writes with an eye to the preoccupations of those allies, even perhaps to their approval. No doubt too he writes with the sense that God is looking over his shoulder. In any case, men are not the same in action as in contemplation. 'A Voice from the Watch Tower' is the record of a man released from those pressures of events which, in even the devoutest politician, will demand practical calculations and responses, and with which the most imperative of spiritual aspirations will mingle. If the *Memoirs* place a heavy layer over the religious experiences of the civil wars, there is a sense in which, during their afflictions at the Restoration, the saints imposed a layer of their own. In particular the martyrological literature (on which the Bodleian manuscript extensively draws) recounting the trials and sufferings of the regicides, those lambs of Christ whom the world despised, blotted out real politics. It also passed over the saints' own earlier, often ruthless exercise of power over their enemies.

Yet when we turn to the surviving letters of Ludlow written during the 1640s and 1650s, we find a voice essentially the same as that which later issues from his watch tower. If the saints of the 1660s interpreted their sufferings at the hands of the ungodly as the smiting of God's rod, the saints of the civil war had assessed their own defeats in the same spirit. During the Puritan upheaval no less than after it, God's chosen ones placed the low points of their cause within a divine timetable which they knew to be on their side. 'Surely,' reflected Oliver Cromwell at a bleak moment in March 1647, 'the Devil hath but a short time.' Countless letters and manifestos of soldiers and sectaries and regicides with whom Ludlow allied during the civil wars speak the saintly language of his manuscript.*

It was not a voice suited to all occasions. The saints habitually spoke their own language to each other, only inhabitually in front of less godly hearers, where they normally accommodated themselves to more conventional modes of address. Though Ludlow knew that the saints were set apart spiritually, he did not suppose that that privilege gave them superior civil or political rights. There was a small minority within the saintly cause, consisting principally of the sect known as the Fifth Monarchy men, who thought it the duty of the saints to win power by force and to subjugate the unregenerate. Ludlow rejected that supposition. Even the godliest of political deeds, he maintained, must have constitutional and legal authority behind them. The reasoning with which he squared the use of a 'good sword' with his respect for constitutionalism is, admittedly, far from persuasive. Even so his concern to reconcile the two reminds us that, however subordinate civil liberties might have been to spiritual ones in his own mind, they figured prominently in the Roundhead cause, with whose other participants he was bound in cooperation.

Besides, differences of political setting demand differences of demeanour. There survive summaries of some of Ludlow's speeches in

* Vivid examples are supplied by two collections of letters: the *Milton State Papers*, edited by John Nickolls in 1743; and the 'Inedited Letters' brought together by J. Mayer in *Transactions of the Historical Society of Lancashire and Cheshire*, 1861.

parliament in 1659, where, as far as we can judge, he mostly spoke not in saintly but in parliamentary language. Defending the 'liberties of the people' and the 'rights' of the electorate, he sounds much less distant from the Ludlow of the *Memoirs* than he does in the Bodleian manuscript. On one occasion he offers the House an explanation of the civil wars, based on recent arguments of the republican thinker James Harrington, that has more to do with economics than with religion. One of Ludlow's allies in parliament was Harrington's close friend Henry Neville, whose own writing displayed that very readiness, which Ludlow's manuscript abhors, to learn as much from the history of ancient Rome as from Scripture. Neville was charged before the Commons with atheism after allegedly remarking that he would sooner read Cicero than the Bible. Ludlow worked still more closely with Neville's friend, and Ludlow's father's friend, the regicide Henry Marten, a freethinker and open adulterer scornful of the moral severity of the Puritans and of their obsession with the evils of popery.

Among Roundheads Marten's anti-Puritanism was exceptional. So was his disrespect for the doctrine of providence. An alertness to God's presence in the world was an inbuilt feature of most mid-seventeenth-century minds, Cavalier as well as Roundhead. It was, however, more often a sobering or consolatory force than the dynamic and energizing one – the impulse to destroy principalities and powers – that it became for Ludlow and his fellow-saints. In that respect, as in their political programme, they were in a minority. Yet it was (mainly) they who radicalized the Roundhead cause, they who demanded and achieved the regicide and planted their convictions in that deed.

Earlier the saints had made the parliamentary soldiery, a force hitherto 'despised by our enemies and little less than despaired of by our friends', the instrument of victory. When Ludlow rode into battle the colours of his regiment showed an open Bible over the pope's crosier, staff and rosary lying on their side, and carried the words 'I yield to the truth, the word of God.' Because Ludlow wrote 'A Voice from the Watch Tower' in defeat and disappointment, perhaps too because he had not been present at the great parliamentary victories of 1644–5 and 1648, his text does not convey the exultation and exaltation known by the saints when God's outstretched arm confounded all human calculation. Other regicides, however, offered ample testimony to the impact of those 'mercies' upon their thinking and their conduct. Out of them there arose the zeal and confidence that would take the saints into the uncharted political territory of the regicide and republic.

The voice that communicates that experience most vividly is Oliver Cromwell's. His interpretation of the world, like Ludlow's, is steeped in biblical reflection. Trust in God's providence is the 'rock', the 'sure refuge', the 'sun and shield' of his life. In the Bodleian manuscript Cromwell's usurpation is so painful to Ludlow not, as it is in the *Memoirs*, because it destroys civil liberty but because it is the apostasy of a kindred spirit. Cromwell remembered the providential deliverance of God's people, and assessed its place in the divine scheme of history, much as Ludlow did. The Lord, he knew, 'hath been pleased to make choice of these islands wherein to manifest many great and glorious things', 'such things amongst us as have not been known in the world these thousand years'. He had wonderfully raised up Cromwell, a 'weak instrument', 'not worthy the name of a worm', and through him had laid low the mighty. Cromwell recognized in his own victories a 'remarkable series' or 'chain' of 'providences'. The saints 'were never beaten; wherever they engaged the enemy they beat them continually. And truly this . . . has some instruction in it.' At Naseby in 1645, riding up and down to inspect the cavalry on the morning of battle, he 'could not but smile out to God in praises, in assurance of victory'. Then there came the triumphs of the second civil war in 1648, 'those wonderful works of God', as he called them, 'breaking the rod of the oppressor as in the day of Midian'. After that there were the 'marvellous great', 'unspeakable mercies' in Ireland in 1649, victories won 'neither from our brains nor from our courage and strength, but that we follow the Lord who goeth before, and gather what he scattereth. . . . What can we say to these things? If God be for us, who can be against us?' After the battle of Dunbar in 1650 he wrote to parliament to report 'one of the most signal mercies God has done for England and his people this war. . . . It would do you good to see and hear our poor foot go up and down making their boast of God.'

That same year, according to Ludlow's *Memoirs*, Cromwell held a discussion with him about the present condition of the Commonwealth's cause, during which Oliver 'spent at least an hour in the exposition of the 110th Psalm'. In 1698 a critic of the *Memoirs* derided that passage. No 'man of sense', he maintained, would believe that Cromwell, a practical politician 'oppressed with ponderous affairs', would have 'wasted above an hour' in theological converse with 'an empty bigot', unless from some ulterior motive to which Ludlow had been blind. By the late seventeenth century the religion both of Cromwell and of Ludlow had become unintelligible. In the account of the conversation in the *Memoirs*, Cromwell's hypocrisy in making use of the Bible is contrasted with the integrity of Ludlow, who takes his stand on civil liberties. If we had the corresponding passage of 'A Voice from the Watch Tower' we would surely find in it an exchange between fellow-saints, accustomed to prolonged deliberation on biblical texts and on their pertinence to current events. Had Ludlow but known it, the accusations of sinfulness and apostasy that he and other saints would heap upon Cromwell after his break with them weighed on the protector's heart with a heaviness almost beyond endurance.

The secularization of Ludlow's manuscript in the 1690s had its parallels in that decade, albeit of a much less ambitious kind. Those who republished pamphlets by Milton – or in some cases plagiarized them – adjusted the texts to reduce their religious dimension. When the autobiography of the prominent Puritan divine Richard Baxter was published in 1696, its editor contrived to replace millenarian emphases with constitutional ones. In the *Memorials* of Thomas Fairfax, published in 1699, the religious language of Fairfax's own text was muted and abbreviated.

The publishers of the *Memoirs*, though they needed to remove Ludlow's Puritan zeal, could have afforded to allow him a larger portion of sober religious reflection. The England of the 1690s had its own providentialism and its own piety. Historians have recently become increasingly alert to the decade's seriousness of mind. Across the political and ecclesiastical boundaries there arose a sense that the political upheavals of the later Stuart period, no less than the chaos of the civil wars before them, had been a divine punishment for godly sinfulness, which must now be purged. But the apocalyptic dimension, and the doctrinal intensity and rigidity, of mid-seventeenth-century Puritanism had retreated. Even among Dissenters there was a theological softening. On the infrequent occasions when the preoccupations of the mid-century with the millennium and with Antichrist can still be glimpsed after 1688, they are mainly expounded by ageing survivors from the earlier time. The belief in divine providence continued to pervade English society, but the decline and discrediting of Puritanism, in which it had assumed most of its volatile forms, had modified its intensity. God's direction of the world's affairs seemed, in the main, less direct and less frequent. There was less eagerness, too, to interpret his interventions as signals to his chosen ones, as aids to the training of the soul on its Calvinist pathway to salvation. Whether England had become a less religious country by the late seventeenth century is a problematical question. What we can say is that religion itself was changing. Protestants had less to say about faith, more about conduct, less about hellfire, more about the scope of human virtue and human reason. Ludlow had been appalled by the claims of 'reason' in religion. In 1695 the publication of John Locke's *The Reasonableness of Christian Religion* showed how far those claims had spread.

The voice from Ludlow's watch tower was by now of a past age. His manuscript, had it been brought before the world in the 1690s, could only have aroused derision and horror. It would have been an easy target for Tories, who loved to find evidence of Puritan 'fanaticism' and of its links with sedition. Even as it was, Tory critics of the *Memoirs* projected their own images of Puritanism on to Ludlow. He was a 'grand fanatic', 'the most holy and sanctified traitor of the gang' of 'king-killers'. If the *Memoirs* were to fulfil the purpose of their publishers, Ludlow's zeal would have to yield to different attributes, more palatable to the new age and more closely related to its politics. We shall now see how Ludlow became, not a Puritan, but a radical Whig.

3

Ludlow the Whig

In November 1692, around the time when the last of the four Ludlow pamphlets was written, an anonymous tract of kindred sympathy, *A Dialogue between Whig and Tory*, bemoaned 'the miserable state we are fallen into from the happy and glorious prospect of things we had in 1688 and 1689'. The sense of loss among radical Whigs intensified in the years ahead. 'The Revolution', remarked their pamphleteer William Stephens in 1701, 'is gone backwards as far as King Charles the Second's reign.' Over the eighteenth century the 'Glorious Revolution' came to be widely accepted as the foundation of modern liberty, a fundamental and binding renunciation of arbitrary and non-parliamentary rule. Within that perspective the nervous uncertainties and constitutional conflicts that endured through the 1690s and beyond them were often forgotten. Only after the accession of the Hanoverian dynasty on the death of Queen Anne in 1714 and the failure of the Jacobite rising the following year, perhaps only after the defeat of the further rising in 1745, did the Revolution seem secure and its constitutional gains decisive. Even then dissentient voices remained.

Among the radicals of the 1690s there were three principal grounds of discontent. The first was the king's unwillingness, once he was settled on his throne, to employ them. The second was the refusal of the government to endorse their interpretation of the Revolution. In their eyes the people had exercised their ancient right, the right which had also been invoked in 1649, to depose a tyrant and erect another government in its place. The nation (or that part of it which articulated its views) was mostly appalled by that version of events. It preferred to think that James had abdicated, that he had left a vacancy on the throne which had had to be filled in order that normality might be restored. The third grievance of the radicals was the continued exercise of royal prerogatives which in 1689 had unwisely been left unimpaired by the Bill of Rights.

Here their disenchantment was more widely shared. William struck few roots in English affections. Few English monarchs have been so little mourned. He was especially unpopular in the late 1690s, when he tried to evade the commitment he had made to parliament to reduce his army. His cold and aloof personality, his dependence on his hated Dutch advisers and favourites, his apparent readiness to put Dutch strategic and financial interests before English ones, created antagonism across a broad political spectrum. So, conseqently, did his insistence on choosing his own ministers and his refusal to concede that they should be accountable to parliament. He retained his legislative veto and resisted (though eventually he yielded to) legislation to guarantee regular parliamentary elections. He opposed the revision of those procedures of treason trials which in the 1680s had made martyrs of Algernon Sidney and the other Whig victims of Judge Jeffreys.

In some radical quarters disillusion was bluntly voiced. 'I thought we called over the Prince of Orange,' declared an exasperated pamphleteer of 1693 in *A Short State of our Condition*, 'to get or give us all the laws we needed.' The same writer judged that 1688 had been no deliverance. 'If we are to be slaves, it's no matter to choose whose we are.' Yet such direct criticism of William was exceptional. The Jacobites aside, most writers, however dismayed by the government's conduct, remembered to applaud the man who had, after all, thwarted Stuart tyranny in 1688. They adhered to the ancient conventions of deference and compliment to the reigning ruler. They blamed, not the king, but his wicked advisers; or they argued that, while prerogative powers could of course be safely entrusted to the present monarch, they might easily be abused by a future one; or they targeted 'the court', from whose sins the monarch was somehow exempted.

Behind those obligatory courtesies, however, there lay a fundamental disquiet. It was not only from the radicals that the king's administration came under attack. A vocabulary of opposition was developing which, though it can often be heard in the later Stuart period, became louder and more insistent after 1688. It would persist through the eighteenth century. It brought together backbenchers of various political creeds. Since the Restoration, the Crown had acquired new resources of patronage from the expansion of royal revenues and of the civil service. By bestowing offices ('places' or 'preferments') and bribes and lands on MPs it could undermine their independence and 'corrupt' them. The demand that office-holders be disqualified from parliament acquired a lasting prominence.

In the 1690s, when the resources of the state swelled still further, 'corruption' came to seem the principal threat to liberty. Bribery appeared endemic to the post-Revolutionary political culture. Protests against 'placemen' became more voluble. They were directed not least at John Somers, the junto leader, a skilful operator of the patronage system and the prime betrayer, as radicals saw it, of their cause. No constitutional action of William caused more fury than his veto in 1693 of a bill to exclude placemen from the House of Commons. The hostility to them belonged to a wider mood of unease. The scale of government patronage and rewards was made possible by a revolution in the state's finances carried out by another junto leader, Charles Montagu, the Chancellor of the Exchequer. Instead of repaying the massive national debt run up by the war with France, the government used parliamentary taxation, itself now massive, to pay the interest on it. Hitherto the refusal of taxation to the Crown had been the Commons' bargaining-weapon. Now its hands were tied, for to deny taxation would be to plunge the fiscal system into crisis.

The Revolution of 1688, though in the long term it weakened the Crown, strengthened the state. The share of monarchs in the running of the state diminished, but the power of the ministers who spoke in their name increased, or at least seemed to do so. Under the later Stuarts as under the early ones, political conflict had been largely about the balance of power between Crown and parliament. Now parliament – or at least the frontbenchers and their henchmen – could seem the Crown's ally against the nation. As the 'old Whig' James Ralph would put it in *The Use and Abuse of Parliaments* in 1744, the evil of 'governing *without* a parliament' had yielded to that of 'governing *by* a parliament'. Against that background the differences between Whigs and Tories could look smaller than those between frontbenchers and backbenchers, between placemen and the independent country gentlemen, between 'court' and 'country'. From around the middle of the 1690s the beginnings of a 'country' alliance brought backbench Whigs and backbench Tories together. Its leaders exploited a dislike, present even among ardent followers of Whig and Tory constitutional principles, of the party system, that instrument of 'faction' through which the executive was tightening its grip on the legislature. The country sentiment of William III's reign had its successes. Its vigilance against the expansion of the executive and the increase of placemen imposed some curbs on both developments. The principal architect of the country coalition was Robert Harley, a man with a Whig past who would become a Tory leader in Anne's reign. As the Whig junto lost its way in 1697, so Harley, speaking from the backbenches, became a dominant presence in the House, his stature enhanced by his own reputation for incorruptibility and for independence of mind.

Behind country values there lay a long tradition of anti-courtly sentiment. Under the Tudors and early Stuarts that sentiment had been directed at the entourage of the king. The expansion of parliament's importance, as a result first of the civil wars and then of the Revolution of 1688, broadened the target. In country-party minds the evils of Whitehall merged with those of Westminster. But if the focus altered, characteristics of the earlier outlook persisted. Under the Tudors and Stuarts, complaints against courtly life had been heard not only from men excluded from it but from courtiers themselves. They preserved a modicum of self-respect by expressing their own superiority to those habits of duplicity, of servility, and of false display which seemed inseparable from Renaissance courts and in which they themselves were implicated. Just so, after 1688, did country values attract MPs with courtly connections. As they and others discovered, the country-party stance had not only its emotional appeal but its opportunist uses. Men on the make adopted it to win influence in the Commons and thus to establish or enhance influence at court. But they could do so only because of the depth and intensity with which country values were held. Like earlier anti-courtly protest, the post-Revolutionary country movement had a strong moral colouring. It is no coincidence that the years 1697 to 1701, when the language and impact of country sentiment peaked, were also the high point of the post-Revolutionary movement, legislative and social, for the improvement of the nation's morals and manners.

The country alliance offered new hope to the radical Whigs. No longer need their hostility to arbitrary power seem a sectional prejudice, doomed to impotence on a dwindling fringe. It could, if skilfully presented, be made to appear the natural stance of the morally upright and the natural sentiment of all who held or aspired to gentility. That, as we shall find, is the ambition behind Ludlow's *Memoirs*. The radical Whigs directed their appeal both to MPs and to the political nation at large. Their predecessors of the exclusion crisis of Charles II's reign had done the same. One of them was an old ally of Ludlow, Slingsby Bethel. His tactics at that time had, in turn, recalled an earlier era. In 1659 Bethel published an account of the parliament held in that year by Richard Cromwell, in which Bethel approvingly described the conduct of the party to which he and Edmund Ludlow belonged. He called the party 'the commonwealthmen', by which he meant the opponents of government by any single person, whether a king or protector. In 1680, during the exclusion crisis, Bethel republished the tract to promote the same anti-monarchical message. But the associations of the term 'commonwealthmen', which summoned memories of England's republican experiences, were too revolutionary to be readily risked under the later Stuarts. Bethel replaced it with a different phrase, 'the country party'. His aim was a synthesis, on the backbenches, of republican and country-party sentiment. Ludlow's *Memoirs* would be a more ambitious exercise in the same strategy.

The development of the country alliance in the later 1690s, which drew on the disillusion of the radical Whigs, took strength too from developments within a section of the Tory party. Indeed Tories contributed more votes to the country cause than Whigs did. A telling instance of country Toryism is the behaviour of the MP Sir Edward Seymour, a close neighbour and old enemy of Ludlow. In 1681, when the Whig cause was crushed by the dissolution of the parliament held in Oxford, it was in Seymour's coach that the king left the city. Seymour was then at the height of his influence. Yet there had always been country sentiment in him. By the late 1690s it was to the fore. He was now visible principally as an opponent of the court. Appalled by the government's methods of controlling parliament, he had begun to emphasize the obligations of MPs to their constituents and their duty to preserve their independence of voice.

Another issue inflamed Seymour too: William's resolve to maintain an army after the Peace of Ryswick. The opposition to the army was not one solely of principle. The high cost of its maintenance played an important part. Most MPs, Harley among them, accepted the inevitability of a standing force of some kind. Their objection was essentially to the size of William's military establishment. But Harley found it useful to encourage opposition to the very principle of a standing army. In the debates of 1697–9 such sentiment became, as the nineteenth-century historian T. B. Macaulay would write, a 'mania'. The presence of army officers among the placemen added to the frenzy and helped to tie anti-army to anti-courtly feeling. 'We have enough to do to guard ourselves against the court without having an army thrown into the scale against us', declared the widely read pamphlet of 1697, *An Argument Showing that a Standing Army is Incompatible with a Free Government*.

As it had under the later Stuarts, the issue of standing armies provoked learned oratory. MPs paraded their historical knowledge. A long tradition of Renaissance thinking explained how standing armies had destroyed the liberties, and created the tyrannies, of ancient Greece and Rome and the modern Italian city-states. Standing armies, it was held, fight, ignobly, for 'pay'. So long as it suits them they will do their master's bidding, however evil. But they are equally ready to topple him and choose another. England, warned country-party voices, already had 'mercenary parliaments', controlled by placemen, who served not their electors but their paymasters. Now it faced the prospect of a 'mercenary army'. Even if William did not abuse the power which it gave him, the army might easily abuse him. In 1688, after all, James II's 'mercenary' army had gone over to William. Might not William's revert to a Jacobite allegiance?

To those who opposed standing armies on principle, there was only one solution. The county militias must be reformed and revitalized, so that a standing force would become superfluous. History showed that, whereas hired armies are imposed on the nations that finance them, militias have roots in the communities they serve. Their interests being identical with their country's, they fight, not for wages, but for its survival and its liberties. The reformed militias would be England's equivalent to the citizen army of ancient Rome. They would be led by the nobility and gentry, England's parallel to Rome's senatorial class. England's model senators, or independent landowners, would thus have two functions. At Westminster, resisting all inducements of fear or favour, they would guard liberty and the constitution against the encroachments or misuses of the prerogative. In the localities they would have a comparable protective role at the head of the militias. Alongside the enduring eighteenth-century campaign against placemen there emerged a no less tenacious tradition of protest against standing armies. It was in large part the opposition to placemen and standing armies that shaped an ideal which would have a powerful hold on eighteenth-century thinking, that of the independent country gentleman. The parliamentary debates of the late 1690s were a critical phase of its emergence.

Pamphleteers who opposed the maintenance of William's army emphasized the connection between standing armies and the issue of constitutional freedom. 'No author,' they averred, 'ever treated of a free government that did not express his horror of an army'; 'we shall find in no country, liberty and an army stand together, so that to know whether a people be free or slaves it is necessary only to ask whether there is an army amongst them'; ''tis well known, all the world over, wherever the sword is in the hands of the people, it is a free government'. The MPs and writers who made that case found illustrations of it not only in classical antiquity or Renaissance Europe but in an example nearer to hand: in the political record, which the *Memoirs of Edmund Ludlow* so vividly illustrated, of the army of Oliver Cromwell. As the publishers' preface to the third volume of the *Memoirs* explains, 'Men may learn from the issue of the Cromwellian tyranny that liberty and a standing mercenary army are incompatible.' We shall now see how adroitly, both on that and on other issues, the *Memoirs* were shaped so as to address the backbench anxieties of the 1690s. Some of those anxieties were the province of radical Whigs. Like the Ludlow pamphlets before them the *Memoirs* were a radical Whig document. Yet they also spoke, as the pamphlets had not, to a country-party audience. At every point the correspondence of the story told in the *Memoirs* to the preoccupations of the 1690s either certainly or *ſtent with the Publick Safety. Men may learn from the Iſſue of the* Cromwellian *Tyranny, That Liberty and a Standing Mercenary Army are incompatible. For 'tis as clear as the Sun at Noon-day, that the Parliament by neglecting to put a Period to the exorbitant Greatneſs of* Oliver Cromwel *immediately after the Battle at* Worceſter, *drew Deſtruction upon themſelves and the whole Common-wealth; and gave the Army ſuch an opportunity to feel their Strength as naturally led them to Counſels deſtructive to the Government. This produced that monſtrous Tyranny of the Uſurper and his Baſha's under the Name of Majors General, and afterwards compelled the People to ſuffer the return of*

The preface to volume three.

probably involved the distortion – in many cases the severe distortion – of Ludlow's own narrative.

Until the Peace of Ryswick the resentment of the radical Whigs at the conduct of the junto was rarely made public. In 1697 it exploded. Betrayal, the resentment which animated the radicals, is also the animating theme of the *Memoirs*. In Ludlow's mind it was God's cause that had been betrayed. In the *Memoirs* the cause is secular. Their opening words – 'Having seen our cause betrayed, and the most solemn promises that could be made to the assertors of it openly violated' – announce the theme. The analogy between the 1690s and the civil wars is transparent. Like the radical Whigs in and after 1688, the Ludlow of the *Memoirs* 'thought the justice of that cause I had engaged in to be so evident that I could not imagine it would be attended with so much difficulty'. Yet the 'good old cause' deserted by the Whig junto was deserted in mid-century too. Those men who, in the 1640s and the 1680s alike, had borne the heat and burden of the day found themselves abandoned. The 'apostasy' of politicians of that earlier era affords a series of parallels to the conduct of the 'apostate Whigs'.

In the earlier case the arch-betrayer, the man at whom the opening words of the *Memoirs* are directed, was Cromwell. It is he whose 'solemn promises' were 'openly violated', he who 'betrayed the public cause' and 'treacherously advanced himself upon the ruins of the Commonwealth', so that 'those who had hazarded all for their country found themselves cheated'. In adjusting, here as so often, Ludlow's own anti-Cromwellianism to their purposes, the publishers give Cromwell a modern parallel. In the 1690s, Jacobite propagandists openly compared William III to Cromwell. In their bitterness and extremism, Jacobites and radical Whigs reached, from opposite approaches, common ground, as commonwealthmen and royalists had occasionally done in the 1650s. Some commonwealthmen of the 1690s, among them the prominent conspirator and pamphleteer of the previous decade Robert Ferguson, went over to the Jacobite cause. The *Memoirs* are very far from being a Jacobite publication (even if in the short term their publishers were ready to find allies where they could). The comparison they offer between William and Cromwell is implicit rather than, as in some Jacobite propaganda, explicit. It is none the less hard to mistake. Both rulers, in acquiring and entrenching their power, claim to be defending the liberties they are in reality undermining. We are alerted to the parallel by the observation made in the main preface to the *Memoirs* that Ludlow was 'an enemy', not merely to Stuart and Cromwellian rule, but 'to all arbitrary government, though gilded over with the most specious pretences'.

One lesson learned by the Ludlow of the *Memoirs* from the replacement of Stuart by Cromwellian tyranny has melancholy implications for the revolutionaries who deposed James II. It is indicated by a generalization, the vehicle of persuasion that usually figures in passages where the recasting of Ludlow's text for present-day purposes has been particularly ruthless: 'Certainly it can never be esteemed by a wise man to be worth the scratch of a finger to remove a single person acting by an arbitrary power, in order to set up another with the same unlimited authority.' Failings of William that were emphasized by Jacobite propaganda, his 'pride' and 'ambition' and his susceptibility to 'sycophancy', are persistent features of the Cromwell of the *Memoirs*. The use of generalization (or epigram, or maxim) again points the parallel. 'Sycophants,' explain the *Memoirs*, are 'a race of men never wanting in great councils.'

The two rulers have common failings of policy too. William affronted the Whigs by bringing Tories into his administration and seeking to balance the two parties. In the 1650s the Cromwell of the *Memoirs* finds 'new friends' among the Cavaliers, 'thereby provoking his ancient friends to a just jealousy and indignation' and finding 'no other way to support himself, but by balancing his new with his old enemies'. William appalled radicals by his 'lenity' to the instruments of later Stuart tyranny, at whose hands they and their friends suffered: the *Memoirs* charge Cromwell with an equally misguided clemency towards royalists. At the same time both rulers use the threat posed by supporters of the previous regime as a pretext for the exercise of arbitrary power. Another correspondence is often hinted at. Cromwell's usurpation, by depriving the parliamentarian cause of its base of national support, paves the way for the return of the Stuarts. The suspicions aroused by William's refusal to yield prerogative powers to the nation's representatives restrict his own base and could have the same result.

*

The resemblances between the two rulers, telling as they are, are secondary to more fully sustained parallels between the eras in which the two men rose and ruled. It is here that, in the rewriting of Ludlow's manuscript, radical Whig perspectives blend with country-party ones. One reason why the attainment of liberty proved such a struggle in the civil wars, the *Memoirs* explain, was the court's resources of patronage. 'Vast numbers' opposed the Long Parliament because they 'depended on the king for preferments'. The more lukewarm of the Roundheads prove to have been similarly motivated. Having initially 'appeared most forward to engage themselves' on liberty's behalf, they 'found themselves disappointed of those preferments they had expected' from parliament, and proposed peace terms to the king in the hope of 'places and advancements under him'. Then, in the 1650s, Cromwell, that 'public robber', 'lavished away the public treasure' on 'bribes' and 'exorbitant salaries' in order to 'procure such instruments as he thought would be subservient to his unjust designs'. Then as now, 'preferment', 'grants of land', 'great estates' are liberally squandered on the regime's supporters. There had been complaints against such evils during the civil war itself. In 1644 Cromwell acknowledged the public complaint 'that the members of both Houses', having 'got great places', had departed from their ideals. Attacks both on the office-holding and on the corruption of men in power persisted through the 1640s and 1650s. Yet never were they the daily diet of complaint that they would become by the late 1690s, and they would not have figured anything like as emphatically in the pre-1660 section of Ludlow's manuscript as they do in the *Memoirs*.

Alongside the villains of the civil wars, it transpires from the *Memoirs*, there was, as there needs to be now, a party of virtue. Its members were 'frugal of the public purse', firm in resisting temptations to personal enrichment and personal favour. Despite the obstacles posed by the apostates who sought peace with Charles I, that party triumphed in the winter of 1648–9 and prevailed during the Commonwealth. It was then that servants of the regime learned that they were 'not placed in employments to serve themselves, but to serve the public'. It was then, perhaps only then, that a parliament was what a parliament should be. The triumph of public virtue, an ideal to which backbenchers of the 1690s were instinctively attracted, is thus linked to republican rule, a thought to which most of them were instinctively resistant. It is the subtle aim of the *Memoirs* to overcome the resistance. Where there are single rulers, they imply, there will be courts, and where there are courts there will be corruption. Only in republics does public virtue triumph. A radical Whig pamphlet of 1698, *The Danger of Mercenary Parliaments*, a work we shall find to have been intimately related to the *Memoirs*, reviewed the corruption, the tyranny, and the apostasies of William's reign and concluded that 'fatal experience' showed 'courts' to 'have been the same in all ages'. The *Memoirs*, which describe the monarchical courts and regimes of Charles I, of Cromwell, of Charles II, point the same message.

The virtue and prowess of the Commonwealth are made manifest in its actions both abroad and at home. Its spectacular record of victories against its external enemies, and its triumphs over the Irish and Scots and Dutch, were a trump card of republicanism. Seventeenth-century England, whose diplomatic and military record under the early and later Stuart kings was so shameful, had achieved greatness abroad under republican rule. There were noble feats of domestic policy too. The *Memoirs* recall that in 1651, at the instigation of an MP 'zealous for justice, especially against such as betrayed the public trust', another member, Lord Howard of Escrick, was expelled from parliament, and massively fined, for having 'taken divers bribes'. 'So just and equitable a spirit then governed' that the House was unmoved by the lobbying on Howard's behalf. Again a maxim, which encapsulates timeless evils and thus points to present as well as past ones, reminds readers of the 1690s of a phenomenon in their own experience: Howard was expelled 'nothwithstanding all the art of counsel learned in the law, who are very skilful at putting a good appearance upon a bad cause'.

The *Memoirs* show another issue of concern to backbenchers of the 1690s being tackled by the Commonwealth of 1649–53: the manipulation of parliamentary elections from the centre of power. The rotten boroughs are swept away. That measure was reversed by Richard Cromwell, the *Memoirs* explain, because 'it was well understood mean and decayed boroughs might be more easily corrupted than the numerous counties and considerable cities'. The *Memoirs* notice, in language familiar from complaints of MPs of the 1690s, the 'arts' used under the protectorate by 'the emissaries of the court', which 'caused the elections in most places to be decided in favour of such as pleased them'. The elections to Richard's parliament in 1659, as described in the *Memoirs*, have features which were once more familiar to readers of William's reign, and which are likely to owe at least something to editorial initiative: 'The officers of the admiralty and navy had a great influence not only upon the Cinque Ports, but also upon all sea-towns whatsoever, and could press at their pleasure any inhabitant to serve at sea, and thereby ruin both them and their families.'

The influence of naval officers on elections in the 1690s seemed part of a wider problem of naval corruption. Opponents of standing armies looked to the navy, together with the militias, to secure England's defence. They knew that, if the militias were in need of reform, the navy was no less so. A series of disasters at sea during William's war with France produced deep dissatisfaction with the venality and ineptitude of the naval administration. Here again, in the *Memoirs*, maxims are the instrument that brings home the lessons of the Commonwealth to the present. The Commonwealth knew 'of how great importance the sea-affairs are to this nation' and 'of what importance it is to this nation always to guard the seas'. Thanks to the 'care and diligence' of the navy commissioners, the administration of the fleet was purged, a rapid programme of shipbuilding carried out, a triumphant fleet sent to sea. There is special praise for the leading commissioner, Sir Henry Vane. His administrative gifts, we read, were accompanied by a stern financial probity, an indifference to the inducements of power, and 'a resolution and courage not to be diverted from the public service'. Those qualities put his counterparts of the 1690s to shame. In the manuscript, Vane, 'this choice martyr of Christ', is distinguished principally by his 'eminent zeal' for 'the cause of Jesus Christ'. In the *Memoirs* he cares most for 'the liberties of England'.

It is another issue, however, that supplies the most frequent and forceful parallels between then and now: the controversy provoked by William's determination to keep up his army after the end of the war with France. It was on the same subject that the *Memoirs* were most often quoted and echoed in the period immediately following their publication. In the civil wars themselves the 'rage and violence' of 'insolent mercenaries' had caused exasperation, but only in the later seventeenth century did opposition to 'mercenary' and 'standing' soldiers harden into a principle. The publishers of the *Memoirs*, exploiting the hostility, went to great lengths to underline one particular point of contemporary relevance. It is, declares the preface to the third volume, 'as clear as the sun at noon-day' that the moment of the mid-century conflict that proved fatal to liberty was parliament's decision to keep up its army, and to extend Cromwell's command of it, after the conclusion of the civil wars at the battle of Worcester in 1651. Here the Commonwealth, so prudent in other respects, fatally erred. Being committed to 'the common good', explain the *Memoirs*, it was 'supported by the affection of the people' and so 'needed not the military sword to uphold it'. By prolonging Cromwell's command it drew 'destruction' upon the cause. It was with his standing army that he broke the Long Parliament and Barebone's and seized power for himself. The danger that the standing army of the late 1690s might likewise move against parliament is a recurrent theme of the literature of the controversy. Ludlow's *Memoirs* indicate what the consequences would be. Having usurped power by military means, Cromwell ruled by them. The climax of his despotism was the rule of those 'bashaws', the Major-Generals, that 'monstrous tyranny', when 'so confident had the soldiery grown, that they openly avowed themselves to be our lords and masters'.

The *Memoirs* emphasize the contrast, which supplied a central argument of the opponents of William's army, between the virtues of militia forces and the vices of standing ones. A passage which was much plundered in the debates and pamphlets of 1698–9 reports, quite inaccurately, that after the battle of Worcester Cromwell 'dismissed', 'with anger and contempt', the county militias that had come to the assistance of his 'standing army' in the battle, 'well knowing that a useful and experienced militia was more likely to obstruct him in his ambitious designs; which was all the acknowledgement they could get from him for their service and affection to the public cause.' Later we meet the freshly recruited militia of Dublin, whose commitment to 'our just rights and liberties' contrasts starkly with the tyrannical impulses of the New Model. Friends of William III's standing army pointed out the frailties and inexperience of militias, but the account of the Dublin regiments shows how, in a more virtuous time, that disadvantage was obviated. We see them 'drawn up on the College Green', 'all very well equipped, and drawn up in good order, indeed so exact in the performance of their exercise that one would have thought them to have been long in the service'. They stand in contrast to those frequent targets of the *Memoirs*, 'soldiers of fortune', 'mercenary' officers and men, who 'make a trade of war'. Fighting for 'pay' instead of their 'country', for 'tyranny' instead of 'liberty', they make bad soldiers, as the defeat on Hispaniola in 1655 humiliatingly demonstrates.

In the pre-1660 section of the *Memoirs*, most of the passages which tell us about militias and standing armies are likely to have been largely or wholly fabricated by the publishers. In the post-Restoration section, for which we have the corresponding portion of the manuscript, almost all of them are fabrications. When regiments of the New Model greet Charles II's return, the publishers invent for Ludlow the words:

> And, I confess, it was a strange sight to me, to see the horse that had formerly belonged to our army now put upon an employment so different from that which they had at first undertaken; especially when I considered that for the most part they had not been raised out of the meanest of the people, and without distinction, as other armies had been; but that they consisted of such as had engaged themselves in a spirit of liberty in the defence of their rights and religion: but having been corrupted under the tyranny of Cromwell, and kept up as a standing force against the people, they had forgotten their first engagements, and were become as mercenary as other troops are accustomed to be.

Equally baseless is the statement, likewise much copied and cited in the standing army controversy, that the disbandment of the New Model by Charles II

> was not caused by the king's aversion to a standing army; for the whole course of his life demonstrates the contrary; but being persuaded that they who had already made so many changes in England were able to bring about another, and to turn him out again with as little consideration as they had brought him in, he thought it most safe and necessary to free himself at once from such dangerous companions.

In that respect, at least, Charles was more prudent than is William, who proposes to leave himself at the mercy of soldiers who 'turned out' James II.

Ingenious as they are, and influential as they proved, it is not primarily in the inventions and distortions visited on the narrative of Ludlow's manuscript that the literary achievement of the *Memoirs* lies. Those changes could carry conviction only because the passages incorporating them issued from a vivid and convincing personality. It is the characterization of Ludlow, the creation of a voice so different from his own, that reveals the workings of genius.

Once that voice had been found, the rewriting of the manuscript may not have been a demanding or laborious exercise. Indeed there are occasional signs of carelessness or haste. Mostly the publishers followed the structure of Ludlow's long, breathless sentences, pruning, tidying, imposing shape and tightening form. Ludlow's prose was, to borrow a verb from the period which produced the *Memoirs*, 'polited'. Its urgency and stridency were muted, its nouns and adjectives softened. Its leaps of mood yielded to evenness of temper, its cries of anger and bitterness to measured reflection. Those changes, by answering to the taste of a more decorous literary era, also served another purpose. They eliminated or reduced the differences of value and perspective between the Puritan age and the present one. The narrative, even as it recovered, for a generation drawn to the history of the civil wars, the drama of distant events, presented the difference between past and present as one only of time. No one spotted, on their publication or indeed at any point before the discovery of the Bodleian manuscript, the anachronisms of the *Memoirs*. The doubts which were raised about the authenticity of the text during the century following its publication derived solely from knowledge or rumour about the conduct of the publishers. They did not arise from the language or arguments of the text itself, which its readers evidently found historically authentic.

The publishers, who transformed the Puritan age, likewise transformed the personality of their narrator, not merely by dissolving his Puritanism but through the creation of other characteristics in its stead. The 'fanciful Swiss dress' in which the manuscript had reached them makes way for country-party clothing. In the main preface to the

Memoirs, which compares Ludlow's virtues to those of Scipio and Cato, the clothes acquire Roman trimmings. In his hatred of arbitrary power, in his advocacy of the regicide, the Ludlow of the *Memoirs* is a radical Whig. And yet he rises above partisanship. He has the integrity, the independence of mind, the indifference to favour and reward, the immunity to the claims of 'faction', that the country party took for its ideals. His courage and energy blend with a capacity – a half-Roman capacity – for Stoic detachment. With it there come engaging qualities of modesty and diffidence, traits conveyed by words which have no basis in the manuscript, which indeed are far removed from its frenetic dogmatism: 'For my part, if I may be permitted to deliver my opinion'; 'if I may be permitted to deliver my sense'; 'I hope a man in my condition may mention, without incurring the charge of ostentation'.

The virtue and constancy of his public life rest on gentlemanly foundations. A series of social accoutrements is invented for him which hint at a background of unostentatious rural self-sufficiency, so that we almost seem to glimpse him running his estates, reading in his library, occasionally even meditating (in no fanatical spirit of course) in his chapel. He acquires an interest in the breeding of horses. He is given a decorous platitude to deliver, derived from Tacitus, about the purpose of historical writing in general and of the *Memoirs* in particular, which a backbench MP of the 1690s might have been pleased to have entered in his commonplace book:

> As the memory of those men whose lives have been remarkable for great and generous actions ought to be transmitted to posterity with the praises they have deserved, that others may be excited to the imitation of their virtues: 'tis as just that the names of those who have rendered themselves detestable by the baseness of their crimes should be recorded, that men may be deterred from treading in their steps, lest they draw upon themselves the same infamy.

The adjective 'generous' ('great and generous actions') is one of which the publishers, in rewriting the manuscript, were specially fond. In religion, Ludlow's providentialism – or the diminutive proportion of it that survives – becomes a spur not to political destruction but to devout and gentlemanly reflection. His revolutionary Puritanism gives way to a poised (and only rarely conspicuous) piety, his 'enthusiasm' to sobriety, his Calvinist faith to a concern for good conduct. Ludlow's manuscript complains repeatedly of the spread of 'wickedness', a sin against biblical injunctions. The *Memoirs*, deferring to the preoccupation current in the 1690s with 'the reformation of manners', replace 'wickedness' with 'immoralities', which are made to sound affronts at least as much to society as to God.

His character thus redefined, Ludlow meets the fearsome challenges facing England's ruling class in the civil wars. Both as an MP and as a military commander he passes every test. Unfortunately he achieves a less prominent role in the war than his merits deserve, for, 'solely applying myself to the public interest', he is 'not fit to promote a faction'. That virtue explains why he is not given a leading or lasting post in the parliamentary army, and why he is mainly confined to the fighting within his native shire. Yet that ill fortune is a blessing to his publishers, for his exploits at the head of his Wiltshire forces make him a model for the gentle leaders of the revitalized county militias envisaged by the radical Whigs of the 1690s. Thanks to the 'integrity and firmness to the true interest of his country' he showed in parliament, explains the main preface, 'he was thought worthy to be entrusted with an independent regiment of horse, to defend the county for which he served against the incursions of the enemy'. The same preface invites the reader to notice 'the military honours he received', and 'how great a progress he made in the science of war', 'in a time when rewards were not blindly bestowed'. As Firth remarked, the *Memoirs* convey a uniquely lively picture of 'what may be termed the everyday life of the war'. We watch Ludlow enduring, with unstinting fortitude, the hardships of cold, sickness, hunger, siege, imprisonment. Alas, 'faction' still undermines him. Because of its influence on the wartime administration, the pay of his forces does not reach them. Their response to that deprivation happily illustrates the radical Whig case for the militias, for 'I and my men had nothing to keep us faithful to the cause but our own affection to it. Yet were we not wanting to improve every opportunity in the best manner we could to the service of the country.'

Early in his military career, conscious of his youth, the Ludlow of the *Memoirs* tends to defer to the judgement of his elders, though events always vindicate his own assessments. But if he is open to persuasion over military tactics, his 'integrity' in sticking to his principles is unshakeable. All readers of the *Memoirs* notice a mulish streak in their narrator. If it can seem a flaw it is also a guarantee of the uncompromising virtue that distinguishes him from the opportunists parasitic on his cause. In the narrative of the *Memoirs* as in the politics of the 1690s, too many men sell their cause and principles for advancement. The firmness of the published Ludlow against that temptation is unflinching. He is 'never solicitous' to procure 'employment' and 'could be well contented to withdraw' from his 'public station'. Nothing will persuade him to become a placeman. In 1659 he is 'earnestly pressed' to accept the command of a regiment, an appointment that would have put him in the same category as the military 'placemen' of William's reign; 'but being unwilling to intermeddle with any employment of advantage under the parliament, that I might give my voice [= vote] in the House with more freedom and impartiality, I desired to be excused'. If the material rewards of power hold no attraction for him, then neither, it is often emphasized, does its 'pageantry'. He is puzzled to find 'that so many men delight in numerous and magnificent trains'.

It is the implication of the *Memoirs* that, at the crisis of the civil wars in 1649, men of upright country-party virtues committed themselves to the regicide, while self-interested politicians drew back. Given the general hostility to the memory of the king's death, that was not an easy point to transmit. The publishers' tactics in proposing it were not constant. Ludlow's manuscript shows the trial and execution of the king to have been the pivotal moment of his life. The prefaces to the *Memoirs* do not mention the regicide. In the narrative itself it is merely one point in his career. Once the king's punishment has been described the narrator does not hark back to it, as the Bodleian manuscript does. Though Charles I is a villain we hear less of his villainy than of Cromwell's, which becomes a more profound and enduring source of Ludlow's anger. In the third, separately published volume of the *Memoirs* a change occurs. Now the publishers treat the king's punishment more boldly, though still not without inhibition. The long accounts of the trials of the regicides in 1660–62 bring its memory into prominent view. A long appendix of civil-war documents, many of which had been cited in the Ludlow pamphlets of the early 1690s, is added by the publishers to illustrate the depths of the ill conduct of Charles, who, we are told, may be said to have 'passed sentence on himself, and absolved the high court of justice'.

What caused that shift? Perhaps the publishers were emboldened by the success of the first two volumes or by the extremity of emotion aroused by the standing army debate. Or they may have recognized that it would be easier to vindicate the regicides in volume three, where they could be portrayed as helpless victims of the tyranny of Charles II, than it had been in the first two volumes, where the narrative of their calculated destruction of king and monarchy would have stood much less chance of attracting late seventeenth-century sympathy. Whatever the thinking behind the alteration of tactics, however, the broad strategy is unchanged. Volume three, no less than the first two, presents a radical Whig case in a country-party mantle. Among the documents with which the appendix builds its case against Charles I, for example, the publishers slip in a transcript, irrelevant to the surrounding matter, of a resolution of the House of Commons in 1645 to take action against the bribing of MPs.

Whether the *Memoirs* converted any of their early readers to the regicide we cannot say. Both in the short term and in the long the work would be most often invoked by readers who were against what the *Memoirs* were against – tyranny, standing armies, corruption – but not in favour of Ludlow's constitutional aims or methods. It was as a country-party manifesto that the *Memoirs* made their principal impact. There survive the notes and speeches of one of their early readers, Sir Richard Cocks, MP for Gloucestershire in the late 1690s. In his image of himself, Cocks had the purity of the country-party MP. 'Preening himself,' as his modern editor D. W. Hayton says, 'on his non-partisanship', he 'adopted the standpoint of the unsophisticated country squire.' He shared in the 'idealisation of the country gentleman as the prime agent of prosperity and harmony in society, the regulator of morals, and the guardian of his country's liberties', that was carried by his generation 'almost to a fetish'. Cocks's reflections reveal his revulsion at the 'fawning', 'proud', 'ambitious' hunters of preferment, at the tendency of placemen to 'vote in matters of state all one way', at the 'corruption' of the House of Commons by 'bribes' and 'pensions'. He notes the pertinence of Roman history to England's present troubles, and fears that venality, which he judges to have cost Rome her liberty, will end England's. Cocks was no radical. He venerated William III and refuted the charge that the king had designs on the nation's liberties. He thought badly of the parliamentary cause in the civil wars and especially of the regicide. Yet he was attracted instantly to the *Memoirs*, on which he drew in addressing the Commons. He noted their account of the Commonwealth's reform of the electoral system. He recorded their salute to that regime's achievements against its external enemies. But what gripped him were the descriptions of Cromwell's mistreatment of the militia regiments after Worcester and of his expulsion of the Long Parliament, actions with a chilling pertinence, he noticed, to the present menace of a standing army.

Cocks's reading of Ludlow would have many eighteenth-century parallels. Time and again, passages about Cromwell's standing army in the *Memoirs*, or reproduced from them in pamphlets around the time of their publication, would be appropriated (usually without acknowledgement) by commentators as loyal as Cocks was to the constitution, as unfriendly as he to the memory of the regicide and the Rump, but as fearful as he of the uses to which the present-day standing army might be put. Through those and other uses of the *Memoirs* during the century after their publication there runs a general rule: that the passages most widely reproduced from them were those with which the publishers, in their own political cause, had taken the largest liberties.

I have used the phrase 'the publishers' with intentional looseness, to refer to a group of people who were involved in the production of the *Memoirs*. Now that the purposes behind the publication, and the differences between it and the manuscript, have been established, we can try to discover who those people were. In particular we can seek the identity of Ludlow's editor. Whose pen was it that transformed the manuscript and so deceived posterity? To find the answer we must enter the world of late seventeenth-century publication from which the *Memoirs* emerged.

4

Ludlow's Editor

Printers and publishers of seventeenth-century books normally liked to advertise their names on the title-pages. In politically risky publications, however, that practice was often dropped. It was dropped in the Ludlow pamphlets of 1691–3, and again in the *Memoirs*. The title-pages of the pamphlets proclaimed their place of publication to be Amsterdam, a familiar pretence among radical London printers. The *Memoirs* are stated to have been printed at Vevey, Ludlow's home in exile. The blind fooled no one. In 1700 William Baron, in attacking the *Memoirs*, commented: 'had they said at Darby it might have been nigher home, and nigher truth too; nay certainly so, by a little quibbling transition from place to person'. In other words the printer was John Darby of Bartholomew Close. Every circumstance supports Baron's imputation.

John Darby had long been a leading printer of radical Whig works. He produced perhaps the most daring and influential attack on the tyranny of Charles II, Andrew Marvell's *An Account of the Growth of Popery and Arbitrary Government* of 1677–8. He helped to keep the radical Whig cause alive during the dark days of the early 1680s and was charged with seditious libel after publishing, 'within an hour' and on a massive scale, a version of the dying speech of the Whig martyr William Lord Russell, a victim, like Algernon Sidney, of Judge Jeffreys in 1683. That text probably owed a great deal to invention. Darby promoted the radical cause again in the wake of the Revolution of 1688. By the late 1690s he was sharing much of his work with his son John, who would carry on the radical tradition of the firm after his father's death. The elder Darby had habitual collaborators in the book trade. There was the Whig publisher (or 'bookseller') Richard

Baldwin, whose business was taken over on his death in 1698 by his widow Anne (or Abigail), who preserved her husband's political affiliations. And there was another Whig publisher, Andrew Bell, who married Darby's daughter Elizabeth in 1696.

A pamphlet of 1698 that is sometimes attributed to Daniel Defoe, *A Brief History of Standing Armies*, included Ludlow's *Memoirs* in a list of publications that had all been 'hammered from the same forge'. The other works in the list carried Darby's name on their title-pages or were included in the advertisements for his publications. They included publications whose connection with the *Memoirs* will become apparent: pamphlets against standing armies, and Algernon Sidney's *Discourses concerning Government* (1698). In 1699 Darby printed the *Memoirs of Sir John Berkeley*. They were taken from a manuscript which had either been copied by Ludlow into 'A Voice from the Watch Tower' or been among other papers of his that had reached the publishers of the *Memoirs*. The text of Berkeley's *Memoirs* is incorporated into Ludlow's *Memoirs*, where it is tidied and shortened in just the manner in which Ludlow's own manuscript is rewritten. The connections of other publications of Darby with Ludlow's *Memoirs* will become plain too. There was the three-volume *Collected Works* of John Milton (1698), which included a life of the poet by John Toland that was also printed separately by Darby in 1699. Linked to those publications was another. Under the date 1700 (though the publication appeared in the autumn of 1699),* Darby printed Toland's edition of the *Works* of the leading republican theorist of the civil wars, James Harrington. In 1712, in *The Fourth Part of the Caveat against the Whigs*, the Tory Charles Hornby would recall that, 'in the latter end of King William's reign', the title-pages of the Milton, Ludlow, Harrington and Sidney publications were 'affixed to the gates of the royal palaces, as if it were in open defiance of monarchy'. In the eighteenth century the same publications would dominate what Caroline Robbins has aptly called 'the canon of real Whig doctrine'. The canon was Darby's creation. When and how the idea of it emerged

* Publishers, perhaps in order to make their productions seem as novel or up-to-date as possible, often gave to books published late in one year the date of the next, a practice that can confuse posterity.

in his mind we cannot say. The *Collected Works* of Milton had been ready for the press in 1694, but the publication had been held back, perhaps because of the decline of the radical Whig cause around that time. At all events it was only amid the excitement of the standing army controversy that the series of publications to which Ludlow's *Memoirs* belonged was placed before the world.

If Darby printed the *Memoirs*, who wrote the text? Unless new evidence appears, which might settle the matter at a stroke, we can never be certain. But we can, I believe, establish an overwhelming probability. It would be a mistake to assume that any editor of such a work was a solitary agent. Yet it does seem likely that a single writer did at least most of the editorial work, whatever pressures he may have come under from within either the publishing or the political world. The *Memoirs* have a distinctiveness of voice and a consistency of stylistic technique and habit that are rarely sustained, at least for so long, in collaborative writing.

William Baron, who identified Darby as the printer, could not identify the editor. He does, however, name a figure with a crucial part in the story:

> 'Tis generally presumed the last of [Ludlow's] acquaintance was S——by B-thel [Slingsby Bethel], with whom those many reams of paper he had, whilst grumbling in Switzerland, emptied his galls into, were entrusted: and report speaks that he was tricked of them by a republican confidant who best understood to make the best of them, as well for the Good Old Cause as for his own advantage; which 'tis further said the said churlish Nabal was very angry at, and would have resented accordingly, had not death put an end to that dispute. The usurper of the copy, having got quiet and sole possession, consulted more than once the whole Calves-head fraternity,* not without some representatives, as to the most creditable way of publishing; where in conclusion it was resolved to cut off the superfluities of that slovenly Swiss dress 'twas left in, and . . . send it forth in that *à la mode* way of Memoirs.

* The 'Calves-head fraternity' was the Calves Head Club, a body which may have existed only in Tory imaginations, if indeed even Tories believed in it. Its members, it was alleged, fed ghoulishly on that dish on each anniversary of the beheading of Charles I.

In 1705 Archbishop Tenison, too, expressed the belief that Ludlow's manuscript had been left in the hands of Slingsby Bethel. Though the story is a little more complicated than either Baron or Tenison knew, they were on the right lines.

Bethel, who had been born in or around the same year as Ludlow, travelled to Switzerland in 1662, where he apparently stayed with him for at least a year. In 1663 the two men's wives travelled together from England to visit them. After his return to England Bethel remained in touch with Ludlow, even though they quarrelled over Edmund's refusal to collaborate with the Dutch republicans. Like Ludlow, Bethel was a survivor of the republican cause of the civil wars. After the Restoration he became a key figure in the community of radical Whigs and Dissenters in London. He was Sheriff during the exclusion crisis and, as a result of his prominent role in that episode, was savagely immortalized in Dryden's allegory *Absalom and Achitophel*, where he 'curst the king when he was by', 'packed a jury of Dissenting Jews', and maintained that, 'in the godly Cause', 'the suffering saint' was free 'from human laws'. After 1688 Bethel collaborated with John Darby and Richard Baldwin in radical Whig agitation. Some hostile contemporaries attributed to him the composition of the Ludlow pamphlets of 1691–3. His book *The Providences of God*, whose arguments complement those of the pamphlets, was published by Darby's ally Richard Baldwin in 1691 and again in 1694, and republished by Darby's son-in-law Andrew Bell in 1697. Though Bethel died in February 1697, a year before the publication of the *Memoirs*, he has a place in them, for the *Memoirs* silently appropriate passages about Oliver Cromwell's domestic tyranny, and about the failings of his foreign policy, from Bethel's tract of 1668 *The World's Mistake in Oliver Cromwell*.

In November 1696, three months before his death, Bethel laid a deposition before the Court of Chancery which has only recently come to light. It gives us our nearest glimpse of the process by which 'A Voice from the Watch Tower' was turned into the *Memoirs*. Bethel had become involved in a quarrel with Awnsham Churchill, a prominent Whig publisher. Its subject was the publication of Ludlow's manuscript. In 1674 Ludlow, who had temporarily resolved to bring his narrative to a close, had inserted into 'A Voice from the Watch

Tower' a note giving directions about the posthumous fate of his treatise. If the text were thought worth publishing, he stipulated, the arrangements should be made by 'my dear wife, if living', and 'if not' by 'those of my dear friends and relations into whose hands by providence it shall fall'. Ludlow's widow returned to England after his death and remarried in 1694. If she had inherited the manuscript she had ceased to possess it by 1695. Bethel told the court that he had 'good reason to believe' that Ludlow, his 'very intimate friend', had 'left' the manuscript to his own 'care and disposal and inspection about the printing of the same'. It was, he explained, in order to 'perform' that 'trust' that in the midsummer of 1695 he had approached Churchill with a view to publication. How and when the manuscript got into Bethel's hands, and whether Ludlow had really hoped that it would, we cannot be sure. At all events, in 1695 Bethel wanted to move fast. The lapse of the Licensing Act in the spring of that year had made the publication of radical literature easier. Bethel, fearing – needlessly as it proved – that new legislation would soon be passed to restore the restrictions on printing which the act had imposed, aimed to get the book published beforehand. To that end he passed the manuscript over to Churchill.

Churchill and Bethel offered conflicting versions of what had happened thereafter. The accounts by both men obviously held much back, and Bethel's version is shifty. Churchill claims two things: first that Bethel agreed that Churchill should publish the work; secondly that, even while discussing with Churchill the arrangements for publication, Bethel reached a separate agreement to the same purpose with the publisher Richard Baldwin (Darby's collaborator and the publisher of Bethel's *The Providences of God*). Bethel's account, though acknowledging that he had talked both to Churchill and to Baldwin, denied that he was contracted to either of them. Churchill wanted the Court of Chancery to confirm his own right to publish: Bethel wanted a court order obliging Churchill to give the manuscript back.

There was an awkward problem for Bethel. Whatever the means by which the manuscript had come into his possession, he could claim no legal title to it. Initially it suited Churchill to overlook that difficulty. But when Bethel tried to extract himself from his dealings with Churchill, the publisher placed him on the defensive by claiming that the text had been 'only lent to [Bethel] or casually put into his hands'. The title had passed – we do not know by what process – from Ludlow's widow to his younger brother Nathaniel, who was aged seventy-two when the Chancery proceedings took place, and who entrusted the management of the affair to his son Henry. A battle ensued between Churchill and Bethel for the support of Nathaniel and Henry Ludlow. Churchill won.

There was one thing about which Churchill and Bethel agreed. The manuscript was too disordered to be published as it stood. Churchill described its contents as 'divers collections and memoirs which were therein set down in a promiscuous, confused and unmethodical manner'. After obtaining Ludlow's text, he explained, he 'did employ an ingenious and learned person to methodise and prepare the said manuscript for the press'. He contracted to pay 'a considerable sum of money' to the 'person', who by late September 1695 had 'made a considerable progress' with the writing (though it was in the interest of Churchill, whom it suited to emphasize the cost he had incurred, to make the progress sound as considerable as possible). According to Churchill, Bethel had endorsed the revision of the manuscript and, when shown the opening passage of the revised version as a specimen, had approved of it. Bethel's own recollection was different. He was, he said, 'very much surprised' that Churchill had commissioned someone to 'intermeddle' with the text without Bethel's knowledge. When shown the opening of the revised version he had expressed his 'dislike' of it. Churchill, Bethel had realized, intended to have the manuscript 'gelt'. The revision was being conducted on an excessive scale and in a spirit unfaithful to Ludlow's treatise. Indeed at one point (said Bethel) Churchill had talked of 'abridging or contracting' it to 'about forty sheets', the length of a longish pamphlet.

There was a further source of contention. Bethel was 'very desirous to know the name' of the reviser. Churchill informed the court that he would have been happy to satisfy Bethel's 'curiosity on that point', had not the 'ingenious and learned person . . . signified his desire to have his name concealed'. As it was, Churchill insisted, he 'must not tell his name without his order'. Bethel had wanted the preparation of the text to be entrusted to someone approved by himself, indeed supervised by him. A 'house or room' would have been 'pitched upon' where the preparer would have carried out the work. There Bethel and Edmund Ludlow's other 'friends' would have been able to call and 'inspect and judge of the proceedings of such person therein to the intent that the mind and intentions of the author [Ludlow] might be fully and punctually pursued and not otherwise'. Churchill repulsed those demands.

Bethel's death in February 1697 appears to have terminated the court proceedings. What happened next we have to guess. The likely answer is that Churchill, with the approval of Nathaniel and Henry Ludlow, came to some agreement with Baldwin, who then entrusted the printing of the work to Darby. What became of the text with which the 'ingenious and learned person' employed by Churchill had 'made a considerable progress'? It is conceivable that Baldwin replaced it with a revision by another hand. Yet that seems unlikely. Bethel had apparently approached Baldwin about the manuscript only after it had been passed over to Churchill, in whose hands it remained at least until November 1696 and probably, we may surmise, until after Bethel's death three months later. Only when Churchill had surrendered it could a second reviser have set to work. Such an agent would have had to proceed with improbable rapidity, for the *Memoirs* were in print by February 1698, a year after Bethel's death.

The hypothesis that a second reviser was involved raises another difficulty. Churchill, a prominent and tight-fisted publisher, had incurred either a payment or a debt to the 'ingenious and learned person'. He would hardly have given up a claim on the manuscript without due compensation, and Baldwin would hardly have wanted to pay for two revisions. In any case Bethel's death removed what seems to have been the only source of objection to the version produced by Churchill's employee, to which Nathaniel and Henry Ludlow, the proprietors of the manuscript, had agreed. It is evident too that the revision commissioned by Churchill was of the same character as that effected in the *Memoirs*. Bethel indicated that the opening passage of the revision, which was shown him by Churchill, broke a rule laid down by Ludlow in his note of 1674. There (as we shall see) Ludlow had stipulated that his text, if revised for publication, should be 'made to speak no other than my principle . . . in relation to' religion. The text of 1698 broke the same rule at every turn.

The likelihood is, then, that the 'ingenious and learned person' who began work in the summer of 1695, and who had made 'considerable progress' by September, went on to complete the *Memoirs* in time for them to be printed by Darby early in 1698. Who was he?

During the eighteenth century two men were named as the reviser of Ludlow's text. The first was Isaac Littlebury, a man otherwise known to literature as a translator of Herodotus's *History* and of Fénelon's *Télémache*. In 1758 Thomas Hollis, that connoisseur of 'real Whig' literature, wrote in a presentation copy of the 1751 edition of the *Memoirs* the words 'By Isaac Littlebury, Esq.' at the head of the preface. Hollis gave no sign of suspecting that Ludlow's text had been rewritten, so perhaps he took the writing of the preface to have constituted Littlebury's sole involvement. There were others who believed his role to have been larger. In the years 1777–80 a version of events was given by two people, whose words closely resemble each other's. One was John Douglas, who would later be Bishop of Salisbury, the other the writer Thomas Tyers. They had heard that the *Memoirs*, far from being 'authentic', had been 'compiled' or 'fabricated' by Littlebury from Ludlow's papers. The source of Douglas's and Tyers's statements was a politician named Andrew Stone. Stone had died in 1773, and we do not know when he passed his information on. His own source, according to Douglas and Tyers, was the printer and scholar Samuel Buckley, who had given him the information in or soon after 1727. Douglas and Tyers were not the sort of men to invent or imagine such a story. Neither was Buckley. He would have taken a scholar's interest in Littlebury's translations; and if Isaac Littlebury is the 'Mr Littlebury' mentioned in John Dunton's survey of the book trade in 1705 as a 'stationer' (a supplier of paper), then Buckley would have been likely to encounter him in that world too – though Littlebury had been dead for at least six years when the conversation between Buckley and Stone (assuming it occurred) took place.

The reliability of Stone – the link from Buckley to Douglas and Tyers, and thus from the early eighteenth century to the late – is harder to assess. Horace Walpole thought him a 'dark, proud man, very able but very mercenary'. He had high Tory views, but managed to prosper under Whig patronage in the reign of George II. He may have orchestrated the publication of pamphlets friendly to the Whig regime, a role that could have brought him into contact with Buckley, a supporter of the Whig establishment. None the less at least a part of Stone's account was flawed. Douglas records that Stone, in telling him about the *Memoirs*, related 'a curious instance of Littlebury's republican spirit', but the episode Stone described cannot have occurred, for it turns on the description of Littlebury as the editor of the *London Gazette* under William III, a post he did not hold. Tyers's remarks on the same episode reveal his own considerable uncertainty about the course of Littlebury's career.

We have, then, an attribution made eighty years after the publication of the *Memoirs*, deriving from a conversation said to have taken place thirty years after it, and supported by an inscription – Hollis's entry over the preface – written sixty years after it. Though not to be lightly dismissed, no more is the story to be lightly accepted. Is it true?

That Littlebury, whose preface to his translation of Herodotus indeed hints at the 'republican spirit' mentioned by Stone, was involved in some way in the publication of the *Memoirs* is likely enough. It is easy enough to see him as a member of the circle from which the Darby publications of the late 1690s emerged. We know very little about his career, but we do know that in November 1697, two or three months before the *Memoirs* appeared, 'Mr Littlebury carried to the press' an anonymous pamphlet against standing armies, printed by John Darby, whose author, as we shall see, had seen the text of the *Memoirs*. Our source, the diarist Narcissus Luttrell, evidently did not think that Littlebury had been involved in the writing of the pamphlet. But an eighteenth-century hand did write the words 'By Isaac Littlebury Esq.' beneath the preface of the 1704 edition of another work intimately connected with the *Memoirs*, the *Discourses* of Algernon Sidney.

Is that evidence strong enough? With the discovery of Ludlow's manuscript, the claim that Littlebury edited the *Memoirs* can be freshly assessed. Eighteenth-century commentators were not in a position to trace the process of rewriting or be aware of the flair it had involved. Did Isaac Littlebury possess that quality? If he is the 'stationer' described by Dunton he sounds a colourless figure. Isaac Littlebury's translations, the only works we know him to have written, are patient, self-effacing, slightly dull achievements. The historian Edward Gibbon, who read Littlebury's Herodotus in his youth, pronounced the translation 'lame'. It could be that there was another side to Littlebury, brought out by the editing of the *Memoirs*, but if so it left no other trace.

There is a second candidate. His claim, too, has eighteenth-century support. In 1770 the books of the Oxford antiquary Francis Godwyn, who had been a Fellow of Balliol College since 1722, were bequeathed to the Bodleian Library. Among them was the first edition of Ludlow's *Memoirs*. On a flyleaf of volume three, Godwyn – we cannot say when – inscribed the words 'Written by Toland'. He can only have meant John Toland, the deist and republican, whose character and writings had made him a highly controversial figure in the years around the publication of the *Memoirs*. Godwyn's claim is seconded by an eighteenth-century reader (whose identity is not known) of a copy, which again is in the Bodleian, of the ten-volume English version of Pierre Bayle's *General Dictionary* (1734–41). The reader wrote, against the dictionary's entry on Toland, that Toland 'wrote the third volume of Ludlow's *Memoirs*'.

John Toland (1670–1722) is known to history chiefly for his pioneering assault on received doctrines and texts of Christianity, and for his search for a religion which would transcend credal traditions and rigidities and unite Christians and Jews and Mahometans and pagans. Recently his significance on a second front, as a republican thinker, has also come to be appreciated. If Godwyn and the reader of Bayle's *Dictionary* were right, Toland has a third claim to celebrity.

Were they right? Francis Godwyn took an informed interest in the history of the civil wars, annotating works of the period (Sidney's *Discourses* among them). The reader of Bayle's *Dictionary*, as the handful of comments he placed against other entries reveals, was a careful and learned man. But we do not know the source of Godwyn's and the reader's information. Equally we do not know why they singled out the third volume. There are two possible explanations. One is that they believed the first two volumes to have been 'written' by someone other than Toland, but that they did not know (or say) who. The other, to my mind the more probable, is that they did not know that the first two volumes, like the third, were inauthentic. At all events, if Toland 'wrote' the third volume he surely wrote the first two as well. The distinctive stylistic techniques and habits and mannerisms of the first two volumes persist into the third. The brief surviving passage of 'A Voice from the Watch Tower' that corresponds to the end of the second volume of the *Memoirs* was transformed by the editor on exactly the same lines as the material that corresponds to the third volume. There is, as we shall find, material in volume three where the evidence suggesting Toland's involvement is more conspicuous, at least to a reader who has not met Ludlow's manuscript, than it is in the first two volumes; and that material could explain the emergence of the belief recorded by Godwyn and the reader of Bayle's *Dictionary*. Yet on inspection the evidence in favour of Toland's candidacy proves to be spread across the three volumes.

If he did edit only volume three he must have worked at a superhuman rate. Between early in 1698, when the first two volumes appeared, and March 1699, when the third was published, he was a very busy man, writing, or preparing for the press, a range of publications. There were two books on John Milton, a major edition of James Harrington, political pamphlets, and, we shall find cause to suspect, other works too. (In 1695–7, when it is likely that the essential work for the the first two volumes was done, there was much less on Toland's plate.) It is not difficult to imagine an editor who had already fashioned the literary form of the first two volumes of Ludlow's *Memoirs* – particularly an editor with the gift for quick and nimble writing which Toland possessed – compiling the third volume with some speed and ease. An editor starting afresh in volume three, and having to learn to imitate exactly the techniques and style fashioned by another writer, would surely have found the going far harder and slower. Certainty on this as on many matters relating to the editing of the *Memoirs* is unattainable. But so, for most readers, is a taste for endless qualification. To avoid it I shall henceforth assume that a single editor was responsible for all three volumes, and leave readers to make any mental reservations they deem appropriate.

No more than the eighteenth-century tradition behind Littlebury's candidacy can the assertions of Godwyn and the reader of Bayle's *Dictionary* be taken on trust. But when we test them we find that

Toland's candidacy has two immediate advantages over its rival. The first is literary. Toland's prose has in abundance a dexterity, an ingenuity, and what his own modern editor Justin Champion calls a 'ludic quality', that the editor of the *Memoirs*, whoever he was, amply possessed. It also displays a capacity to create and sustain voices separate from its author's own, voices moreover often close to that acquired by the narrator of the *Memoirs*. Secondly, and more decisively, Toland's name takes us, as Littlebury's does not, to the centre of the activities, literary and political, to which the publication of the *Memoirs* belonged. There is thus a double reason for an exploration of Toland's candidacy. Not only will it (I submit) answer our question. It will be the best means to recover the context from which the *Memoirs* emerged.

John Toland (christened Joannes Eugenius) was an Irishman, born in Londonderry in 1670, apparently the illegitimate son of a Catholic priest. Even among the vivid annals of Anglo-Irish literature he is a colourful figure. In his childhood he worked as a shepherd. In his teens he cast off his Catholicism, a faith he would revile for the rest of his days. By 1688 he was in Scotland, where he studied at Glasgow and then Edinburgh before making his way to London in the summer of 1690. There he formed ties with the clergyman Daniel Williams, the 'presbyterian pope'. In the autumn of 1692 Williams arranged for him to move to Holland to study at Leiden and Utrecht.

It was during Toland's stay in London that the four Ludlow pamphlets were published. They were probably a collaborative venture, and we cannot tell who wrote what. Alongside the contemporaries who attributed them to Slingsby Bethel there were others who ascribed them to Milton's nephew John Phillips, a figure consulted by Toland at some stage during the preparation of his *Life* of Milton. A different view was expressed, sometime between the autumn of 1693 and around the end of 1694, by a cataloguer in the Bodleian Library. The third of the pamphlets, *Ludlow no Liar*, was, he stated, 'wrote by J. Toland'. At that time Toland was little known in the nation at large. His *Christianity not Mysterious*, the work that made his name by scandalizing orthodox Christians, would not appear until the end of 1695 (and bears the date 1696). Paying tribute in its title to John Locke's *The Reasonableness of Christianity*, also of 1695, it was the first and most famous of the works in which Toland attacked the foundations of revealed religion and the exclusive claims of Christianity to religious truth. Even before the publication of *Christianity not Mysterious*, however, Toland was a notorious figure in Oxford. Back from Holland, he arrived there in January 1694 (and worked in the Bodleian during his stay). As so often in his life he provoked dismay and alarm by his excitable conduct and by the extremity of the political and religious views which he was given to announcing when, on his own rueful acknowledgement, 'keeping too much tattling company in coffee-houses'. Eventually he was obliged to leave Oxford after 'commending commonwealths' and 'justifying the murder of King Charles I', views which the Ludlow pamphlets had been designed to promote and which the *Memoirs* would be designed to promote too.

There are significant differences between the Ludlow pamphlets and the *Memoirs*. The pamphlets are not autobiographical and they carry no memorably distinctive voice. They differ from the later work, too, in their attention to historical detail. In the *Memoirs*, which are littered with inaccuracies, Ludlow's forgetfulness about long-past events is an intelligible, even sympathetic feature of his character. Even so a continuous thread of purpose runs through the two enterprises. The pamphlets illustrate the tyranny of Charles I partly by passages narrating events of his reign, partly by the reproduction of incriminating documents. Sections of the pamphlets which pursue those methods reappear in a number of publications of the late 1690s. One of them is the third volume of Ludlow's *Memoirs*, where the documents are printed in the appendix. Another is Toland's *Life of John Milton*, which takes up points that the third of the Ludlow pamphlets, the one attributed to him by the Bodleian cataloguer, had particularly stressed. Others are two pamphlets of 1698, *A Defence of the Parliament of 1640* and *King Charles I no such Saint, Martyr or Good Protestant as Commonly Reputed*. The first, *A Defence . . .*, is the publication of the late 1690s that draws most extensively on the Ludlow pamphlets. It is attributed to Toland in the attack on the *Memoirs* by William Baron, who also suspects him of having penned *King Charles I. . . .* The second of the Ludlow pamphlets describes itself on its title-page as 'Vindicating the Parliament which began in November 1640'. The third calls itself 'a Further Vindication of the Parliament of The 3d of

November, 1640'. The title-page and preface of Ludlow's *Memoirs* hail the 'Parliament which began on November 3, 1640', the parliament of which the *Memoirs* are indeed another vindication.

By January 1695 Toland was back in London. It was in midsummer of that year that Awnsham Churchill employed 'an ingenious and learned person' to rewrite Ludlow's manuscript. Two other pieces of evidence from 1695 merit attention here. First, in that year Toland was reported to have boasted that he had won the backing of Anthony Ashley Cooper, third Earl of Shaftesbury, whom we shall meet as his principal literary patron in the years ahead. Shaftesbury was also a patron of Churchill, who ten years later would recall his own 'long experience' of the earl's 'good opinion and goodness towards me'. It would have been characteristic of Shaftesbury, that assiduous promoter of radical Whig and country-party writing, to put Churchill and Toland in touch with each other. Secondly, it was in 1695 that Richard Baldwin, with whom Slingsby Bethel was also negotiating about the publication of Ludlow's manuscript, published a work by Toland, *Two Essays Sent in a Letter from Oxford*.

In the first two months of 1697 Toland signed contracts, probably not for the first time, with Baldwin and John Darby. They do not refer to Ludlow's *Memoirs*, but they do show that Toland was negotiating with the two men in the weeks on either side of Bethel's death, a period when Baldwin, Darby and the editor of the *Memoirs* are likely to have been making dispositions for the completion of the text. The contract with Baldwin was for a book entitled *Christianity Restored*, which never appeared. With Darby, to whom he owed debts, Toland agreed to produce 'original copy or translations of his own composition' towards repayment. After signing the contracts Toland left for Ireland, where the House of Commons ordered his arrest and trial as the author of *Christianity not Mysterious*, which was condemned to be burned. (In England it had already been cited before the Middlesex Grand Jury.) He avoided imprisonment by slipping back to England in September – three or four months before the publication of the *Memoirs*, and with time enough, if the deed was his, to put finishing touches to them and give them colouring suitable to the current political mood. Early in 1698, about the time the *Memoirs* appeared, Darby printed Toland's tract against standing armies, *The Militia*

Reformed. Toland's *Life* of Milton, its sequel *Amyntor*, and his edition of Harrington's works would follow from Darby's press over the next two years.

In 1705 Toland wrote in a private letter that, in the service of the political 'party I had espoused', he had 'published the lives and works of Harrington and Milton, with some other authors', all of them advocates of 'democratical schemes of government'. Which 'other authors' can he have meant? One possibility is Harrington's disciple Henry Neville, whose book *Plato Redivivus*, first published in 1680, was reprinted in 1698 by Richard Baldwin's newly widowed wife Anne. Only two others suggest themselves. One is Edmund Ludlow. The other is Algernon Sidney. As we shall now find, whoever edited either Ludlow's *Memoirs* or Sidney's *Discourses concerning Government* is likely to have edited the other work as well.

We noticed that an eighteenth-century hand attributed the preface to Sidney's *Discourses* to Isaac Littlebury. But in 1763 Thomas Hollis, in his new edition of the *Discourses*, ascribed the preface to Toland. He also implied that Toland had 'collected' the text. His words on that occasion weigh more than his handwritten attribution, in a copy of the 1751 edition of Ludlow's *Memoirs*, of the preface of that work to Littlebury. Hollis was not the editor of the Ludlow text of 1751: his edition of the *Discourses* was a labour of love. The attribution he makes to Toland is persuasive. Time and again the thought and language of the works of Toland, a writer with a propensity to pick up habits of phrasing from authors he admired, are notably close to those of the *Discourses*. In a tract of 1701 Toland praised a passage of the *Discourses* 'very much deserving every man's perusal, but too long to be transcribed here, and too well expressed to be done by any other'. Toland's *Life of John Milton*, which was probably completed just after the publication of the *Discourses*, contains a shamelessly gratuitous tribute to 'the incomparable and golden *Discourses* of that heroic patron of liberty, Algernon Sidney'. Later in the *Life* Toland, who was investing labour and pride in his imminent edition of *The 'Oceana' of James Harrington and his Other Works*, inserted an equally otiose reference to 'Harrington's *Oceana*, which for the practicableness, equality, and completeness of it, is the most perfect form of such a government that ever was delineated by any modern pen'. The Sidney and Harrington publications were widely advertised as a pair, and were regarded as such by contemporaries (who were also quick to associate the printing of Sidney's *Discourses* both with Ludlow's *Memoirs* and with Toland's Milton publications of 1698–9). Toland's own political philosophy is a subtle blend of Sidney's and Harrington's teaching.

Whether the manuscript of Sidney's *Discourses*, which does not survive, underwent treatment of the kind visited on 'A Voice from the Watch Tower' is a vexing question, to which we shall return. Whatever the answer, there is a telling similarity between the *Discourses* and the *Memoirs*. It is to be found in their opening words. Italic will bring it home. The *Discourses* start:

> *Having* lately *seen* a book entitled *Patriarcha*, written by Sir Robert Filmer, concerning the universal and undistinguished right of all kings, *I thought* a time of *leisure* might be well *employed in* examining his doctrine . . .

Ludlow's *Memoirs* begin (in language far remote from that of his manuscript):

> *Having seen* our cause betrayed, and the most solemn promises that could be made to the asserters of it openly violated, I departed from my native country. And hoping that my retirement may protect me from the rage and malice of my enemies, *I* cannot *think* it a misspending of some part of my *leisure*, to *employ* it *in* setting down . . .

It seems a fair inference that either the editor of the *Memoirs* borrowed the formula from Sidney's as yet unpublished manuscript, or he fabricated both passages, using in the *Discourses* the form of wording that had already served him in the *Memoirs*.* There is another link between the Ludlow and Sidney publications. Ludlow's editor, who in revising the Bodleian manuscript freely invents opinions for him, only rarely

* During his dispute with Awnsham Churchill in 1696, Slingsby Bethel claimed that Ludlow's 'Introduction' to his manuscript was 'much better' than the opening 'sheet or two' prepared by Awnsham Churchill's employee. His wording suggests that the two passages were fundamentally different.

inserts factual information which has no basis in the manuscript. The exceptions can be suggestive. One of them discloses an arcane piece of knowledge, about Sidney's possession of a pair of Italian pistols, which indicates that the editor took an unusual interest in Sidney and was unusually well-informed about him.

Ludlow, Sidney, Milton and Harrington were all figures from the civil wars. In March 1699 there appeared another publication of the same genre: the *Memoirs of Denzil Holles*, a leading parliamentarian of the 1640s who accepted the Restoration in 1660 and was ennobled by Charles II the following year. (The editor of Holles did not have a large job to do, for his text faithfully reproduced Holles's own, which has none of the frenzied Puritanism of Ludlow's manuscript.) If Ludlow's editor is likely to have been the editor of Sidney, so is he to have been the editor of Holles. Holles's *Memoirs* were evidently designed as a companion to Ludlow's. They contain an illustration of Holles by the engraver R. White which corresponds to White's engraving of Ludlow in the equivalent position of Ludlow's *Memoirs*; the dedicatory epistle is dated 28 March 1699, two days later than the preface to the third volume of Ludlow; and the preface to Holles's *Memoirs* explains that they are 'communicated to the world, that by comparing them with those of Ludlow, and such as appeared before, or will be published hereafter relating to the same times, they may afford mutual light to each other'. The third volume of Ludlow's *Memoirs* contains a series of points about the life of Holles that have no basis in Ludlow's manuscript.

A number of contemporaries identified Toland as the editor of Holles's *Memoirs*, among them Toland's dependable biographer Pierre Desmaizeaux, who reports that the publication was commissioned by Holles's kinsman and Toland's patron John Holles, Duke of Newcastle. The editor's dedicatory epistle is addressed to Newcastle, and contains the statement that 'the following papers of the famous Lord Holles, your great uncle, happened to fall into my hands'. The dedicatory epistle of Toland's tract *Anglia Libera*, published in 1702, is likewise addressed to Newcastle, whom it congratulates on 'having been the darling, and (as it were) the pupil, of the famous Lord Holles your great uncle'.

Holles and Ludlow, though both Roundheads, had been profoundly divided by the course of the civil wars. In the later 1640s Holles bitterly opposed Ludlow's radical cause. Pride's Purge, so glorious a deed in Ludlow's eyes, disgusted Holles, whom it evicted from power. His opposition to tyranny in the 1670s (when the honeymoon of the Restoration had passed) would, it is true, make him a Whig hero. He was lauded alongside Ludlow by radicals in the early 1690s. But he was no commonwealthman. The editor's preface to Holles's *Memoirs* makes a virtue of the contrast between Holles's views and Ludlow's. 'Such as really desire to know the naked truth, and propose for their chiefest aim the common good . . . have ever expressed a desire in their writings of seeing the memoirs of all parties made public as the most effectual means of framing a true General History.' The *Memoirs* of Holles, Ludlow and others are being published so that, 'after distinguishing the personal resentments and private biases of every one of them, the truth wherein they are found to agree (though dressed by them in different garbs) may by some impartial hand be related with more candour, clearness, and unanimity'. The words recall a passage in Toland's *Life of John Milton* which regrets that no Englishman has yet 'produced one good or approved *General History of England*', and which welcomes the progress of the composition of the *General History of England* currently being written by James Tyrrell. They are also a reminder of Toland's frequently voiced conviction that, within the broad spectrum of Whig principles, diversity of opinion was an antidote to political and intellectual 'stagnation'. He often observed that (as he put it in 1701) ''tis a thing never to be expected (nor perhaps so desirable as some may fancy) that all men should agree about all things'. The main preface to Ludlow's *Memoirs* carries a statement, which bears a strained relationship to the context in which it is set, that 'it can never be expected that all men should be of the same mind'.

Toland's *Life of John Milton* itself points us towards Ludlow's *Memoirs*. Again it is a detail that directs the way. As in relation to Sidney and Holles, so in relation to Milton, the editor of Ludlow's *Memoirs* slips in information which has no basis in Ludlow's manuscript. It concerns John Diodati, the father of Milton's friend Charles Diodati. Toland, who acquired letters of Charles to the poet, was the first writer on Milton to mention the friendship. The *Memoirs* identify the father, as the corresponding passage of Ludlow's manuscript does not, as minister of the Italian church at Geneva. The same information appears in Toland's *Life* of Milton. A second connection between the *Life* and the *Memoirs* takes us into the standing army controversy, the focus of Darby's end-of-century publications and a prominent issue in Toland's own writing and thinking. The wilfully anachronistic insertions about standing armies in the *Memoirs* have a counterpart in an abrupt digression in the *Life*. If Cromwell's army, Toland there asks, 'was capable of enslaving their country, what may be expected from any other, as most are, of a worse disposition?' That point, which was repeatedly made during the standing army controversy, appears in a passage of the *Life* which closely resembles one in the *Memoirs*, one moreover without a foundation in Ludlow's manuscript.

The standing army controversy connects Toland to the *Memoirs* from other angles too. His pamphlet *The Militia Reformed*, published, like the first two volumes of the *Memoirs*, early in 1698, makes a series of observations that have their counterparts in the *Memoirs*. One parallel is striking. Opponents of standing armies liked to stress that the soldiers of a citizen army will have their own occupations, to which they will return when their period of service is finished, whereas standing forces, to the hazard both of their own character and of their country, remain idle in peacetime. *The Militia Reformed*, in describing the attitude of William III's army to the prospect of disbandment, notes the healthy desire of 'the body of the common soldiers' to 'return home to their wives, or their relations, or their callings', but warns that if they remain in arms, 'tasting the pleasures of idleness and ease, they will every day become less willing to disband. . . . War being their trade, 'tis no wonder if they be always for continuing it.' Two passages of the *Memoirs* correspond to those statements. Though parallels to them can be found in the literature of the 1640s and 1650s, the wording of the *Memoirs* has a distinctive ring. The first passage explains that, at the end of the civil war in 1646, many soldiers of one parliamentary brigade 'were glad of the opportunity to return home to their several callings, having taken up arms and hazarded their lives purely to serve the public', but were resisted by 'divers idle and debauched persons [who did not know] how to betake themselves to any honest employment'. The second reports that, in 1659, the 'private soldiers' of the

Cromwellian army were easily deluded by their officers into betraying their country's liberties, for they 'had either utterly forgot their trades, or were unwilling to return to an industrious life . . . in order to get a living'. On two other occasions the *Memoirs* hit at men who 'make a trade of war'.

The Militia Reformed was one of a group of interdependent pamphlets, printed by Darby, which complemented each other's approach to the standing army question. Of the others there were two, published anonymously, which made a profound and lasting impact. The first was *An Argument Showing that a Standing Army is Incompatible with a Free Government*, published in the autumn of 1697. This was the work 'carried to the press' by Littlebury. Even though it appeared two or three months before the *Memoirs* came into print, its author or authors had plainly seen the text, on which the pamphlet drew for its account of Cromwell's army. The second was *A Short History of Standing Armies*, published late in 1698. It would be endlessly quoted and many times reprinted through the eighteenth century. It relied heavily on the *Memoirs*, a work which, it explained, answers 'any doubt whether a standing army is slavery', and from which it took a number of passages and points that would in turn be often lifted from the pamphlet in the century ahead. So extensive and influential were the borrowings that the pamphlet must be reckoned a significant element in the long-term impact of the *Memoirs*, perhaps almost as large a one as the successive editions of the *Memoirs* themselves. Who wrote the two pamphlets? The claim made by defenders of the standing army in 1697–9 that they and other tracts attacking it were written by a group (or 'club') was probably accurate. *An Argument* and *A Short History* would come to be attributed to the radical Whigs John Trenchard and Walter Moyle, both of whom are indeed likely to have played leading parts in their composition. But Toland was reportedly 'proud' to have them 'thought his', and there were contemporaries who believed him to have written them. Certainly there are striking overlaps and similarities of wording between them and pamphlets we know to have been Toland's.

Collaboration with John Toland was not something the collaborators cared to remember. People who befriended him learned to regret it.

That was partly because of his opinions, which usually proved to be more radical than he had let on, and which, together with his involvement in a series of embarrassing quarrels and brawls in England and on the Continent, could embarrass the thinkers and statesmen who had taken him up. It was also because of the untrustworthiness of a man who was said to maintain '*qu'il est permis de mentir à certaines occasions*'. His dishonesty, which served sometimes his opportunism, sometimes his vanity, sometimes both, was notorious. Yet he projected an earnestness and a charm that captivated – for a time – some of the leading thinkers of the age.

In April 1699 the government, convinced that he was an 'incendiary', was anxiously seeking to identify his 'encouragers'. Two of them were particularly important to him: Robert Harley, and Anthony Ashley Cooper, third Earl of Shaftesbury. Both relationships, like so many in Toland's life, ended in bitterness, but they were of critical significance while they lasted. Harley we have met as the creator and leader of the country party. Toland's polemical gifts made him an ideal recruit for a statesman keenly aware of the political power of the press, though the partnership was shrouded in secrecy. It was Harley who encouraged Toland to edit James Harrington's *Works* and to write his country-party manifesto of 1701, *The Art of Governing by Parties*. Whereas Toland's publications for John Darby were normally remunerated, Toland paid him to produce the handsome edition of Harrington, something Toland could not have done from his own pocket. Perhaps Harley supplied the money. We do not know whether he gave encouragement to the publication of Ludlow's *Memoirs*. What we can say is that their country-party stance conformed to his own.

It conformed to Shaftesbury's too. Where Toland's relationship with Harley was born of shared convenience, that with Shaftesbury was, on the earl's side, one of emotional intensity. The second partnership can be traced more fully than the first, though it too had its secretive side. Shaftesbury was a year younger than Toland. Their friendship has been obscured by their subsequent estrangement and by the efforts of the fourth earl to write the relationship out of his father's life. An undated letter from Shaftesbury to Toland, probably belonging to the later 1690s, breathes devotion and dependence. Even in 1701, when the earl had become aware of at least some of Toland's shortcomings, he called himself 'your best and truest friend'. A common friend was Robert Viscount Molesworth, whose *An Account of Denmark*, a warning against absolutism in England published in 1694, was one of the most influential radical Whig works of the decade.

Shaftesbury's political career was dominated by what he called 'the much injured memory' of his grandfather, the first earl, the Whig leader during the exclusion crisis. Here Toland saw his chance. In 1695 he 'boasted much of the young Lord Ashley, how he had framed him, and how he should outdo his grandfather'. Ludlow's *Memoirs*, we saw, omitted passages from 'A Voice from the Watch Tower' which were hostile to the first earl and of which Locke made copies. Toland, the cultivator of the third earl, would have had every reason to omit them. (In 1714, when he had broken with him, Toland freely attacked the earl's grandfather in a pamphlet about the Restoration.) Toland and Shaftesbury were close literary allies. They collaborated in 1698, the year of the *Memoirs*, to produce the radical Whig pamphlet *The Danger of Mercenary Parliaments*. The third earl probably encouraged Toland to write *The Militia Reformed* of the same year. Shaftesbury is an alternative (or additional) candidate for the sponsorship of Toland's edition of Harrington's works, for upon the publication of the volume he helped to organize its distribution in the Netherlands, where he had friends among what he thought of as the 'Holland Whig party'. In the month following the publication of the third volume of Ludlow's *Memoirs* Toland slipped over to Holland, where he reportedly intended to 'print some book' (we do not know which).

In 1699, at Toland's instigation, John Darby printed Shaftesbury's philosophical work *An Inquiry concerning Virtue*. Later the earl would repudiate the tract, which, he said, Toland had 'surreptitiously' caused to be 'printed from a rough draft'. He did not complain at the time, but it does seem that Toland acquired and published the text without Shaftesbury's knowledge. Toland's capacity to get his hands on, and keep possession of, other people's manuscripts is a persistent, sometimes astonishing feature of his career. His insouciant remark about the manuscript of Denzil Holles's *Memoirs*, that it 'happened to fall into my hands', might have been made about any number of documents. Seemingly on any subject he could locate or acquire manuscripts with uncanny ease: the early Church, primitive Ireland, Renaissance

France, seventeenth-century England. His *Life* of Milton and his edition of Harrington drew on fresh manuscript material that he had acquired. Some of the manuscripts in Toland's possession may, for all we know, have been gained by honourable means, but accusations of theft and deception – and plagiarism – were rife. We get a glimpse of his methods in an account by John Sharp, Archbishop of York and the leading ecclesiastical adviser to Queen Anne, of an interview he gave Toland in 1702. Toland secured the meeting by professing regret for his own theological lapses and a novel devotion to the Church of England. By the time he had left he had flattered the archbishop into giving him a copy of his recent Coronation sermon, which Toland subsequently used to his own advantage and the prelate's disadvantage. It is not difficult to imagine Toland persuading Awnsham Churchill in 1695 that he was the person to entrust with the rewriting of Ludlow's manuscript, or hanging on to it – in whatever circumstances – after Churchill had fallen out with Slingsby Bethel. William Baron, we saw, heard that Bethel was 'tricked' into handing over Ludlow's manuscript 'to a republican confidant', who, 'having got quiet and sole possession', proceeded with its preparation for publication. It was, as we also saw, not Toland who got the manuscript from Bethel; it was Churchill, who was not a 'republican'. Yet if Baron's version simplifies, it is easy to envisage conduct on Toland's part that could have given rise to the simplification.

The year 1699, when Shaftesbury's *An Inquiry concerning Virtue* was published, also saw Toland taking lodgings with another of the earl's protégés, the clergyman William Stephens. Though a much older man than Toland, Stephens was very close to him at this time. His writings in 1699–1700 are so similar to Toland's in thought and language that it can be hard to tell them apart. On 30 January 1700, the anniversary of Charles I's execution, Stephens preached a sensational sermon before the House of Commons (which was published by Anne Baldwin). The previous year's anniversary had been eventful too. Then the House had heard a Tory preacher make an attack on Toland for his disrespectful treatment of Charles I in his *Life* of Milton. Stephens's sermon exacted revenge. It assailed men who used the anniversary commemorations 'to flatter princes with notions of arbitrary power'. 'Many paragraphs' of the sermon were 'said to be given him by [John] Trenchard',

Toland's collaborator in the campaign against standing armies. In a tract of 1699 Stephens argued that the Nineteen Propositions, the terms of settlement which had been proposed by parliament to the king in 1642, should be the basis for present constitutional reform. The Propositions are reproduced in the text of Ludlow's *Memoirs*, where they are given a quite disproportionate space and prominence that must owe everything to editorial intervention. In the end Stephens's relationship with Shaftesbury, like Toland's, would break down. The earl learned, painfully, of Stephens's capacity for 'forgery and abuse'. Toland's response to that trait may have been more appreciative.

Shaftesbury's reputation as a philosopher rests on his book *Characteristics*, which appeared in 1711. By then he was an altered man from the nervous, impetuous figure of William III's last years. He had mellowed both in his personality and in his views. By 1705, when he and Toland had gone separate ways, he was ready to think of his grandfather's times as having 'laid the foundation' for 'the present glorious ones and for the happy Revolution that gave birth to them'. The Shaftesbury of Anne's reign was, admittedly, by no means always so sanguine, but he would never have spoken in such terms in the later 1690s, when the 'Revolution' seemed to him dangerously insecure and incomplete. 'Mercenary parliaments' and 'mercenary soldiers', he had then written, were grave evils, to be blamed on the 'compliance' of the 'apostate Whigs' with 'the court'. In 1698 he wrote to Locke of the 'shipwrecks' that had ruined English political life. In 1700 he looked, as the sole means to preserve the nation's liberties, for 'total reform', for the 'reducing' of parliaments 'solely and wholly to the country bottom'. Later he would remember that, at the outset of his career in the early 1690s, he had been drawn more to the Tories, who were 'so patriot-like', than to the Whigs, who were 'corrupt'. Only when the Tories' own capacity for corruption revealed itself had he abandoned them. He summarized his political life in note form: 'This [corruption] the foundation of all. An enemy to corruption. This monster to be subdued. Nothing else.'

Shaftesbury's and Toland's impassioned pamphlet of 1698, *The Danger of Mercenary Parliaments*, rounds on the Whig traitors in the language in which Ludlow's *Memoirs* assail the betrayers of Ludlow's cause. Now as under Cromwell, 'places and preferments', 'public robbers', the court's 'creatures', 'bribery' ('so sure and unavoidable a way to destroy our nation'), the political servility of the clergy, have played into the government's hands. Just as, in the *Memoirs*, Oliver Cromwell exploits the Cavalier threat as a pretext for the tyrannical measures of the protectorate, so *The Danger of Mercenary Parliaments* complains that the present regime has used the Jacobite menace 'as a footstool to ascend the throne of absolute power'. The government is supported by 'apostates', men who hitherto seemed 'possessed with [the] spirit of liberty' but who 'infamously fall in with the arbitrary measures of the court, and appear the most active instruments for enslaving their country'. One parallel between the two texts seems particularly telling. At the time of Cromwell's coup of 1653, recall the *Memoirs*, 'the nation [was] likely to attain in a short time that measure of happiness which human things are capable of'. *The Danger of Mercenary Parliaments* remembers how, during the Revolution of 1688, men expected 'happiness' and 'all manner of blessings a nation is capable of enjoying'. In both cases shattering disappointment was to follow.

The political stance of the *Memoirs*, then, corresponds to those of Toland's principal patrons: to the country-party position shared by Harley and Shaftesbury, and to the radical Whig in Shaftesbury. It also corresponds, as we shall now find, to Toland's own opinions. The identification of Toland's opinions is a difficult pursuit. It may seem a misguided one, so slippery and shifting and evasive are his statements, so easily do his ambitions and resentments convert into principles, so ready is he with the tactically apposite posture. Even so a consistency of thought and feeling can be identified.

The sense of betrayal voiced both in *The Danger of Mercenary Parliaments* and in the *Memoirs* is also a motif of writing we know Toland to have produced on his own. Bitterly and repeatedly he recalled the apostasy of the junto Whigs (and their rejection of his own literary talents). The Ludlow of the *Memoirs* retains, while others fall away, a 'constant and hearty affection to the public cause': Toland's own theme is the 'inviolable constancy' of the radical Whigs to their 'cause'. He is particularly aggrieved by the complicity of leading Whigs in William's resistance to the bills for triennial parliaments and the reform of treason trials. Then there was 'the business of the standing army', which in Toland's mind, as he recalls, 'finished all'. He shares the discontent of the published Ludlow on other fronts too. Both men bemoan the court's capacity to control parliamentary elections, and both look to an overhaul of the electoral system to thwart that practice. The criticism of the 'corrupt' legal profession that runs through the *Memoirs*, and in particular the protrusive complaint that 'counsel learned in the law' are 'very skilful at putting a good appearance on a bad cause', recall Toland's own attacks on the 'extremely corrupt' proceedings of the law courts and on 'counsel abominably mercenary'.

Those and several more sentiments that are paralleled in the *Memoirs* had other expositors in the 1690s too. But sometimes the *Memoirs* reflect distinctive sentiments of Toland. Above all there is his impassioned hatred, which has an intensity unique among the radicals of Toland's generation who went into print, of Cromwell as an apostate and usurper and tyrant. Toland time and again denounces the 'usurpation' of that 'dissimulating tyrant', a man 'forever to be remembered with detestation', that 'enslaver of his country' and 'monstrous betrayer of the liberties with which he was entrusted' by it. Toland's Introduction to his edition of Harrington's *Works* underlines a point also made in the *Memoirs*, that under Cromwell too many friends of liberty were 'seduced by the honours and preferments whereby they were retained in the service of the ruling powers'. Toland's commentary glosses Harrington's thinking so as to emphasize, more than he, the evil of Cromwell's rule by 'the sword', just as, on a larger scale, the editor of the *Memoirs* adjusts Ludlow's thinking so as to dwell on the despotism of 'the sword'. The text of the *Memoirs*, the preface to their third volume, and Toland's Introduction to Harrington all concentrate on the tyranny of the Major-Generals, 'bashaws' as they are called in each case. If Cromwell is the chief villain of the *Memoirs*, he has a partner in crime no less duplicitous, George Monk, the architect of the Restoration. In two tracts of 1714 Toland drew detailed parallels between Monk's conduct in 1660, which engineered the return of the Stuarts, and the behaviour, as the death of Queen Anne approached, of Robert Harley, formerly Toland's patron but now his enemy, whom he charged with the same purpose.

*

Behind the local points of agreement between the *Memoirs* and Toland's writing there lie more general correspondences of outlook. To grasp them we need to meet patterns both in Toland's ideas and in his promotion of them. First there is his republicanism. In 1711, reminding Harley of their cooperation in getting Harrington's *Oceana* published, he observed that 'neither of us imagined the model itself to be practicable'. The 'model' was Harrington's scheme for a republican constitution without king or House of Lords. Toland may indeed not have thought the model practicable, but he surely did think it desirable. Harley did not. He did not want a republic. He merely welcomed the circulation of literature likely to promote hostility to the court. Toland professed not to want a republic either, though his disavowals were less firm during the crisis of 1697–9 than after it. But in print Toland's radicalism, in politics and religion alike, is always modified or concealed. Open republicanism would not only have confirmed the allegations of his Tory enemies, who longed to see him 'called to account' for his seditious, as well as for his blasphemous, views. It would have been counter-productive. To approve of the regicide in the 1690s was risky enough. But regicide could be a step short of republicanism. After all, kings had been slain or deposed before, and been replaced by other kings. In 1688 a deposed king had been replaced by another king. What was widely feared during and after the Revolution of 1688 was that England, having rid itself of the Stuart tyranny, would stumble into the opposite danger of 'a commonwealth', a term which, as Toland himself acknowledged, the experience of the Interregnum had discredited in the nation's eyes.

Toland's pamphlets offered reassurance. The word 'commonwealth', he pointed out, deriving as it does from the Latin word *respublica*, properly means 'the common good'. In that sense England was already 'undeniably a commonwealth, though it be ordinarily styled a monarchy because the chief magistrate is called a king'. So there is no necessity to change the constitution. It need only be purged of the defects which were introduced by the Stuarts and which, because of 'the insufficiency of our hasty Bill of Rights' of 1689, are present, or at least dormant, still. Yet, as we read, it becomes clear that that operation will be far more fundamental than Toland has made it sound. It will involve a shift of constitutional balance, away from the royal prerogative, so profound as to reduce the monarchy to a detail: a convenient detail, certainly, but a disposable one. There are, explains Toland, two kinds of constitution. There are 'free governments' which serve 'the common good', the best examples being England and Toland's beloved Holland. The first of those nations happens to have a king, the second not. On the other side there is 'arbitrary' or 'tyrannical' monarchy, which the Stuarts imposed. Only 'besotted' men, he remarks, would prefer the second form to 'the most glorious republic'.

Ludlow's *Memoirs* applaud a glorious republic. In their narrative it is the Commonwealth whose leaders stand firm to the cause of liberty which others have betrayed, the Commonwealth that makes England great abroad, the Commonwealth that clamps down on bribery and instils probity and frugality into public life, the Commonwealth that reforms the navy, the Commonwealth that overhauls the electoral system. In Toland's own mind, such achievements and reforms are not attainable without republican constitutional change. In his Introduction to Harrington, and again in commending Sidney's *Discourses*, he contrives to intimate that political corruption is a symptom of constitutional disorder, beyond cure by mere *ad hoc* legislation. Yet he hesitates to make the point explicitly. In his writing the superiority of republican to monarchical rule is normally left to the reader to deduce.

So is it in the *Memoirs*. Both there and in Toland's own writing the contrast between republics and monarchies is tactfully subsumed under looser and less provocative ones between private and public interest, between freedom and slavery. Just as Toland's own writing explained that 'commonwealth' properly means 'the common good', so in the *Memoirs* a letter of Oliver Cromwell in 1650 is glossed so as to disclose that a true 'commonwealth' is one that serves 'the common good'. The editor of the *Memoirs* is free with the word 'commonwealthmen', the term often used by radical Whigs to describe themselves in the late 1690s. Yet the basic quarrel of the 'commonwealthmen' in the civil wars, first with Charles I and then with Cromwell, proves not to be between monarchical and non-monarchical rule. It is, like the quarrel of the 1690s as depicted by Toland, between 'arbitrary' or 'tyrannical' rule and government which serves 'the public good'. 'The question in dispute' during the civil war is 'whether the king should govern us as a god like beasts: or whether the people should be governed by laws made by themselves, and live under a government derived from their own consent'. 'Consent', remarks *The Danger of Mercenary Parliaments*, is 'the best of titles' for 'kingship'.

If there is a parallel of political position between the *Memoirs* and Toland's own writings, so is there one of social philosophy. Harrington's model republic, that 'most perfect form' of government in Toland's eyes, rested on the participation of 'the people' (a term which in Harrington's and other seventeenth-century hands normally excluded the servant class and omitted the 'rabble', but none the less extended well beyond England's customary rulers, the nobility and gentry). Under Charles II many of Harrington's followers had softened, even inverted his social teaching so as to adapt it to the revival of aristocratic power after 1660. After 1688, however, his commitment to 'popular government' found new supporters among the radical Whigs. Toland's *The Militia Reformed* in 1698, and his friend William Stephens's *A Letter to King William III* in 1699 (printed by Darby for Anne Baldwin), endorsed it. Walter Moyle, Toland's collaborator in the standing army controversy, concluded from his reading of Harrington that the post-Revolutionary regime must 'widen' its 'popular' support by 'multiplying property into many hands'. The *Memoirs* reproduce Toland's Harringtonian thinking. In his own writing, Toland notices that in parliamentary elections 'the populace', especially 'the better sort of them', are truer to the cause of liberty than most of the gentry. So when England 'had any tolerable parliaments, it was owing to the little interest the clergy and gentry had then over' the electorate. In the *Memoirs* it is 'commoners' whose 'interest' it is 'to stand firm for liberty'. Their outlook is contrasted with that of 'the nobility', those ready betrayers of the parliamentary cause, who like to 'insult over such as are of a lower order' and whose 'defensive principle' undermines the war effort. In the elections for Ludlow's native Wiltshire in 1656, report the *Memoirs*, it is 'the people' who vote for 'the common good' and seek a government supported by 'the affections of the people' – and who defy the persuasions of 'the imposing clergy'.

The crowning achievement of Ludlow's editor is the measured, semi-Stoical, country-party voice of the narrator. Toland's own prose achieves a poise and a reflectiveness that are as remote from his own excitable personality as the parallel qualities in the prose of the *Memoirs* are from Ludlow's excitable Puritanism. It is a prose, like that of the *Memoirs*, suited to country-party teaching. Toland likes to write, he invites us to believe, in 'a country retirement', free from 'the tumult of business or faction', from 'all the pomp and delicate entertainments of the court', from 'all the wealth and splendid luxury of the city'. His ideal legislator, he explains, is the independent country gentleman, whose roots and values are proof against those malign pressures. The published Ludlow is a legislator in that mould. In portraying him, the editor of the *Memoirs* created more than a voice. He created – indeed inhabited – a personality. In his *Life of John Milton* Toland proved that gift to be within his grasp. He revered Milton, as he did Sidney and Harrington, all figures to whom he was closer in mind and spirit than to the Ludlow of 'A Voice from the Watch Tower'. Yet the figure whom we get to know in the *Life*, like the Ludlow of the *Memoirs*, is artfully adjusted from the personality portrayed in the written material on which the characterization drew. Twentieth-century commentators noticed how the 'glow' and 'wit' of Toland's account of Milton created an 'animated' and 'rounded portrait', but one heavily influenced by Toland's own perspectives.

That achievement is most conspicuous in the field of religion. Toland, as a contemporary noticed, saw Milton's religion through the prism of his own. He conveyed nothing of its intensity, nothing of its apocalyptic dimension. For Toland a good religion is a civic religion, conducive to the virtuous service of the community and contending against everything 'that contributes to enslave [men's] minds and bodies', everything that serves 'the purposes of princes or priests against the interest of mankind'. That is the role of such religion as the Ludlow of the *Memoirs* is granted. So is it the function of religion in Toland's *Life* of Milton. Even the millenarian passage at the end of Milton's anti-episcopal tract of 1641, *Of Reformation*, becomes, in the context Toland creates for it, less a vision of the 'shortly expected' Second Coming than a denunciation of political 'tyranny'. In the same spirit Toland's Introduction to Harrington's *Works*, and the preface to the 1698 edition of Sidney, pass over the religious concerns of those writers and present their works as antidotes to 'tyranny'. The two prefaces to Ludlow's *Memoirs* do the same. All of the Darby publications of 1698–1700 that were intended to revive the political enthusiasms of the mid-seventeenth century – Milton, Harrington, Sidney, Ludlow – removed or subordinated the religious ones. Toland, who was responsible in the first two cases, was surely responsible in the others too.

Far more radical surgery was needed on Ludlow's religion than on that of Milton or Harrington or Sidney. Ludlow's Puritanism ran counter to Toland's every instinct. Ludlow was the self-professed enemy of 'reason' in religion, Toland its avowed friend. Ludlow was horrified by the challenges he saw around him to the doctrines of predestination and salvation by faith: Toland thought those notions to be 'nice speculations', 'mere jingle', and the controversies about them a symptom, perhaps even a cause, of mental and moral darkness. Ludlow complained of the tendencies of his time that 'struck at the mystery of the Trinity': Toland's *Christianity not Mysterious* became notorious for its anti-Trinitarian implications. If anyone could have been impelled to cut so energetically and ruthlessly through Ludlow's Puritanism it was Toland.

The Ludlow of the *Memoirs* is not merely deprived of Puritanism. He is hostile to it – or rather to those features of it that irritated Toland. The Puritan clergy are for the most part as unpalatable to the Ludlow of the *Memoirs* as the Puritan (or Dissenting) clergy are to Toland. The secularization effected by the editor of the *Memoirs* went beyond the requirements of late seventeenth-century values. Ludlow – like Milton and Harrington and Sidney in Toland's accounts of them – is allowed surprisingly small portions of the discreet piety and undemonstrative providentialism which characterized the public mood of the 1690s, but which in Toland's eyes were permeated by irrationality. During the 1690s Toland fell out with the Dissenters, the survivors of Puritanism, who had fed and supported him early in the decade. In the *Life* of Milton he portrays them, or at least the less tolerant of them, as bigots, and fears what will happen if, like their predecessors of the civil wars, they should 'get the sword into their hands'. Toland had a nose for what he called the 'canting' of the Puritans. The published Ludlow has one too, as we find on the occasions when religious enthusiasm – especially Cromwell's – is presented as a self-evident mark of hypocrisy and as an instrument of political advancement. In the *Life* of Milton, Toland glances at the 'reputation' which Cromwell gained by 'his supposed piety'.

A heavy weight of evidence, then, indicates that Toland edited the *Memoirs*. But if he did, one question remains. How did he escape detection? The process by which Ludlow's manuscript was converted into the *Memoirs* was a closely guarded secret, which defied every Tory attempt at penetration. Toland would have been more exposed to suspicion than most. Since the publication of *Christianity not Mysterious* in 1696 he had been a marked man, his movements closely inquired after by his enemies. Yet his foes found his deeds tantalizingly difficult to trace.

As an author Toland had two opposing instincts. Robert Sullivan has described 'the compulsion to prove his own importance' which made him eager to claim the credit for his anonymous productions and left him 'galled' by 'anonymity'. How proud he would have been of the *Memoirs* it is hard to say. Perhaps he would have rejoiced in so inspired a contribution to his own political cause; but perhaps too, working on a text soaked in what he would have thought Puritan cant, he would have seen the revision as hack-work, akin to the translations he was obliged to undertake to meet his debts to Darby and others. The second instinct was that of a man who, notes Sullivan, 'habitually covered his tracks'. His perpetual juggling of patrons and allegiances made furtiveness a way of life for him. In 1705 (when his lodging had a door 'by which any man may come to me *incognito*') he wrote to Shaftesbury urging him to conceal his knowledge of Toland's authorship of the recently published tract *A Memorial of the State of England*, a secret that Toland had withheld even from the printer. The 'ingenious and learned person' employed by Churchill in 1695 to rewrite Ludlow's manuscript, we recall, 'signified his desire to have his name concealed'. At that time Toland, who was preparing his explosive pamphlet *Christianity not Mysterious* for the press, was already risking trouble enough without incurring a public reputation for republicanism. It was not merely – though it was mainly – the guardians of religious and political orthodoxy whom he would have had grounds to fear. His former patrons among the Dissenters, to whom the deism of *Christianity not Mysterious* was so offensive, would have been affronted too (as the response of the Dissenter Slingsby Bethel to the passage shown him by Churchill indicates) by the secularization of Ludlow's manuscript – or at least by the extent of that operation.

After the publication of the *Memoirs*, likewise, Toland would have had every motive for secrecy. The legal action taken against *Christianity not Mysterious* had been warning enough. It was soon after the appearance of the third volume of Ludlow's *Memoirs* that a government source referred to Toland as 'an incendiary'. His associates discovered that daring publications could lead to trouble with the government or in the courts. John Trenchard was interrogated by the Secretary of State on the publication of *An Argument* against standing armies. According to the pamphlet *The Seaman's Opinion of a Standing Army*, published by Richard Baldwin's widow in 1699, Richard had been threatened with prosecution for one of his productions and had had to pay handsomely to 'buy' off the action. William Stephens would be sentenced to the pillory in 1706 for his authorship of one pamphlet, and was spared only at the last moment when the spectators had already gathered. From around the turn of the century Toland would have had another ground for concealment. As the centre of political gravity shifted towards the Tories, so he became increasingly anxious to disown his radical past, the more so, perhaps, since he had apparently quarrelled with his former associates of the late 1690s. Perhaps – though this can only be speculation – he at some point found it useful to have it thought that Isaac Littlebury had been the editor. The ruse would have been in character.

If he did edit the *Memoirs* there is a certain irony, though one again entirely compatible with what we know of his personality. Writings which Toland owned to have written, especially those on religion, warred against the fraudulent creation of texts and of textual 'canons'. If the *Memoirs* are his work, he is revealed as a triumphant exponent of the practice he condemned. Renowned as he was for his fondness for 'paradoxes', he would have savoured that one.

To avoid wearisome qualification I shall henceforth assume that Toland was the editor of the *Memoirs*, and again leave readers to make any mental qualifications they judge fitting. I shall assume too, in the same spirit, that he edited Algernon Sidney's *Discourses*, the subject of the next part of this book. Before we move to it we owe Ludlow a parting word. What would his response to the rewriting of his manuscript have been? He indicates the answer in the note of 1674 which Bethel cited in his dispute with Churchill. I reproduce it in its original spelling and punctuation.

If the Lord please to put an end to my pilgrimage, before I have brought this narrative to its perfection, its my desier, that my deare wife, if liveing, if not, those of my deare friends, and relations, into whose hands by providence it shall fall, will take care that if it, or any part of it, bee thought of use unto others, it may not bee made publique, before it hath ben perused, rectifyed, and amended by some one, or more iudicious friends, who have a fluent style, and [are] of the same principle with mee, as to civill, and spirituall governmement, the liberty of men, and Christians, and well acquainted with the transactions of the late times, to whome I give full power to deface what hee, or they conceive to be superfluous, or impertinent, or what they know to bee false, to change or alter what they find misplaced in respect of time, or other circumstances, to adde what they conceive to bee deficient, or may conduce to render it more usefull, and agreable, and to that end to cloth it in a more full, and liquid stile, and to illustrate what is therein asserted with such reasons, similes, examples, and testimonys, as they shall think fit. Provided that in the maine, they make it speake noe other then [= than] my principle (which as I judge is according to the minde of the Lord) in relation to the gouvernement of church, and state, and Christs ruleing, yea ruling alone by his spirit in the hearts of his people, and carrying on his worke in them by his owne weapons, which are spirituall, mighty through his blessing for the beating downe of the strongholds of sin, and Sathan, and bringing into captivity every thought to the obedience of Christ. In testimony heereof I have heereunto set my hand this 27th of November 1674. Edmund Ludlowe.

Between that call from the heart of the ageing Ludlow, and the manipulative opportunism of the young Toland, there lay a chasm of human experience. Perhaps Ludlow would have regarded the style of the *Memoirs* as 'more full and liquid' than his own. It was his misfortune that his editor, though his 'civil principle' may have overlapped transgressed against him; whose worme shall not dye, nor their fire be quenched, but they shall be an abhorring to all flesh. For the Lord will be glorified in his justice on such, as are not willing that he should be glorified in his mercey towards them. For to him belongs the kingdome, power & glory, and happy yea happy only are those who in trueth of heart can say heereto Amen.

Edmund Ludlowe.

228

Ludlow's note of 1674. The words at the top of the page (in the hand of an amanuensis) are those with which he intended to conclude his narrative. They read: 'transgressed against him; whose worme shall not dye, nor their fire be quenched, but they shall be an abhorring to all flesh. For the Lord will be glorified in his justice on such, as are not willing that he should be glorified in his mercey towards them. For to him belongs the kingdome, power & glory, and happy yea happy only are those who in trueth of heart can say heereto Amen.'

Ludlow's, cared nothing for the 'spiritual' one for which the author of 'A Voice from the Watch Tower' had lived.

In 1699 the country party began to crack. A series of events near the end of William's reign gave country Whigs alarming reminders of the menace of France and of the precariousness of the Protestant succession. Opposition to standing armies appeared untimely if not irresponsible. The impeachment of the junto leader Lord Somers in 1700 brought home to Toland's patron Shaftesbury the need for Whig unity against the Tories. The moment that had produced the *Memoirs*, and with them the editions of Sidney, Milton, Harrington and Neville, had passed.

Yet its legacy would be momentous. The authors and editors of the 'canon of real Whig doctrine' would have a profound influence in the eighteenth century. They supplied an essential component of what Bernard Bailyn has termed 'the ideological origins of the American Revolution'. They had an influence on the French Revolution the extent of which is only now beginning to be appreciated. Our concern is principally with the impact of the canon in England. We can best approach it through a study of the author in the canon whose prose, on both sides of the Atlantic, made the widest eighteenth-century impression: Algernon Sidney.

5

Algernon Sidney the Republican

Algernon Sidney (or Sydney) won his eighteenth-century fame on two counts. First there was his martyrdom. In 1683 he was executed for treason after a trial, presided over by Judge Jeffreys, that shocked contemporary opinion and outraged posterity. Secondly there was his book *Discourses concerning Government*, published in 1698, fifteen years after his death. In the eighteenth century he commanded intense admiration. It became a commonplace that the *Discourses* were a compensation to posterity for the loss of the missing books of Cicero's work *de Republica*. Richard Baron, who edited Sidney (and Ludlow and Milton) in the early 1750s, went further, claiming that 'all antiquity cannot show' a writer equal to Sidney. In 1781 the republican historian Catharine Macaulay ruled that in him 'all the dignity of the Roman character, and all the literature of the Greeks, were happily united'. Charles James Fox described him and his fellow-martyr Lord Russell as 'two names that will, it is hoped, be ever dear to every English heart', and predicted that 'when their memory shall cease to be an object of respect and veneration . . . English liberty will be fast approaching its final consummation'. The most energetic and influential of Sidney's eighteenth-century admirers was Thomas Hollis, who re-edited the *Discourses*, which he judged 'one of the noblest books that ever the mind of man produced.' It was Hollis who commissioned the engravings that made semi-classical images of Sidney and other Whig heroes familiar. He found in him 'piety enough for a saint, courage enough for a general or martyr, sense enough for a king; in a word, if ever any, he was a perfect Englishman'.

There were other, less immaculate features of his character, from which his eighteenth-century admirers turned their eyes but which

Algernon Sidney in 1663. After Justus von Egmont.

his contemporaries had less chance of avoiding. The clerical Whig politician and historian Gilbert Burnet, who had dealings with Sidney and was impressed by his courage and learning, remarked also on the 'rough and boisterous temper' of a man who 'could not bear contradiction'. Time and again in his dealings with colleagues we find Sidney 'waxing hot' or voicing 'high discontents'. In 1659 the MP Bulstrode Whitelocke refused to accompany him on a diplomatic mission because he 'well knew the overruling temper and height of Colonel Sidney'. Algernon himself acknowledged 'the heat and violence of my disposition'. His fury found many targets, some within his own family, others among his political colleagues, but perhaps its leading objects were the two men whom he joined Edmund Ludlow in detesting: Oliver Cromwell and Charles II. Like Ludlow he hated Cromwell's protectorate. For most of Charles II's reign he longed for the king's overthrow. For much of it he plotted to achieve it. His quarrels with his fellow-conspirators undermined any chance his plans had.

Sidney's posthumous reputation converted a hot-headed insurrectionist into a plaster saint. But if the eighteenth century was indulgent to his character it also distorted and impoverished his ideas. Like Ludlow's, Sidney's writing introduces us to dimensions of seventeenth-century thinking that later generations would find it convenient to forget. The key to Ludlow's writing is his Puritanism. The key to Sidney's is his republicanism, intellectually an altogether more sophisticated creed than Ludlow's (a palm which Ludlow, who mistrusted intellectual sophistication, would readily have yielded).

Algernon Sidney was born in 1622, the second son of Robert, Earl of Leicester, the owner of Penshurst in Kent, and of Dorothy Percy, daughter of the ninth Earl of Northumberland. His great-uncle was the Elizabethan poet and courtier Sir Philip Sidney, whose early death after the battle of Zutphen in 1586 would make as powerful an impression on posterity as would Algernon's death on the scaffold in 1683. Like Philip he achieved more in politics by his death than by his life. Yet in both cases posthumous memory was a distortive force. Philip's unavailing radicalism was obscured by the seventeenth-century Cavalier culture that claimed him for its own. Algernon's was muted by the eighteenth-century country-party culture that absorbed the canon created by John Darby and John Toland.

Shortly before his execution Algernon recalled that 'from the year 1642', when the civil war broke out, he had contended for 'the common rights of mankind, the laws of the land, and the true Protestant religion, against corrupt principles, arbitrary power, and popery'. That summary suited the more radical of his posthumous admirers, who liked to think of him as a constant enemy to Stuart tyranny, but it was a convenient simplification. At the start of the war, when he was not yet twenty, Sidney's views and commitments had still to form. He took up arms only belatedly, and even then, it seems, from economic rather than principled motives. Like many younger sons of aristocratic descent he was plagued through his life by debt and poverty. Only 'extreme necessity', he intimated, made him 'bear arms in England', 'the only way of living well for those that have no estates'. (His financial plight may be one reason why he never married, though he loved like a lovesick Elizabethan.) He was given a regiment, fought bravely at Marston Moor, and for the rest of his life 'carried the marks' of the wounds he incurred there 'in many parts of his body'.

He did not fight again. Like Ludlow he entered the Commons after a by-election in 1646. He represented Cardiff, a seat close to lands owned by his family. At Westminster he took time to make his mark, owing such initial influence as he possessed more to his aristocratic connections than to any exertions of his own. For some years his conduct as an MP showed few foretastes of his subsequent radicalism. He seems to have opposed the execution of Charles I – a deed he would later call 'the justest and bravest action that ever was done in England'. He continued to sit in parliament after the king's death, but for some time attracted little attention in the Commons other than by his feuds with fellow-members. Ludlow's *Memoirs* tell us that in 1650 Ludlow advised Cromwell that 'a fitter man could not be found than Algernon Sidney' for the post of second-in-command of the forces in Ireland, a story that is likely to have had a basis in Ludlow's manuscript. But Sidney had quarrelled with Cromwell and the suggestion came to nothing. Then, in 1652–3, the last year of the Long Parliament, his standing rose. He was elected to the Council of State and threw himself into the formation and implementation of foreign policy. He involved himself especially in two causes, the running of the Anglo-Dutch war that began in 1652 and the negotiations that paved the way for the incorporation of Scotland into the English Commonwealth. For Sidney this was a stirring time, a period of epic endeavour and achievement on the government's part. Three decades later his *Discourses* would compare

the integrity of those who for a while managed the public treasure; the discipline, valour and strength of our armies and fleets; the increase of our riches and trade; the success of our wars in Scotland, Ireland and at sea; the glory and reputation not long since gained, with that condition into which we are of late fallen. . . . I think I shall offend no wise or good man, if I say that . . . neither the Romans nor Grecians in the time of their liberty ever performed any actions more glorious than freeing the country from a civil war that had raged in every part, the conquest of two such kingdoms as Scotland and Ireland, and crushing the formidable power of the Hollanders by sea; nor ever possessed more examples of valour, industry, integrity, and in all respects complete, disinterested, unmoveable and incorruptible virtue, than were at that time seen in our nation.

Cromwell had a very different view. The abusive speech in which he announced the dissolution of the parliament in April 1653 railed at the wickedness of its members. Sidney, who was present at the coup, was one of those who bore the brunt of Cromwell's anger. He was ordered from the chamber by Major-General Thomas Harrison, who had 'continually opposed' him since a parliamentary quarrel four years earlier. To Sidney as to Ludlow, Cromwell's assumption of power was a vile and calamitous usurpation. After the Restoration he wrote a life of Cromwell, though it does not survive. It must have been vituperative. During the protectorate he may have involved himself in conspiracy against the government. He did not resume an open role in politics until 1659, when the restored Rump sent him on an embassy to The Sound. It was during the mission that he inscribed, in the visitors' book of the University of Copenhagen, words with which his name would come to be indissolubly associated on both sides of the Atlantic: *Manus haec inimica tyrannis* ('this hand hostile to tyrants'). By the end of the century it was believed – perhaps accurately: we cannot be sure – that he had added, to that phrase, *Ense petit placidam cum libertate quietem* ('seeks with a sword quiet peace with liberty'): words that would be adopted in the late eighteenth century as the founding motto, which survives to this day, of the State of Massachusetts.

In the short term the incident at Copenhagen was disastrous. News of it soon reached the Stuart family. When the republic collapsed Sidney was still abroad. Like everyone else he was surprised by the backlash against Puritan and republican rule that followed the Restoration. At first it was widely supposed that the new king would be content to rule as a 'limited', parliamentary monarch, tolerant of political and religious dissent. Sidney acknowledged that the nation had consented to Charles's return and that the restored monarchy was thus, at least to begin with, a legitimate regime. He had thoughts not only of returning to England but of securing political office. He soon knew better. For the greater part of two decades he was to 'wander as a vagabond through the world, forsaken of my friends, poor, and known only to be a broken limb of a shipwrecked faction'. Like Ludlow he was pursued by assassins in Charles's or his allies' pay. At first he found a safe retreat in Italy, but 'it was an ill-grounded peace that I enjoyed' there 'because I lived only to myself, and was in no ways useful unto God's people, my country, or the world'. In 1662 he was shocked to learn of the execution of that leading parliamentarian Sir Henry Vane, whom he revered, as Ludlow did. Of all the exemplars of 'complete, disinterested, unmoveable and incorruptible virtue' among the rulers of the Commonwealth, Vane was in Sidney's eyes the doyen. His death seemed an outrage of vindictiveness, for alone among the executed Roundheads he had not been involved in the trial and execution of the king, events from which Sidney too had stood back. In 1663 Sidney moved north, with the aim of drawing the regicides exiled in Switzerland and Holland into conspiracy against the Stuart regime. He visited Ludlow, and while at Geneva wrote another striking entry in a university visitors' book: *Sit sanguinis ultor justorum*: 'let there be a revenger for the blood of the just'.

Sidney was better at rhetorical gestures than at the practicalities of conspiracy. His fellow exiles, he soon realized, were unprepared for his plans. But late in 1664 the outbreak of hostilities between England and the United Provinces gave him fresh hope. He went to Holland and pressed the republican government there to enlist the exiles in its cause, to invade England with their help and to restore the Commonwealth. The Dutch, who had suffered from the Commonwealth's might, were understandably doubtful. Ludlow was doubtful too. His insistence that the Dutch repent of the blood of the regicides who had been seized on their soil seemed 'ridiculous' to Sidney, who sent him, as a rueful Ludlow noted, a letter 'stuffed with invectives from the beginning to the end'. Sidney's relations with other exiles were marked by 'great heats'. Eventually he turned to France, offering to lead a regiment of exiles under Louis XIV. 'Most' of them, however, declined to serve under Sidney, and in any case Louis judged the asking price too high.

Meanwhile Algernon was also busy with his pen. His treatise *Court Maxims, Refuted and Refelled*, which came to light in Warwick Castle in 1976, a few years after the sale of Ludlow's manuscript from there, was written in the mid-1660s. It was evidently prepared for publication, either by the men who published his *Discourses* in 1698 or else by a like-minded group around the same time, but the plan fell through. Only in 1992 was the work first printed. It is a vehement indictment of the Restoration regime, intended to incite an uprising against Charles II. 'All that are friends to reason and justice', it declares, are 'obliged' to rise and 'destroy' that 'monster' the king. Sidney's *Discourses*, an enormous work, would be written with the same purpose. There is no sign that either treatise was ever read in its author's lifetime. The Sidney family had a tradition of meditative political writing that went back at least a century. Their reflections had been confined to manuscript and been kept, mainly or wholly, within the family. Hard as he tried, Algernon found the leap from that instrument of expression to propaganda unmanageable.

With the Anglo-Dutch peace of 1667 his hopes of inciting insurrection subsided. For the next ten years he lived quietly in France, mostly in the south. Then in 1677 he was permitted to return to England, on condition that he did not act against the government. He soon broke the contract. His purpose in returning was personal and financial, not political. As so often he had family and property disputes to attend to. But in 1678 the lure of politics proved too strong. The Popish Plot of that year, and the exclusion crisis of 1679–81, restored the political temperature to the high level of 1641–2. Sidney, drawn naturally to the Whig side, was active on many fronts. Again looking to external aid he entered into talks with the French ambassador in London, Paul Barillon. He also made a series of determined but unsuccessful attempts to win a seat in parliament. He immersed himself too in the politics of the city of London, a community of which the Crown had lost control. In 1680 he helped secure the election of Slingsby Bethel as Sheriff, a post of high political and electoral influence in the capital.

The dissolution of the Oxford Parliament in 1681 ended Whig hopes of a parliamentary solution to the crisis. Sidney responded to that new situation as he had done to the Anglo-Dutch war of the 1660s, by simultaneously writing and plotting. It was now, from 1681 to 1683, that the *Discourses* were composed. They argued that the people have not merely a right but a duty to disobey bad laws and kill or depose a tyrant. If possible Charles II, who 'despises the law' and deserves the consequences, should be brought to trial like his father before him. If not, 'extrajudicial' measures will be needed. By 1683 Sidney was planning extrajudicial methods himself. At his trial the prosecution failed to marshal conclusive evidence of conspiracy, and won a conviction only with Jeffreys's connivance. Even so there is no doubt of Sidney's prominent involvement in plans for a general rising in England, which was to be supported by an invasion from Scotland.

In the cult of Sidney his two legacies, the martyrdom and the *Discourses*, were closely linked. Both of them had features attractive to men of political views different from his.

The methods that were used to secure Sidney's condemnation for treason were no more ruthless than those deployed earlier by his friends to achieve the convictions of the victims of Whig hysteria after the Popish Plot. His death may have been an act of calculated revenge for the procedures used by his close allies, Slingsby Bethel among them, to procure the execution of the alleged plotter Lord Stafford in 1680. But there was one aspect of Sidney's trial to chill the blood of any gentleman or politician outside the orb of courtly favour. The offence of treason had long been held to include intent as well as deed. But in trials in which the case against the accused rested solely on words spoken or written by him, as it did in Sidney's, the prosecution was required to supply at least two witnesses to the offence. Sidney's prosecutors could find only one, Lord Howard of Escrick, whom everyone despised and few trusted. (It is he whose expulsion from parliament for bribery under the Commonwealth receives emphatic attention in Ludlow's *Memoirs*.) With Jeffreys's approval the prosecution produced, as a second 'witness', passages of the manuscript of the *Discourses*, a few sheets of which had been seized in his study at the time of his arrest. At his trial Sidney protested that the Spanish Inquisition would not have gone so far. It was the 'right of mankind', he declared, to 'write in their closets what they please for their own memory, and no man can be answerable for it unless they publish it'. The manuscript, he claimed, bore no relation to the conspiracy alleged against him. It was concerned only with 'general principles', not with current events. It was the fruit of private and leisurely reflection, written 'long since', 'perhaps twenty or thirty years ago'.

Those assertions were untrue, but they made their mark. If the prosecution's device 'holds to be law and comes to be followed in practice', reflected Gilbert Burnet, 'England is the miserablest nation in the world'. Even John Evelyn, the Tory diarist, dismayed as he was by Sidney's 'aversion to government by a monarch', sympathized with those who pronounced the verdict 'very hard measure'. In the 1690s men opposed to Sidney's principles shuddered to recall the invasion of his study. His ripostes to the use of his manuscript against him, it was claimed in parliament in 1698, showed his 'love to liberty and the good of his country'. The memory of the prosecution's insistence that 'compassing and imagining the death of the king is the act of the mind, and is treason while it remains in the heart', took long to fade. Transcripts of the trial, circulating in print and in manuscript, helped keep the memory alive. The horrible circumstances of his death obscured the recollection of his violent intentions against the king. So did the demeanour with which he met his end. He accepted the death-sentence and his ordeal on the scaffold with a serenity that surprised those who knew him. Posterity was struck by Burnet's observation that Algernon faced death 'with an unconcernedness that became one who had set up Marcus Brutus for his pattern'. At his execution he produced a paper which, at least in the form in which it rapidly got into print, linked him to that Roman model, addressed as it was to his 'Friends, Countrymen and Strangers!' In the eighteenth century Sidney became known as 'the British Brutus' (or, sometimes, a 'Cassius'). The classical mantle distanced him from the turbulence of circumstance and character that had brought him to the scaffold.

The preface to Toland's edition of the *Discourses* in 1698 aided the taming of Sidney. Toland was gingerly, in the same year, in handling the radicalism of Ludlow, whose emphasis on the regicide, as we saw, he diminished. His caution in the instance of the *Discourses* took a different form. His preface says nothing of the incendiary origins and purpose of the work. It presents it, as Sidney himself did at his trial, as a work of philosophical reflection. That impression is heightened by the opening words of the text, which (we saw) describe the composition of the book as the occupation of 'a time of leisure'. The very similar opening to Ludlow's *Memoirs* imparts a sense of detachment to that work too.

Is the opening of the *Discourses* Sidney's or Toland's? Did Toland, who took so many liberties with Ludlow's text, take liberties with Sidney's too? He is unlikely to have done so on anything like the same scale. There are three reasons for thinking this. First, we have Sidney's *Court Maxims*, a work of which a high proportion appears to survive in the form in which he left it. Though it has some differences of character from the *Discourses*, they are mostly of a kind explicable by reference to contrasts of subject-matter or to the passage of time – fifteen years and more – between the two compositions. The similarities between the treatises are more striking than the contrasts. Secondly we can compare the printed *Discourses* with the short passages of Sidney's manuscript that were seized from his study and produced in evidence against him. Toland did not have access to them, and his edition of the *Discourses* records the gaps in the text where they would have appeared. The seized passages are encouragingly consistent in style and character with the text prepared for publication by Toland.

Thirdly the *Discourses* are very long and very repetitive. Ludlow's *Memoirs* show Toland's capacity for ruthless pruning. If he had ruthlessly pruned Sidney we would surely have a far shorter text. Sidney's manuscript was probably in a disordered state at the time of his arrest, and Toland is likely to have had to do some tidying. Perhaps the opening sentence of the *Discourses* emerged from that process. There are grounds, as we read the *Discourses*, for wondering if Toland has sometimes intervened in more essential ways, but there are never grounds for certainty. One difficulty is the high degree of similarity of argument and wording between the *Discourses* and writings of Toland's own. Not only that, but passages of Ludlow's *Memoirs* where Toland's presence is particularly conspicuous – especially on the subject of standing armies – are closely resembled in the *Discourses*. Did Toland insert his own points and language into the *Discourses*, or did he take them from them? We cannot be sure. But Toland's habit of appropriating arguments and words from authors he admired supplies the likely explanation. We probably have, in the *Discourses*, more or less the text that Sidney wrote.

If Toland did not interfere substantially with Sidney's text, perhaps he should have done. How many people have read Sidney through? The *Discourses* belong to a genre of which the seventeenth century was fond but which has not travelled well down the centuries: the page-by-page refutation of another work. Sidney's target was the *Patriarcha* of Sir Robert Filmer, published in 1680 though written much earlier. It is thus Filmer, not Sidney, whose thinking imposes the shape of the *Discourses*, or such shape as they possess. Filmer's book, an argument for the unlimited powers of kings, shocked everything in Sidney's mind and heart and soul. Its arguments, he explains, 'seem so far to concern all mankind that, besides the influence upon our future life, they may be said to comprehend all that in this world deserves to be cared for'. Sidney knew the power of ideas. 'The whole fabric of tyranny will be much weakened if we prove that nations have a right to make their own laws, constitute their own magistrates; and that such as are so constituted owe an account of their actions to those by whom and for whom they are appointed.' The import of Filmer's treatise was to 'corrupt the people' by 'false and slavish doctrines' which 'poison the springs of religion and virtue'. At its best Sidney's prose is a rare blend of elegance and fire. Eighteenth-century readers warmed to his eloquence. They applauded the 'propriety of diction' and 'dignity of expression' of a work so 'admirably written'. But to an increasing number of them Filmer's theses, with which Sidney engages so closely, were absurdities, relics of a tyrannical age now happily past, scarcely deserving detailed refutation. In reading Sidney it was tempting, and easy, to skip and dip. He became known, more than most writers, through excerpts and quotations. He was read selectively.

Selection muted the impact of his radicalism. In 1689 he had the most radical of credentials, on account both of his judicial murder and of his thought. He was the hero of extreme Whigs, who were busily creating a martyrology of the years 1683–8. First during the 'Tory revenge' at the end of Charles's reign, then as a result of the proscription of Monmouth's followers under James, numerous radicals had suffered death or exile. Now, in 1689, the survivors among them reasserted their cause. Sidney's friend and fellow-conspirator John Hampden, grandson of the famous Hampden who opposed Charles I, insisted that the overthrow of James had been merely a delayed fulfilment of the plans made by Sidney and the other leaders of the conspiracy of 1683 that had cost Algernon his life. The tract *Sidney Redivivus*, published in 1689, kept Sidney's radical affiliations in the public eye. Over the eighteenth century they would retreat. Late in that century, it is true, the emergence of populist radicalism (as, for shorthand, I shall call it) revived them; but not for long.

There are two faces of the radicalism of the *Discourses*. One is its championship of the people's right to resist tyranny. The other is its republicanism. On the first front the *Discourses* were intended to incite their readers to overthrow the Stuart tyranny. On the second they offered principles of government to replace it.

The question whether oppressed subjects are entitled to rise against their rulers has been one of the most inflammatory issues of European political thought. Under the Tudors and Stuarts, when kings were portrayed, at least by their apologists, as divinely appointed, claims for a right of resistance were explosively unorthodox. Charles I's opponents in the civil war, or at least the more moderate of them, were quick to deny that their defiance of the king was an act of resistance. They claimed to be fighting for king and parliament, not for parliament against the king. Charles's execution discredited that claim. John Milton explicitly vindicated the regicide as an assertion of the right to resist. After the Restoration, when the regicide was execrated, it was easy for royalists and Tories to identify the Roundhead challenge to

Charles I with the wicked principle of resistance. The persistence of the principle in radical circles strengthened the regime's polemical hand. When Sidney, in statements published at the end of his life, linked his own recent behaviour to the Roundhead cause he delighted radicals but horrified others.

The year 1688 altered perceptions of the principle of resistance. It was hard to deny that the Revolution had involved resistance. In many quarters justifications of resistance acquired a novel respectability. It was partly for that reason that in 1698 the publication of Sidney's *Discourses*, on whose seditious principles the prosecution had swooped in 1683, provoked less alarm and hostility than the appearance of Ludlow's *Memoirs* – though it was also because allegations of tyranny against Charles II, the immediate target of the *Discourses*, remained less contentious than those levelled at his father. In the first half of the eighteenth century points made by Sidney and other radicals in demanding the overthrow of the Stuarts were assimilated, in muted form and for the most part silently, within orthodox Whig thought. Yet they were cautiously advanced. Though orthodox Whigs occupied power, they knew how slowly and reluctantly, in the society around them, the doctrine of the divine right of kings was retreating. They were wary of bringing Sidney's insurrectionary conduct and outlook to public attention. Hardly ever did they mention his name. Sidney's claims for resistance had been couched in rhetorical and inflammatory language. Orthodox post-Revolutionary Whigs generally preferred a more sober and discreet approach. Even though the right of resistance had become an essential component of their justification of the Revolution, they mostly said no more about it than they needed. Jacobite risings and conspiracies, and the fear of popular insurrection, showed how dangerous were the uses to which the right might be put. As the Whig leader Charles James Fox observed near the century's end, the right to resist 'is a principle which we should wish kings never to forget, and their subjects seldom to remember'.

So resistance was what, in the emergency of 1688, had legitimately been done, not what anyone should want to do again. Only an unfree people could have reason to resist, and 1688 had set the English free. Sidney's exclamatory justification of resistance could sound less like a warrant for the post-Revolutionary regime than a threat to it. From the 1690s to the accession of George III it presented problems for his admirers. Walter Moyle, Toland's ally in the campaign against standing armies in 1697–8, felt obliged to address the charge that in the *Discourses* Sidney 'makes the grounds and obligations of subjection and obedience to government too loose'. 'This objection,' he maintained, 'seems to be taken from some incorrect expressions which have fallen from his pen, and does not arise from the regular hypotheses he advances.'

Under the Hanoverians Sidney's arguments for resistance proved less influential than those of John Locke, the second of whose *Two Treatises of Government*, written, like the *Discourses*, as a warrant for resistance to Charles II, had been composed at the same time as Sidney's treatise and bears close resemblances to it. Locke's case, though no less revolutionary than Sidney's, was formulated in more measured and reflective language. In the reigns of the first two Georges it was Locke's political thought that was the more comfortably absorbed by establishment Whigs. In George III's reign, as we shall see, there were times when new threats to English freedom inspired Whigs of various colours – Fox among them – to invoke Sidney's name on their behalf. It now seemed possible that what had happened in 1688 might have to happen again. Yet it was again Locke's name that was the more often cited. Sidney's arguments for resistance tended, in eighteenth-century minds, to yield to other, less troubling aspects of his teaching.

So did his republicanism.

We saw that during the exclusion crisis the opponents of Charles II, though agreed in their opposition to arbitrary government, were divided over the means of replacing it. The first Earl of Shaftesbury, the Whig leader, favoured the policy of exclusion. The king's heir and brother James, as an avowed Catholic, should be removed from the line of succession. Sidney despised Shaftesbury, who returned the feeling. With Ludlow, Sidney regarded Shaftesbury as an opportunist politician. If the earl was willing to mount parliamentary opposition, Sidney thought, it was in order to pressure the Crown into giving him office. On the radicals' reading, Shaftesbury wanted not the reform of the constitution but a king whom the Whigs could control. He was, as it were, a junto Whig in the making. Sidney and his friends wanted curbs on arbitrary power to be written into the constitution. If that were done, the character and religion of the monarch – even supposing there remained one – would matter far less. In the division between Shaftesbury and Sidney the conflict between the court Whigs and radical Whigs in the 1690s was foreshadowed.

Sidney not only aimed at an end to arbitrary rule. He wanted, if he could get one, a republic. In modern times English republicanism has for the most part become (at least outside academic circles) a mere voice of grievance. In Sidney's time it was a system of ideas. It went against the grain of conventional seventeenth-century political thought. The premise of most political argument of the era was respect for the ancient, and monarchical, English constitution, a body of law and observance that was sanctioned by time and custom. Politicians competed to show that ancient practice was on their side. Innovation, a dirty word, was charged upon their opponents. No one before the civil war, and hardly anyone before the execution of the king, argued openly for the monarchy's removal. It was the novel abuse of royal power that was condemned.

In 1649 the ancient constitution was swept away, for reasons that had more to do with religious zeal and political necessities than with constitutional ideas. England's new rulers, far from designing a novel constitution, merely preserved the remnant of the old, the purged House of Commons. No one thought it could last long, but no one knew how to replace it. All the governments of the Interregnum rested on armed force. All of them collapsed. Out of that combination of tyranny and anarchy a new movement of political thinking arose.

Its most powerful exponent was James Harrington, whose work *Oceana*, published in 1656 and reverently edited by Toland at the end of the seventeenth century, would fascinate political thinkers down to the nineteenth. Harrington did not take sides between Crown and parliament. He knew and loved Charles I and hated the New Model Army's uses of force to get its political way. But he came to think the king's cause doomed. He found the explanation of the civil war not in the wrongs of which the two sides accused each other but in long-term and irreversible economic developments, of which quarrels about politics and religion had merely been the symptoms. For political power,

Harrington argued, always follows economic power: a claim that would exert a wider influence in the generations ahead than the republican inferences he drew from it. The ancient constitution, he maintained, had been the product of feudalism. The slow death of feudalism since the later middle ages had brought the demise of the ancient constitution with it. Under Henry VIII the sale of monastic lands had produced a transfer of landed wealth from the Crown and the peerage to the gentry and freeholders, the social groups represented in the House of Commons. Subsequently the Commons had striven for a new political power commensurate with its new economic power. The civil war, or something like it, had been inevitable. Only when politics and economics were newly aligned could stability return to the afflicted land.

Harrington's ascription of the English upheaval to long-term and impersonal causes drew strength from the simultaneous convulsions not only in the rest of the British Isles but in much of Europe – in France, Spain, Italy, Portugal, Germany, Sweden, the Netherlands. England's turmoil seemed part of a general crisis of monarchy, which evidently transcended the policies and personalities of particular monarchs. Only in England, however, had the mid-century troubles produced the termination of the ancient constitution. For that reason England was uniquely equipped to achieve a healthy and durable form of rule. How should it set about it? Harrington, who refused to pine for the nation's feudal past, took the end of kingship and the House of Lords for granted. England needed a republic – but not the sort of republic it experienced from 1649 to 1653. The rule of the Rump was single-chamber rule, government without check or balance. What the country required was what its new rulers lacked: principles of constitutional design. To discover them it must abandon its insular preoccupation with its extinct constitution. It must look to the principles of rule which had governed the republics of classical antiquity, and of which he found a modern exemplar in the republic of Venice.

Harrington was a prophet whom the Restoration proved wrong. In 1660 the ancient constitution was restored. Henceforth, as before its breakdown in the 1640s, it was difficult to win respectability or wide support for any constitutional argument that did not pay homage to it. In the public mind republicanism was linked, however unjustly in Harrington's case, to the hideous memory of the regicide. It could not be openly advocated as an alternative to the traditional constitution. But there were subtler methods of promoting it. Sidney, writing after the Restoration, adopted them. His republicanism was by no means identical to Harrington's. Where Harrington despised the memory of the Rump, Sidney revered it. Harrington's economic thesis, though passingly deployed by the *Discourses*, is not integrated into their main argument. What Sidney shared with him was the conviction that England would find political salvation only if it looked beyond its own history and constitution to those of republican antiquity.

Even within that fundamental agreement there lay significant differences. Where Harrington, contrasting the ancient English constitution with the ancient republics, says a glad farewell to the first and urges the emulation of the second, Sidney treats the two categories as essentially the same. In modern times, he maintains, England's ancient constitution has been profoundly perverted. If we examine it in its proper form, the form it took in the middle ages, we find that it is much closer to the republics of antiquity than to the tyrannical rule at which the Stuarts have aimed. What is true in England is also true abroad. For Sidney, like Harrington, thinks in European terms. In the Continental 'mixed' or 'regulated' monarchies of the middle ages, as in England's medieval constitution, he locates principles that also prevailed in the Greek and Roman commonwealths. Both in and outside England it is only by a return to the principles of constitutional architecture which were understood in the classical and medieval worlds that political health can be restored.

Sidney's argument rests on an ingenious premise. Classical political thought, as everyone knew, located the best form of government in the mixture or balance of three components of rule: the one (the kingly element), the few (the aristocratic), and the many (the democratic). Harrington, brushing the kingly element aside, devised elaborate schemes for balancing the few and the many. Sidney returned to the classical premise. 'There never was a good government in the world,' explain the *Discourses*, 'that did not consist of the three . . . species of monarchy, aristocracy and democracy.' How the single-chamber rule of the English Commonwealth of 1649–53, which he represented as so glorious an epoch, had embodied that virtue he did not explain, but it was his analysis of the nation's ancient constitution, not of the republic that had replaced it, that mattered for his constitutional thesis. Sidney was not the first writer to discover the classical principle of mixture in England's ancient constitution. The same claim had been advanced, in a spirit of expediency, by both parliamentarians and royalists during the approach to civil war, though not to republican ends. Sidney's argument is born of expediency too. It enables him to represent the republicanism of the *Discourses* not as a challenge to the ancient constitution but as happily compatible with it. In ancient Rome, the republic to which Sidney most warms, he locates the kingly element in the power entrusted to the consuls. The medieval world, he explains, entrusted it to kings. That difference, we learn, is essentially trivial. Consuls and kings alike were public officers, their powers bestowed by and answerable to the nation which had appointed them.

Where Sidney pointed in the early 1680s, John Toland would follow in the late 1690s. Toland, we saw, distinguished between two kinds of government, 'arbitrary' or 'tyrannical' monarchies which 'enslave' their peoples, and 'free governments' which rest on 'consent' and serve 'the common good'. In the second category there are some, England among them, which happen to have a king, others, Holland among them, which do not; but the distinction is incidental. As so often, Toland's argument and language echo Sidney's. In both cases, professions of respect for the existing constitution are a ruse. Both men hope for a constitution very different from the one England knows or has known. If it finds room for a king, his powers will be narrowly limited. Neither writer intends to be curbed by the backward-looking character of conventional constitutionalism or by the fear of innovation. There prove to be limits to Sidney's idealization of the middle ages. He knows that medieval kings were more powerful than Roman consuls. That was because, for all its virtues, the initial design of the English constitution had unnoticed flaws, of which, with time, kings learned to take advantage. The errors ought to have been rectified long ago, and they must be rectified now. The nation is not chained to original forms, for as 'time can make nothing lawful or just that is not so of itself', so 'in matters of greatest importance wise and good men do not so much enquire what has been as what is good and ought to be'.

Toland agrees. He and Sidney both think that the existing constitution needs to be 'added to' or 'perfected'. Neither man ventures to say what that means in practice. Both realize that the achievement of a republic would take time. In the 1640s, after all, it was only when the constitution had broken down that the possibility of a republic could be so much as broached. Sidney hoped for a similar outcome to the crisis of Charles II's reign. In 1683, in the company of his fellow-conspirators, he made plain what the *Discourses* do not: that while other plotters were aiming merely at a moderated monarchy, his wish was a 'commonwealth' or republic. He looked, as the Duke of York observed, for 'a gentle way of dropping into a commonwealth'. Toland looked for a 'gentle way' too. So did other 'real Whigs' of the 1690s. When John Wildman, that ageing survivor of the Roundhead cause, was asked why he and his radical friends had not pressed openly for a republic in 1689, he reportedly replied that 'Rome was not built in a day'.

For Sidney – as for Toland – free governments promote virtue, unfree ones slavery and corruption. 'Virtue' being inseparable from 'liberty', mankind's 'happiness' is indivisible from its constitutional arrangements. The servitude, the degradation, the licentiousness of Restoration England grieve Sidney's soul. He yearns for the virtue, the discipline, the frugality, the public spirit, of ancient Rome. He longs too for its martial ardour and glory. 'All governments', he maintains, 'deserve praise or blame as they are well or ill constituted for making war.' Here as elsewhere Sidney is the disciple of Niccolò Machiavelli, the Florentine republican. Harrington was Machiavelli's disciple too, but on one subject Sidney follows the Italian where Harrington did not. In designing his model republic Harrington looked for stability, tranquillity, longevity. It was the ordered republics of Sparta and Venice that he urged his countrymen to emulate. So unconventional in other respects, Harrington shared the conventional seventeenth-century fear, to which the experiences of civil war added their measure, of mutability and chaos. He did not care for the turbulent conflicts of republican Rome. Machiavelli by contrast had seen in those 'tumults' evidence not of disorder but of vitality. So does Sidney. They 'sharpened the spirits' of the Romans, he says, and 'kept up good discipline'. On his Italian travels Sidney noticed the grim, defeated silences of the Tuscan landscape, which until the extinction of republican life by the Medici had boasted the political life that thrives in 'turbulent, contentious cities'. Echoing Tacitus, Rome's mourner of republican vitality, Sidney insists that the 'peace' and 'quiet' commended by orthodox thinkers is in reality a 'wretched slavery and solitude'.

There is no more eloquent a testimony in the English language to the imaginative hold that classical images of political liberty can exert than Sidney's *Discourses*. Posterity responded more readily to the eloquence than to the republican substance. In the years between his death and the Revolution, Whigs found it easier or safer to promote the memory of that other aristocratic victim of Judge Jeffreys in 1683, William Lord Russell, who was repelled by Sidney's republicanism, than that of Algernon himself. In later times, too, many cautious Whig spirits would more readily cite Russell's name than Sidney's. When reference to Sidney's *Discourses* was made, the veil of traditionalism and of ancient constitutionalism in which he had covered his radicalism, even as it gave the work a broader audience than it could otherwise have reached, encouraged readers to bypass the unorthodoxy of his purpose. The concessions he had offered to conventional Whig thought were mistaken for a commitment to it. As absolutist and divine-right doctrines slipped into the past, so the gap between his convictions and the uncontentious assumptions of the present was ever more easily ignored. Sidney commended a constitutional balance of the one, the few and the many: in the eighteenth century it became a commonplace that the Revolution had established such a balance. In the *Discourses* Sidney affects to dislike only 'absolute' monarchy, 'professing much veneration for that which is mixed' and 'regulated by law'. The ideal of 'mixed' and 'regulated' monarchy appealed across the broad spectrum of Whig opinion. Before 1688 moderate Whigs hoped for it, as Sidney professedly did. After 1688 they told themselves that they had got it. The new approach is audible in an echo of Sidney's words in Toland's Introduction to the *Works* of Harrington. Outwardly deferring, like Sidney, to moderate opinion, and declaring that 'there's not a man alive exceeds my affection for a mixed form of government', Toland commends the excellence of the 'regulated' monarchy that has prospered since 1688.

It is not that Sidney ceased to be a critic of power. That, we shall see, would be his eighteenth-century function. But the criticism would be submitted, and confined, within a constitutional framework alien to his thinking. Like Edmund Ludlow's, Sidney's radicalism was merged in the late 1690s with country-party virtues. We shall find that in the eighteenth century, again like Ludlow's, it took second place to them.

We saw how Edmund Ludlow was made presentable to the post-Revolutionary world at the expense of his religion. What of Sidney's religion?

He was not a Puritan of Ludlow's stamp. In his mind Christian beliefs merge with pagan values of classical antiquity. In that as in much else in his thinking he is at one with Milton, in whose *Paradise Lost* Christian and classical inspiration blend. Ludlow was a Calvinist fundamentalist for whom pagan and classical virtue, though he allowed a place to it, was at best a supplementary guide to the life of the spirit and potentially a distraction from it, even an affront to it. In his thinking the 'elect', whom God has redeemed from perdition, owe their salvation solely to God's grace and not in the least to their own merits, for mankind is helplessly fallen and depraved. Sidney, like Milton, has a more favourable view of man's capacities. Where Ludlow distrusts the presumptuousness of human 'reason', Sidney and Milton insist on our duty to exercise it. For them the word did not only mean, as it would come to do, ratiocination or logical thinking. It had a spiritual resonance. Sidney thinks of reason as 'the remains of divine light' that are left to us after the Fall. It spurs man towards his 'reunion from that good from which he is fallen'. Virtue is the 'dictate of reason', demanded of Christian and pagan alike. James Harrington, the writer promoted by Toland alongside Sidney and Milton, thought the same. Yet across the gulf between Ludlow and the others there stretches a common Christian seriousness. The Christianity of Harrington and Milton and Sidney had a theological content, and an apocalyptic dimension, that can be legitimately called Puritan. By Toland's time those features of their religion had become puzzling, even deterrent. Toland in his commentaries squeezed it out. So did the interpreters who followed him.

The eighteenth century was able to square Christian with classical values, but only by making the Christian religion one ever more of conduct than of faith. Since Toland's time the closeness between the Puritan and classical values of Sidney and Milton and Harrington has seemed barely intelligible. The favoured solution has been to forget the Puritanism. Through the Enlightenment's thinking on the civil wars there runs the influence of an observation by Gilbert Burnet, first published in 1723, whose legacy is with us still. 'The Commonwealth party' of Cromwellian England, he explained, had two components, one 'the Fifth Monarchy men and enthusiasts', the other 'those who pretended to little or no religion, and acted only upon the principles of civil liberty, such as Algernon Sidney, Henry Neville, Marten, Wildman, and Harrington'. So there were fanatics on one side of the movement and heathens on the other.

In Sidney, Burnet mistook an indifference to the outward observances of worship and to doctrinal precision for a want of religious conviction. Sidney's religion is much indebted to Plato. Like Platonism it is a matter more of spirit than of forms or creeds. 'That my Redeemer liveth' was a sustaining conviction of Sidney's life, but not one on which he elaborated. As was often the case in aristocratic households his religion had a certain independent-mindedness about it. Though he wrote again and again of his love of 'God's people', of his longing to serve them, of his need of their prayers, those 'people' are always 'they', never 'we'. He worked closely with Independents (or Congregationalists)* and had ministers of that Dissenting denomination with him at his death, but he seems to have been with Independency rather than of it. What evidently drew him to it were the Independents' seriousness of life and purpose and the steadiness with which, under persecution and among the transitory frivolities of Restoration England, they held to the things eternal. Here Sidney's classical taste for austerity fuses with a Christian one. He contrasts the 'frugality' of the 'sober and godly people', their scorn of 'sensual pleasures', their love of 'those treasures that perish not', with the 'lewd', 'light', 'profane' values of men who thrive under Charles II's monarchy. Those men, often young, are contemptuous of England's Puritan past. 'God's people', like Sidney, sigh for its earnestness.

* 'Independents' allegedly crowded into Ludlow's house during Edmund's time in England in 1689.

Sidney's alliance with Nonconformity had its parallels among the opponents of Charles II. The poet and politician Andrew Marvell respected the Dissenters and protested vigorously against their persecution, without ever indicating that he was one of them. Like Sidney, Marvell was steeped in classical as well as Christian culture. Then there is Henry Neville, Harrington's disciple, whose republican tract *Plato Redivivus* was reprinted in 1698. He too felt a bond with the 'godly and sober party', especially the Independents, and was dismayed by the persecution of Dissent. Yet neither Marvell nor Neville left any record of inner religious experience of a kind the Dissenters would have recognized. Sidney's case is different. His *Court Maxims* of the mid-1660s have a millenarian streak reminiscent of Ludlow's manuscript. Some passages of the work might almost have been lifted from Ludlow's text. 'The blood of the saints' – the regicides executed in 1660 and 1662 – 'cries out' for vengeance; 'the measure of the iniquity' of the restored monarchy, a regime imposed by God as 'a punishment for the sins and exercise of the graces of his people', 'seems to be full'; 'God will not long suffer the rod of the wicked to rest on the lot of the righteous, though for the sins of his people he suffers them for a season to be a scourge to them' – here as elsewhere we find the arguments, the language, the biblical colouring familiar from 'A Voice from the Watch Tower'.

In the early 1680s similar thought and language can be found in Sidney's second main work, the *Discourses*, but much less often and for the most part in a muted form. How do we explain the difference? It is possible that the answer lies partly with Toland. If there is a major theme of the *Discourses* where his interference can be suspected it is here. Yet it is improbable that he intervened on a large scale. The apocalyptic component of *Court Maxims* has nothing like the centrality and insistence that its counterpart in Ludlow's manuscript has. There is very unlikely to have been a more prominent one in the manuscript of the *Discourses*. In any case Toland's hand, though it can be guessed at, cannot be proved. A different explanation of the slimness of apocalyptic language in the *Discourses* is possible. The responsibility may lie not – or not only – with Toland but with Sidney himself. The *Court Maxims* were written to appeal above all to the religious Nonconformists in England. Sidney may have thought, amid the royalist reaction of the Restoration, that the Dissenters offered the only serious hope of an uprising. The *Discourses*, written when hatred of the regime was more widespread, aim at a larger audience. Another shift of public mood is discernible between the mid-1660s and the early 1680s. In the earlier period Ludlow's millenarian thought and language have many counterparts in radical Nonconformist writing in England. The pamphlets written against the Crown towards the end of Charles II's reign rarely breathe the same spirit. Puritan zeal is on the retreat. By the time of the *Discourses* the Crown's critics take their stand more often on constitutional grounds, or on grounds of natural rights or natural morality, than on biblical ones.

So Sidney, either in *Court Maxims* or in the *Discourses* or in both, may have tailored his language to his intended audiences. Whether he did or not, the language of the first work may be truer to Sidney's inner convictions than the second. As he faced death, the apocalyptic vocabulary of *Court Maxims* resurfaced. Sidney assumed the mantle of the executed regicides of 1660–62. They, in speeches which Ludlow incorporated into his manuscript, dwelt on the passage of Revelation (6.9–10) where the Evangelist

> saw under the altar the souls of them that were slain for the word of God, and for the testimony which they held. And they cried with a loud voice, saying, How long, O Lord, holy and true, dost thou not judge and avenge our blood on them that dwell on the earth?

In the same vein Sidney's dying 'Apology' beseeches the Lord to 'let not my soul cry though it lay under the altar', to spare the nation 'inquisition' for his death, 'or, if innocent blood must be expiated, let thy vengeance fall only upon the heads of those who knowingly and maliciously persecute me for righteousness' sake'.

When Sidney cited the Bible at his trial, Jeffreys pounced. He pointed out to the jury that Sidney had 'coloured' his treason 'with religion' and had 'quoted Scripture for it too; and you know how that went in the [civil wars]'. Jeffreys recalled the use made of Psalm 149.8 by the army preacher Hugh Peter at the time of Charles I's execution to vindicate the 'binding' of 'our kings in chains, and our nobles in fetters of iron'. The text figures among the justifications of the regicide in

Ludlow's manuscript – but not, of course, in the *Memoirs*. Soon after Sidney's death a Tory writer, aiming to stem the tide of public sympathy for him, remarked that 'this departing enthusiast made his exit like a perfect second Harrison': that is, like the Fifth Monarchist Thomas Harrison, whose spiritual fervour at his execution in 1660 is diligently recorded in 'A Voice from the Watch Tower' – and omitted from the *Memoirs*. In Anne's reign another Tory writer sought to discredit Sidney by recalling his 'canting prayers' on the scaffold.

Many of Sidney's eighteenth-century devotees, like Toland before them, were deists. Though admiration for him persisted among some Nonconformists, theirs was a marginal voice. In 1763 Thomas Hollis was pleased to conclude that Sidney's 'piety' lay 'as far from enthusiasm as any man's.' Hollis deceived himself. At his death Sidney caused a sensation by his bold endorsement of the 'OLD CAUSE', by which he meant the godly cause that united him to the martyrs of 1660–62, and especially to his hero Sir Henry Vane. Sidney's own words at the approach of death echoed those with which Vane had prepared for his own. On the scaffold Vane too had asked 'How long O Lord holy and true . . . ?' He had prophesied 'a speedy and sudden revival' of 'the CAUSE of GOD', and been confident that 'this cause shall have its revival in my death' – much as Ludlow had predicted that God's 'seemingly dead and buried cause' would shortly be resurrected. On Sidney's death government publicists were quick to emphasize the religious fanaticism implicit in his use of the phrase 'old cause', which would embarrass his more cautious admirers for decades to come. Hollis put a different slant on Sidney's language. By the 'old cause', he decided, Sidney had meant the cause of his country and its freedom. For by Hollis's time Algernon's name was widely linked to a 'cause', a 'glorious cause', of an altogether more secular cast, that of civil or political liberty. The eighteenth century, which averted its eyes from Sidney's political radicalism, turned them from his religion too.

6

Sidney the Whig

In 1697 there was published 'The Honourable Algernon Sidney's Letter Against Bribery and Corruption'. It appeared in a very popular work entitled *Familiar Letters written by the Right Honourable John Late Earl of Rochester and Several Other Persons of Honour and Quality*. Over the following century Sidney's 'Letter' would be printed and quoted time and again, and its pertinence to present circumstances much remarked on. It was probably read more widely than Sidney's *Discourses* and more widely than the documents relating to his trial and execution. The 'Letter' is likely to have been based on something Sidney wrote. But it is also the product of fabrication. As in the Ludlow 'Letters' of the early 1690s, as in Ludlow's *Memoirs*, the Whig history factory has been at work.

The document is inauthentic in both style and content. Its prose has a histrionic element which, though having its momentary parallels in writing we know to be Sidney's, has no sustained equivalent in them. (A puzzled nineteenth-century biographer of him, not suspecting the inauthenticity of the 'Letter', found the style 'at first so unlike Sidney's'.) The document is not dated, but its allusions to contemporary events place it in the early 1660s, when Sidney had yet to form some of the sentiments it voices. Again the use of italic will help us. The 'Letter' makes transparently anachronistic protests against the prevalence of 'bribery' and 'corruption'. We learn that '*detestable* bribes' and 'infamous *traffic*', which flourish in 'this mercenary court', have made 'all things vendible'. One would not know of that development from Sidney's own correspondence of the 1660s. In the *Court Maxims* of the mid-1660s – as in the Bodleian portion of Ludlow's manuscript, written at the same time, which Toland would transform into a critique of corruption – the venality of the court is touched on only passingly. The anachronism of the 'Letter' becomes plainer still when 'Sidney' addresses that central country-party preoccupation, the transformation of parliament from a body independent of the executive to one fatally intertwined with it. 'Parliaments', which 'in all preceding ages . . . have been the palace of our *liberty*, the sure defenders of the *oppressed*; they, who *formerly* could bridle kings, and keep the *balance* equal between them and *the people*, are *now* become the instruments of all our *oppressions*'. That claim is characteristic of the 1690s, not of the 1660s.

Indeed it is strikingly paralleled in writings of 1697–8 by members of the circle from which Ludlow's *Memoirs* and Sidney's *Discourses* emerged. Sometimes the similarities of argument give rise to repetition of wording. In 1698 Walter Moyle, that leading figure in the campaign against standing armies, composed a study of ancient Sparta. In it he remarks that, in states in which the legislative power escapes 'control' and 'check', '*the people*' become '*oppressed* by their own representatives'. The 'consideration' of the Spartan constitution, he observes in the same place, was 'of equal use to Sidney as well as Harrington'. In 1697, the year of the 'Letter', Moyle was one of the authors of a pamphlet which we saw to have been intimately connected to *Ludlow's Memoirs*: *An Argument Showing that a Standing Army is Incompatible with a Free Government*. In one passage of it the role which the 'Letter' attributes to parliament is given, in a more cautious spirit, to the nobility and the House of Lords; but despite that difference there is again a suggestive resemblance. It was, we read, the nobles who kept 'the *balance*' of the constitution, they who 'were *formerly* the bold assertors of their country's *liberties*' and 'are *now* only the ensigns and ornaments of tyranny, and *the people's* beasts of burden'.

It is not hard to guess who wrote the 'Letter'. In his tract of 1701, *The Art of Governing by Parties*, John Toland, who had been Moyle's collaborator in the standing army controversy and probably in the composition of *An Argument*, reproduced a long passage from a chapter of Sidney's *Discourses* – the chapter he thought 'very much deserving every man's perusal', 'too well expressed to be better done by any other'. There, Toland explains, Sidney attacks the 'bribery' that has corrupted English politics. 'The picture of corrupt ministers', observes Toland, was 'never so well drawn to the life as by the great

Colonel Sidney', who 'sums up the character of evil ministers, charging them with the most *detestable traffic* in procuring or disposing of preferments'. There is another link between the 'Letter' and Toland, the editor of Ludlow. The 'Letter' is ostensibly written to Sidney's father, the Earl of Leicester, on whose papers other material in the Rochester volume is based. Ludlow's *Memoirs* contain details about Oliver Cromwell's behaviour at the expulsion of the Long Parliament which correspond strikingly to information in Leicester's diary, so strikingly that C. H. Firth thought it 'remarkable' that 'these two independent accounts agree so closely'. An easier explanation is that they were not independent, and that Leicester's papers were a source for the *Memoirs* as for the Rochester volume.*

Venality, the target of the 'Letter', is not the principal target of the *Discourses*. There Sidney's main concerns are the tyrannical powers of the Crown and the political theories which sanctioned them. 'Corruption', eloquently as he attacks it, is a subordinate theme. He sees that patronage and bribery have extended the Crown's capacity to control parliament. That development, however, had become conspicuous only in the 1670s, when his political ideas were for the most part already formed. For him corruption is a symptom of constitutional disorder. Change the constitution and corruption will cure itself. After 1688, when corruption became the dominant preoccupation both of the radicals and of the country party, Sidney's interpreters placed it at the centre of his thought. Toland – trying, like Sidney before him, to project a radical message in a reassuring form – does struggle to sustain the connection that Sidney made between corruption and the defects of the constitution. 'The senates of free governments,' he remarks, 'are not so subject to venality as the courts of princes.' In the eighteenth century, however, corruption was for the most part represented not as the product of an ill-designed constitution but as a threat to the well-designed one which had been secured in 1688.

Anxiety about the condition of the English polity did not diminish. The eighteenth century was no less alarmed by the advance of corruption than the seventeenth had been by the progress of absolutism. In

* Doubt has been cast on the authenticity of the letters published in the name of the Earl of Rochester (the Restoration poet) in the collection.

January 1737 the country-party journal *The Craftsman* was angered when a court Whig writer asserted that Sidney's principles – 'the mischief of absolute monarchy, or being subject to the will of one man; and the happiness of being governed by wise, just, and equitable laws' – were precisely those which the post-Revolutionary world had secured. *The Craftsman* remonstrated that if Sidney, 'that great man', were alive now, he would see that placemen, bribery and corruption had brought the executive 'more real power, with the sanction of law, than it ever enjoyed by the claim of prerogative'. The preoccupations on which Toland had played in the late 1690s – venality, moral degeneration, the loss of independence among England's legislators – supplied the dominant theme of political protest for a hundred years. Corruption, financial and ethical, was blamed not merely for the distortion of the constitutional balance in the Crown's favour but for the rage of party conflict, and for the sway of 'faction' and self-interest, that were preventing the nation's unity and corroding its virtue.

Like Sidney, eighteenth-century readers turned intuitively to ancient Rome for instructive parallels to their own circumstances. Yet there is a difference. Sidney compared the overthrow of the English Commonwealth and the subsequent rules of Cromwell and Charles II to the collapse of the Roman republic and its replacement by imperial tyranny. Eighteenth-century readers regretted Rome's fate not because it deprived her of republican institutions but because Rome had succumbed to an ethical threat, one similar to the menace to modern virtue. From the pages of Sallust and Tacitus they learned how corruption and degeneration had cost Rome her liberty and had subjected it to tyranny and slavery. England owed its liberty, judged the eighteenth century, to its constitution. Would not the forces which had wrecked the republican constitution of Rome likewise destroy the monarchical one of England, at the same cost to liberty?

The passage about venality in Sidney's *Discourses* that Toland thought 'very much deserving every man's perusal' made a lasting impression. It may have attracted widest attention in the wake of the South Sea Bubble scandal of 1720. The passage was reprinted in the *London Journal* in 1721, which commended Sidney in one of a long series of essays that were brought together in a succession of publications of

1720–24 as *Cato's Letters*. 'Cato' praises Sidney as 'a great enemy to bribery'. The *Letters* were written jointly by John Trenchard, who had been Toland's and Moyle's ally in the standing army controversy of 1697–9, and Thomas Gordon. They were reprinted in 1733, 1737, 1748, 1754 and 1755. On both sides of the Atlantic they were widely read and widely influential. *Cato's Letters* pay homage to the 'old Whig' cause, which declined at the end of William's reign and was on the retreat in Anne's and which 'Cato' seeks to revive. The *Letters* recall the junto's apostasy in the 1690s and its infamous conduct during the standing army controversy. The 'deliverance' promised in 1688, they declare, is still 'expected'. Indeed 'the Revolution is worse established than when it began'. Yet such complaints were losing their edge. The radicals' tribulations under the later Stuarts were fading from public memory, a development that suited establishment Whigs. 'New generations', 'Cato' complained, 'are risen up, which knew nothing of the sufferings of our fathers and are taught to believe there were never any such.'

Sidney's *Discourses* are a pervasive presence in *Cato's Letters*. He is 'an author who can never be too much valued or read; who does honour to the English nobility, and to the English name'; and whose 'love of liberty was as warm' as Cicero's, 'his honesty as great, and his courage greater'. 'Cato' allows no room to Algernon's republicanism: 'I know it is objected' that Sidney 'is a republican', but 'the passages which I take from him are not republican passages', and anyway 'Mr Sidney's book, for the main of it, is . . . agreeable to our constitution'. A quarter of a century later, in his *History of England* in 1746, the 'real Whig' James Ralph, who worshipped Sidney and whose own writings were deeply indebted to him, did acknowledge Algernon's 'republican' principles and his readiness to 'try practices on the constitution', but declared those tenets 'mistakes in point of judgement'. The renunciation of Sidney's republicanism by establishment Whigs was more emphatic. The accounts of him by Gilbert Burnet, White Kennett, John Oldmixon and Paul Rapin de Thoyras in the early eighteenth century all disowned his 'republican principles'. Orthodox Whigs were against what Sidney was against, tyranny and divine-right rule, but were not for what he was for.

Under the first two Georges very little if any republicanism is visible in England. Country-party sympathizers looked for political redemption, not to a commonwealth, but to the 'patriot king' in waiting, the heir to George II's throne, Frederick Prince of Wales, on whom so many hopes of reform centred. They longed for a ruler – another Alfred or Edward III or Henry V or Elizabeth – whose uprightness and leadership would restore England's health and greatness. As a cure for corruption an ideal king was a more attractive and more plausible prospect than a change of constitution. When, under George II, the poet James Thomson, in his poem *The Seasons*, praised the 'fearless' Sidney as 'the British Cassius', as a hero 'warmed' by 'ancient learning to the enlightened love/ Of ancient freedom', he placed him in the company of Frederick, to whom the poem was dedicated, and of England's great monarchs, among them William III, who as Prince of Orange had been Sidney's old enemy.

If republicanism did continue to appeal, it was in a hypothetical spirit. A republic was an ideal but not a practicality. There is republicanism in *Cato's Letters*, but it is resigned to defeat, its aspirations being purely hypothetical. Again James Harrington is a decisive presence. He believed that the post-medieval balance of property favoured government in the interests of the whole community rather than in the sectional interests of the nobility, the social group that had previously sustained the monarchy. His post-Revolutionary successors, who had seen aristocratic politics return in 1660 and emerge triumphant from 1688, were driven to an opposite conclusion. A balance of property favourable to 'popular government', they believed, would have to be artificially created by legislation for the redistribution of land. In the late 1690s Walter Moyle and John Toland and William Stephens did allude to the need for such legislation, but by the 1720s the notion seemed too risky and impracticable to be seriously advanced. 'Cato' accepted that land redistribution, though desirable, was not an option; and without it only 'disordered brains' would pursue the 'phantom' or 'utopia' of a republic. So we should 'make the best of our own constitution'. With Toland, 'Cato' professes to regard that constitution as a free and healthy one. In words which echo his, and which share their insincerity, 'Cato' explains that the 'constitution' to which Sidney's *Discourses* are 'agreeable' is 'the best republic in the world, with a prince at the head of it'. But where Toland contrived to combine his praise of the existing constitution with the promotion of republican alternatives, 'Cato' is content to lace his own commendations with sarcasm. The republics which Toland ventured to commend are repudiated in the *Letters*. Where Toland hails the 'glorious republic' of the United Provinces, 'Cato' thinks of that constitution as a 'jumble' of 'confusion' with 'all the causes of dissolution in its contexture'. Where Toland published encomiums of the Commonwealth of 1649–53, 'Cato' condemns that 'detestable' regime. Across the eighteenth century, voices akin to that of 'Cato' would scorn the constitutional arrangements of the Rump, that 'anarchy' of 'infamous memory'.

After the accession of George III we do find the occasional voice explicitly opposed to kingship. Catharine Macaulay and Sylas Neville, pure republicans in the earlier part of George III's reign, revered Sidney. But most of his other devotees of that time were advocates of mixed or limited monarchy who welcomed those of his views on constitutions which appeared to conform to that ideal and turned their eyes from the rest. Thomas Hollis, Sidney's most influential eighteenth-century champion, made his own unwillingness to embrace republicanism clear. With others, Hollis admired the regicide – the exemplary punishment of a tyrant – but not the abolition of monarchy that followed it. He was anxious to explain that John Milton, whom he revered perhaps even more amply than Sidney, had been an enemy only to tyranny, not to 'regal government as such', an assertion which overlooked the republican pamphlets the poet wrote at the approach of the Restoration. Hollis presented Sidney in the same light. Another admirer of Sidney, Hollis's friend the radical politician and journalist John Wilkes, that thorn in the flesh of George III's ministries, declared himself 'firmly attached to a limited monarchy' and reflected on the anarchic tendencies of 'republican government'.

Cato's Letters were born of the national revulsion and resentment provoked by the bursting of the South Sea Bubble. They made their impact among those angered or dismayed by the long ascendancy, from 1721 to 1742, of Sir Robert Walpole, the Whig prime minister. Like the dominance of the junto, his supremacy left 'old' and 'true' Whigs in the cold. It was an unusually exclusive supremacy, for Walpole would brook no rivals and dealt briskly with dissent within his party. Again a Whig ministry was held to be concerning itself not with the promotion of public virtue but with the extension of its own power and patronage. Like its predecessor it was marshalling placemen, handing out bribes and favours, fixing parliamentary elections, maintaining standing forces. What was new was the scale of the patronage and the prolonged monopoly of power by one party. Reward had become a system of government. Walpole saw it as the necessary instrument of national stability. To his enemies it was a symptom of national degeneracy.

If those developments gave new scope to radical Whiggism, they also reanimated the country-party sentiment with which, in the 1690s, it had allied. Now the alliance re-formed. Alongside the success of *Cato's Letters* there ran the influence of another publication by Trenchard and Gordon, *The Independent Whig*. Its title merges the ideal of the independent country gentleman with the Whig cause. It is the country values that predominate. They predominate in *Cato's Letters* too. In their attacks on 'places and employments sold, salaries augmented and pensions multiplied', in their criticisms of standing armies, the *Letters* became at least as much a country-party voice as a radical Whig one. Like Sidney before him, 'Cato' turns to Roman history to explore the themes of liberty and slavery. Where Sidney's perspective was essentially republican, the *Letters* see Rome through country-party eyes. Marcus Brutus, the slayer of Julius Caesar, was revered by Sidney essentially as a 'deliverer' of his country from slavery. The interest of 'Cato' in Brutus's deed is different. The *Letters* note that other writers, in condemning the killing of Caesar, have charged Brutus with ingratitude to a man who, after all, had bestowed 'places' and 'favours' on him. On the contrary, remonstrates 'Cato', the nobility of Brutus's soul was nowhere better illustrated than in his refusal to be swayed by the 'mercenary employments' which Caesar gave him 'as hire for that great man's assistance to support his tyranny'. Caesar, aiming to extinguish Rome's freedom through 'corruption' and 'immense briberies', was trying to 'bribe' Brutus 'to be his slave'. 'Cato' adds that Brutus later demonstrated his immunity to the inducements of power no less admirably by resisting the efforts of Cicero to reconcile him to Octavius Caesar.

Sidney admired the Romans for what they did, not for what they refrained from doing. With Machiavelli he applauded the vitality, the contention, the risk-taking of political life under the republic. He wanted, through a citizen militia, to recover those qualities for England. So, in the late 1690s, did Toland. Yet the men of country-party sentiment to whom Toland appealed had no wish for political risks. They wanted not the political excitement of an Italian city-state but to be left alone. Toland reassured them. His scheme for a *Militia Reformed*, explains his title-page, will 'maintain perpetual quiet at home, without endangering the public liberty'. Though Toland brought Sidney's appetite for Rome's 'turbulence' and 'tumults' into print, he did not dare to advertise his own. In the eighteenth century only a few wanted to know about the benefits of tumults. Sidney, explained a biographical sketch of him early in George III's reign, had proved that liberty gave 'order and stability' to Rome.

'Cato' was named after Cato the Younger, who like Brutus had killed himself rather than live under Caesarian rule (though sometimes he became merged, in eighteenth-century minds, with the earlier, equally austere Cato, 'the Censor'). The Stoic virtues of the younger Cato made him a cult figure in the eighteenth century, following the sensational success of Joseph Addison's play *Cato* in 1713. In the influence of the Catonic ideal we see how profoundly the period equated virtue with distance from political corruption and with indifference to preferment. An obituary tribute by Thomas Gordon to his fellow-author of *Cato's Letters*, John Trenchard, observed that 'no man was ever more remote from all thoughts of public employments'. Just as, in Toland's hands, Edmund Ludlow was made to despise the 'pageantry' of power, 'Cato' mocks its 'mighty pomp and retinue', its 'glaring equipages', those 'burdens of greatness rather than proofs of happiness', a condition which is rather to be sought in 'quiet passions and an easy mind'. 'Cato' absorbs the Horatian ideal – so prominent a theme of English poetry from the mid-seventeenth century to the early nineteenth – of 'the happy man'. 'Happiest of all men, to me, seems the private man', who can be 'perfectly disinterested', free from the temptations of 'faction' and 'ambition'. To be 'disinterested', to defy 'faction' and 'ambition', became essential attributes of the eighteenth century's heroes, Sidney among them. Just as Ludlow's mulishness towards men in power came to seem proof of his integrity, so the 'obstinacy' noticed by Gilbert Burnet in Sidney was taken as evidence of his 'inflexible' superiority to politics and to corruption.

Some expositors of country values maintained that, in an age so poisoned by corruption, men of virtue should stay clear of politics altogether. Others recognized that power had to be occupied. They held that evasion of the duties of office, especially in hours of national need, could be as reprehensible as the abuse of it. England needed leaders who would sacrifice the honourable pleasures of Horatian retreat to save their country. But it was the very indifference of such figures to the customary appetites and rewards of politics that would equip them for effective rule. They alone could harness those energies of the nation which the contamination of corruption had subdued.

In one sense the cult of Cato belongs to a long tradition of anti-political literature. It recalls the persistent criticism of courts that flourished in the literature of the Renaissance, much of it written and read by courtiers or would-be courtiers seeking self-respect or consolation amid the frenzy of power-seeking. Then too men turned to the literature of ancient Rome, in this case particularly to Tacitus's grim account of the imperial courts, to understand the developments of their own time. But between Renaissance perspectives and eighteenth-century ones there is a difference. In the Renaissance almost everyone had endorsed Cicero's maxim that 'virtue consists in action', not least political action. From Cicero's writings, and from guidebooks to conduct that were based on them, the nobles and gentlemen of the sixteenth century drew lessons on how to behave in the political arena. By contrast the conduct-books addressed to the nobility and gentry of the eighteenth century tend to say very little about involvement in politics.

Cicero's own moral authority, though still powerful, came under question. That was partly because Walpole's supporters identified the prime minister with him. *Cato's Letters*, we saw, sided with the incorruptible Marcus Brutus against Cicero. In the same spirit George Lyttelton, a leading promoter of country values, wrote in 1731 *Observations on the Life of Cicero*, which challenged the Roman's representation of himself as an 'unspotted' servant of his country. Rome's true heroes, opined Lyttelton, were Cato, Brutus and other 'quite untainted' figures who 'gallantly stood in the breach, and struggled hard for liberty'. By contrast Cicero's 'ambition', and his 'servility' to Octavius Caesar, were 'pernicious failings', which at critical moments induced him to 'yield to the corruption of the age' and to 'sacrifice the welfare of his country to his private interests and passions'. Cicero could still be invoked in the cause of virtue. In the middle decades of the eighteenth century, admirers of the age's model of upright incorruptibility, the elder William Pitt, 'delighted' to call him 'England's Cicero'. But when he appeared to sell out to the court the parallel was turned against him: Pitt was said to have been driven, like Cicero, by 'mercenary ambition', and by the pursuit of courtly 'favour', to 'turn his back upon liberty and the commonwealth'. In its assessments of Cicero and Cato, as so often in its comments on Roman history, the eighteenth century passed judgement on itself.

The Hanoverian Sidney, with his 'uncorrupt hands', his 'probity' and 'integrity', is less a Machiavellian republican than a Cato. His 'elevated' character was deemed to have raised him 'above' covetousness. There had been a Stoic side to his own thought and character, which his accounts of himself heightened, as did his bearing at his death. Recalling, before his execution, the attempts made to assassinate him in the 1660s, he explained that he had been selected for pursuit because 'it was known that I could not be corrupted'. Even after his return to England in 1677 he was, in his own well-publicized account, not a seeker or subverter of power but a victim of it. 'When I only looked over a balcony to see what passed at the election of sheriffs of London,' he avouched, 'I was indicted for a riot.' There would have been other ways of describing his conduct during that episode, when he and his radical Whig associates, standing on the balcony inside the Guildhall, egged on the crowd that was agitating below, in vain, against the Tory coup in the shrievalty election of 1682. It was that defeat that drove Sidney and his friends into the plots which would bring him to the scaffold. Sidney's eighteenth-century Stoic image was aided too by the words he was believed to have inscribed in the album at Copenhagen: *Ense petit placidam cum libertate quietem*. They inspired images of rustic detachment. In America John Adams, a devotee of the *Discourses*, decided that Sidney had 'from his infancy sought a tranquil retirement under the shadow of the tree of liberty'. The opening passage of the *Discourses*, referring to the 'leisure' in which the book was written, also helped. In 1776 a medical student at Edinburgh 'spoke in raptures of the character of Sidney, and said that he once got out of his carriage in passing by Sidney's country house [Penshurst] and spent several hours in walking in the wood in which [Sidney] was accustomed to meditate when he composed his famous treatise on government'. Such tributes would have been enjoyed by John Toland, who affected to have written works of his own 'from under an elm' or in other postures of rural retirement.

Sidney's republicanism was international in perspective. His mind roamed across the histories of nations, biblical, classical, medieval, Renaissance. For him the struggle between liberty and tyranny was confined by no boundaries of time or place. Stuart misrule, to which he found so many parallels in ancient and medieval history, also seemed to him to have its recent and present ones. It belonged, in his mind, to a European phenomenon that had begun with the erosion of representative institutions in many parts of the Continent in the late fifteenth and the early sixteenth century. Only in the Netherlands had that process been significantly resisted, and even there the cause of liberty was under siege from the Stuarts' ally, the House of Orange. Under Charles II, as Jonathan Scott has emphasized, the anti-Stuart cause was an Anglo-Dutch cause, which brought radical English and radical Dutch thinkers into regular contact. The links persisted for a time after 1688. Sidney would have been pleased by the publication of his *Discourses*, in a French translation, in Holland in 1702 and by its dedication to the Estates of Holland and West-Friesland, the heartland of Dutch republicanism. Ludlow's *Memoirs* had already been translated into French and (apparently) into Dutch. English radicals had been involved in those publications. Thereafter the *Discourses* did retain an influence on the Continent. French and Dutch translations were published in 1755, and there were further French editions in 1789 and 1794. Yet until late in the eighteenth century the English Sidney and the Continental Sidney seem to have largely gone separate ways. The memory of Algernon's internationalism had evaporated.

Edmund Ludlow's outlook, like Sidney's, was international. His country's cause, though dear to him, was inseparable from the cause of God across Europe. In his mind the political convulsions which shook the Continent in mid-century, and the persecution of the godly across national boundaries before and during and after them, testified to the operation of a divine apocalyptic force which no national frontier could hope to contain. That was not, in its time, an unusual view. Even James Harrington and his friend Andrew Marvell, men whose thinking was in some ways much more secular than Ludlow's, saw Europe's upheavals of the 1640s and 1650s in an apocalyptic light. In Toland's version of Ludlow's text the cause of God becomes the cause of England, Ludlow's love of God a love of England. Toland was in tune with his own time. From the 1690s ever more is heard about our obligations to our country. The trend is represented in the writings of Charles Davenant, a critic of standing armies in the late 1690s whose writing would influence eighteenth-century ideals of patriotism. 'All thoughts, endeavours and designments' of the good citizen, he explained in 1699, 'should tend to the good and welfare of our country.' 'The public virtue which must preserve a state,' he maintained, is 'a constant and perpetual will to do our country good.' The fourth of the Ludlow pamphlets of 1691–3, *Truth Brought to Light*, proudly recalled Ludlow's refusal to hearken to offers of help from Louis XIV to the exiles in the mid-1660s. Ludlow's 'soul was too great and loyal to his country to seek revenge' on it for his exile and persecution. In Ludlow's manuscript, however, it is no consideration of native loyalty that holds him back from allying with foreign powers, rather a doubt whether it could work and, in the case of the Dutch, his Puritan obsession with that nation's bloodguilt. Sidney's own love of country is not in doubt. In the civil war, as his eighteenth-century admirers were pleased to discover, his standard bore the motto *Sanctus amor patriae dat animus*: 'Sacred love of country gives courage'. But when his country was ruled by enemies to its liberty and virtue he was ready to seek foreign assistance, Dutch or French, to overthrow them.

As duty to country becomes, from 1688 onwards, more insistently emphasized, so do the qualities proper to 'an Englishman'. Toland caught the mood when, in rewriting Ludlow, he replaced the Puritan sentiments voiced by the regicide John Barkstead at his execution with the statement that Barkstead met his death with 'the character of a true Englishman'. Sidney became a true Englishman too, or, as Hollis had it, 'in a word, if ever any, a perfect Englishman'. He was never an

AT THE TIME WHEN MR. ALGERNON SYDNEY WAS AMBASSADOR AT THE COVRT OF DENMARK MONSIEVR TERLON THE FRENCH AMBASSADOR HAD THE CONFIDENCE TO TEAR OVT OF THE BOOK OF MOTTOES IN THE KING'S LIBRARY THIS VERSE WHICH MR. SYDNEY ACCORDING TO THE LIBERTY ALLOWED TO ALL NOBLE STRANGERS HAD WRITTEN IN IT

MANVS HAEC INIMICA TYRANNIS
ENSE PETIT PLACIDAM SVB LIBERTATE QVIETEM

From the 1763 edition of Sidney's *Discourses*.

exclusively English property: eighteenth-century writers were clear that he had written for the liberties not merely of England but of all 'mankind'; but his English loyalties were judged to have come first. Perfect Englishmen did not seek aid from foreigners. If they had international sentiments they kept them under control. During his exile at Vevey, Ludlow had a Latin inscription carved above the door of his house. Their source was a line of Ovid, *Omne solum forti patris*: 'every land is to the brave his country' – though Ludlow's inscription amended that pagan wording, at a cost to its metre, by inserting a Christian sentiment. But when, in the mid-eighteenth century, the elder Pitt, that hero of the country-party thinking of his age, reflected on Ovid's maxim, he found it 'big with fatal casuistry'. It was true, he acknowledged, that it had 'supported some great and good men', Ludlow and Sidney among them, 'under the persecution of faction and party injustice and taught them to prefer an honourable retreat in a foreign land to an unnatural mother-country'. But if the maxim were generally accepted the effect would be the 'dissolving all the nearest and dearest ties that hold societies together'.

Not only Sidney's international instincts, but his classical ones too, shrank under eighteenth-century inspection. For if the eighteenth century is the most self-consciously classical of ages its classicism is generally less exploratory or challenging than his. It finds in classical politics reflections of the present rather than alternatives to it. As England's power and confidence grew, comparisons with Roman politics, though they could still be keenly felt, lost some of their awe. Where Sidney and Harrington and Toland had exalted the Roman militia and urged the English to emulate it, in 1762 a self-styled 'old Whig', in demanding the reform of the English militia, remarked that his case 'carries its own conviction, without resorting to Greece or Rome'. The classical republics were to be imitated in spirit but not in form: a principle encapsulated by Charles James Fox when he commended the early leaders of the Long Parliament, who

> never conceived the wild notion of assimilating the government of England to that of Athens, of Sparta, or of Rome. They were content with applying to the English constitution, and to the English laws, the spirit of liberty which had animated and rendered illustrious the ancient republics.

Before the Revolution of 1688, Whigs could hardly escape the international dimension of English politics. The French alliance and French funds enabled the later Stuarts to defy their parliaments. The Revolution of 1688 ended the French dependency. Henceforth England would largely rely for its security on its own resources. Its rivalry with France, which would endure until 1815, sharpened the sense of England's – and Britain's – national identity.

The Revolution of 1688 had another consequence for England's self-perception. Henceforth the nation's constitutional developments seemed not so much a part of European ones as an exception to them. Sidney had seen, in the aspirations of the houses of Stuart, Orange and Bourbon, manifestations of a European trend towards absolutism and tyranny, which the English seemed as powerless as their Continental counterparts to prevent. After 1688 his successors generally acknowledged that England had been delivered from that tendency. They were torn between two impulses: revulsion against William's regime, which had betrayed the Revolution, and fear lest it fall to the Jacobite threat. Should they argue that England still lived under tyranny, or rather that it had escaped it but might still revert to it? Their own predilection was for the first position, which emphasized the failure of fundamentai constitutional reform in 1689. Nevertheless the world had changed. Popery had been defeated. Parliaments, however corrupt they had become, at least met regularly and, from 1694, were elected regularly. How much most Whigs of the later Stuart era might have given for those blessings! Radicals, if they wanted to win converts, had to recognize the advantages of the regime about whose disadvantages they had so much to say.

Their acknowledgements were grudging. Under William III they maintained that the Revolution, because it had been so incomplete, was dangerously insecure. It was no cause for national self-congratulation. 'The best that can be said' of it was that it was 'a piece of luck', owed to a fortuitous 'combination of circumstances (which may never happen again)' and dependent on the 'dangerous remedy' of 'a foreign force'. The preservation of English 'liberty' was more indebted to the 'accident' of geography than 'to our own wisdom, integrity or courage'. There was every danger that it would soon be extinguished, either through the restoration of the Stuarts, a prospect which according to 'real Whigs' was being made all too concrete by the government's deficiencies, or through the instruments of power being fashioned by the junto. Radical argument had shifted even so. Under Charles II radicals had attacked existing calamities. After 1688 they more often warned of impending ones, of what would happen 'if' corruption 'shall' or 'should' make further inroads. In 1694 Robert Molesworth's highly influential tract *An Account of Denmark*, a work often close in spirit and argument to Sidney's *Discourses*, showed how that nation's corruption had facilitated the coup which subjected it to tyranny in 1660. His point was not that post-Revolutionary England laboured under a parallel tyranny but that it was in danger of succumbing to one. At least while Englishmen clung to their liberty, conceded *An Argument* against standing armies in 1697, they were 'freemen and not slaves in this unhappy age when an universal deluge of tyranny has overspread the face of the earth'.

In the eighteenth century innumerable writers who saw corruption as a grave peril to the constitution none the less told themselves that, as Richard Beckford's journal *The Monitor* put it in August 1755, England had managed to 'preserve' its balanced constitution whereas 'the liberties of our neighbours have been long swallowed up by arbitrary power'. It was as the 'Eden amongst the nations' that in July 1763 England was warned by the same journal to 'beware'. The admiration of foreigners, especially Frenchmen, for the Hanoverian constitution encouraged, even among radicals, England's sense of its own distinctiveness. The 'beloved patriot' John Wilkes contrasted the despotisms of the European continent with the freedoms of England, which he ascribed to the Revolution of 1688, that 'great era of English liberty. From this most auspicious period, freedom has made a regular uninterrupted abode in our happy island.' The tone of such statements, which can sound so complacent, is easy to misjudge. The very frequency of eighteenth-century praises of the English constitution hints at the unease behind them, at the awareness of the frailty and instability of the constitutional balance and of the post-Revolutionary political world that depended on it. Even so the preservative instincts bred by such anxiety were far removed from Sidney's subversive ones.

The radical Whig case against the Revolution did persist. Some radicals, when they declared their reverence for the constitution, managed to indicate that it had been allowed to operate properly only in some distant past. In the eighteenth century the claim that an 'opportunity' to secure the people's fundamental constitutional rights had been missed in 1688–9 was made time and again. In 1744 Sidney's devotee James Ralph complained that, because the revolutionaries of 1688–9 'had not an eye to corruption', 'such an opportunity was lost of resettling our old constitution as England is not like to have again'. A stronger tug, however, pulled in the opposite direction. The radicals of the 1690s described the shortcomings of the revolutionary settlement as a 'betrayal': *Cato's Letters* warn against the 'hirelings', not who have betrayed, but who 'would betray', the 'late Revolution'. Thus it was that the *Discourses*, which had been published in 1698 as a protest against the Revolution's failings, gradually came to seem a vindication of it, and Sidney's own career a struggle for it. The same thing happened to John Locke, who pleaded for radical change in 1689, and whose *Second Treatise*, like Sidney's *Discourses*, was published only after the Revolution and in a form that revealed nothing of its incendiary genesis. Something similar happened to James Harrington, whose *Oceana* came to seem a perceptive if flawed anticipation of the eighteenth-century balanced constitution. Even Edmund Ludlow, whose departure from England in 1689 so graphically illustrated the shortcomings of the Revolution in radical eyes, was absorbed by the post-Revolutionary world. The preface to the new edition of the *Memoirs* in 1751 urged Englishmen to put party quarrels behind them and unite in 'promoting the prosperity and happiness of Great Britain, and transmitting down to future ages the blessings we now enjoy'. Thomas Tyers, who remarked in his book *Political Conferences* (1780) that the 'patriots' of 1641 had 'paved the way to the Revolution of eighty-eight', commended Ludlow in the same work for seeking 'the recovery of the rights of the people, for which he first drew his sword, and which were restored (though with no benefit to himself) in 1688'.

The linking of Sidney with 1688 had its irony too. In *Court Maxims* Sidney urged the English to 'extirpate the two detestable families of Stuart and Orange'. Later he told the French ambassador Barillon (admittedly with a tactical intention, but with at least an element of truth) that he 'feared the Prince of Orange' – particularly the thought of him 'with an army behind him' – 'more than the Duke of York', the future James II. In 1688, five years after Sidney's death, William arrived, 'with an army'. When, the following year, Sidney's devotees portrayed the 'blood' of Sidney and other 'patriots' as the 'seed' of the Revolution, their aim was to help steer that Revolution in their own, radical direction. Yet by 1732 the *Free Briton* could, in a single breath, commend the 'great and virtuous' Sidney, who 'lived and wrote and acted for the liberties of mankind', and hail 'the Revolution of 1688', which, together with 'the wisdom of succeeeding parliaments', had brought England the 'free' constitution it had lacked in his time. Sixty years later, in 1792, the journal *The Patriot* carried a letter, over the pseudonym Algernon Sidney, in commendation of the 'noble and magnificent fabric' of 'the English constitution', a constitution which is 'the theme of praise in the mouth of almost the whole enlightened part of the globe'. Sometimes, it is true, admirers of the Revolution, rather than portraying Sidney as its prophet, regretted his want of 'moderation', and claimed that 1688 had produced, thanks to 'our glorious deliverer' William, 'a better remedy' than the republican solution envisaged by Sidney. But his excesses were indulgently attributed to the desperation of the nation's circumstances near the end of his life. He could be forgiven for having been unable to imagine, under the extremity of Stuart tyranny, any but an extreme alternative to it. Had he lived in present times he would have known better.

As 1688 receded into the past, ever less attention was paid in political commentaries to the disagreements among those who had opposed the later Stuarts. The constitutional conflicts of the Stuart age were of diminishing relevance to present-day debate. 'The Revolution,' declared the former Tory leader Lord Bolingbroke in 1733, 'is looked upon by all sides as a new era.' The political theories that had endorsed the Stuart bid for absolutism retreated. It was a gradual process, so slow indeed that conventional Whigs, in their contest with divine-right Toryism, for long found it useful to draw (even if mostly without acknowledgement) on Sidney's attacks on the 'slavish doctrines' that had supported the Stuarts. The *Discourses* themselves remained vulnerable to Tory criticism. None the less the nation's political thought was changing. In 1735 the Tory writer Nathaniel Salmon, even as he attacked Sidney's 'deposing doctrines', distanced himself from the principles of divine-right rule and passive obedience. A little earlier Bolingbroke had observed that

The whole bulk of the people hath been brought by the Revolution, and by the present settlement of the Crown, to entertain principles which very few of us defended in my younger days. The safety and welfare of the nation are now the first and principal objects of regard. The regard to person and to families of monarchs hath been reduced to the second place.

David Hume, who mocked the cult of Sidney, nevertheless allowed that his 'principles', which Hume summarized as 'the original contract, the source of power from the consent of the people, the lawfulness of resisting tyrants, the preference of liberty to the government of a single person', were 'such as the best and most dutiful subjects of all ages had been known to embrace'. Hume noticed the prevalence of an opinion, which he seems to have at least half-shared, that since 1688

most people, in this island, have divested themselves of all superstitious reverence to names and authority . . . [and that] the mere name of kings commands little respect; and [that] to talk of a king as God's vicegerent on earth, or to give him any of those magnificent titles which formerly dazzled mankind, would but excite laughter in everyone.

Bolingbroke, seeking to replace what he called 'absurd' divine-right principles of opposition with the country-party ones that might win a broader base, and Hume, whose Toryism was of a distinctly sceptical cast, may have exaggerated the shift of opinion. Even so their words point to developments within Toryism with significant consequences for the eighteenth century's understanding of the seventeenth. Certainly there were Tories who, with one half of their minds, were reluctant to abandon the creed of Stuart absolutism. None the less the party's long exclusion from power under Walpole made the Tories predominantly a body as suspicious of executive power as the radical Whigs were. Alongside the clash of party histories there flourished country-party perceptions of the civil wars that could draw Tory and disaffected Whig together. Against that background Toland's investment in the commonwealthmen of the civil wars yielded new dividends.

As in the 1690s, so in the earlier eighteenth century, the 'country' was a loose and fragile coalition, which could disappear from sight at moments of heightened party animosity. Yet the groups that were excluded from power by Walpole's ascendancy, and increasingly desperate to end it, found plenty of common ground, as, over a much shorter period, men kept out by the junto of the 1690s had done. The term 'country' had a serviceable ambivalence. By alluding to the countryside, to the rooted permanence of the 'landed interest', to the honourable rewards of pastoral retirement and political disengagement, it could be turned against the restless world of London, against the temptations of power, against the ephemera of fashion, against the fickle economy of credit and paper which sustained the ever-expanding 'moneyed interest' and which divorced wealth from social responsibility.

Yet the appeal of country-party programmes had never been solely rural. The 'country' was not only the countryside but the nation, whose communal interests were contrasted, in country-party programmes, with the sectional ones of courtiers and factions and parties. Urban support for country measures grew with the expansion of the press over the later seventeenth and the earlier eighteenth century and with the accompanying widening of public political consciousness. Country sentiment crossed the barriers not only of town and country but of social rank. It was given social breadth by the iniquities of the electoral system. The control of large numbers of constituencies by the Crown and nobility excluded a high proportion of the politically literate from representation. It also gave spice to those contests, in electorally 'open' areas, where public opinion might still be made to count. Resentment was fuelled by the passage in 1716 of the Septennial Act, a measure which, in the light (or on the pretext) of the Jacobite rising the previous year, enabled ministries to call elections, which were often tumultuous events, only once every seven years. The Triennial Act of 1694, which it replaced, was 'often said' to have been 'all the nation got by the Revolution' of 1688; now it was lost. The demand for frequent elections was a staple eighteenth-century country-party one. Alongside it the grievances which Toland had felt and exploited in the 1690s – standing armies, placemen, bribery – were ever to the fore.

The term 'country' co-existed with, and often merged with or yielded to, another with a comparably useful ambivalence: 'patriot'. The word had been a feature of English political vocabulary at least since the early seventeenth century. In 1645 Edmund Ludlow's ally in the civil wars Sir Arthur Hesilrige remembered 'what a good patriot' Edmund's father had been. At that time, however, the term was merely applied to virtuous individuals or groups. In the eighteenth century it was used to characterize a movement. So frequent did its use become that it sometimes looks as if everyone – or at least everyone either young or outside the centre of power – who cared for self-respect had to pay tribute to the patriot ideal. A patriot was a defender of his country's liberties against those evils which the country party had identified. He was also one who cared for his country's standing abroad and blushed at its moments of international ignominy. In the seventeenth century that second meaning had been linked to the first by the weaknesses of Stuart diplomacy. In the eighteenth the association was intensified by Walpole's refusal to confront England's enemies. Corruption, tyranny and weakness abroad were judged to go together.

The word 'patriot' gave legitimacy to opposition to the government. In the modern world the legitimacy of parliamentary opposition is taken for granted. In the early eighteenth century it remained vulnerable to the charges of disloyalty, faction, even sedition. Like 'country', the term 'patriot' shifted the balance of ethical authority away from the Crown and court. Patriots, like the country party, represented the community at large: the ministries they attacked, corrupt and unprincipled, were the true sources of faction, division, instability. All definitions of patriotism agreed that the patriot was 'impartial', above 'party' and 'party spirit'.

The truth was more complicated. There were many elements of patriotism. Some were outside the Tory and Whig parties but a number were within or half-within them, ready when occcasion demanded to rally behind conventional party stands. Though the patriot ideal gave its various components a common language, they competed to annexe it to their several purposes. There were thus a number of patriot readings of the civil wars, some hostile to the parliamentary cause of

1641, some sympathetic to it, some – at points where patriotism merged with the 'real Whig' tradition – even in favour of the regicide. There were likewise various readings of 1688. To some patriots the Revolutionary settlement had supplied a perfect design of constitutional balance, only for the subsequent development of corruption to endanger it. To others, in or close to the radical tradition, it was the failure of the Revolution to secure proper guarantees of liberty, and to restrict the Crown's revenue, that had made the ministerial corruption of the Hanoverian age possible. That position, generally a radical Whig one, had its attraction to Tories too.

The appeal of patriotism was never stable. It often broadened or shrank in response to events. The movement could temporarily draw in men who had mocked it earlier or would do so later. Dr Johnson, who famously derided patriotism as 'the last refuge of the scoundrel', had had his own intense patriot phase. Although the term had acquired a persistent presence in public discussion by the 1720s, it was in the later 1730s, when frustration at Walpole's hegemony merged with contempt for his unwillingness to stand up to England's enemies abroad, that it acquired the prominent position in the nation's political vocabulary which it would retain for the remainder of the century. Towards the end of Walpole's ascendancy it attracted an array of poets to its ranks: Thomson, Pope, Johnson and many more. Thomson's sympathies were Whiggish, those of Pope and Johnson high Tory. To Pope, the Whig historian of the civil wars John Oldmixon was 'a perverter of history'. Pope shared, as perhaps Johnson did, the Jacobite sympathies of Pope's patron and ally Lord Bolingbroke, the former Tory leader. Yet he followed Bolingbroke down the patriot path too. It was Bolingbroke who in his writings, among them *A Letter on the Spirit of Patriotism* and *The Idea of a Patriot King*, did as much as anyone to bring the vocabulary of patriotism to the centre of political debate. Party rule, which he had promoted under Queen Anne but which he now disowned, was for him the enemy of patriotism. Charles I, defended by orthodox Tories, was reproached by Bolingbroke for having been a 'party man'. Valuing his patriot credentials, Bolingbroke liked to be compared to Cato.

In 1732 Pope tried to arrange the publication of some of the republican Algernon Sidney's letters. Pope was a regular visitor to that focus of patriot activity, Stowe in Buckinghamshire, the home of Viscount Cobham, a Whig who, like other leading patriots, broke with Walpole. In the gardens at Stowe Cobham laid out classical temples and statues and porticos that celebrate the patriot ideal. Among them is the Temple of British Worthies, where, among the figures whose 'unspotted names', as George Bickham's mid-eighteenth century guidebook *The Beauties of Stowe* put it, 'humbled the torrent of corruption', are Pope and the republican Milton. A leading figure in Cobham's circle was his nephew William Pitt, later Earl of Chatham, 'that worthy patriot', whose ability to combine Whig and Tory affiliations, and yet to rise above both, recalls the career of Robert Harley earlier. Pitt used his reputation for 'disdaining the aid of party', and for 'disinterestedness' towards the disposal of preferment, as the foundation of his career and popularity. Beckford's *The Monitor* portrayed him as Britain's Cato and Cincinnatus, as a statesman above the intrigue and corruption of politics. 'Like an old Roman' he liked to 'retire to his farm, where temperance and frugality reign'. Though often 'implored to take hold of the helm', the man 'who had given signal proofs of his contempt of riches', a man whose 'principles are purely constitutional, not to be biased by private gain or other temptations', was finally prevailed on only by 'the best of motives': his love of country, his devotion to the nation which won its spectacular victories of the Seven Years' War (1756–63) under his leadership. Pitt, who called himself 'the oldest Whig in England', read Sidney and Ludlow and was painted standing beside an altar which bore a bust of Sidney next to a flame of liberty. On his death an anonymous poem put into Sidney's mouth a tribute to that 'Patriot Minister' and simultaneously applauded 'Sidney's fire in freedom's glorious cause'.

Pitt, the modern hero of patriotism, became its betrayer. Just as in the 1690s radical Whigs were shocked by the abandonment of their cause by the party's leadership, so the patriot ideal was repeatedly shaken by apostasy. On Walpole's fall in 1742, when patriots were expected to insist on an end to corruption as a condition of taking office, they scrambled for power within the prevailing system. The decision of Walpole's leading opponent Sir William Pulteney to accept a peerage was a heavy blow. Pitt's acceptance of a pension in 1761 and then of a peerage in 1766 were others. Later Pitt's aberrations

The Temple of British Worthies at Stowe. The heads individually reproduced here are those of Milton, Hampden and Pope. King Alfred, the Black Prince, Queen Elizabeth, Shakespeare, Raleigh, Drake, Newton, Locke and William III are also represented.

would come to be indulgently judged by patriots, who preferred to remember his merits. At the time their impact was shattering. Horace Walpole acknowledged himself to have been 'a dupe to virtue and patriotism. I adored Mr Pitt, as if I was just come home from school and reading Livy's tales of Brutus. . . . Alack! Alack!' Thomas Hollis, 'that matchless patriot', had a similar experience. As part of what he thought of as his 'patriotizing' activities, which promoted visual images of the heroes he wished his age to emulate, Hollis had had medals made in honour of Pitt's patriotism. Now he ordered them to be re-engraved with words that recorded his descent from it. Betrayals played into the hands of ministries, which were enabled by them to portray the ideal of patriotism as a front for everyday political appetites. Yet while desertions impaired country sentiment they did not destroy it. As in the 1690s, they hardened the resolution, and the sense of distinctiveness, of those who remained true.

Between the late seventeenth century and the late eighteenth there are essentially two stages to the cult of Sidney. The first, which lasts until around the middle of the eighteenth century, is the period of Sidney 'the independent Whig', who, being independent, can appeal to patriot sentiment across the party divide. To the patriot writer James Ralph, Sidney was 'a patriot indeed', 'one of the best and bravest men that ever did honour to the English name'. Not every patriot, it is true, could stomach Sidney, even the Sidney whose radicalism had been posthumously muted, but his appeal was wide. The only element in the political nation to which, in the first half of the century, it did not extend was the ruling one, the Whig establishment. Sidney was a patriot and a country Whig or independent Whig, but not a court Whig. Walpole's administration, which was troubled by the cult of Sidney, did make some efforts to appropriate the *Discourses* for its cause, but in terms which implied that, thanks to the new Whig hegemony, the book had lost much of its point. Readers were reminded of the 'immortal memory' of Sidney, 'who, had he lived in these days, would never have wrote his book'. The ploy was unavailing. Even so the Whig ascendancy, like that of the junto before it, inhibited the radicals. It was always harder for them, especially for those of them who hoped for office, to oppose Whig administrations than Tory ones. Sidney's devotee Thomas Hollis remarked in 1761 that the very 'moderation' of George II's reign, from 1727 to 1760, had left Sidney 'in some degree of neglect'.

That statement owed something to retrospective distortion. It was only when they experienced the rule of George III that 'real Whigs' such as Hollis came to value the 'moderation' of his predecessor, and it was only in comparison with the cult of Sidney after 1760 that the earlier enthusiasm for Algernon looked tepid. None the less the reign of George III transformed his standing. The Whigs, who had more or less controlled the first two Georges, were now confronted by a king determined to break their hold on power and to be his own master. At the outset of the reign there were patriot hopes of him. It seemed that he might be what his father Frederick, whose early death in 1751 prevented his own succession, had promised to become, a patriot king, above party and above corruption. *The Monitor*, which in the twilight of George II's reign had equated Pitt with Cato, quickly compared the new king to that Roman model. Though some patriots retained hopes of George III until well into the reign, more were rapidly disillusioned. His rule inspired fears of a return to Stuart absolutism and to civil war. Early on he made the Earl of Bute, a descendant of the Stuarts and seemingly an admirer of their principles, his leading adviser. Whigs believed that they had established, under the first two Georges, the principle that the Crown's ministers must have an independent power-base in the House of Commons. Bute lacked one. He was a mere royal favourite, of the kind that had flourished under James I and Charles I.

George III's determination to appoint his own ministers, and his insistence on exercising his legislative veto, were hardly innovative. William III had made the same claims. Even so the 'influence' of the Crown became a source of mounting anxiety. The virtue of the English constitution, deemed its admirers, was that its three separate components, King, Lords and Commons, which represented the principles of monarchy, aristocracy and democracy, checked and balanced each other's ambitions. In the earlier eighteenth century, patriots had protested that corruption, and the swelling revenues that financed it, were heightening the power of the Crown (that is, of its ministers) at the expense of the other estates. Under George III that complaint was levelled not merely by patriots but by orthodox Whigs; and it was aimed not merely at ministers but at the king himself. The arrest of the 'beloved patriot' John Wilkes in 1763, the Stamp Act crisis of 1765–6, and Wilkes's re-imprisonment and his exclusion from parliament in 1768, raised the temperature. Many Whigs sympathized with the resistance in America, which seemed to them merely a reassertion of the principles of 1688 against a despotic Crown. The constitutional crisis of 1782–4, when the king stood on his right to determine the composition of the ministry, produced fresh alarm among the Whigs. In the 1790s the new laws and practices designed to suppress political dissent, and the rallying of Tory sentiment behind the war against revolutionary France, convinced leading Whigs, especially Fox, that the peril to the constitution was grave once more.

It was the dismay provoked by the king's constitutional aspirations that produced the second stage of Sidney's eighteenth-century reputation. Thomas Hollis's edition of the *Discourses* in 1763 appeared, as Hollis's biographer Francis Blackburne would explain in 1780,

> at that critical period when it began to be visible that the management of our public affairs was consigned into the hands of men notoriously known to have entertained principles unfavourable to liberty, the principles upon which those men acted who sacrificed Sidney, without law or justice, to the tyranny of a profligate and licentious court and ministry. . . . It was never more necessary than it has been within these last seventeen years to let such men as Sidney speak for themselves. Their principles have been obnoxious to the rulers of the times for that whole period.

Memories of Sidney's trial were revived by the afflictions of Wilkes, whom Hollis urged to write a life of Sidney. Hollis's widely read and widely influential edition was republished in 1772. The following year a pamphleteer proclaimed that Sidney and his fellow-conspirator Russell 'will remain objects of a nation's veneration and love while the names of Bute and Mansfield' – Lord Chief Justice Mansfield, who had ruled against Wilkes – 'will ever be uttered with contempt and abhorrence'. Sidney's claims for the right of resistance acquired a new appeal. A broadside printed in London in 1775, *Sidney's Exhortation*, urged the Americans to resist their English oppressors by force. In the first half of the century Sidney's praise of that most daring feat of resistance, the regicide ('the justest and bravest action that ever was done in England'), had been barely mentioned by his admirers. Now Hollis and others gratefully remembered it.

It was not only among radicals that opposition to George III enhanced Sidney's memory. Orthodox Whigs began to embrace it too. Excluded from power, they became less the butt of patriotism than its ally. Fox and other leading Whigs were now habitually called patriots. As Whig and patriot thinking came together so Sidney became not merely a country-party or radical Whig but a mainstream one. In 1792 Fox, losing 'all temper and patience' with the 'monstrous and unheard of wickedness' of the ministry, called on his fellow-Whigs to defend 'the rights of the people' as Sidney had done. Even the regicide, which had horrified orthodox Whigs in the early eighteenth century, now found its defenders among them. In 1780 Thomas Tyers, a writer with conventional Whig views, remarked that 'if Charles had not lost his head . . . the nation would have no liberties at this time'. Tyers noticed that under George II the patriot politician Lord Chesterfield had said the same thing. Chesterfield's remarks, however, had been confined to a private document. Under George III the document was published. Sidney's rise to Whig respectability is reflected in the correspondence of Horace Walpole, a client of orthodox Whiggism but temperamentally sympathetic to patriotism, who described Sidney as a 'saint'. In 1780 Walpole placed Sidney in unimpeachably orthodox Whig company. Replying to Tory attacks on 'our patriots, martyrs, heroes and geniuses', he named Algernon among those worthies but also included not only William III, whom the radicals of the 1690s had judged to have thwarted their cause but whose memory their successors had sometimes been willing to compliment, but the Duke of Marlborough, who had crushed Monmouth's rebellion and been deeply mistrusted in radical quarters thereafter.

Sidney acquired other respectable company too. Earlier in the century, patriots of cautious outlook had been readier to commend Sidney's fellow-martyr Lord Russell than to praise Algernon himself. Now the two names frequently appeared together. Sidney also came to be ever more often associated with John Hampden, who had earned his fame by that courageous protest against tyranny in 1637, his refusal to pay ship money; by his leadership in the early stages of the Long Parliament; and by his death on the battlefield at Chalgrove in 1643. Like Sidney, Hampden was often called a martyr to liberty. Like him he could exert an appeal across the party frontiers and be enlisted in cross-party causes. In 1742 the patriot pamphlet *National Unanimity Recommended* proclaimed that the Tories, hitherto the party of divine right, had come to act, 'with many worthy Whigs, . . . like men of honour, by keeping upon such principles as old Hampden himself would not be ashamed of'. In the same decade Chesterfield placed Hampden's 'brave stand' against ship money alongside the coups of 1649 and 1688 as a source of 'our present liberties'. In 1753 we first encounter the slogan 'The cause for which Hampden bled in the field and Sidney on the scaffold'. After 1760 it is everywhere.

The association between the two men was an entirely posthumous creation. It is unlikely that they ever met. The link confirmed Sidney's new status among orthodox Whigs, for Hampden was the respectable face of the Roundhead cause. He died well before the regicide. He defied Charles I in a spirit not of destruction and innovation, the qualities blamed by Tories for the rule of the Commonwealth, but of moderate constitutionalism. Those who aligned Hampden and Sidney remembered the common opposition of the two men to Stuart tyranny and overlooked the radicalism which distanced Sidney from the other man. Algernon's participation in the Commonwealth was rarely mentioned. Indeed ever less about his life (as distinct from his death) was mentioned. He had become, for many who cited his example, more a symbol than a person. The more often the slogan about his and Hampden's deaths was repeated the more historically imprecise it became. Sidney's admirers had contrived to place him, with Hampden, among the heroes of the initial phase of the Long Parliament, when in reality the teenage Algernon had been abroad on a grand tour. Edmund Ludlow, who, though a few years older, had likewise been unheard of in the politics of that time, was placed in the same company by a newspaper of 1766, which urged 'men of England' to say to themselves:

What is become of the noble spirit of your ancestors! Where are your . . . Hampdens, your Ludlows, your Sidneys, and all the illustrious spirits of forty-one! Suffer not the noble memorials of them to be defaced by moths and cobwebs in your libraries. Bring them forth to action; and fear not to be reproached for reviving obsolete maxims . . .

That reproach reflected a widespread eighteenth-century conviction that degeneracy had deprived the present era of the virtue and moral courage of earlier generations, and thus of its capacity to withstand the peril of tyranny. It was a belief expressed across a wide spectrum of Whig and patriot opinion. In 1737 the journal *The Old Whig* contrasted the commitment with which Sidney, Hampden, Milton and Harrington had defended 'our natural rights' with the present 'supine' neglect of them. During the following decade Lord Chesterfield remarked that Charles I's bid for absolutism had failed because 'there was then spirit and virtue enough in the nation to oppose it'. In August 1755 *The Monitor*, observing that 'our history abounds with instances' of the collective defence of liberty, commended the men who 'fought for the liberties of England in 1641 or placed King William on the throne in 1689'. The journal longed for a comparably 'vigorous exertion of our natural rights' and lamented the 'supine indifference to the public good' which impeded it. In 1770 the republican Sylas Neville, upon toasting the anniversary of Charles I's execution, regretted that 'there is not public virtue enough left to make a stand like that made in the days of Charles I'. In the 1790s Fox, believing the constitutional gains of the Long Parliament and of 1688 to be disappearing, and startled by the feebleness of opposition to the Crown, concluded that 'the country is wholly without spirit'. Even those who baulked at Sidney's republicanism could envy his resolution of character. Among them was Thomas Hollis's admirer Francis Blackburne, who observed that Sidney's 'expedients' for the victory of liberty over tyranny 'are easy, obvious, and entirely practicable whenever there is virtue enough among the aspiring patriots to carry them into execution'. Again Hampden was linked with Sidney. In 1792 a letter in *The Patriot*, apparently alluding to the slogan that joined their names, remarked that the 'time seems to be going' when 'the people of this kingdom . . . fought and bled in the cause of liberty'. The shades of the two men rebuked a century softened by corruption.

*

By the early 1770s the transformation of Sidney appeared complete. The respectable, 'incorruptible' Stoic martyr, the 'perfect Englishman' who placed love of country before all else, who wrote so eloquently against 'bribery and corruption', who was immune to inducements of power and profit, seemed securely established. In 1772 Thomas Hollis's edition of the *Discourses* reappeared in another elegant version, which reaffirmed, in italic, Hollis's emphasis on Sidney's purity of character: 'Many circumstances at present loudly call upon us to exert ourselves. *Venality and corruption have well nigh extinguished all principles of liberty*.'

The following year nemesis struck. It was in 1773 that the Scottish historian Sir John Dalrymple published documents from the French archives relating to the embassy of Paul Barillon in England under Charles II. They showed that in 1678 Sidney had received a payment of a thousand guineas from the ambassador. Sidney thus stood charged with the two evils on which eighteenth-century Whigs and patriots had blamed the tyranny he had resisted: venality, and conspiracy with foreigners. The eighteenth century dwelt, much more extensively than Sidney had done, on the venality of Charles II's regime. The king's readiness to sacrifice the nation's interests in order to secure French subsidies was portrayed as its most disgraceful manifestation. James Thomson's poem *Liberty* represented Charles as 'A pensioned King,/ Against his country bribed by Gallic gold'. In December 1755 *The Monitor* remembered how England had been brought to the edge of destruction 'when the King of England debased his Crown by taking a bribe from France'. Now it was Sidney whom French money was seen to have brought low.

By his own lights, and by those of his time, Sidney had committed no offence against political morality. Seventeenth-century ambassadors customarily handed out payments to native politicians whom they wished to sweeten (though not all of them accepted them). During the exclusion crisis, Sidney, thinking in European terms where his posthumous devotees would think in insular ones, had no scruple in treating with a foreign government against his own tyrannical one. He played the English court at its own game. He wanted French intervention on the republicans' side rather than on the king's. His eighteenth-century admirers, who had raised him above politics, could not bear to think of him as a politician like any other. They responded to Dalrymple's revelations as to the slaughter of a sacred cow. The Whigs, though they had lost their political supremacy at the accession of George III, had retained the advantage in political ideology. Now it too was at risk. Dalrymple's charges, Whigs agreed, were a Tory plot, hatched by Dalrymple in revenge for Sidney's hostility to the Scottish Stuart line. Since Sidney was, *a priori*, 'incapable of base actions', it followed that lies had been told by either Dalrymple or Barillon, if not by both. Whigs, who were unable to gain access to the French documents on which Dalrymple's evidence was based, were exasperated when the Tory prime minister, Lord North, gave an assurance to parliament that Dalrymple's evidence could be shown to be authentic. But even to respond to Dalrymple's claims seemed demeaning. 'After almost a century's established fame', expostulated one Whig, it was 'shameful' that the glories of Sidney's character, that model of 'disinterested virtue', were being so much as questioned. Dalrymple's revelations delighted critics of the Whigs. It was 'well', Dr Johnson told Boswell, 'that all mankind' could now see that Sidney and his accomplices were 'rascals'. Hume, who attributed Sidney's exalted stature to the 'blind prejudice' of the Whigs, found it 'amusing to observe the general and I may say national rage'.

More than Sidney's own reputation was at stake. Algernon had become a 'pattern', a model in the instruction of the young, who were urged to read his writing rather than the 'novels and romances' to which they were too readily drawn. Underlying the political corruption of the eighteenth century, believed patriots, there lay an ethical one. As the patriot journal *The Monitor* had put it in March 1757, 'no lasting change in our politics can prevail until a thorough reformation in our morals, our way of thinking and living, be promoted'. The prevailing wickedness was deemed both cause and effect of the want of principle among England's rulers, who, it was alleged, were determined to make politics a matter of mere management, exclusive of morality. The rejoicing of courtiers on learning Dalrymple's news was the predictable response, asserted Sidney's admirers, of men who could not bear to look virtue in the face and who had to reduce it to their own level. In Sidney's character his devotees saw an antidote to the corrosive moral scepticism of the eighteenth century. Remarks of his in the *Discourses* about the 'corrupting' of 'youth' were approvingly quoted in *Cato's Letters* and often echoed elsewhere. Early nineteenth-century commentators reflected on the educational influence Sidney had long commanded. His name, acknowledged his biographer G. W. Meadley in 1813, had been long held up 'to disingenuous youth as an example of pure and disinterested patriotism'. Six years later a Tory writer observed that 'we have been seduced from our infancy to revere the principles of Milton, of Sidney, of Hampden'. Dalrymple's charges, though they failed to destroy that standing, menaced it. The 'republican virago' Catharine Macaulay – who compared Sidney to Cato and who, like Thomas Hollis, reprinted 'The Honourable Algernon Sidney's Letter against Bribery and Corruption' – explained that 'the contemplation of a great character never fails to warm the young and generous student into the noble attempt of imitative virtue'. 'What patterns', then, 'shall we select for the model of youthful emulation' if the 'modern scepticism' characterized by Dalrymple's charges is permitted to stain 'that virtue which we have long adored in the sacred memory of our forefathers?' Other writers, too, detected in the allegations an assault on 'all public virtue'.

For all the blows it suffered – the betrayals by Pulteney and Pitt, Dalrymple's exposure of Sidney – patriotism occupied the high moral ground of eighteenth-century public life. We shall now see how it coloured the era's thinking not only about Algernon Sidney but about a range of figures from the seventeenth-century past.

7

The Patriots

Between 1747 and 1766 there appeared *Biographia Britannica: or, The Lives of the Most Eminent Persons who have flourished in Great Britain and Ireland, from the Earliest Ages, down to the Present Time*. It was published in seven large volumes, the opening one carrying the endorsement of George II. The first substantial attempt at a dictionary of national biography in these islands, it offers a vantage-point from which to observe a set of eighteenth-century perceptions of the civil wars, a conflict in which it takes a close, perhaps even disproportionate interest. The dictionary had been many years in the making, but we know very little about the planning or editing of it. We can however discern a consistency of outlook running through the entries.

It was not a radical outlook. Algernon Sidney and his claims to virtuous incorruptibility are sceptically treated. The volume which carries the entry on him was published in 1763, the year of Hollis's influential edition of the *Discourses* and a time when anxieties about George III's constitutional ambitions were beginning to broaden the public admiration for Sidney. The dictionary remarks that, though so widely commended for his love of his country, he 'would', 'to judge by his writings', 'not have been sorry to have seen it brought to the greatest difficulties, nay to destruction, that he might have had the pleasure of seeing his enemies involved in its ruin'. *Biographia Britannica*'s account of Sidney annoyed his admirers, who responded by emphasizing the 'noble and patriotic sentiments' of his 'Letter against Bribery and Arbitrary Government'. The dictionary even casts a doubtful eye on Sidney's more respectable accomplice, Lord Russell, who, we read, showed 'malice' to his king. Readers are reminded too of John Locke's involvement, which succeeding generations had generally overlooked, in Whig conspiracy against Charles II.

The dictionary is still less enamoured of the radicalism of the civil wars. It regrets the 'violent measures which the House of Commons ran into' and condemns the 'barbarous death' of Charles I. There is corresponding praise for those members of the Long Parliament whose 'zeal for the Church' and 'duty to the king' kept them loyal to Charles's cause. The civil-war figure most warmly commended is the royalist Arthur, Lord Capel. Following Clarendon, the dictionary observes that Capel, having seen the king's 'honour violated' and his 'just rights invaded', was unstintingly 'generous' in his bravery and loyalty. He paid for them with his life in 1649, when the 'passions and revenge' of the new Commonwealth secured his 'sacrifice' on the scaffold. 'In a word, he was a man that, whoever shall after him deserve best of the English nation, he can never think himself undervalued when he shall hear that his courage, virtue and fidelity is laid in the balance with, and compared to, that of the Lord Capel.'

Biographia Britannica supplies a useful reminder of the persistence, in a Whig age, of royalist historical sentiment. In 1746, and again in 1757 (around the time when Thomas Hollis was commissioning the visual representations of Toland's heroes that he would distribute so widely), engravings were printed of Charles I and eighteen 'noble lords and others, who suffered for their loyalty'. 1747, the year of the first volume of *Biographia Britannica*, also produced the opening volume of the *General History of England* by the great Jacobite historian Thomas Carte, who had long been embattled against Whig interpretations of the civil wars. Yet straightforwardly royalist and Roundhead allegiances, though they still satisfied many people, were of diminishing appeal. Sermons on the anniversary of Charles I's execution became less aggressive and more dispassionate. The royalism of *Biographia Britannica* is not straightforward. If the work rebukes the conspirators against Charles II, so does it disown the 'slavish and persecuting principles' which were promoted by high-flying supporters of his rule, and which Sidney, who himself called them 'slavish doctrines', had written to refute. The royalism of the dictionary is a patriot royalism, which shares extensive ground with the patriotism of *Cato's*

Letters.* Sidney himself may be coolly treated, but the ideal of incorruptibility with which his admirers identified him is the ideal of the dictionary too. In disclosing it, it is kinder to some of Charles I's other opponents than to Sidney. In the reigns of William and Anne, biographical dictionaries which had much to say about the civil wars – Anthony Wood's Tory account of Oxford's graduates *Athenae Oxonienses*; the rival compilations in which Edmund Calamy lauded the Puritan ministers who had been ejected from power at the Restoration, and John Walker saluted the Anglican clergymen whom the Puritans had dispossessed – had prolonged the partisanship of the wars themselves. *Biographia Britannica* eschews those stances.

The colouring given to the royalism of Lord Capel is more patriot than Tory. Though he rallied to the Crown when his 'loyalty' was put to the test, we are reminded, he had keenly opposed the personal rule and its instruments of prerogative power. That stand, the dictionary declares, showed him to be 'a true lover of his country and an enemy to oppression of all sorts'. The dictionary is sympathetic to those 'sober and faithful patriots', John Hampden among them, who took up arms to secure redress of the nation's 'grievances'. It is the Roundheads driven by 'mercenary' motives who are condemned. There were, the dictionary concedes, 'mercenary' royalists too. Capel was not one of them. He had 'no other obligations to the Crown but those which his own honour and conscience suggested to him'.

The radical Whigs of the 1690s had targeted 'faction' and 'ambition' as enemies of republicanism. The dictionary represents them as enemies of 'loyalty' to the Crown. The common ground counts for as much as the contrast. The dictionary has kind words for that radical Whig John Trenchard, the 'patriot' author of *Cato's Letters*, and for Trenchard's ally in the campaign against standing armies in the 1690s, Walter Moyle: 'the cause of liberty lay much at his heart'. Sometimes *Biographia Britannica* and *Cato's Letters* are hard to tell apart. The emphasis laid by 'Cato' on the virtues of 'the private man' has its

* In October 1737, when the cult of patriotism was reaching new heights, *The Gentleman's Magazine* advertised, as a new work, *Biographia Britannica; or Select Lives of Eminent Men*, published in five small volumes – perhaps a first attempt at the project that would be completed in 1766. If the work of 1737 did get into print, no copies of it are known.

counterpart in the prominence given in the dictionary to a tribute paid to it by Gilbert West, a nephew (like Pitt) of Lord Cobham and a conspicuous figure in the literary branch of patriotism. West praised the dictionary for 'reviving from obscurity and oblivion examples of private and retired merit; which, though less glaring and ostentatious' than the deeds of men in public life, are not 'of a less extensive or less beneficial influence'. Both works find, in the lives of flawed heroes of the civil wars, a warning lesson. 'While he was yet a commoner,' observes 'Cato', 'England could not boast of a greater patriot' than Thomas Wentworth, who as 'the great Earl of Strafford' was Charles I's leading adviser. 'No man exposed better or more zealously the encroachments and oppressions practised by the court upon the kingdom, or contended more loudly for the redress of grievances. But he was no sooner got into the court but he began to counteract the whole course of his past life.'

Biographia Britannica supplies a parallel example. Where 'Cato' picks on the failings of the royalist Strafford, the dictionary points to the shortcomings of the parliamentary general Thomas Lord Fairfax. If only he had confined himself to the remedy of national grievances, 'he might have been honourably ranked' among the 'patriots', for he was 'inflexibly honest'. 'Inflexibility' was the essential hallmark of patriotism. In 1753 one of the many eighteenth-century journals to be called *The Patriot* explained that 'the true patriot', 'whilst he is engaged in his country's service', 'thinks the most glorious epithets the world can fix upon him are those of a RIGID, INFLEXIBLE, HONEST MAN'. In Fairfax's case, however, *Biographia Britannica* judged inflexibility to have served his own, not his country's, ends. 'His boundless ambition, and his great desire to rule, made him weakly engage, with the utmost zeal, in the worst and most exceptionable parts of our unhappy civil wars.' 'Happy would it have been for the nation, happy would it have been for him,' if he had 'retired sooner'. For, as Addison's *Cato* 'elegantly represents it, "When vice prevails, and impious men bear sway, / The post of honour is a private station."' When in 1737, at a peak of anti-Walpolean feeling, Addison's play had been revived before the patriots' hero the Prince of Wales, those same lines drew a burst of applause, which the prince rose to acknowledge.

If power can corrupt the virtuous, the dictionary allows that superiority to it can redeem men of misguided views. There is Admiral Robert Blake, leader of the navy under the Commonwealth and under Cromwell. Blake had been a national hero since his own time. During the Restoration the victories he had won over the Dutch and Spanish in the 1650s were portrayed as triumphs of 'the English', not merely of the Roundhead cause. The eighteenth century placed him alongside those heroes of Elizabethan sea-power Raleigh and Drake. 'Writers of all parties,' notes *Biographia Britannica*, 'have shown an eagerness to do his memory justice.' Legendary as they were, Blake's naval triumphs were not the only source of his fame. In the eighteenth century, Tories no less than Whigs applauded his immunity to bribery and his readiness to put country before party. Dr Johnson was impressed by his 'disinterestedness'. For Hume, writing in the mid-1750s, he was 'one of the most perfect characters of the age'. *Biographia Britannica* does have its difficulties with Blake. It is troubled by his 'puritanical' inclinations and his 'tincture' of 'republican principles'. Yet, we read, he transcended those defects. He 'loved his country with extraordinary ardour', 'adhering to its interest' and 'doing all he could to exalt its glory' amid the changes of regime wrought by men less 'disinterested and unambitious' than he. He 'never affected the character of a politician', being merely 'solicitous to do his duty' and to serve 'the public good'. Besides, he was immune to financial corruption. In 1704 an account of him in *Lives, English and Foreign* had explained that he 'scorned nothing more than money'. *Biographia Britannica* concurred: 'he was upright to a supreme degree', spurning the opportunities for enrichment from the 'vast sums which passed through his hands'.

There is one opponent of Stuart absolutism for whom the dictionary has unqualified praise. This is Andrew Marvell. The statement in the *Cyclopaedia of English Literature* in 1844 that Marvell 'is better known as a prose writer than a poet, and is still more celebrated as a patriotic member of parliament' would have been uncontroversial at any point in the two centuries after his death in 1678. Marvell's service of Cromwell in the 1650s was for the most part passed over. It was his opposition to Charles II that won praise. Like Sidney he was in the thick of the Restoration political fray. Yet, like Sidney's, his posthumous reputation raised him above it and above the engagement and

Robert Blake. From Frederic Hervey's *The Naval History of Great Britain* (1779).

calculation of party strife. It is Marvell's immunity to corruption, the 'inflexible steadiness' that, in spite of his poverty, was 'proof against all temptations', that the dictionary emphasizes. *Biographia Britannica*, as firm as any radical Whig publication against the erosion of the independence of the legislature, finds a kindred spirit in Marvell. Like many accounts of him in the eighteenth century, the dictionary lifts a passage from the narrative of Marvell's life in Thomas Cooke's edition of his works in 1726. There Cooke describes an (improbable) occasion when Lord Danby, the Lord Treasurer, tried to buy Marvell off with an office. Marvell replied 'that he full well knew the nature of courts . . . and that whoever is distinguished by the favour of princes is always expected to vote in his interest'. When Danby offered a thousand pounds instead, Marvell

> continued equally inflexible to this temptation also, and rejected the money with the same steadfastness of mind with which he refused the proffer of a place . . . so far did the public good overrule all sense of private interest in his honest heart.

To observe the intensity of eighteenth-century admiration earned by Marvell's pecuniary self-denial is to understand the dismay wrought by Dalrymple's exposure of Sidney's acceptance of a thousand guineas from Barillon. Through the eighteenth century, indeed for much of the nineteenth, a litany of praise of Marvell is heard again and again: he was 'an incorruptible patriot', 'virtuous and incorruptible', 'the inflexible patriot'.

The poetry of Marvell's friend John Milton, too, became separated from his prose. Milton had a prominent place in the eighteenth century's pantheon of liberty. Like Sidney he was often linked with Hampden. Hampden and Milton have niches in the Temple of British Worthies at Stowe. Yet the linking of Hampden with Milton, as with Sidney, derived from a moderating impulse. Again like Sidney's, Milton's radicalism was largely bypassed. Where Marvell's prose was better known than his verse, the opposite was true of Milton. Marvell's prose had pleaded only against the 'arbitrary government' of Charles II, a cause that had few eighteenth-century defenders. Milton's had demanded and vindicated the radical transformation of Church and state. Toland, in his biography of Milton in 1698, did try to keep Milton the poet, and Milton the apologist for republicanism and regicide, together. Some eighteenth-century writers, Thomas Hollis to their fore, likewise endorsed the poet's political radicalism. In 1764 the republican Catharine Macaulay had herself painted beside a table on which stood Sidney's *Discourses* and Milton's political works. Occasionally Milton's poems were cited in political causes. Hollis's edition of Sidney's *Discourses*, published in 1763, carries on its title-page a line from *Samson Agonistes* which, as other later eighteenth-century writers noticed, alluded to the trials of the regicides in 1660–62: 'To the unjust tribunals under change of times'. In the era of the prosecution of John Wilkes the words found a fresh application. In 1795 the populist radical Henry Yorke, in his pamphlet *These Are The Times*, invoked a famous phrase from *Paradise Lost*, 'Necessity, the tyrant's plea', to characterize the present government's justifications of its treason trials.

Admirers of Milton's political tracts were none the less dismayed to find how few readers those works attracted. For the most part commentaries on his poetry either bypassed his political radicalism or praised the verse and condemned the politics. Dr Johnson, who knew most of *Paradise Lost* by heart, thought Milton's republicanism the creed of a scoundrel. *Biographia Britannica* is of the same mind. As a poet Milton is 'admirably excellent and in many respects without an equal; an honour to his country and even to human nature'. 'It is agreed on all sides', too, 'that he was a zealous follower of moral beauty and virtue.' But 'his principles', 'gilded with the specious name of absolute liberty, and dislike of the trappings of monarchy', produced 'failings . . . too notorious to deny or disguise'.

Even so, intimated the dictionary, Milton's political career had one redeeming feature. His *The Tenure of Kings and Magistrates*, composed around the time of the regicide, was written 'without any view of a reward'. So at least he was not 'mercenary'. His 'disinterestedness' was dear to the heart of his eighteenth-century admirers. In a transparently autobiographical passage of *Paradise Lost*, Milton has the seraph Abdiel, 'Among the faithless faithful only he', defy the apostasy of his fellow-angels during the war in heaven, as Milton himself, in his own eyes, had remained faithful to his own cause in

1660 while the nation deserted it. In 1740 another journal entitled *The Patriot* quoted the lines about Abdiel's defiance in order to illustrate Milton's hostility, not to the return of Stuart tyranny, but to 'venality' and to 'mercenary' conduct. A series of publications two years earlier had represented Milton as the enemy of the kind of corruption that was thriving under Walpole. Among them was a new edition of his writings, whose sponsors made anti-Walpolean mileage out of one work, the 'Digression' to Milton's *History of Britain*, in which he had denounced 'the ravening seizure of innumerable thieves in office', 'the sweetness of bribery', the wickedness of men who 'huckster the commonwealth'. Even so Milton's own 'disinterestedness' was vulnerable, albeit on a smaller scale than Sidney's, to inspection. He had after all been paid for his secretarial duties during the Interregnum, when a series of Puritan regimes had given him preferment. Not all judges were as charitable as *Biographia Britannica*. The churchman and scholar William Warburton thought Milton's readiness to serve successive masters showed his 'moral character' to have been 'certainly the most corrupt of any man of that age'. David Hume's charge that Milton 'prostituted his pen' during the Interregnum threw the poet's champions on to the defensive.

Edmund Ludlow's involvement in the regicide was not transcended, as Milton's was, by timeless poetic achievement. Yet *Biographia Britannica*, though it baulks at Ludlow's 'exultation' at Pride's Purge and his role in what followed, is more sympathetically disposed towards his politics than to Milton's. Toland's editing had done its work, not only in the short term but in the long. He had won for Ludlow a measure of tolerance, even of respect, across a range of political opinion. In 1726, in his *The Critical History of England*, the orthodox Whig historian John Oldmixon, no friend to Ludlow's radicalism, defended him from the aspersions of Laurence Echard, a historian of royalist sympathies. Oldmixon described his own 'moderate' sentiments and contrasted them with those of that 'errant republican, Algernon Sidney'. While he thought the Roundhead 'resistance' to Charles I to have been 'lawful' until 1648, he 'abhorred' Pride's Purge and the regicide. Yet what right, he asked, had Echard to suppose that Ludlow, merely because he was a 'commonwealth's man', 'can't speak truth or reason?'. Ludlow 'had all the great qualities which Mr Echard informs us are necessary for an historian, as quality, learning, genius, experience, valour and conduct'. Besides, whatever crimes the rulers of the Commonwealth had committed, their rule had been no worse than that of the restored Stuarts. Oldmixon's account reveals the emotional power of the narrative which the *Memoirs* provide of the executions of the regicides, where Charles's judges seem not so much actors against tyranny as its victims. Toland, purging the Puritanism of Ludlow's own narrative of that episode, gave priority instead to a subject much closer to post-Revolutionary hearts, the authorities' brutal disrespect for legal process. Oldmixon is scandalized by the 'inhumanity' of the proceedings.

It is to the country-party theme of the *Memoirs* that *Biographia Britannica* warms. The dictionary endorses their claim that Ludlow's career was impaired by the sway of 'faction'. It quotes them on those royalists – the ones the dictionary calls 'mercenary' – 'who having acquired estates in the service of the parliament, now adhered to the king's party in the defence of what they had got'. For Ludlow, declares the dictionary, 'however he might be mistaken' in his 'republican' aims, was at least true to his own principles, which he held 'sincerely and steadily'. He was thus a cut above those on either side who were selfishly motivated. 'He appears always inflexibly the same, animated by the love, and steady in the pursuit, of what he thought conducive to the liberty of mankind.' That tribute has its counterpart in the dictionary's account of a figure at the opposite end of the political spectrum, William Sancroft, the Archbishop of Canterbury who resigned his see rather than accept the Revolution of 1688. He too, we discover, put principle before advantage. Though 'party zealots who sacrifice truth to prejudice' beleaguer Sancroft's memory, he like Ludlow rose above the passions and prejudices of his own party. The dictionary admires him not for his high Tory views but for his decision to surrender the 'dignities and other . . . greatest advantages' of office. His self-denial is explained by the 'sincerity' with which he adhered to 'what he thought truth and honesty'.

Ludlow's own virtues emerged 'very strongly', the dictionary explains, under the protectorate, when he resisted all Cromwell's attempts to lure him back into the political fold. This was the stand which, to the eighteenth century, proved Ludlow's 'inflexibility'. 'If we except their bravery', rules the dictionary, 'there could not be two more different men in the world' than Ludlow and the 'ambitious' Cromwell, a man whom the dictionary sees largely through Ludlow's eyes. Cromwell 'acted a part' and wore a 'mask' while pursuing his own 'advancement': Ludlow 'spoke his mind plainly and was never taken for any other than he professed himself to be'.

As a parliamentarian narrative of the civil wars, Ludlow's *Memoirs* had one principal rival. This was the *Memorials* of Bulstrode Whitelocke, first published in late 1681 (under the date 1682). They are a far less readable work. A large proportion of the book consists merely of Whitelocke's transcriptions or summaries of printed documents of the 1640s and 1650s. The editor amended Whitelocke's text, though on nothing like the scale on which Toland changed Ludlow's. Working during the exclusion crisis, he cautiously omitted or modified most of Whitelocke's personal reflections, which would be recovered for study only in the later twentieth century. The excisions add to the dullness of the book, but they enhance the sense of impersonal authority at which the publishers evidently aimed and which gave the work, in orthodox Whig eyes, an aura of political safety to which Ludlow's *Memoirs* could never aspire. Those of Whitelocke's own views which the *Memorials* did reproduce were equally reassuring. Whitelocke was no regicide or republican. He 'gives us', explained Oldmixon, 'the sentiments of the sober men in the House of Commons'. Though he sat in the Long Parliament both before and after Pride's Purge and then served the protectorate, his unhappiness at the revolutionary course of events and at military rule was plain. Yet *Biographia Britannica* has less respect for him than for Ludlow. The 'patriot party in the House of Commons', it notices, was opposed to Whitelocke, for he was 'a temporising gentleman', 'of too easy a nature. . . . He had not the resolution vigorously and effectually to oppose what his own words and professions declare he did not like.' He 'always sided with the strongest, and where most was to be gained'. The Ludlow of the *Memoirs* has country-party instincts, the Whitelocke of the *Memorials* court-party ones.

The dictionary's entry on Ludlow bears the influence of the preface to Richard Baron's edition of the *Memoirs* of 1751, a publication which accompanied Baron's edition of Sidney's *Discourses* in the same year. (There seems to have been a plan to reprint the *Memoirs* – and the Ludlow 'Letters' – together with the *Discourses* in 1761; and the 1771 edition of the *Memoirs* would be followed by the fresh edition of the *Discourses* in 1772.) To Baron, Ludlow was 'a man of such excellent spirit, such generous principles, and performed such great services to his country, that his name and memory will ever be dear and precious to the lovers of liberty'. Like Toland, whose hints he followed, Baron cloaked a radical purpose in a country-party message. Again like Toland, he thus presented a Ludlow whose radicalism could seem a secondary characteristic. Where the first edition of the *Memoirs* had been completed by an appendix of documents showing that Charles had deserved his death, Baron included as an appendix the indictment of Charles prepared for his trial by Ludlow's friend John Cook. Yet when Baron's preface touches on the regicide it records merely that Ludlow was 'far from being ashamed' of his part in it. And even if he helped to destroy the king, he was, it seems, no republican. Toland had blurred the edges of Ludlow's republicanism: Baron in effect renounces it. Ludlow fought, Baron implies, only for 'law' and 'liberty' and his 'country', opposing not monarchy itself but 'arbitrary power' and the abuse of 'the prerogative'. He was not to blame for the 'disorders' after the king's death. It was the royal court, not Charles himself, that he disliked. Almost everyone in the eighteenth century could agree about the failings of courts. Ludlow, says Baron, 'vigorously opposed the court-measures', acting 'sincerely' for the public good 'without any private views or sinister ends'. 'A man of serious thought and consideration', he was 'inflexible' once he had decided where right lay. In the Folger Library in Washington there is a copy of the 1751 edition, annotated by an eighteenth-century hand (probably English). The themes which struck the annotator were largely those country-party ones which Toland had introduced or highlighted: the threat to liberty and parliamentary rule from a standing army; the exclusion of patriotism from the conduct of foreign policy; electoral corruption and reform; bribery; Oliver Cromwell's ambition; the conflicting claims of private and public interest.

Toland himself, in introducing the *Memoirs*, compared Ludlow's 'virtues' to Cato's. In 1780 Thomas Tyers revived the parallel. Though no republican, Tyers permitted himself to 'erect' a tribute to the memory of the 'stubborn' Ludlow, 'that gallant Englishman who equalled Cato in disinterestedness, intrepidity, steadiness of principle and conduct'. Charles James Fox, no republican either, linked Ludlow and Sidney with Cato. Joseph Towers's *Biographical Dictionary* of 1766–73, which drew on *Biographia Britannica*, took a similar stance. Though it condemned Pride's Purge and the regicide, it observed that the 'honest' Ludlow 'appears to have acted from principle'. It was Ludlow's 'adherence to principle and affection to the public', his superiority to 'partial feelings', that struck Catharine Macaulay.* Across a wide range of political opinion other seventeenth-century commonwealthmen received comparable praise, the more readily since the republicanism of that era, being now so distant, seemed to some (though by no means all) less than alarming. 'Whatever we may think' of Milton's 'political tenets', urged his biographer William Hayley in 1794, 'let us render justice to the courage and consistency with which he supported them'. Hayley was impressed by the defiance with which Ludlow had stood out against Cromwell's usurpation. He admired the same stand in John Bradshaw, who had been President of the court that tried Charles I and then of the Council of State. 'The odium' which Bradshaw 'justly incurred' from the regicide, Hayley ruled, had unfairly hidden the 'great qualities' of that 'inflexible' figure.

Sidney was viewed by some – even if not by *Biographia Britannica* – in a similar light. If he had republican principles, remarked James Ralph, 'surely he that acts up to his principles, however erroneous those principles may be, is a more worthy being than he who has no principles at all'. John Granger, in his biographical dictionary of 1779, remarked that though Sidney had strayed into republicanism he had

* Earlier in the century the Tory Jonathan Swift, in explaining that 'we read with pleasure the memoirs of several authors whose party we disapprove, if they be written with nature and truth', acknowledged that 'even the violent flat relation of Ludlow, though written in a spirit of rage, prejudice and vanity, doth not want its advocates'. Swift elsewhere described the *Memoirs*, and Sidney's *Discourses*, as 'seditious and republican'. Yet his Toryism, like Pope's, had a country-party dimension. He admitted to having had, in his early career, a 'mortal antipathy to standing armies', and he quoted Ludlow's *Memoirs* to demonstrate the danger of them. The Tory Roger North, in his *Examen* (1740), noted that Ludlow's *Memoirs*, though 'violent', were 'in their way honest' and were thus a 'most useful history'.

at least held that creed 'from speculation and principle', not, 'as others', 'from animosity and faction'. Granger greatly preferred him to his enemy the first Earl of Shaftesbury, the 'flexibility' of whose 'principles' he condemned. Like *Biographia Britannica* Granger discovered patriot sentiment on both sides in the civil wars. In the 'honest' Clarendon, who refused to aid Charles II's attempt 'to enslave millions', he found 'all the virtues of a Cato'. Much earlier in the century, in 1734, even the establishment Whig Lord Hervey, no friend to either Tory or patriot allegiances, had acknowledged Clarendon to have been 'a true patriot', but for whose restraining influence the English would have been made 'as absolute slaves as the Turks and the Persians'.

The eighteenth-century admiration for public spirit, which qualified the age's dislike of the republicanism of the civil wars, also modified, indeed sometimes countered, its condemnation of the Commonwealth. Again Toland's editing, which had brought the eulogies of that regime's integrity and achievements in Ludlow's *Memoirs* and Sidney's *Discourses* into print, had done its work. Those tributes left their mark not only on the accounts of such republican historians as Catharine Macaulay in the later eighteenth century and William Godwin in the early nineteenth, but on writers far less sympathetic to republicanism. In 1751 William Guthrie, who was appalled by the regicide and the abolition of the monarchy, none the less explained in his *History of England* that under the Commonwealth 'the glory of England was now the ruling passion', so that the regime's energies were not distracted by 'private disputes'. Eight years earlier William Warburton declared (in his edition of Pope's *An Essay on Man*) that the 'spirit of liberty was at its height' under the Commonwealth, when the nation was 'conducted by a set of the greatest geniuses for government ever embarked together in a common cause'. Coming from Warburton that was some tribute. Descended from a royalist, he sympathetically annotated Clarendon's *History* (and claimed to have read most of the pamphlet literature of the civil wars). He despised the political virulence of Milton, thought Toland's admiring life of him a work of 'malignity and folly', and described Ludlow as 'furious' and 'mad' (though 'apparently honest').

In the pages of Ludlow and Sidney the Commonwealth looked like a patriot administration, triumphant at sea, overcoming faction and self-interest at home, appointing men to posts on the basis of merit rather than favour. In June 1760 *The Monitor* silently appropriated, as did other eighteenth-century publications, the tribute to the rule of the Commonwealth in Slingsby Bethel's *The World's Mistake in Oliver Cromwell*: 'the kingdom was arrived at the highest pitch of trade, wealth and honour that it, in any age, ever yet knew'. The regime's exploits abroad took a form particularly attractive to eighteenth-century patriots, for once its royalist enemies had been defeated it had concentrated not on military but on maritime power. If only such a policy were adopted now, it would obviate that pretext for national enslavement, the standing army. The emphasis in Ludlow's *Memoirs* on the vigilance of the Commonwealth, and (albeit to a lesser extent) of the Long Parliament in the 1640s, against the waste and abuse of public funds also impressed an age aghast at the expansion of public spending, of expenditure on the army, of the civil list. 'Though the friends to monarchy will always bewail the distractions' and 'oppressions' of the 'anarchy' of the civil wars, reckoned *The Monitor* in April 1758, the Long Parliament's 'care of public money' 'cannot be too much aplauded'. If only, the journal reflected, the same 'watchfulness' had been exerted in the financial negotiations between Crown and parliament under William III, from which England's present evils flowed!

In all eighteenth-century discussions of Edmund Ludlow, one subject is conspicuous by its absence: religion. *Biographia Britannica*, which admired Ludlow in spite of his republicanism, would have been horrified had it known about his religion. The dictionary is at home with seventeenth-century religion only when it can describe it as 'piety', a frame of mind conducive to seriousness of mind and purpose, to right conduct, to civil and social harmony, but not to the 'ungenerous' trait of theological dogmatism and zeal. John Bastwick, that martyr, in Puritan eyes, to persecution by Archbishop Laud, was in the dictionary's view 'a man more remarkable for the great noise he made in the world than for any singular merit of his own'. Ludlow had been mortified when he saw religion being challenged by reason: the dictionary is shocked when it finds reason being undermined by religion. From the colourful career of the Quaker James Nayler, who was punished for blasphemy by the parliament of 1656, we learn that the most plentiful source of error and delusion, and a principle the most mischievous of any of its consequences, is a spirit of enthusiasm, spurred on by ambition and pride. This blind and ungovernable guide has, at different times, led an incredible number of persons of weak judgement and strong imagination through a maze of such strange and unaccountable follies as, one would imagine, could never have entered into the thoughts of a creature endowed with reason: such follies as have rendered persons possessed with them extremely troublesome, a plague to the world as well as to themselves; and their actions have been a disgrace to human nature and a scandal to the Christian name. It behoves therefore every honest and rational person to watch against so troublesome an enemy, and to take particular care not to give so disagreeable a guest any admittance into his bosom; not only for his own sake but also for the benefit of the society to which he belongs.

The manifestation of enthusiasm that most troubles the dictionary is the providentialism of the Puritans. The detection and interpretation of God's interventions in politics, and of his 'judgements' upon them, had been the central preoccupation of Ludlow's 'A Voice from the Watch Tower'. *Biographia Britannica* knew where providentialist thinking led. Of all the 'deep and dangerous errors' of Oliver Cromwell, that 'great pretender to enthusiasms and revelations', the gravest was his belief that 'success was a mark of divine approbation'. In 1739 even Cromwell's sympathetic biographer John Banks had conceded that Oliver's 'continual pretensions of humility and devotion, ascribing the glory of all his actions to the providence of God', were 'one of his most effectual engines' in those 'enthusiastical times'. The eighteenth century was much influenced by Gilbert Burnet's account of Cromwell's religion. Oliver, wrote Burnet, was 'a true enthusiast', who held a 'principle', conducive to 'all the practices both of falsehood and cruelty', that 'moral laws were only binding on ordinary occasions' and that 'upon extraordinary ones these might be superseded'. Cromwell was widely supposed to have also held the blasphemous belief that when he prayed to God he received concrete political advice in return.

In its pronouncements on enthusiasm *Biographia Britannica* again joins hands, across the gap of political allegiance, with *Cato's Letters*. John Trenchard, remarked his fellow-author of the *Letters* Thomas Gordon, was 'obnoxious to bigots' for 'exposing their stupid, sour and narrow imaginations'. 'Cato' declares that men's 'presumption' in 'meddling with the secret councils of God' is the product of worldly 'prejudices'. From the 'religious madness called enthusiasm', that 'fever in the head', there arises 'a flaming conceit that we have great personal interests with the deity, and that the deity is eminently employed about us, or in us; that he . . . sets us far above those who have less pride and more sense than ourselves'. 'Cato', like the dictionary, defends the claims of 'reason' against 'enthusiasm'. We cannot 'serve God by sequestering for a time all the faculties which he has given us, by sending our wits out of doors to make room for grace'. For 'Cato' as for the dictionary, religion properly serves social improvement and harmony. It teaches men to love their neighbours. It 'improves and enlarges the faculties of men, exalts their spirits, . . . inspires them with generous and beneficent affections to one another'. Yet the 'parties and factions' of religion, by 'throwing God's judgements at one another, and impiously confining his providence and mercies to themselves', 'have raised up and inflamed implacable hatred, animosities and uncharitableness amongst men of the same nation'. 'Cato' has in mind the self-styled 'saints' of the civil wars (in whose number Ludlow counted himself) and above all Cromwell, whose supposition that 'all that he did was the Lord's doings' was 'downright impudence'. Other eighteenth-century country and patriot publications disowned the 'fanaticism' and 'enthusiasm' of the civil wars. It was 'the wild rage' of 'mad enthusiasm', observed the patriot poet James Thomson, that had replaced the Long Parliament's honourable struggle for liberty in its early stages with a lawless 'conflagration' and destroyed the balanced constitution.

The eighteenth century's distaste for seventeenth-century Puritanism explains the absence from its pantheon of seventeenth-century patriots of the figure whom modern students of the civil wars might expect to find as its presiding spirit: Sir Henry Vane. If there was a single hero of their time for Ludlow, for Sidney, for Milton, it was Vane. Over the course of the Long Parliament there was no more influential a member. He worked indefatigably for the war effort and outmanoeuvred those who sought accommodation with the king. Under the Commonwealth he carried out, with great energy and skill, the naval reforms that made Blake's triumphs possible.

Both from a republican and from a country-party perspective he was sound on Cromwell, for although he had been Oliver's most formidable parliamentary ally he turned against him after the coup of April 1653. His execution in 1662 gave him a martyr status akin to that acquired by Sidney twenty-one years later. Yet by the time of Sidney's death, Vane's religion had placed him beyond reclamation. There were non-Puritan features of Milton, Sidney, Harrington and Blake that Toland and his successors could bring into the foreground while pushing their faith into the background. Ludlow's Puritanism could be wiped from the record. But Vane's writings, opaque, cloudy speculations on the inner life of the spirit and on the Book of Revelation, would have defied even Toland's ingenuity. No non-religious substance could have been extracted from them. In their own time they had been revered by a group of disciples, 'Vanists' as they came to be called, but had baffled most other people. His faith was despised and mocked after the Restoration. Clarendon's *History*, which remarked on Vane's 'giddiness' in religion, on the corruption of his 'reason and understanding' by his 'perfect enthusiasm', perpetuated the hostility to it.

Toland and his successors did what they could. Though they were unable to make use of Vane's own words, they could adopt or adapt the praises his contemporaries had bestowed on him. They were helped by the sonnet which had been addressed by Milton to him in 1652 and had been defiantly included in a life of Vane published immediately after his execution ten years later. Milton's subject is Vane's belief, which the poet shares, in the separation of Church from state. As usual, Milton's religious instincts combine with classical ones. A 'better senator' than Vane 'ne'er held/ The helm of Rome, when gowns not arms repelled/ The fierce Epirot and the African bold.' So at least Vane could be given Roman trimmings. Toland worked hard, in rewriting Ludlow's manuscript, to convert the spirituality which Ludlow revered in Vane into something secular. Vane's zeal for 'the good of the Commonwealth' and for 'the public service' is emphasized. Toland credits Vane, in words that Ludlow's account of him in the corresponding portion of the Bodleian manuscript does not use, with 'integrity', with 'a just and noble eloquence', with 'an easy and graceful manner of speaking'. It was through Vane's management of the navy

Vane. From George Sykes's *The Life and Death of Sir Henry Vane, Kt.* (1662).

that men 'were brought to understand that they were not placed in employments to serve themselves, but to serve the public'. Vane is credited – wrongly, the research of Violet Rowe has suggested – with an immunity to the financial temptations of office, and with a readiness to give up half his salary as Treasurer of the Navy 'towards carrying on the war for the liberties of England'. That 'generous instance of disinterested virtue', as the *Memoirs* call it, won applause from the later eighteenth century. It won more in the early nineteenth. For Vane's star, for reasons to which we shall come, had begun to rise, just as those of Ludlow and Sidney had begun to fall. For most of the eighteenth century, however, he could not compete with them or with Milton.

Sidney's reverence for Vane – 'Ah, noble Vane!' – surfaces in his *Court Maxims*. The king's aim in bringing Vane to the block, Sidney there says, must have been 'to destroy, as in its root, all virtue, wisdom and godliness, since those who were eminent in any of those qualities looked on him as their master'. There survives, in the Hertfordshire Record Office, a manuscript, in a hand apparently of the late seventeenth or early eighteenth century, entitled 'The Character of Sir Henry Vane by Algernon Sidney'. It was not printed. Is it authentic? Or is it, like 'The Honourable Algernon Sidney's Letter against Bribery and Corruption', a product of the Whig history factory? Was it prepared for publication but – like *Court Maxims* but unlike the 'Letter' – not published? The manuscript tells us of Vane's 'piety and virtue', 'the severity of his manners', 'his invincible spirit and magnanimity', his 'sanctity of life', even his 'great zeal and devotion to God', but not of his religious doctrines. Vane, we read, had Stoic virtues, 'frugality', 'tranquillity of mind', 'constant and steady behaviour and resolution in the greatest adversity', virtues which shone in the calm with which he met his death. Those, admittedly, were qualities to appeal as much to Sidney himself as to the country-party readers whom the radical Whigs of the 1690s would woo. But why does the manuscript of the 'Character' of Vane not so much as hint at that apocalyptic theology to which he subscribed and to which Sidney's own *Court Maxims* give voice? Like Ludlow's *Memoirs* the 'Character' concentrates not on Vane's faith but on his desire to serve 'his country', 'the good of his country', 'the public good'. It resembles the *Memoirs*, too, in explaining that when Cromwell 'corrupted the army' it lost its 'discipline' and became 'subject to bribery'.

If Toland and his circle did plan to launch a non-Puritan Vane, they evidently thought better of it (just as it may have been they who considered but decided against the publication of Sidney's *Court Maxims*). The eighteenth century, except towards its end, barely noticed Vane's virtues. His 'enthusiasm' and 'fanaticism' made him an easy target for Tories. John Oldmixon, the moderate Whig historian of the 1720s, ventured the nearest thing the orthodox Whigs produced to an apologia for him. Shocked by Vane's 'murder', Oldmixon again found the republican cause less objectionable than that of Stuart tyranny. 'We all know,' he remarked in Vane's defence, 'that the religious of those times used a set of pathetic terms.' 'It's now called cant, and perhaps there was too much affectation in it'; but at heart Vane had been 'a man of sense'. It was no use. *Biographia Britannica*, so forbearing towards Ludlow, laid into Vane, 'an enthusiastic rigid Puritan', 'giddy', 'hot-headed', 'always an enemy to peace', a man 'of very ambiguous character' and of a 'working and unquiet fancy'. Admittedly he had 'remained inflexible' under Cromwell, but that patriot virtue could not outweigh his 'enthusiasm'. The dictionary considered the tribute to Vane in Ludlow's *Memoirs* and found it unpersuasive.

Biographia Britannica, which values independence from power, admires too the social status and economic solidity that make it possible. Written in the most aristocratic era England has known since the middle ages, it is unhesitating in its reverence for ancient and honourable descent. It rallies behind one 'very honourably descended politician', the Elizabethan scholar and conspirator Henry Cuffe, who has been 'very unjustly said' to have been lowly born. The eighteenth century liked to bestow nobility and gentility on its heroes of the past. The Roman historian Tacitus, that 'new man' of imperial Rome, whose tense, epigrammatic dissection of tyranny had haunted the political thinking of the Renaissance, appeared before the public in 1728 in a translation of gentlemanly leisureliness by Thomas Gordon, who credited him with 'the good sense and breeding of a gentleman'.

In the late seventeenth century and the early eighteenth the minds of radical Whigs had been divided about the claims of wealth and status. On the one hand the radicals maintained that rich MPs of ancient families would be more resistant to bribery than poor ones. On the other they saw oppressive and selfish instincts in the nobility and would have liked to widen the social base of land ownership and of political participation. They were therefore torn between deferring to aristocratic qualities and questioning them. Toland had it both ways. The 'eternal fame' that 'some' of the nobles of the middle ages had 'worthily acquired', he explained, 'was wholly owing to those glorious actions they performed for their country, and not in the least to that immoderate power they might then exercise over the people'. He has it both ways again in Ludlow's *Memoirs*, remarking in the preface that Ludlow was of 'an ancient and worthy family, if that be anything'. In ensuing generations, remarks about Ludlow's social standing display no such ambivalence. Oldmixon, in repudiating the attack on Ludlow by Laurence Echard, that devotee of Clarendon's *History*, pointed out that Ludlow was 'of as ancient a family as Lord Clarendon, and of a much better fortune'. He noted too that Ludlow's social prominence had secured him election for one of the two prestigious county seats in Wiltshire, whereas Clarendon (at that time a commoner) managed to win only a borough seat in the same county. In the preface to Richard Baron's edition of the *Memoirs* in 1751, no hint of qualification attends the endorsement of Ludlow's membership of 'a family of considerable rank'. The first edition of the *Memoirs*, in 1698–9, had been cheaply printed. The editions of 1751 and 1771, like other eighteenth-century editions of works within the Toland–Darby canon, were elegant productions, fit to adorn the libraries of gentlemen. No one would have guessed now that in his own time Ludlow had been called 'Levelling Ludlow'. The criticisms in the *Memoirs* of the House of Lords and of noble oppression and self-interest were overlooked.

It would not have occurred to Algernon Sidney's contemporaries to bestow the word 'Levelling' on him. His consciousness of his noble ancestry appealed to the eighteenth century, when his admirers liked to think that the recklessness of the conspiracy of 1683 had been the fault of its lower-class adherents, not of Sidney and its other aristocratic ones. Yet the *Discourses* note the suffering wrought by aristocratic rack-renting; they plead for a broadening of the ruling class; they insist that a healthy government, even though it will be predominantly aristocratic, will have a vigorous democratic element too, so vigorous that the term 'popular government', which he derived from the populist republicanism of the Italian Renaissance, can properly be applied to it. For most of the eighteenth century that dimension of his thought escaped notice.

Towards the end of the same century it began to receive it. At that time there emerged the demands for parliamentary reform, and the stirrings of industrial and popular unrest, that would grow into the great nineteenth-century movement for political enfranchisement and social improvement. Sidney's reputation among the new radicals, who at first warmed to him and later cooled, can be as informative a barometer of public values as his earlier standing. In the short term the radical movement gave fresh life to the patriot interpretation of the seventeenth century promoted by the Darby–Toland canon. In the long term it destroyed it. The economic grievances which would come to figure so largely in populist thinking, and would eventually emancipate it from the radical Whig and country-party traditions, were less prominent in the early stages of the movement. Radicalism grew out of patriot sentiment and inherited many of its assumptions. John Wilkes, in some respects the launcher of populist radicalism, for most of his career pursued a programme of reform that stood within the country tradition. 'Corruption', that obsessive theme in patriot minds, was likewise to the fore in populist ones. Populism, like patriotism, grew up as an anti-political movement, suspicious of the executive and determined to purge it. The movement for parliamentary reform, which in time became an assertion of the right to vote, was in its earlier phases dominated by different concerns: the removal of the rotten boroughs, those instruments by which governments controlled the Commons, and the provision of a firm electoral base for watchfulness against the power of the state.

Many populist radicals of the later eighteenth and earlier nineteenth centuries adopted the term 'patriot'. It had the advantage, for them as for those opponents of Walpole who had given the word a wide currency, of bestowing legitimacy on protest. In Walpole's time it was parliamentary opposition that sought legitimacy against charges of disloyalty: now it was popular agitation. In both cases the language of patriotism served to separate the nation from its government. There were admittedly reservations in the populist camp, for the supporters of government had begun to make their own bids for control of the term patriot. They had started to make the word what in the nineteenth century it would generally become, an uncritical appellation betokening support, especially in foreign affairs, for one's country right or wrong. Perhaps in reaction against that tendency the populist radical John Thelwall described patriotism, in his *The Tribune* in 1796, as 'a narrow sectarian principle', the source indeed 'of very splendid actions, but the parent at the same time of much illiberality and injustice, of contentions, massacres and devastations'. The loyalist sentiment stimulated by the Napoleonic wars encouraged patriotism in the new, uncritical sense. In the songs prompted by the renewal of the wars in 1803, Sidney was recruited, along with King Alfred, Queen Elizabeth, Hampden, William III, Marlborough and Nelson, to the needs of national defence, his death transformed into a symbol of the harmony of king and country:

> Repel the foe that, desperate, dares invade
> The land protected by great SIDNEY'S shade.
> And in the cause for which your HAMPDEN bled,
> Should every Briton's blood be freely shed.

Yet if there was a loyalist Sidney there was a much more conspicuous populist one. The new radicalism initially took him to its heart. The eloquence of his paeans to Roman liberty, and of his attacks on courtly corruption and standing armies, proved no less attractive to the new generation of radicals, to Wilkes and Horne Tooke and James Burgh and John Thelwall and Major Cartwright (who wanted his country run by 'men who reason and feel like Locke and Sidney'), as it had to Toland and to 'Cato'. The Society for Constitutional Information, founded by Tooke, which aimed to bring historical and political knowledge to a popular audience, publicized the *Discourses*. The work appears to have been made available in a cheap format in the 1790s, and would be serialized in a similar form early in the next century. In 1794 a series of 'Political Classics', intended for popular instruction, included a memoir of Sidney and a number of documents relating to his life and death, but not the more demanding *Discourses*.

In the service of populist sentiment, as of country-party and patriot feeling before it, Sidney was recast. His allusions to 'the people', a term which in his as in most seventeenth-century writings had included only men of some independence of means and character, were now interpreted in a more extensive light. Not for the first time, readers swooped on statements in the *Discourses* that are peripheral to the main arguments of the work. In passages near the end Sidney briefly addresses the question of the relationship between members of parliament and their electors. He describes MPs as 'delegates' and 'deputies', to whom their constituents do not give 'absolute power' and who merit infamy if they 'betray the trust' of those who choose them. Those passages were emphasized by eighteenth-century country-party commentators, who used them to remind MPs that their obligations lay to the nation, not to the court, and who found in them support for the practice of issuing 'instructions' by constituents to their members. The populist radicals found in the same passages an argument not only for that practice but for the extension of the franchise.

The influence of Sidney's writings remained intertwined with the memory of his martyrdom. When Horne Tooke was charged with high treason in 1794, Charles James Fox told parliament that his case resembled Sidney's, 'the very sound' of whose 'name is still animating to every Englishman attached to the glorious cause' of liberty. Tooke's fellow-victim John Thelwall, finding himself charged, like Sidney before him, with aiming to kill the king, proposed to base his defence at his trial on Sidney's before Jeffreys. Thelwall would remember the moment in the Tower when he and Tooke, 'from the bars and grates of our respective windows, at the still hour of midnight, the moon scattering her rays over the still surface of the river', called to each other the names of 'those murdered patriots' of 1683, Sidney and the Earl of Essex, 'who had been the preoccupants of our dungeons'. They 'exulted in the sacrifice' they 'were possibly to make', though in the event they were acquitted and the prosecutors were covered in ridicule. To Thelwall, Sidney was a living presence. While impatient with aristocratic Whiggism, Thelwall conceded that at least it had 'stamped with authority and approbation the political speculations of a Sidney' and had 'consecrated the memory of the holy martyrs of liberty', Hampden, Sidney and Russell, 'engraving them as upon adamantine pillars in the temple of eternal fame and virtue'. Thelwall named one of his sons Algernon Sidney Thelwall and another John Hampden Thelwall. 'The cause for which I suffered', he pronounced, was that 'for which a Hampden fell, a Sidney bled'. It was also, he added, that for which the Gracchi, the champions of popular rights in late republican Rome, perished. For Thelwall was drawn to the classical, not the Christian resonances of Sidney's travails. As readily as patriot writers earlier in the century, he condemned the 'fanatics' of 1649. In the same spirit Henry Yorke, though he admired the Rump, was repelled by the 'religious cant' of that era, when 'every sect' was 'impelled by fanaticism'.

Sidney's arguments for resistance to tyranny, already revived in response to George III's constitutional aspirations, were given a fresh edge by the suppression of free speech in the 1790s, by the trials of Thelwall and Tooke and others in 1794, by the suspension of Habeas Corpus in the same year, and by the passage of the Treasonable Practices Act and the Seditious Meetings Act in 1795. Henry Yorke, bidding defiance to those measures, cited the *Discourses* and recalled

> the fate of the British patriots who perished in the last century. . . . Let us invoke the spirits of Hampden, Russell, Pym, Vane and ALGERNON SIDNEY! And now that I mention Sidney I feel my heart glow with a patriotic fervour, and I glory to hold up his life, writings, courage, and even his death to the imitation of Englishmen. He was ever plotting and scheming the subversion of a government which he considered as a cruel and iniquitous system of oppression.

Cautious spirits among Whigs and patriots had preferred to dwell on the fate of Russell rather than Sidney. Yorke reversed that priority. Somewhat fancifully he noted that, if tears of pity met Russell's death, 'no symptoms of effeminate grief were visible' upon that of Sidney, 'THE GREAT CONSPIRATOR', when instead 'the spectators glowed with the fire of republican freedom and were roused to animation'.

The appeal of Sidney the victim of oppression spread abroad, to

Germany and more markedly to France. In the years from the outbreak of the French Revolution in 1789 many prisoners found that images of Sidney came into their minds. Parallels between Bourbon and Stuart tyranny were frequently drawn. French revolutionaries carried busts of Sidney on demonstrations. It was in France that William Wordsworth developed, under the influence of his friends among the Girondins, his enthusiasm for Sidney, Harrington and 'others who called Milton friend'. In England there was added, to Sidney the populist reformer, Sidney the Romantic. Shelley's 'blood boiled' to think how 'Sidney's and Hampden's blood was wasted'. In a poem written in or around 1814 the young Keats, shocked by the 'infatuate Britons' who continued to commemorate 29 May, the anniversary of the Restoration, urged them instead to 'revere' England's seventeenth-century 'patriots', 'gallant Sidney' at their head. Byron's notes to *Childe Harold* honoured Sidney. Browning and Tennyson warmed to him in their youth. When, in the 1790s, Sidney's body was exhumed by devotees and found to be 'very perfect', the young poet Southey, still in his radical phase, wrote an 'Epitaph on Algernon Sidney'. Coleridge, to whom Sidney was 'a lifelong hero', annotated the *Discourses* 'with a beating heart'. The influence of the Darby–Toland canon endured. Sidney, Milton and Harrington were, to Coleridge, 'sages and patriots that being dead yet speak to us'.

By now adulation of Sidney had again become what it had been in the years after his death, a badge of unorthodoxy. The radicals and Romantics knew they were defying a public mood, which had been succoured by the French Revolution and by England's war against French republicanism. For a time orthodox Whigs saw the Revolution as a French 1688, and were appalled by the hostility of their fellow-Englishmen to it. But most of them drew back from the execution of Louis XVI in 1793 and its attendant violence. The French Revolution probably inflicted more lasting damage on Sidney's standing than Sir John Dalrymple's charges had done twenty years earlier. In 1808 the Whig writer Francis Jeffrey lamented in the *Edinburgh Review* that it had become 'unfashionable and, we are afraid, not very popular to talk of the tyranny of the Stuarts and the triumph of [1688] in the tone' that until recently had been 'universal and established'. 'A sort of tacit convention' had been entered into to say nothing for a while of the follies and vices of princes, the tyranny of the court and the rights of the people. The Revolution of 1688, it was agreed, could not be mentioned with praise without giving some indirect encouragement to the Revolution of 1789; and it was thought as well to say nothing in favour of Hampden or Russell or Sidney, for fear it might give spirits to Robespierre, Danton or Marat.

The year of Jeffrey's remarks did produce a flicker of hope. At the time of the Spanish uprising against the Napoleonic regime, according to Coleridge, 'Englishmen of all parties recurred, *in toto*, to the old English principles, and spoke of their Hampdens, Sidneys and Miltons with the old enthusiasm.' If so the mood did not last.

The Tory reaction of the Napoleonic wars would pass too. More fundamental and enduring objections to the patriot pantheon came not from conservative forces but from radical ones. The radicals and Romantics who embraced Sidney's memory were in the main of middle-class rather than working-class background and outlook. Coleridge contrasted Sidney's prose, which 'differs not at all from that which every well-educated gentleman would wish to write', with 'the vulgar seditions of Corresponding Societies and Manchester Clubs'. It was the rise of working-class agitation in the nineteenth century that gradually destroyed Sidney's radical credentials. As early as 1813 his biographer G. W. Meadley conceded that Algernon's views, 'being chiefly directed to the circumstances of the higher and middling classes of society', offered no hope to the suffering 'lower ranks'. The eighteenth century had deprived Sidney of such chance of lasting working-class appeal as he had, partly by emphasizing his aristocratic qualities, partly by absorbing him within respectable Whig thought. The extent of the second process is illustrated in a remark of the future Whig leader Lord John Russell in 1819. It was to such men as Sidney and Lord John's own ancestor William Lord Russell, he wrote, 'that we owe the permanency and excellence of our constitution'. Sidney's courage, and his 'attachment to the ancient principles of the constitution and the inalienable right of resistance', he ruled, had been a chief cause 'of that Revolution to which we owe our present liberties'. Fourteen years later Richard Carlile, an ally of working-class radicals, derided Lord John Russell and other leading Whigs who had 'throughout their lives toasted the names of Hampden, Russell and Sidney'. 'There must', he told his friends, be 'nothing Whiggish' in the radical programme, 'no toasting of "Hampden that died in the field, and Russell and Sidney on the scaffold." That was all very well in its day; but that day has gone by, not again to return.'

Not everyone agreed. Sidney and other patriots had been recommended to working-class readers in the 1790s. In the first half of the nineteenth century the old patriot hatred of 'party' and 'politicians' often resurfaced in the literature of popular radicalism. The clubs for young working men founded by the Chartist Thomas Cooper had classes named after 'the worthies of old England': the 'Algernon Sidney class', the 'John Hampden class', the 'Andrew Marvell class'. As late as 1854 we find *The People's Paper* printing (or at any rate launching) a serialization of 'The Trial of Sidney the Patriot'. Eleven years earlier the *English Chartist Circular* paid tribute to another patriot hero, Andrew Marvell. It commended his opposition to standing armies, a resonant theme for some radicals of the Industrial Revolution, among whom the enthusiasm of seventeenth-century republicans for a citizen militia was transmuted into an insistence on the right of working people to bear arms. But though the Chartists kept the Whig heroes alive, they were the last substantial radical group to find inspiration in them.

Sidney himself recalled the lost liberties of classical antiquity and medieval England. Many radicals of the early nineteenth century turned their backs on the liberties of the past, which, they maintained, had benefited only aristocrats. The thinking of John Wilkes and of Charles James Fox, those admirers of Sidney, had remained rooted in the knowledge and love of the classics. John Thelwall's writings, too, made extensive use of classical literature, partly as a way round censorship, which found observations on distant history harder to deal with than directly contemporary ones, but also because of his own classical instincts. He republished Walter Moyle's *An Essay upon the Constitution of the Roman Government* under the title *Democracy Vindicated*, assisting his own popular readership by translating passages which Moyle had left in Latin. He was troubled, however, by some of Moyle's undemocratic sympathies. By the early nineteenth century the ancient republics were out of favour among the radicals, thanks not least to the rise of anti-slavery sentiment. In 1828, in an aside from a commentary on the English civil wars, the republican John Rutt remarked that 'the people of England' had been 'as little concerned by Magna Carta as the numerous slave-populations of Greece and Rome were protected by' the institutions of 'the mis-called free states of antiquity'. In 1846 Edmund Clarke, addressing the Manchester Mechanics Institute on Cromwellian England, paused to glance at the history of Rome under the rule of those 'freebooters' the senators. To the eighteenth century, which had savoured and decorated the classicism of Sidney, Algernon was the 'British Brutus': Clarke judged that schoolboys had the story of the death of Julius Caesar drummed into their heads because 'it is a lesson pregnant with aristocratic morality'. Indeed the whole 'history of Rome is a manual of political wisdom for the use of all young noblemen, and most of them learn the lessons which it professes to teach'.

In the ancient and medieval governments which he admired, Sidney located the principle of constitutional mixture or balance, the ideal for which he 'professed much veneration'. The eighteenth century counted the balance of its own constitution its principal political blessing. From the time of Tom Paine, however, mixed government was condemned by radicals and republicans as a fiction, designed for the convenience of Crown and nobility, who had used it to divide the spoils of government between themselves. For republicanism had changed its character and purpose. In the seventeenth century its target had been the power of kings, which in Sidney's eyes it was the function of the nobility to restrain. By the late eighteenth century its target was the power and privileges of the ruling class, of which the king was merely the head. Across the Atlantic, John Adams, his thought steeped in seventeenth-century English republicanism, was troubled by the new attack on constitutional checks and balances. Paine's system of government, he protested, was 'so democratical, without restraint or even attempt at any equilibrium or equipoise, that it must produce confusion and every evil work'. English radicals of and after Paine's generation – Henry Yorke, James Mackintosh, William Godwin, Rutt – took his side: constitutional 'balance', they maintained, was 'farcical', a mask for corruption, 'a government not of check, but of conspiracy'. To approve of a constitution as a set of checks by separate interests on each other, rather than as the servant of a common interest, seemed to Yorke a 'blasphemy against human nature'.

Sidney, the venerator of mixed government, had found it hard to explain how the Commonwealth of 1649–53, that unchecked unicameral government, had achieved the wondrous deeds that he lauded. To radicals of the late eighteenth and the early nineteenth century the Commonwealth's refusal to allow any balance to its power seemed a virtue. Eventually such changes of perspective would help to make Sidney's name redundant to populist radicalism. For a time, however, he was read not as the advocate of balance but as its enemy. In 1792 *The Patriot* carried, under the pseudonym Algernon Sidney, a letter attacking the principle of balanced constitutions and describing the English constitution as 'a downright aristocracy'.* In 1795 Henry Yorke commended the rule of the Rump and called for a similar government now, one 'not formed on the crude and undigested materials of Gothic barbarism'. For Sidney, Gothic constitutions were models of mixed government. Yorke, overlooking that taste, decided that Sidney had favoured 'an unintricate form of legislation'.

The later eighteenth century drew Sidney into the orthodox Whig fold. The early nineteenth pushed him out again. Whig thought was changing. The 'inflexibility' which the eighteenth century revered in the seventeenth century's patriots came to seem less a recommendation than a defect. The Napoleonic wars, and the strengthening of populist radicalism, gravely damaged the Whig party, which found itself stranded between Tory and populist sentiment. Gradually it reconstructed itself, ideologically as well as politically. In the eighteenth century it had been a party of preservation, defending the settlement of 1689. It had allied with patriot sentiment against the threat to the Revolution posed by George III. Now it severed that tie. The Whigs became a party not of preservation but of reform, and a party less interested in theoretical vindications than in practical measures.

* Populist and patriot aims merged in the journal, which carried a series of other appeals to patriot heroes, King Alfred, Hampden, Milton, Harrington, Marvell, Molesworth, Bolingbroke. Another letter bearing Sidney's name attacked the use of corruption to destroy parliamentary independence.

It was in that new context that flexibility, hitherto a sin, became a virtue. In 1827 the prominent Whig historian Henry Hallam acknowledged that, thanks to the trial and execution of Sidney and Russell, an episode with which he trusted his readers to be 'familiar', their names 'have always been united in grateful veneration'. But, he ruled, Sidney's martyrdom had produced exaggerated notions of his virtue. His 'inflexible and haughty character', his 'pride and inflexibility', 'though they gave a dignity to his character, rendered his views too narrow and his temper too unaccommodating'. Hallam objected, on grounds not of principle but of pragmatism, to Sidney's involvement in conspiracy. He allowed that Sidney would have been perfectly entitled, had the circumstances been right, to act against a government which lacked that essential basis of legitimacy, the consent of the nation. But 'resistance to established authority can never be warrantable until it is expedient'. Sidney's acceptance of money from the French ambassador Barillon was reprehensible, in Hallam's eyes, not as evidence of corruption but because of the irresponsible republican designs on which he aimed to spend it. Republicanism, to Hallam, was no friend to liberty. It was an enemy to the English constitution, which, when it was allowed to function properly, was liberty's friend. Only by armed force, observed Hallam, could Sidney have imposed his republican 'utopia' on England. Yet 'for this idol of his speculative hours' he would have been 'content to sacrifice the liberties of Europe'.

In Hallam's wake came the author of the greatest historical work Whig history had yet produced, Thomas Babington Macaulay's *History of England*, which was published between 1848 and 1855 and which had the Revolution of 1688 as its focus. Macaulay was born in 1800, twenty-three years after Hallam. In his radical youth he paid rapturous homage to Sidney, hailing him alongside Hampden and Milton. Even thereafter he sometimes found it useful to invoke that pedigree of freedom. 'The good old cause, as Sidney called it,' he once told the Edinburgh electors, 'is still the good old cause with me.' But he could not take it seriously. 'The cause for which Hampden bled on the field and Sidney on the scaffold,' he noticed, 'is enthusiastically toasted by many an honest radical who would be puzzled to explain the difference between ship money and the Habeas Corpus Act.' Macaulay's *History*, though condemning Sidney's judicial murder, passes rapidly over it. Macaulay, like Hallam, had no time for the radical and republican strains within Whiggism. 'The history of England during the seventeenth century', he wrote approvingly, is that of 'the transformation of a limited monarchy constituted after the fashion of the middle ages into a limited monarchy suited to a more advanced state of society'. He paid no attention to Sidney's *Discourses*, or indeed to any theoretical discussions of politics. In the eighteenth century Dalrymple's charges had indicated that Sidney, far from being, as patriots claimed, inflexibly superior to politics, had been all too political and all too flexible. In the eyes of Macaulay, a practising politician for whom practical politics were the essential means to national wisdom and progress, Sidney's failure was not to have been political or flexible enough.

There is a patriot strain in Macaulay. He admired the 'disinterestedness' of 'stainless' politicians. He conceded that the Revolution of 1688 had introduced, alongside its blessings, 'corruption and faction'. But the idea of a patriot administration or a patriot king struck him as 'childish' in its impracticality. The eighteenth century's corruption, he believed, could never have been wished away by legislation against placemen or by virtuous sentiments. Only if parliament had been made answerable to the nation could the evil have been cured. Like Hallam, Macaulay admired Whigs who had operated within the mainstream, with respect for the realities of power. He revered Lord Somers, the pragmatic junto leader whom the publishers of the *Discourses* had seen as an apostate. He had no time for the inflexibility of Edmund Ludlow, whose *Memoirs*, by 1825, he found 'foolish and violent'. Though the *Memoirs* remained a central source of information, they were by now much less often a source of political inspiration. Nineteenth-century Whiggism stood back from the ideal of political purity. François Guizot, in a work which was translated into English in 1850 and which was both indebted to and soon absorbed by Whig thinking, observed that Sidney, Ludlow, Harrington and Milton 'were men of lofty ambition for their country and for mankind; but so injudicious and so insanely proud that they learned nothing from power or from defeat'. 'Credulous as childhood and obstinate as age', they had created the 'anarchical tyranny' of the Commonwealth in the belief that they were 'founding the freest and most glorious of governments'.

In 1881 the writer and social critic Goldwin Smith declared the 'patriotism of the seventeenth century', to which Sidney's 'Roman morality' had 'contributed largely', to be 'obsolete'. In its place, Smith recognized, new criteria of heroism had arisen. Into the vacuum of admiration left by the decline of the saints of the Darby–Toland canon there stepped the man who had united most of them in vehement hatred of him: Oliver Cromwell.

8

Oliver Cromwell: from Villain to Hero

From time to time a historical anniversary touches a nation's nerve. It answers to perceptions of national identity, or it prompts the deployment of the past to support present causes. The centenary of the 'Glorious Revolution' in 1788 was one such event. No English centenary, however, has produced a more prodigious intensity of sentiment than the three hundredth anniversary, in 1899, of the birth of Oliver Cromwell. Across the country there were fervent gatherings of his admirers. In the City Temple in Holborn, which held more than 3,000 people, a series of meetings lasted from noon to night. Hundreds had to be turned away. The tercentenary prompted a series of biographies of Cromwell, most of them laudatory and deeply felt. His rule as Lord Protector was widely hailed as one of the best periods of rule in English history. Praise of the man assumed extreme proportions. He was described frequently as the greatest of Englishmen, sometimes as the greatest figure, or one of the greatest figures, in the history of the world.

The years around the tercentenary saw the climax of a cult of Cromwell which had grown up over the nineteenth century. A hundred years earlier, in 1799, a public commemoration of him would have been unthinkable. From the Restoration of monarchy in 1660 until around the accession of Queen Victoria in 1837, historians and politicians mostly portrayed him not as hero but as villain. They condemned his seditious deeds: the regicide, the establishment of a republic, the imposition of military and sectarian rule. They assailed his character, which was generally held to have been one of ruthless ambition and cunning and dissimulation. They reviled his Puritanism. Some deemed his religious 'enthusiasm' or 'fanaticism' the source of his evil actions. Others judged it a hypocritical pretence, a mask for selfish and treacherous designs and the principal instrument by which he had built up his following. Clarendon's observation that 'Cromwell, though the greatest dissembler living, always made his hypocrisy of singular use and benefit to him' made a deep impression.

Yet hostility to Cromwell, wide and deep as it was, was only one side of the story. His late Victorian admirers, who congratulated their century on having transformed his reputation, exaggerated that achievement. Their interpretation of him owed more to pre-nineteenth-century images than they knew. There was Cromwellianism before 1800. Anti-Cromwellianism, it is true, had then prevailed in the written word. Yet the spoken one may have been a different matter. The published attacks on Cromwell across the later seventeenth and the eighteenth century were prompted by the fear that he retained a hold on the public's heart. Anti-Cromwellian books and pamphlets of Charles II's reign observed a 'mistaken' public tendency to 'adore' or 'idolise' his memory, especially his rule as Lord Protector. In 1739 Cromwell's biographer John Banks, though carefully limiting and qualifying his own praise of Cromwell, noted that 'the present age begins to see through' the contumely favoured by its predecessor. Eighteenth-century patriots and commonwealthmen were dismayed by the signs of enthusiasm for him. In June 1760 the patriot journal *The Monitor*, noticing the respect 'so often' shown to Cromwell 'in political conversation', warned that 'they who adore the remembrance of that usurper, as the idol to which all statesmen in this nation ought to look, . . . are greatly mistaken'. *The Monitor* felt it necessary to return to the theme the following spring. On both ocasions it borrowed material from Ludlow's *Memoirs*, and from pamphlets related to them, to counter the habit of praising Oliver. In 1796 John Thelwall, whom we have met as a devotee of Algernon Sidney, was troubled to find that Sidney's enemy Cromwell had 'even at this day many enthusiastic admirers, who do not scruple to uphold him as the greatest champion that liberty ever had in this country'. In 1827 the *Westminster Review* judged, in a similar spirit of regret, that Cromwell's devotees had got the upper hand. Perhaps the most striking assessment of pre-Victorian Cromwellianism is the young T. B. Macaulay's in 1828. Even though Cromwell's memory had enjoyed the 'patronage' of 'no party',

Macaulay declared, even though it was 'constantly attacked and scarcely ever defended', even though admiration of him had necessarily been 'secret', yet 'even to the present day his character . . . is popular with the great body of his countrymen'.

Such observations are impossible to test but also to ignore. Admiration for Cromwell had a number of sources. From the time of the Restoration we catch occasional whispers of a Cromwellianism born of political or social grievance. Men are overheard lauding Cromwell's readiness to kill a king. There was a fanciful but persistent supposition that he had been a defender of the poor against the rich, and that the protectorate had been a period of popular prosperity which the Restoration had cruelly ended. Then there were the Dissenters or Nonconformists, to whom Cromwell had given the liberty of worship of which they were deprived by the restored monarchy. Charles II's reign had also stripped them of their civil rights, which they regained only in the nineteenth century. Before that century, it is true, Dissenting Cromwellianism dared not speak its name. For Dissenters, the memory of the civil wars was a cross to be borne. They had no hiding-place from the popular charges, sometimes ribald, sometimes vitriolic, that linked them to the regicide and the rule of the Rump. It was as well for them that their accusers did not know of Ludlow's 'A Voice from the Watch Tower', which would have confirmed, not to say intensified, their views about the seditious properties of Nonconformity. If there is a single force behind Dissenting treatments of the civil wars before Victoria's reign, it is the desire to be free of the memory of them. The Dissenters were eager, sometimes desperate to convince governments of their loyalty. They stayed clear of political agitation – to the dismay, in Charles II's reign, of Algernon Sidney, who aimed to mobilize them in his conspiratorial cause. They concentrated on the spiritual, not the political achievements of their Puritan ancestors. So defences of the Roundhead cause were mostly left to men of more secular outlook. And yet, amid so much caution, there are hints of an underground Cromwellianism in Nonconformist circles. Portraits of Cromwell were reportedly preserved in Dissenting households. George Crabbe's poem 'The Frank Courtship', published in 1812, described a Dissenting congregation, possibly modelled on a real one of the 1770s, whose members rejoiced in the memory of the regicide and of Cromwell. He 'was still their saint, and when they met, / They mourned that saints were not our rulers yet.'

Cromwell's nineteenth-century admirers brought to the surface sentiments that had long lain below it. Even so his Victorian standing was won only after long and bitter battles. An imposing weight of traditional hostility had to be countered. Only gradually did the old allegations against his character and religion recede. In the middle third of the century, lecturers and public speakers found that Cromwell's name fiercely divided their audiences. Not until late in Victoria's reign did the battle for approval seem securely won.

In pre-nineteenth-century historical writing, anti-Cromwellianism had two main streams: one royalist, the other radical Whig or republican. The royalist tradition, rooted as it was in ancient loyalties and bitter memories, took some extreme forms. On 30 January 1661, the twelfth anniversary of the beheading of Charles I, Cromwell's body, which had been laid to rest in Westminster Abbey, was exhumed together with the corpses of two other leading regicides. The bodies were dragged to Tyburn and hanged in front of a huge crowd. Then they were taken down, decapitated and thrown into a pit. Their heads were taken to Westminster and left to stand on spikes before the public view. If Cromwell's corpse was insulted at the Restoration, his character was vilified then and in the years ahead. Satires and plays and dramatic dialogues portrayed him as a Machiavel, void of religion and morality, even in league with the Devil. James Heath's vituperative biography *Flagellum* (1663), which would be reprinted six times during Charles II's reign, was a sensationalist caricature embellished by a wealth of slanderous invention. In a pamphlet of 1665, *The Loyal Martyrology*, Cromwell is 'this wicked monster', 'the centre of mischief, a shame to the British chronicle, a blot to gentility, a pattern for tyranny, whose horrid treasons will scarce gain credit with posterity, whose bloody tyranny will quite drown the names of Nero, Domitian, Caligula, etc.' The demonic Cromwell would have a lasting impact in folklore and popular consciousness. Flora Thompson's *Lark Rise to Candleford* tells us that, in the 1880s, misbehaving children in an Oxfordshire village were told by their mothers that 'Old Crummell'll have 'ee' or 'Here comes old Crummell.' Popular hostility continued to surface in the twentieth century, when proposals to name colleges or roads after Cromwell were thwarted, to the surprise of their sponsors, by irate local resistance.

There has been sophisticated anti-Cromwellianism too. By the end of the seventeenth century, when few participants in the civil wars survived and when the bitterness bequeathed by them had begun to recede, Heath's coarse caricature had ceased to satisfy lettered sympathizers with the royalist cause. At the start of the eighteenth century Clarendon's *History of the Rebellion*, while attributing to Cromwell 'all the wickednesses against which damnation is denounced and hell-fire is prepared', allowed that that 'brave bad man' had 'some virtues which have caused the memory of some men in all ages to be celebrated'. Unlike Heath, Clarendon made Cromwell a recognizable human being and gave his deeds a realistic historical context. In 1754 David Hume's *History of England*, a book that would assume a stature in anti-Roundhead literature – and a demonological status among Whigs – to rival that of Clarendon's work, did the same. In Clarendon's and Hume's accounts of Cromwell there is a vein of magnanimity that can be found too in a number of other royalist or Tory assessments of Oliver in the eighteenth century.

The anti-Cromwellianism of radical Whigs was without magnanimity. It kept alive quarrels that had torn the Roundhead cause. Tory sentiment was not much interested in those quarrels. It tended to lump the evils of Cromwell's protectorate with those of the Commonwealth, which he had usurped. To the radicals the usurpation of 1653 was a catastrophe. In their eyes Cromwell was as wicked and tyrannical as Charles I, perhaps more so. In Ludlow's *Memoirs* John Toland created the most powerful and lasting of the weapons of anti-Cromwellian historiography. Whereas most royalists of the civil wars had only secondhand knowledge of Cromwell's character, Ludlow knew him well, watched him closely, talked often to him, collaborated with him in politics and government. Even under the protectorate, when he had broken with him, he was summoned to his presence and allowed to argue with him. His descriptions of him, as rewritten by Toland, have an immediacy and conviction that no royalist history could match. There was nothing new about the charges of ambition, hypocrisy and dissimulation that run through the *Memoirs*. They had been staple elements of anti-Cromwellian literature since Cromwell's own time. It was Toland's text, however, that gave them verisimilitude. From the time of its publication until well into the nineteenth century its portrait of Cromwell was persistently appropriated by royalist writers.

Three features of the anti-Cromwellianism of the *Memoirs* were especially influential, even among readers hostile to Ludlow's republicanism. First there is the account of Cromwell's conduct from the battle of Worcester in 1651 to the dissolution of the Rump in 1653. That, in the *Memoirs*, is the critical period when Cromwell's ambition was revealed and Ludlow's own cause sacrificed to it. Secondly there is the theme, that guiding preoccupation in the preparation of the *Memoirs*, of the tyranny achieved by a standing army. Thirdly there is Toland's incorporation into the *Memoirs* of material from Slingsby Bethel's pamphlet of 1668, *The World's Mistake in Oliver Cromwell.* Some of the charges brought by Bethel and reproduced in the *Memoirs* cover the domestic policies of the protectorate and its assaults on the rule of law. More extensively influential was the accusation that Cromwell's foreign policy had been fundamentally flawed.

That claim ran counter to convention. If there is a single subject where admiration for Cromwell has persisted across the generations it is the greatness he achieved for England abroad. From his own time onwards, writer after writer acknowledged the 'honour' he had brought to his country and remembered how the powers of Europe had 'dreaded' his name and 'trembled' at it and been reduced to 'courting' his favour. In 1738 the Dissenting historian Daniel Neal, no friend to the regicide or Cromwell's usurpation, allowed that 'he carried the reputation and glory of the English nation as high as it is capable of being raised'. Times of national emergency or shame have been especially conducive to such approval. In the eighteenth century, diplomatic or military irresolution or failure, especially under the ascendancy of Walpole and again during the prelude to, and the early mishaps of, the Seven Years' War, brought Cromwell's achievements to the public mind.

There had been still lower points under the later Stuarts. In 1667, the year before Bethel's pamphlet, the Dutch navy was able to sail up the Medway unopposed and set fire to the English fleet. By that time the political honeymoon of the Restoration was long past. Charles II's regime was weak and divided. After the Dutch raid Samuel Pepys recorded in his diary that 'everybody doth nowadays reflect upon Oliver and commend him, so brave things he did and made all the neighbour princes fear him'. Next year it was 'the undeserved approbation and applause that Cromwell's memory seems to have with his adherents' that prompted Bethel's tract. It was not under Cromwell, Bethel insisted, that England's army and navy had awed Europe. It was under the Commonwealth, whose record Cromwell had slandered and from whose principles of foreign policy he had foolishly departed. His decision to ally with France against Spain, argued Bethel, had fatally destroyed the balance of power in Europe, which the Commonwealth had skilfully sustained, and had paved the way for the European dominance that, by the time of Bethel's tract, the France of Louis XIV had acquired. It was a thesis to which the servile dependence of English to French diplomacy under the later Stuarts gave a continuing plausibility. Its pertinence would be sustained by the long series of Anglo-French wars between 1689 and 1815, which, it was sometimes intimated, would have been unnecessary but for Cromwell's error of policy. Across the eighteenth century the claims of Commonwealth and protectorate to the credit for England's greatness abroad in the 1650s would continue to compete.

The Commonwealth was more readily praised for its foreign than for its domestic deeds. So was Cromwell. One of the *Letters of Junius* remarked in 1771 that he had contrived 'to make a great nation at the same moment unhappy and formidable'. None the less his internal policies won an altogether wider degree of admiration than the Rump's. Royalist historians were ready with expressions of approval, which the criticisms by Bethel and in Ludlow's *Memoirs* were unable to discourage, of some of his achievements at home. In a biography first written in Latin, and then published in English in 1685, the royalist George Bate, who had been Cromwell's physician, vouched that Cromwell 'had two attendant spirits, a good and a bad'. Bate supplied a list of domestic accomplishments that in succeeding generations would be reproduced or drawn on in history after history. Cromwell's appointment of impartial judges, his concern for the reform of the electoral and legal systems, his immunity to financial and courtly corruption, his antipathy to vice and immorality, his patronage of learning, were virtues not merely acknowledged by royalist historians but sometimes exaggerated by them.

They were remembered by country-party and patriot sentiment too. Cromwell could never have belonged to the patriot pantheon. He was a manipulator of power, not a Cato. Besides, he could not be secularized, that first requirement of Puritans up for patriot status. His religion, whether genuine or feigned, was conspicuous at every turn of his career. One could not imagine him among the statuary and engravings and poetry that commemorated the patriot saints: alongside Hampden or Milton among the British Worthies at Stowe, or with Hampden and Sidney among the heroes of James Thomson's verse. A cartoon of 1757 shows the wicked Cromwell in confrontation with the virtuous patriot Pitt. 'It's all over, it's foolish to be honest,' Cromwell advises him. 'Ancient traitor, I defy thee,' comes the reply. Eleven years later, when Pitt had yielded his patriot credentials, another cartoon lauded the patriots Hampden, Marvell, Sidney and Russell but showed the apostate Pitt 'well mounted' on a broom inscribed 'Oliver Cromwell'. There were eighteenth-century admirers of Cromwell who did try to link his name to those of two 'patriots' of the civil wars, Hampden and Milton, but the compliments were not returned by the devotees of those heroes. Sidney and his fellow-heroes were credited with the virtues of Rome's great republicans. From that perspective Cromwell was either Julius or Octavius Caesar, figures with whom he was often paralleled by critics of military rule. Thomas Gray's 'Elegy written in a Country Churchyard' (probably composed between 1746 and 1750) did grant Cromwell a place alongside 'some village-Hampden' or 'mute inglorious Milton', but only on terms that recall his 'guilt' for 'his country's blood'. In a draft of the poem the place which the final version gives to Cromwell is occupied by 'Caesar', while Hampden and Milton are prefigured by Cato and Cicero.

Even so, as our look at *Biographia Britannica* showed, patriot sentiment knew how to pick and choose. Like the Commonwealth, the protectorate could seem, in one light, a patriot administration, incorruptible and public-spirited at home and great abroad. Cromwell's overhaul of the electoral system, which swept away courtly patronage, was one sign of patriot virtue. In reality, though he implemented that reform, it was the Commonwealth that designed it, as

Ludlow's *Memoirs* claim; but it was the protector who received much of the praise of posterity. Here as elsewhere it helped that, whereas the Commonwealth had been born of the regicide, the protectorate, which began nearly five years later and which repudiated the rule of the Rump, was less immediately associated with Charles I's death. A Lord Protector, though not exactly a king, was closer to kingly than to republican rule, and was thus less distant from normality than the regime which his government replaced. His rule earned patriot marks on other fronts too. There were the frugality and probity of his court, an institution which in Ludlow's *Memoirs* thrives on preferment and bribery but which other writers presented as an enviable contrast to the corruption of eighteenth-century administrations. Then there was the protector's readiness, in his choice of men to help him rule the country, to value ability above the ties of favour or party or connection, another virtue which Toland's editions had claimed for the Commonwealth but which again came to be associated at least as often with the protectorate. Oliver's exploits abroad touched another patriot chord, the more readily since, like the Commonwealth's, they principally relied on maritime more than on military power. The prominent patriot George Lyttelton, in his *A Letter from a Persian in England* in 1735, was torn between revulsion at the usurpation of a man who 'trampled on the laws of the nation' and respect for him for having 'raised the glory of it; and it is hard to say which he deserved most, a halter or a crown'. Even Thomas Hollis, that devotee of the seventeenth-century commonwealthmen, admired Cromwell's exertions for his country's greatness – though, remembering Oliver's uses of his standing army, he added that 'the patriot' in him had 'sunk into the colonel'.

So Cromwell, however ill the methods by which he had gained power, had put it, as it was often said, to some good 'uses'. 'No man,' wrote Robert Southey in the *Quarterly Review* in 1821, 'was so worthy of the station which he filled, had it not been for the means by which he reached it.' When judged, not as a Puritan or a regicide, but as a ruler responsible for the maintenance of his country's interests, he commanded wide respect. In 1801 Lord Shelburne, who had been Prime Minister under George III and who had patriot sympathies, reflected that the protector had 'never had justice done to him' and that as a reformer he 'set more things forward than all the kings who reigned in that century, King William among them'. It was acknowledged, too, that the chaos amid which Cromwell came to power had presented him with extraordinary challenges, which he had surmounted. Alongside the revulsion at the use of military force in the coups of 1653, and alongside the assumption that his elevation had been motivated by personal ambition, there ran the judgement that the protectorate had put an end to anarchy and had restored at least an element of domestic stability. The suspension, in exceptional times, of parliamentary rights and liberties seemed to some writers to have been a price worth paying for those achievements. 'No other genius, it may be,' conceded Daniel Neal's *History of the Puritans* in 1738, 'could have held the reins, or steered the commonwealth, through so many storms and hurricances.' And as Clarendon acknowledged, Cromwell was 'not a man of blood'. As Lord Protector he had sought at least a measure of national reconciliation.

Whatever animus his name might arouse, no one found Cromwell dull. As Alexander Pope had it in *An Essay on Man*, Oliver was 'damned to everlasting fame'. Lives of him were in heavy demand. Between the Restoration in 1660 and the Revolution of 1688, when victorious royalism dominated historical writing, they were uniformly unfavourable and unfair. After 1688 the mood changed. Nathaniel Crouch's non-partisan life of Cromwell appeared in 1692 and had run to seven editions by 1740. In 1698 Ludlow's *Memoirs* provoked an influential reply, *A Modest Vindication of Oliver Cromwell*. In 1725 a biography of Cromwell by Isaac Kimber entered into competition with Crouch's life, to which it was indebted. It too ran to seven editions, the last of which appeared in 1788. John Banks's biography of 1739 had run to eleven editions by 1779. William Harris's life of 1762, though less markedly successful, was widely read. Whether liked or disliked, Cromwell inspired awe and wonder. Even men who saw no goodness in him could be moved by his greatness. How was it, readers wanted to know, that a provincial squire of modest means had raised himself to supreme power in his own country? How had he, within so short a time, overcome his enemies on both the Cavalier and the Roundhead side, secured a personal supremacy over a parliament determined to prevent it, subjugated England, Ireland and Scotland, become the terror of Europe? As a soldier, politician, statesman, he had displayed a vigour, an energy, a courage, a resolution, an artfulness, a dexterity that took posterity's breath away. He had towered above his age. The history of his times, explained *Biographia Britannica*, 'in truth is no other than the personal history of Cromwell; for his and his friends' intrigues either moved or gave motion to all the parties in the kingdom'.

Only on the extremes was antipathy to Cromwell unqualified. Jacobites and high Tories were mostly irreconcilable. So were most radical Whigs and republicans. In the later eighteenth century the radicals Catharine Macaulay, James Burgh, John Thelwall, Henry Yorke and Horne Tooke propounded a view of Cromwell, as the hypocritical and ruthless destroyer of the Commonwealth, that in all its essentials derived from Ludlow's *Memoirs*. In Cromwell's breast, ruled Catharine Macaulay, there 'rankled the most sordid principles of self-interest, with their concomitant vices, envy, hatred and malice'.

Thus before the early nineteenth century there was, amid so much execration, a large degree of admiration for Cromwell's deeds. Yet, at least in print, it had always to be balanced against his misdeeds and his defects of character. It was only in the 1820s that there began a movement towards what was called a more 'kindly' balance of opinion. That development was aided by the publication in 1810 of *Cromwelliana*, a miscellany of documents which brought much material relating to his personality and career into print. Only gradually did the work acquire wide notice, and only with time did it work to Oliver's advantage. It represented him unsympathetically. Yet the evidence it supplied made him easier to know; and it was by getting to know him that hosts of nineteenth-century readers learned to like him. Influential as *Cromwelliana* was, the work of two writers of the 1820s, the young T. B. Macaulay and the ageing William Godwin, was more so. Their judgements on Cromwell would long carry weight. Macaulay's early essays paid tribute to the figure whom, in his *History of England*, he would call 'the greatest prince that has ever ruled England'. William Godwin's *History of the Commonwealth* (1825–8), though sharing the traditional republican revulsion at Cromwell's usurpation, presented the ambition that led him to supreme power as a tragic flaw, akin to Macbeth's, which had destroyed the wonderful 'elevation of his soul'. In the 1830s, while hatred of Cromwell remained widespread, admiration of him gathered into a current. By the end of the decade it was a torrent. The 1840s produced an extraordinary range of publications, much of it hostile but a growing proportion of it admiring. There are biographies, essays, novels, poems, songs, at least two plays, even a phrenological study. The movement of Cromwellianism that would reach its climax in 1899 was fully launched.

It was not only Cromwell's standing that rose from the earlier nineteenth century. So did that of the Roundhead cause which he had come to dominate. In the 1690s John Toland and his associates, critics of the shortcomings of the Revolution of 1688, had emphasized the merits of the more far-reaching revolt of the middle of the century, even if only up to the moment of Cromwell's apostasy. In the eighteenth century few outside the radical ranks followed their lead. If the Cromwell tercentenary of 1899 is the great political anniversary of the late nineteenth century, its eighteenth-century equivalent is the commemoration of the centenary of the Revolution of 1688. Among the radicals, however, discontent with 1688 was tenacious. In the later eighteenth century it found a new boldness. Previously critics had complained that the Revolution had not gone far enough. Now it was rejected *tout court*. Catharine Macaulay wrote of the 'moral and political evils that took place at the Revolution' and of the 'fatal encroachments' made on constitutional rights by the 'tyranny' of William III, who 'broke like an enraged lion from the toils of patriotism'. The Bill of Rights, she ruled, had 'opened a wider field for more corrupt abuses than ever were produced by all the monarchical, oligarchical and aristocratic tyrannies in the world'. Catharine Macaulay's republicanism was suffused with patriot and country-party sentiment. It was on the failure of the parliaments of William's reign to secure independence from the executive that she particularly blamed the subsequent spread of corruption.

Tom Paine, in *The Rights of Man* (1790–92), supplied criticism from a different quarter. He spoke against 1688 on behalf not of country sentiment but of the poor. At the Revolution, he wrote, an oligarchy had 'imported' the 'detestable' William and Mary, just as in

1714 it would 'send for' George I, in order to preserve its oppression of the people. The Bill of Rights was 'more properly a bill of wrongs, and an insult'. Paine had another objection to the Revolution. It had involved England in 'the destructive system of Continental and foreign intrigues, and the rage for foreign wars and foreign domination'. A similar objection had been voiced earlier in the century by patriots, who looked to maritime supremacy for the defence of England's interests and who saw land wars as pretexts for the swelling of government revenue and the maintenance of a standing army. In July and October 1757 *The Monitor* lamented the consequences for liberty of the wars which, as a result of the Revolution, had been fought in the reigns of William – 'a king not entirely English in his heart' – and his successors. Paine objected not to the damage those conflicts inflicted on patriot ideals but to the slaughter and sufferings of humble soldiers in conflicts conducted for the sake of aristocratic sport and plunder. It rejoiced him to observe that the reputation of 1688 was 'already on the wane, eclipsed by the enlarging orb of reason and the luminous revolutions of America and France'. Until the American Revolution, he declared, there had been no true revolutions, merely 'changes of persons' which 'worked within the atmosphere of a court, and never on the great floor of a nation'.

To repudiate 1688 was one thing. To embrace the Puritan revolt in its stead was another. In the eighteenth century even commendations of the patriots of 1640–41, the figures of the civil wars whom it was safest to praise, were often defensive in tone. More was said in praise of their characters than of their deeds. Unease about the civil wars can be found even among radicals. In 1792 *The Patriot*, whose 'main design' was the securing of parliamentary reform, regretted the want of 'honesty' of the leaders of 1640 and their readiness to assault 'the constitution'. Only in the early nineteenth century did the claims of the civil wars to the nation's gratitude come to be boldly reasserted. A contributor to that process was the zealous Whig Francis Maseres, who brought a number of mid-seventeenth-century texts back into print. He also reprinted the first three of the four Ludlow 'Letters' of the early 1690s. Those pamphlets had explained that if the armed resistance to James II had been justified, that of the Long Parliament to Charles I had been no less so. Maseres revived that claim.

In the following decade T. B. Macaulay repeated it. Here was a significant breakthrough. Mainstream Whiggism had embraced the Roundhead cause. Macaulay's great *History of England* (1848–55) would centre on 1688. Yet in his early career he found more to warm to in the earlier and, as it then seemed to him, more manly revolt, whose leaders braved the king themselves rather than bringing in a foreigner to do their work. Other writers proceeded in a reverse direction to Macaulay's, starting with the study of 1688 and moving back to the 1640s. Gradually, and in spite of Macaulay's *History*, the balance of sympathy shifted in favour of the first upheaval. In 1840 John Forster, whose own writings on the civil wars commanded a wide readership, pronounced it

> a grave reproach to English political biography that the attention so richly due to the statesmen who opposed Charles I, in themselves the most remarkable men of any age or nation, should have been suffered to be borne away by the poorer imitators of their deeds, the authors of the imperfect settlement of 1688.

In the decades ahead, school textbooks registered the new priority. J. R. Green's hugely influential *History of the English People*, published in 1874, reflected it. In 1888 the bicentenary of 1688 made little impression. It was not that 1688 had come to seem unimportant, rather perhaps that the very ease with which Macaulay's triumphalist thesis had won acceptance had largely deprived the Revolution of controversy and thus of appeal.*

There is one sense in which the civil wars themselves were less controversial than they had been. Jacobite and high Tory interpretations had virtually vanished. Once the Napoleonic wars were past, much of the revulsion and unease that had marked so many accounts of the Roundhead cause disappeared. Though it was Whig historians

* The two conflicts could be placed respectfully alongside each other. In 1852 Tennyson, the Poet Laureate, eager to illustrate Englishmen's readiness to fight for freedom, remembered that 'From our first Charles by force we wrung our claims/ . . . / We flung the burden from the second James.' In the 1690s radical Whigs had struggled to connect the two upheavals: now it could easily be done.

whose advocacy reclaimed the Puritan revolt, the shortage of intellectual resistance on the Tory side is almost as conspicuous. Toryism had become a thoroughly parliamentary creed. The nineteenth century saw much sentimental affection for the person of Charles I, much nostalgic representation of royalist chivalry, much sympathy – prompted and exploited by such paintings as William Frederick Yeames's 'And when did you last see your Father?' in 1878 – for royalist sufferings; much Anglican admiration for the Caroline Church. There was plenty of dislike of rebels, plenty of readiness to condemn the disloyalty of Charles's opponents, plenty of distaste for Puritanism. It was those sentiments that sustained the vigour and animus of anti-Roundhead views. But if many Victorians were against what Charles had been against, by the middle of the century few people were in favour of what, in political and constitutional matters, he had been for. *1066 And All That* (published in 1930) would hit the mark: from Victorian times onwards the Cavaliers were indeed wrong but romantic. By the mid-nineteenth century it was difficult to argue that Hampden had been wrong to refuse to pay ship money. Even the raising of arms against the king in 1642 was generally acknowledged, however grudgingly at times, to have been a necessary step.

The twenty or thirty years after the Napoleonic wars are probably the period in English historiography when condemnations of Charles I's tyranny were most widespread and intense. Whig or Whiggish writers who wrote or grew up in that time, Macaulay and John Forster at their head, agreed that his reign had set 'the friends of liberty' against its 'enemies'. Forster pronounced that the personal rule of the 1630s, that calculated attempt 'to trample into the dust . . . the laws and liberties of England', had been 'the most vexatious and intolerable tyranny that ever tortured body and soul at once'; and that only 'the gallantest fight for liberty that had ever been fought by any nation in the world' had thwarted it. It was, Whigs declared, to key moments in the years before the civil wars – the king's suicidal attempt to impose an English Prayer Book on Scotland; the passage through the Commons, by so narrow a vote, of the Grand Remonstrance of 1641, that rallying call of the parliamentary cause – that England 'owes her freedom'. The nation's exemption from the epidemic of European revolutions in 1848, and its growing prosperity and social stability in the 1850s, gave it renewed confidence in the superiority of its institutions, a virtue for which Charles's defeat was given an increasing share of the credit. Had he won the civil war, affirmed Victorian after Victorian, England would now be like Spain or Russia. The readiness of Roundheads, quite as much as that of James II's opponents, to risk civil war seemed a cause of England's modern immunity from it.

The execution of Charles I, admittedly, remained a divisive subject. The old tension within Whig and republican historiography re-emerged in the 1820s. William Godwin, at the republican end of the spectrum, praised the regicide unreservedly. Macaulay, at the Whig end, though he found it an intelligible step, judged it an 'error' and a 'crime' (though not, as earlier critics would have said, a 'sin'), which had wrenched the Roundhead cause from its course of constitutional propriety. Over the century, approval of the regicide was perhaps always a minority view, but the minority expressing it became ever larger. While it remained easy to impugn the motives that impelled the coup it became harder to argue that it had been unnecessary. In 1858 the statutory annual lament for the regicide was abolished; it seems anyway to have largely fallen into desuetude. By the late Victorian era it was often contended that Charles I's death had put a stop to absolutist aspirations in England, that it had supplied a grim but necessary 'object-lesson' to kings, who 'have sat differently on their thrones ever since'.

The credit for the Roundheads' achievements did not go entirely to Cromwell. The Long Parliament, which defied Charles I's tyranny, exerted its own claims on the nineteenth century's gratitude. Since the late seventeenth century, Whigs of many shades had lauded – though with varying emphases – that 'great', 'celebrated', 'ever-memorable' assembly. It was its early deeds, when it defied Charles's bid for tyranny, that won broadest acclamation. Incantatory references to the first day of its meeting passed down the generations. Again Macaulay gave such sentiment a new breadth of appeal. He annexed it, more decisively than any Whig before his generation had done, to the cause of constitutional respectability. 'On the third of November 1640,' he wrote, 'a day long to be remembered, met that great parliament,' 'that renowned parliament', which 'is justly entitled to the reverence and gratitude of all who in any part of the world enjoy the blessings of constitutional government'. Over the earlier nineteenth century, reverence grew for the parliamentary leaders to whom modern liberty was indebted: for John Hampden, for his ally John Pym and for their precursor in Charles I's early parliaments, Sir John Eliot. The formation of the Hampden Club in 1812 for the promotion of parliamentary enfranchisement, and the proliferation of local clubs carrying Hampden's name thereafter, were symptoms of that development and a stimulus to it.

The parliamentarian cause, Whigs told themselves, had been, in its prime, a constitutionalist cause. After all, Hampden, Pym and Eliot were safely dead long before the parliament lurched into what Macaulay called its 'disasters', the radical moves of the late 1640s. For the rule of the Commonwealth the nineteenth century had little love. In the mid-eighteenth century, we saw, it had won admiration in unexpected quarters as a patriot ministry, pure at home and triumphant abroad. In the later eighteenth and the early nineteenth century there were republican admirers of it too. In 1771 Catharine Macaulay called the Commonwealth 'the brightest age that ever adorned the page of history'. In the 1820s Godwin's eloquent four-volume *History of the Commonwealth* portrayed the era as the proudest point in the nation's annals. Godwin's work, however, was a final flowering, the last influential work in the line of celebrations of the Commonwealth that stretched back, and owed so much, to Slingsby Bethel and to Toland's editions of Ludlow and Sidney. Like Catharine Macaulay's in the late eighteenth century, Godwin's republicanism had its patriot flavour. His life of the elder Pitt pronounced it to have been 'the glory of Mr Pitt's government to abolish the spirit of party'. But patriot republicanism was on the wane. Radical Whiggism had always been dependent, for its influence, on country-party sentiment. As the sentiment abated, radical Whiggism declined too. The long era of English history, from the Renaissance to the late eighteenth century, in which anti-courtly sentiment had been the dominant theme of political commentary was over. The republican component of the Whig historical tradition subsided with it.

Ironically the republican Godwin, who charged Cromwell with wicked apostasy in destroying the Commonwealth but who saw virtues in him none the less, did more for the protector's public standing than for the reputation of the Commonwealth. Cromwell's indifference, which the coup revealed, to constitutional propriety did trouble many of his Victorian admirers. Yet they found ways of extenuating it. Only the pressures of exceptional events, it was maintained, had 'driven' him into 'arbitrary measures'. Once those pressures were allowed for, it could be seen that he had tried to rule constitutionally and had accepted legal curbs on his rule. The protectorate, so different in that respect from the Commonwealth before it, was commended as an experiment in those principles of parliamentary government that the nineteenth century would hold dear. There was admiration for the protectoral constitution introduced in 1657, the Humble Petition and Advice. Together with parliament's Nineteen Propositions of 1642, and with the Heads of the Proposals of 1647 (the peace terms favoured by the Cromwellian army), the Humble Petition was deemed to have precisely anticipated the nineteenth century's own constitutional arrangements. There was renewed praise, too, for Cromwell's redistribution of the parliamentary constituencies, which anticipated the nineteenth century's electoral reforms. In that as in other respects the debt of Cromwell's measures to the Commonwealth was now generally forgotten.

The eighteenth century, we saw, had sometimes overlooked it too, but its respect for the parliamentary or constitutionalist reformer in Cromwell had been altogether less prominent. It had also had a different focus. He was then praised for challenging those bugbears of backbenchers and patriots, 'corruption and ministerial influence'. In the nineteenth century that country-party perspective was adjusted to accommodate principles more easily compatible with the exercise of power. In admittedly 'rudimentary form', judged Cromwell's biographer the Liberal statesman John Morley at the century's end, the Humble Petition and Advice settled the protectorate 'on the same principles . . . that have developed our modern system of government by parliamentary cabinet'.

The eighteenth century sometimes remarked that Cromwell had saved the nation from anarchy. In the nineteenth century the point was made more frequently and assertively. In 1864 Alfred Bisset, clinging to the defeated ideals of patriot republicanism, complained that 'well-informed writers' were constantly 'asserting that a Cromwell or a

Napoleon is needed to prevent anarchy'. From Macaulay onwards the 'order' achieved by Cromwell was seen less often as an enemy to 'freedom' or 'liberty', more often as its precondition and its necessary partner and balance. To the eighteenth century the maintenance of order was a preservative process. To the nineteenth it was also a creative one. Amid the rapid social changes of the Industrial Revolution the unitive capacity of an energetic and decisive leader, able to hold a society or nation together through his vision and resolution and his power to shape events, became an ever more attractive ideal. Somehow Cromwell had held mid-seventeenth-century England together, an achievement made the more conspicuous by the chaos that followed the fall of the protectorate and the restoration of the Commonwealth, that rule of many heads, in 1659. From one angle, constitutional arrangements seemed vital to the Victorians. Yet from another they could be judged to occupy only the surface of political life.* In times of crisis constitutional forms must expect to yield to the deeper forces of society and to the energizing force of leadership. A new, more dynamic conception of the hero had replaced the patriot Stoicism of the previous age, when the nouns 'hero' and 'patriot' had been regularly coupled.

There was a new reverence too, created by the Napoleonic wars, for martial heroism, which earned Cromwell a place alongside Wellington and Nelson. No longer did rejoicing at the triumphs of English armies need to be inhibited by fears that their generals would turn, like Julius Caesar, on the civilian powers they served. By now the British army had become so much a source of national esteem, and so firmly integrated into the society it defended, that antipathy to the corrupting and tyrannical tendencies of standing armies, that emphatic theme of Ludlow's *Memoirs* and of eighteenth-century echoes of them, had become antediluvian. Military despotism, as witnessed abroad or in history, did retain a power to shock, even to alarm. Cromwell reminded many of Bonaparte. In 1827 the *Westminster Review* lamented the tendency of people 'who adore alike the powers of good and evil' to 'adore Cromwell . . . along with his modern counterpart Napoleon'.

* S. R. Gardiner, who is sometimes represented as a devotee of English constitutionalism, emphasized its narrowness and ineffectuality at those hours of national need, such as 1642, when it did not answer to the country's broader aspirations and anxieties.

Thirty years later the Tory politician and writer J. W. Croker saw the two men as wreckers of constitutionalism. Yet comparisons with Napoleon could work to Cromwell's advantage. Some saw him as a superior version of the Frenchman, who combined Bonaparte's genius and energy with more English qualities of decency and constitutionalism. 'Bonapartism' was one of the forces invoked by Goldwin Smith in 1881 to explain why Cromwell had replaced the Whig saints.

The transition to a new kind of heroism was not abrupt. In the first half of the nineteenth century we find leading figures of Cromwellian historiography – Godwin, Macaulay, John Forster – divided between the old claims of Stoic disinterestedness and the new ones of dynamic leadership. They liked their heroes to blend the two virtues. By the late Victorian era the Stoic ideal earned respect only when subordinated to the dutiful exercise of power. The transformation was not always fatal to the patriot saints, but they could survive only by adapting to it. As we shall now find, they were increasingly judged in relation not to patriot merits but to the greatness of Cromwell.

John Hampden, the 'sober and faithful patriot' of *Biographia Britannica* and the 'Cato' of Thomas Gray, was admired in the eighteenth century above all for his superiority to power and his vigilance against its abuse. His devotees – who had to contend with the hostile account of him in Clarendon's *History* – were troubled to learn that he had come close to taking office under Charles I in 1641, when the king contemplated taking his leading critics into his administration. Mercifully he had survived that hazard. Even if his life had not been abbreviated on the battlefield, his admirers told themselves, he would still have proved immune to power's temptations. Unlike Cromwell he would have been 'unblemished' by the Roundhead victory. Over the early decades of the nineteenth century, comparisons of Hampden with Cromwell are still generally favourable. But there is a shift of emphasis. Gradually he becomes, not an opponent of power, but England's lost leader, his early death depriving the nation of the one man whose authority might have prevented the radicalization of the Roundhead cause and Cromwell's usurpation. Macaulay's essay on Hampden in 1831 was a critical moment in that transformation. For all his admiration for the protectorate, Macaulay wished that its rule had not been necessary. Knowing that 'a good constitution is better than the best despot', he would have preferred statesmen of Hampden's rank to have guided the nation into a peaceful settlement at the end of the civil war. Cromwell aside, Hampden is the Roundhead statesman to have been most admired by the Victorians, as perhaps by any age. Yet his elevated virtue was of diminishing appeal. John Pym, who had earlier been thought of as Hampden's subordinate ally, came almost to match his stature. Clarendon's description of Pym as a 'man of business' had done Pym little good in the eighteenth century. John Granger's biographical dictionary of 1779 was troubled by his 'excessive application to public affairs'. In the nineteenth century Clarendon's phrase helped Pym to be thought of, to his advantage, as a man who got things done. To the more ardent Cromwellians Hampden came to seem too cautious a spirit, lacking Oliver's 'zeal and resoluteness of purpose'.

Hampden the opponent of state power did retain a hold, as Peter Karsten has shown. In 1874 an Oxford don wanted his countrymen to look 'with reverence' on men like Hampden, who represent the 'purer virtues' and constitute 'the moderate party of all ages'. The nation, he urged, should 'recoil from the picturesque attractions of a strong government', whether the absolute monarchy of a Charles I or the 'military despotism' of a Cromwell. Two years later a critic of state funding of education, signing himself 'John Hampden, ratepayer', compared the 'despotic' London School Board to 'the old Star Chamber'. Mildly-spoken Anglicans seem to have had a soft spot for Hampden. Even so the modern conception of patriotism was dimming his light. By the time of the international tensions and military preparations of the 1890s his refusal to pay ship money, always his chief claim to fame, was coming under criticism for having obstructed the build-up of the navy.

The decline in the status of those patriots of the Commonwealth, Edmund Ludlow and Algernon Sidney, who broke with Cromwell in 1653, was swifter and fuller than Hampden's. In 1846 Ludlow's 'cold nature and narrow views' were contrasted, in the *British Quarterly Review*, with Cromwell's 'practical' greatness. Sidney's admirers had shrunk by late Victorian times to a small and eccentric minority. Two other figures of the Commonwealth fared altogether better. For unlike

Ludlow and Sidney they had not broken with Cromwell on his assumption of the protectorate. They had remained at their posts. One was Admiral Blake. Though some eighteenth-century commentators had portrayed his and Cromwell's glorious deeds abroad as a shared achievement, others had been glad to infer, from Clarendon's *History* and Ludlow's *Memoirs*, that Blake disliked the usurpation of Cromwell and that the protector in turn mistrusted and mistreated him. In 1739 the patriot poet Richard Glover commended 'unconquerable Blake' while presenting 'perfidious Cromwell' as a 'ruffian'. In Victorian times such contrasts were outdated. It was now common to portray Blake as Cromwell's willing partner in the nation's service. What England needed, explained a critic of the nation's current diplomatic weakness in *The Reasoner* in December 1860, was an 'Oliver-Cromwell-Admiral-Blake-combined-into-one-sort-of-person'.

The second figure was Milton, who after 1653 had continued to act as Latin Secretary in the office of John Thurloe, Cromwell's Secretary of State. Among his eighteenth- and early nineteenth-century admirers that loyalty caused discomfort. By patriot standards Milton appeared to have committed a cardinal sin: he had yielded to the temptation to serve an evil ruler. In 1749 a life of Milton by Thomas Newton, a clergyman with patriot credentials, acknowledged that the poet's 'attachment to Cromwell must be condemned'. In 1796 William Hayley's admiring biography reflected that 'the severe enthralment of his country under the severe despotism of Cromwell must have wounded very deeply the tender and patriotic feelings of Milton'. With many others Hayley defended Milton from the charge of 'sycophancy' towards Cromwell. The poet had, it is true, been 'duped' by that 'impostor', whereas 'the prudent unheated Ludlow' had seen through him. But 'in contemplating' Cromwell and Milton together, 'the real lover of truth and freedom can hardly fail to observe the striking contrast of their characters: one was an absolute model of false, the other of true grandeur'. Even so doubts persisted. Milton's praise of Cromwell in his treatise of 1654, *Defensio Secunda*, which in Dr Johnson's eyes displayed 'grossness of . . . flattery', was particularly disturbing. To Coleridge it was 'the only passage of his life and writings I find it impossible to defend'. How was it, Coleridge asked himself, that Milton had been 'misled' into supporting the 'Tiberian' Cromwell?

Over the nineteenth century Milton's relationship with Cromwell became, for the poet's admirers, a source not of embarrassment but of pride. He became his partner in greatness. Macaulay, in his essay on Milton in 1825, took a characteristically practical view. The choice in 1653, he remarked, was not, as republicans had liked to tell themselves, 'between Cromwell and liberty but between Cromwell and the Stuarts'. Only Oliver's resolve and dexterity could have withstood the return of that calamitous dynasty. In the wake of Macaulay's judgement, Milton's support for Cromwell came to seem evidence not merely of good sense but of divinity of soul. The eighteenth century had on the whole liked Milton's poetry and disliked his politics. It was dismayed by his readiness to suspend his major poetic ambitions during the central decades of his life for a political cause. Now admirers delighted to find him setting aside his 'purely literary interests', which, however uplifting, were ultimately self-centred, and to discover that he 'did not flinch' from immersing himself in the 'dirt' of politics.

In 1927 Hilaire Belloc said what might equally well have been said at any point since the middle of the nineteenth century: that 'if there is one name consistently associated with Oliver Cromwell it is that of the poet John Milton'. Wordsworth, seeking to animate his sluggard countrymen in liberty's cause, had urged on them the example of the republicans who 'called Milton friend'. Over the course of the nineteenth century, Cromwell took those republicans' place. 'Were he to have a new tomb,' judged the popular mid-nineteenth-century lecturer George Dawson, 'the noblest and best inscription that could be written upon it would be, "Here sleeps Milton's friend."' A century earlier Thomas Newton had been pleased to discover that Cromwell and Milton had not worked closely together, that under the protectorate Milton 'had no share in the secrets and intrigues of government'. Thomas Hollis, who revered Milton, had likewise been relieved to conclude from a perusal of Cromwellian state papers that Milton 'does not appear to have been' in the 'confidence' of the usurper. Those eighteenth-century judgements were correct. There is no evidence that Milton and Cromwell were ever alone together, and nothing to tell us what, if anything, Cromwell thought about Milton. Victorians none the less imagined an intimate and inseparable relationship between the two men. Milton, in reality a civil servant, becomes Cromwell's 'personal secretary', living 'under his roof' and 'sitting every day at the same table', where the 'poet-statesman' discusses and helps to shape the protector's decisions about foreign policy. Mid- and late nineteenth-century paintings and prints show the two men communing in spirit. Sometimes the viewer is fancifully shown Milton playing the organ for Cromwell, who is rapt by the poet's playing.

Victorian imaginations went to work too on Milton's sonnet on the slaughter of Protestants in Piedmont in 1655, 'Avenge, O Lord, thy slaughtered saints'. Though the protectorate's protests against the massacre were a key episode in its diplomacy, there is nothing to suggest that the poem was written for Cromwell or read by him. Yet it came to be read, especially when the Bulgarian agitation against Turkish oppression in the 1870s afforded a modern parallel to the Piedmont episode, as the ultimate testimony to the sympathy between their souls. The evidence of Milton's deep misgivings about the protectorate was passed by. As a duo Cromwell and Milton became in nineteenth-century mythology what Hampden and Sidney had been in its eighteenth-century counterpart. The eighteenth century hailed the cause for which Hampden fell and Sidney bled. A candidate in a parliamentary election in Banbury in 1857 appealed to 'those mighty principles for which Milton sang and Cromwell fought'.

Among the men who in Wordsworth's poem 'called Milton friend' was 'the younger Vane'. Sir Henry Vane (who was known as the younger to distinguish him from his father Sir Henry, another prominent member of the Long Parliament) had been the hero of Milton, as of Ludlow and Sidney too. Allowed no place among the patriot heroes for most of the eighteenth century, the younger Vane gained a prominent one in the pantheon's final phase. Toland's emphasis on Vane's energetic reform of the navy and on his financial probity at last reaped rewards. Vane still had plenty of critics. In 1832 Hampden's biographer Lord Nugent drew an orthodox Whig distinction between Hampden's sane desire for a limited monarchy and Vane's 'darling scheme' of 'a Platonic republic'. Yet Vane, no less than Hampden, seemed to a growing number of early nineteenth-century readers a happy blend of drive and disinterestedness. The problem for his eighteenth-century reputation had been the intensity and opacity of his religious faith, especially of what Thomas Tyers called his 'pretences to inspiration'.

Cromwell visits Milton. By the nineteenth-century engraver Daniel Neal.

By 1800 that characteristic was becoming less of an obstacle. From the later eighteenth century there was a development in religious appreciation which corresponds to, even if it was slower to spread than, the tendency which (as we saw from the treatment of Ludlow by *Biographia Britannica* and other patriot works) bestowed increasing admiration on integrity and sincerity in the realm of politics. The 'sentimental revolution' of the earlier part of George III's reign, and the respect for piety that accompanied it, had made possible the beginnings, however tentative, of the nation's reclamation of its Puritan past. The sincerity and sensibility behind a religious principle could now seem at least as important as its content. It was in line with that premise that Catharine Macaulay endorsed those remarks of Algernon Sidney at his death which spoke the godly language of the old cause, and which had so embarrassed earlier admirers of him. His words, she claimed, revealed his 'sincerity', his 'elevation of sentiment', his 'dignity of soul'. Vane, whose words at his own death Sidney's had echoed, gradually became a beneficiary of the same development. Like Sidney too he profited from the rise of Romanticism, a movement sometimes drawn to the emotional ardour of the Puritans.

Besides, Vane had sustained a profound commitment to the principle of liberty of conscience, a merit in him which had largely escaped the eighteenth century's notice but which won high respect in the nineteenth. It had barely occurred to the eighteenth century that enthusiasts were capable of wanting toleration, except for themselves. In 1827 the *Westminster Review* saw that Vane had managed that feat. Not least he had tried, exceptionally among politicians of the civil wars, to extend liberty of conscience to those who embraced the heresy that most alarmed the seventeenth century, the denial of the doctrine of the Trinity. His tolerance towards them now pleased the Unitarian (or anti-Trinitarian) movement, which supplied the intellectual leadership of early nineteenth-century Dissent and which produced some of the most influential commentary on the civil wars to have been written in that era. Over the first four decades of the early nineteenth century Vane's memory was widely revered. He was the hero of William Godwin. Edward Bulwer Lytton wrote a dramatic dialogue representing his heroic resistance to the evil Cromwell. Even the nineteenth century's dislike of the Commonwealth, a regime in which he had played so central a part, now barely touched Vane. Writers behaved as if anxious to compensate for the earlier neglect of his 'spotless', 'incorruptible', 'disinterested' qualities.

The same virtues were complimented later in the nineteenth century, but with a shift of emphasis. Previously his integrity had been cited to explain his breach with Cromwell in 1653. John Rutt remarked in 1828 on the 'contrast' between Vane's 'generous adherence to the public cause' and 'the selfish character' of Cromwell's 'ambition'. For the more adventurous of the Whig spirits of the same era he was what Hampden was for the more cautious ones, the lost leader of the civil wars, the man who should have guided England's destiny in Cromwell's place. From the 1840s, however, it became conventional to regard his split with Cromwell as evidence not of his stature but of his limitations. 'Much stress is laid,' observed Daniel Wilson in his study of the protectorate in 1848, 'on the incorruptible integrity of Vane. But it was not incorruptibility or integrity alone that was needed' in the crisis of 1653. 'It was the ability to govern. Cromwell alone proved to be the master-spirit of the age.'

At two critical moments, it was decided, Vane had shirked the responsibilities of power. First there was Pride's Purge in December 1648, when instead of trying to control the course of events he had withdrawn from Westminster. Secondly and more critically there was Cromwell's assumption of protectoral power in December 1653. Vane's admirers now regretted that he had not seen the necessity of the protectorate or stood at Cromwell's side during it. His earlier nineteenth-century champions, lauding his administrative achievements, had represented him as (in John Forster's words) 'the most practical of politicians'. Now he was called 'unpractical'. Like Ludlow he was judged a 'narrow' figure beside the pragmatic Cromwell, whose readiness to work with men of views different from his own illustrated that 'largeness' of character and of vision with which Victorians often credited him. 'Narrowness' had become the term used to disparage the very quality which the previous century had praised as 'inflexibility'. Though Vane retained his followers, they generally conceded that his talents and exertions had been secondary to the protector's. Cromwell came, in the same way, to seem a greater figure than Blake, that 'faithful agent' and 'efficient instrument' of a 'master spirit'. In many accounts Milton, Cromwell's 'secretary', assumed a comparably secondary role. Wordsworth had famously invoked the spirit of Milton, who 'shouldst be living at this hour', for 'England hath need of thee'. A number of late Victorian writers and speakers, appropriating Wordsworth's words, substituted Cromwell's name for Milton's.*

Cromwell's rehabilitation, won at the expense of the Whig saints, was complete. To see how it was achieved we now look more closely at the bases of Victorian Cromwellianism.

* Another leading figure of the civil wars to benefit from the change of attitude towards heroism was the parliamentary general Thomas Fairfax, whose 'ambition' had been rebuked by *Biographia Britannica*. His offence in eighteenth-century eyes had been his decision to remain in his post as Lord General in the late 1640s, when, had he been faithful to his own moderate instincts, he would have broken with the army upon failing to withstand its lurch into radicalism. By contrast Clements Markham's reverential and influential biography of 1870 explains that 'a strong sense of duty alone' dissuaded Fairfax from 'deserting his post' when, 'had he simply consulted his own ease', 'every personal consideration would have led him to throw up his command'; and that in adhering to 'his patriotic resolution to serve his country under whatever form of government the ruling powers might introduce' he 'chose the part of a true patriot'. Markham can thus credit Fairfax with 'disinterestedness', with 'unswerving uprightness', with an immunity to 'extraordinary temptations', with a life led 'without a stain upon his honour' or 'taint of self-seeking' – the very qualities which, in the dictionary's eyes, had succumbed to his 'ambition'.

9

Victorian Cromwell

Nineteenth-century Cromwellianism, still more than eighteenth-century patriotism, was a coalition of enthusiasms. It had various faces, some aggressive, some accommodating. It began, as patriotism had done, as an anti-establishment impulse. By the end of the nineteenth century the establishment had more or less come to terms with Cromwell, but it was not establishment writers who had made the running. In the new era of mass politics and mass publication, anti-establishment Cromwellianism acquired a breadth of social appeal, and at times a ferocity, which the patriotism of the earlier age had not commanded. It spoke for the other England: the England, it was said, for which Cromwell had stood and which had been oppressed ever since. It is the other England, speaking sometimes for political and social causes, sometimes for religious ones, that supplies the drive of the Cromwellian movement.

Anti-establishment Cromwellianism took its strength from the economic distress and discontent of the early nineteenth century. Its initial focus was the episode of Cromwell's life that John Toland had succeeded in highlighting, his forcible dissolution of the Long Parliament in April 1653. That event had long held the nation's imagination. Eighteenth-century readers, even as they were appalled by the coup, thrilled to the drama of its assault on every parliamentary decency and privilege. Cromwell's arrival at the Commons with a troop of musketeers at his back, his violent harangue against the depravity of the members, his seizure of the mace ('Take away that bauble!'), the forcible eviction of the members from the chamber, the locking of its doors when they were gone: that sequence of events entered the nation's collective memory. At the coup Speaker Lenthall, who had famously defied Charles I before the House when the king came to arrest the five members, was no less famously led from his chair by a Major-General. Dr Johnson had no love for either the perpetrator or the victims of the deed. To him Cromwell and the Rump were twin betrayers of parliamentary legitimacy. Yet in 1759 he suggested in *The Idler* that a painting of the moment when Cromwell 'ordered the bauble to be taken away' would make 'a picture of unexampled variety and irresistible instruction'. In 1783 Benjamin West obliged with a picture of Cromwell ordering the mace to be removed. The painting acquired a lasting fame and influence.

Later generations were equally impressed by the coup. Macaulay wrote that watching the passage of the Great Reform Bill of 1832 through the Commons, that high moment of nineteenth-century parliamentary conflict, was 'like seeing . . . Cromwell taking the mace from the table'. In 1845 Thomas Carlyle, who thought the coup Cromwell's 'big hour', noticed the 'shudder' with which it was still remembered. The episode is a set-piece in Gilbert Beckett's celebrated *Comic History of England* (1848) and in Charles Dickens's *A Child's History of England* (1852–4). It was, remarked Cromwell's biographer Frederic Harrison in 1889, 'one of the most famous scenes in our history'. In 1891, at the Australian Federal Conference which discussed the Commonwealth of Australia Bill, it was argued that the word 'Federation' was preferable to 'Commonwealth' because the latter term was 'connected with republican times', and that if it were adopted 'a future Oliver Cromwell' might arise 'who would say, "Take away that bauble", meaning by the bauble the allegiance we owe to her Majesty the Queen and the United Kingdom'. During the famous debate of May 1940 which produced the fall of Neville Chamberlain, Leo Amery dramatically quoted – with some embellishment – words spoken by Cromwell at the coup. Michael Heseltine's seizure of the mace in 1976, a protest against the conduct of the Labour government Whips in securing the passage of a vote, was a perhaps less conscious but a no less indebted tribute to Cromwellian memory.

It was one thing to dwell on or allude to Cromwell's military coup, another to approve of it. Yet, down the centuries, approving voices can be heard. The Walpolean oligarchy was often equated with the Rump and by implication was deemed to merit similar treatment. Later

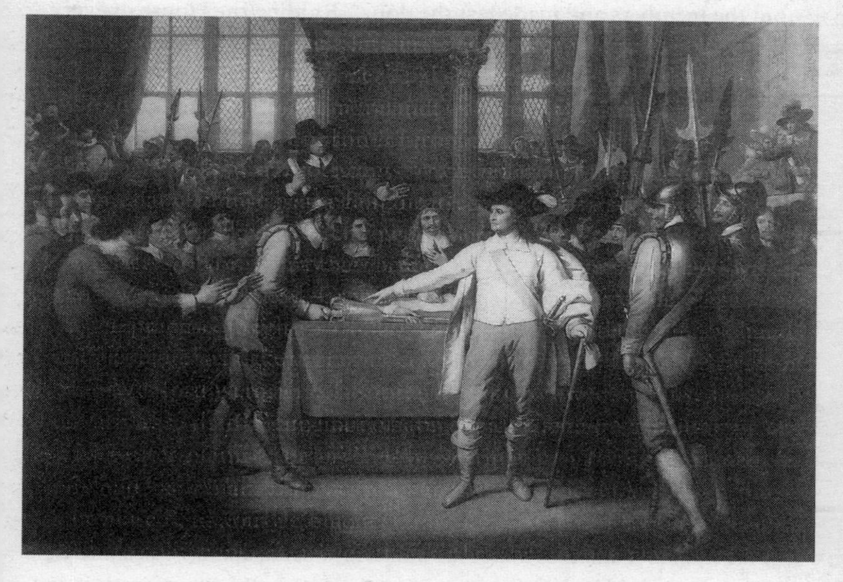

Benjamin West, *Cromwell Dissolving the Long Parliament* (1783).

Hanoverian ministries suffered the same comparison. The eighteenth-century Dissenting congregation described in Crabbe's poem 'The Frank Courtship' liked to recall the moment when Cromwell 'turned out the members and made fast the door, / Ridding the House of every knave and drone.' In 1767 the *Annual Register* carried a forged version, inspired by parliament's behaviour to John Wilkes, of the speech delivered by Cromwell at the Long Parliament's dissolution, in which Oliver was made to say: 'Your country, therefore, calls upon me to cleanse the Augean stables.' With the rise of populist agitation in the early nineteenth century, such invocations of the coup became more common. In 1811 a letter from starving and unemployed workmen to the Home Secretary warned him of impending 'vengeance': 'It's time a second Oliver made his appearance to cleanse the Augean stable.' When, around 1816, the radical weaver and poet Samuel Bamford first visited the House of Commons, in the old chamber of St Stephen's chapel, he was shocked by what he saw:

> And are these, I thought, the beings whose laws we must obey? This 'the most illustrious assembly of free men in the world'? Perish freedom then and her children too. O! for the stamp of stern old Oliver on this floor; and the clank of his scabbard, and the rush of his iron-armed band, and his voice to arise above this babel-howl – 'Take away this bauble' – 'Begone; give place to honester men.'

There was a belligerent strain, a sometimes despairing instinct to smash, in working-class radicalism, which the memory of Cromwell's destruction of the Long Parliament gratified. In September 1836 an article in praise of Cromwell in the *Political Penny Magazine*, signed 'Wat Tyler', met objections to Oliver's political morality with the argument that 'in matters of state there is no right and no wrong except what the strongest choose to declare. Might is right', and 'the labouring people of England' will be free only when they acquire the strength to 'regain their rights' as they did in Cromwell's time. Sometimes such sentiments had the memory of Charles I as their target. In 1834 Robert Lowery, attacking the verdict against the Tolpuddle martyrs, warned England's rulers that 'the spirit which brought first Charles to the block is not yet extinct'. But Cromwell, the breaker first of the king and then of the parliament, pleased early nineteenth-century radicals as much by the second achievement as by the first. In 1831, at the crisis over the Great Reform Act, the following notice appeared in Henry Hetherington's journal the *Poor Man's Guardian*:

> Wanted, a man of the most uncompromising honest and enterprising activity, who will undertake to clear St Stephen's, and the whole country, of a host of vermin who are fattening themselves upon the productions of our poor starving and miserable fellow-countrymen. Any person of the name of Cromwell would be preferred.

Though there were some radicals during the early and mid-nineteenth century – William Cobbett and Richard Cobden among them – for whom Cromwell was the people's enemy, to many more he was their friend. Cromwell had come of (modest) gentle origins, but in the nineteenth century he was held to have 'belonged to the people', from whom he had 'sprung' and for whose 'drift' he had 'an unerring instinct'. Earlier ages, though dazzled by the rise of Cromwell, a commoner, to sovereignty, could not approve of it. They too gave him plebeian associations, but in a hostile spirit. In particular they derided his family's connection with the brewing trade. In the nineteenth century that apparently lower-class link became a matter for indifference where not for approbation. In recruiting and inspiring his troops, it was observed, he had set the claims of 'conscience', which crossed and challenged social frontiers, against the 'delusive' aristocratic values of 'honour' and 'chivalry'. With the 'bright flash of his sword' he had 'smashed our feudal gyres [= bonds]'. 'The aristocracy of England', remarked Edmund Clarke to the Manchester Mechanics Institute in 1846, 'have always regarded' Cromwell 'as their chief enemy', for he 'infused the loftiest energy into the common people, and showed that there was a soul in the plebeian, and a might in his arm, before which the aristocrat and his retainer were as dry twigs before the blast'. Clarke attacked, as a mask for aristocratic selfishness, the language of 'disinterestedness and patriotism' which had been dear to the previous century. A detail will register the shift from patriot to anti-aristocratic sentiment. In the eighteenth century the Self-Denying Ordinance, the measure of 1645 which, with Cromwell's support, forbade members of parliament to hold public or military office, had been approved in some patriot quarters as a 'corruption bill', an assault on placemen. In the nineteenth century it was hailed for having purged from the parliamentary command those 'titled incapables' who feared that, if the king lost battles, 'aristocracy would be in peril'.

Working-class radicals applauded not only Cromwell but what the Chartist Henry Vincent, who around the middle of the century gave a series of lectures on Oliver and his age, called 'that wonderful period' of the civil wars and of its struggle for liberty. Cromwell himself came to be viewed not only as a socialist but as a republican. To earlier republicans, who stood in the Whig and patriot tradition, he had been the vile apostate of their cause. Now that republicanism viewed the Crown less as an enemy to parliamentary liberties than as the head of a system of aristocratic oppression, it was able to make common cause with Chartism and with socialism. Whig republicans had attacked the divine right of kings: in 1845 the *Bradford Observer* approvingly described Cromwell as the man who armed 'the people' against 'the divine right of the nobility'. It is perhaps around 1850 that socialist and republican Cromwellianism is at its peak. 'A spirit of Cromwellian might,' proclaimed George Harney's *The Red Republican* in that year, 'is stirring at this hour.' Also in 1850 the memory of the dissolution of the Rump stirred once more, when the Chartist George Thompson, while making a speech attacking parliament, was interrupted by cries of 'Cromwell!' Four years later the *Northern Tribune* likewise drew on that memory. Praising Cromwell as 'the first man to draw the sword on the people's side' it called for a leader who 'shall again lead the Ironsides to victory, and sit at England's council-board'.

There was middle-class Cromwellianism too, which found in Cromwell middle-class virtues. To Macaulay he embodied 'the best qualities of the middling orders'. Sometimes images of him were rural and static. To Carlyle in 1846 he was a 'solid farmer'. Sometimes he was portrayed as a self-made man, a witness to the merits of Samuel Smiles's principle of self-help. In the eighteenth century the readiness of the protectorate to recruit its leaders and advisers from a wide range of talent and opinions had been explained as a policy of political (rather than social) inclusiveness. Now it fed the middle-class Victorian demand, which inspired the introduction of competitive examinations for the Civil

Service, that the state's servants be appointed on grounds of merit rather than social rank.

Despite their many differences, working-class and middle-class Cromwellianism often merged. Writers who stressed Oliver's middle-class credentials tended to think of the middle class, in the seventeenth and the nineteenth century alike, as the ally or partner of the working class or at least of its more respectable or aspirational elements. Middle-class and working-class thinking came together in a social interpretation of the civil wars. Since the wars themselves, royalist and Tory history had portrayed the Roundhead cause as a socially inferior movement, motivated by the envy, resentment or desperation of the low-born, the rootless, the indebted. Over the earlier nineteenth century the social inclusiveness of the Roundheads became, to much respectable Whig thought as well as to working-class radicalism, a mark of virtue. Parallels were discerned between the social movements underlying the civil wars and the challenge to aristocratic dominance in the present time. In 1845 one observer, rejoicing in the retreat of hostile accounts of the Puritan revolt, attributed it to the spread of 'enlightened' opinion among the 'bulk of the community', to the meanest cottager and artisan. The parliamentary cause itself, it seemed, had given voice to a comparable enlightenment. Its origins, it was commonly said, had lain in the weakening of the aristocracy under the Tudors, in the rise of the commercial classes in its place, and in a consequent appetite for civic and moral independence among social groups hitherto denied them. It was a 'popular' cause, devoted to 'popular progress' and 'popular rights' and 'popular privilege', to political emancipation beyond Westminster and the ruling class, to the cause of 'the despised yeomanry and mechanics' and to the defeat of 'the tripartite league of the king, the noble, the priest'. Again the Revolution of 1688 suffered by comparison. In 1849 the popular lecturer George Dawson declared that only a nation reprehensibly 'ashamed' of Cromwell would have so 'magnified' the 'small affair of 1688' and undervalued 'the mighty business of 1642'. In 1867 Goldwin Smith, who thought of the second conflict as a merely 'aristocratic revolution', observed that 'there were other interests for which men had given their lives at Marston and Naseby, and with which, when Cromwell died . . ., all was over for many a day'.

From the 1840s a great movement of middle-class and working-class discussion of Cromwell arose. Debating clubs and Mechanics Institutes and Mutual Improvement Societies gathered to assess the protector's character and motives and stature and achievements. In Oxfordshire in 1852 the Watlington Mutual Improvement Society, after a debate which lasted seven evenings and which produced, according to the local newspaper, speeches of 'great research, power and eloquence', resolved that 'a better Christian' than Cromwell, 'a more noble-minded spirit, a greater warrior, a more constant man has scarcely ever appeared on the face of the earth'. Comparable meetings took place in many parts of the country, above all in the north. In northern towns and cities a heavy demand for library books on the Cromwellian period was recorded. There too a touring exhibition of a painting of Cromwell refusing parliament's offer of the Crown caused a sensation in 1859–61. In 1877 the Wycliffe Mutual Improvement Society at Warrington decided, following an animated debate but with only one dissenting vote, that Cromwell 'was a benefactor to his countrymen, and that many of the privileges that we enjoy at this day were secured by him'. At Hebden Bridge in Yorkshire in 1889 an earnest discussion after an Oxford University Extension Lecture on Cromwell ended with a vote in favour of the regicide.

In the first half of the nineteenth century, Cromwellianism, like the Whiggism and republicanism of the previous age, was predominantly secular. Cromwell was admired less often because of his Puritanism than in spite of it. In the eighteenth century his tendency to 'enthusiasm' had been admitted by his friendly assessors. They argued sometimes that it had been exaggerated, sometimes that, 'how little soever his behaviour would take at present', it had merely been characteristic of 'the times in which he lived', an excuse that was sometimes extended, by admirers of the commonwealthmen of the civil wars, to them too. The charge of hypocrisy against Cromwell was occasionally repudiated, partly on the ground that it is not for men to judge truthfulness of soul, which is known only to God. But the overwhelming weight of published opinion was mercilessly against his professions of faith.

By the end of the Victorian age his Puritanism was a prominent part of his appeal. Signs of the change are visible early in the nineteenth century, when the spread of Nonconformity brought a new interest in Cromwell's religion. Hitherto Nonconformist historians had normally ventured to praise seventeenth-century Puritanism only in its pre-civil-war and post-Restoration guises, its eras of persecution. From the late 1820s some of them began, nervously and tentatively, to commend it in the form it had taken in the civil wars, its era of power. No less nervously and tentatively they began to find merits in Cromwell. Where their secular counterparts praised his deeds, the Nonconformist historians Thomas Price, Charles Mann, William Jones and Robert Vaughan started to reassess his character and his faith. They detected sincerity, or at least a measure of it, where most still saw hypocrisy. For a time their lead was not widely followed. Most Nonconformists remained wary of invoking Cromwell's name. They knew how gravely the cause of liberty of conscience, their highest priority in public affairs, had been damaged since 1660, and could be damaged now, by memories of his radical politics.

The argument that the mid-seventeenth-century record showed Dissent to be inherently seditious met unavailing protests. In 1726 the Whig historian John Oldmixon condemned it as 'groundless and scandalous', the concoction of 'bigoted clergymen'. A century later, Independent (or Congregationalist) historians, William Orme at their head, had to mount a comparable defence. With the Baptists, Independents were the denomination which had owed most to Cromwell's rise and protection and which, since the Restoration, had been readiest to remember the liberty of conscience extended by the protectorate across the Puritan fold. Cromwell's politics, however, were a different matter. Early nineteenth-century Dissent generally kept quiet about politics. Nonconformists who mixed religion with politics encountered disapproval from their colleagues on both spiritual and prudential grounds. The political achievements of Puritanism did win admiration in other quarters. In the 1820s Macaulay and William Godwin acknowledged that the movement, by virtue of the zeal it instilled into Charles I's opponents, had helped to thwart the Stuart tyranny. But it was only as an ally of 'civil liberty' that they endorsed it, not for its religious content, which they could not stomach. The nineteenth century transformed the reputation of Puritanism, as of Cromwell. To Macaulay the distance kept by John Hampden from fanatical Puritan doctrine was a sign of his superiority to his Roundhead allies. Subsequent admirers of Hampden searched for Puritan instincts in him. Macaulay explained too that Milton, whom he revered as much as Hampden, was 'not a Puritan'. The poet's later followers deemed his virtue 'Puritan'.

It was the swelling of Nonconformity that brought Cromwell his firmest and most devoted Victorian following. Above all he was, as a prominent Baptist declared in 1877, 'the hero-saint of all true Baptists and Congregationalists'. Those and other denominations, or at least the more militant elements within them, had cast political inhibition aside. The struggle for, and advances of, political and educational emancipation wrought the change. By 1873 the Independent journal *The Congregationalist* could declare that 'the least active and satisfactory members of the Church are, for the most part, those who have a pious horror of strong political views and decided political action'. One commemorator during the tercentenary maintained that Christianity was 'worthless unless it led to practical religion on this earth'. He condemned the 'miserable', 'selfish' idea, which 'finds no support in the Bible', that 'religion only consists in ensuring the safe passage to heaven of your own soul, leaving the world to welter in the mire'.

The rise of Nonconformist political radicalism brought a reassessment of Dissent's political past. Nonconformity, it was argued, had dwelt too much on its history since the Restoration, too little on its period of Cromwellian triumph. It had been too proud of its endurance under persecution after 1660, too grateful for the limited gains won for Dissenting worship by the Toleration Act of 1689 and by Whig patronage and protection thereafter. *The Congregationalist*, calling in 1873 for an end to two centuries of humiliating subordination to Whig leaders, looked behind them 'to those sublime days when our forefathers held sway in England. If we have served under Somers, Walpole, Fox, Grey and Russell, we have reigned with Cromwell.' Late nineteenth-century Congregationalists were proud to remember the era when Independency 'ruled the destinies of England'. At the tercentenary they and other Nonconformist denominations recognized their duty to 'work for England and the world precisely as [Cromwell] did'. They urged each other to 'awake' to meet that challenge. They told themselves that Cromwell was 'the man of the hour', that in spirit he was 'alive' or 'living now', or that 'living Cromwells' were needed now. In 1902 the National Council of the Evangelical Free Churches, outraged by the Anglican bias of the Education Bill of that year, heard its leaders warn the government to expect 'noble instances of stubborn and heroic resistance', even a readiness to 'die', from men whose 'proud boast' it was to be 'descendants of men like Oliver Cromwell'.

In and around the tercentenary year it was mainly political militants who wrote Nonconformist biographies and studies of Cromwell. They celebrated the protector's 'clear recognition of our fundamental principles'. During the commemorative meetings in the City Temple, that 'Nonconformist cathedral', an event organized by the National Council of the Evangelical Free Churches, allusions to present-day political evils produced crescendos of acclamation. No one could remember such excitement in the building. The principal preacher, Joseph Parker, soon to become Chairman of the Congregational Union, was 'renowned for his strong language', which he now aimed, in a manner 'worthy of the Cromwellian Puritans', 'to men who sit in high places'. He electrified the congregation by calling, in a house of God, for the return of the Liberals to power. Other speakers and writers used the tercentenary to address a range of contemporary evils: drink, gambling, prostitution, poverty.

Above all there was the high church movement, which had been a main source of Victorian antagonism to Cromwell. A fresh wave of 'Puseyism' had gathered strength in recent years. It reached its climax in and around 1899. Hatred of popery and of Puseyism had been potent forces within Victorian Cromwellianism, but were never more so than during the tercentenary commemorations, of which Cromwell's 'anti-Ritualism', and the sinister influence (in the seventeenth and the nineteenth century alike) of 'priestcraft', supplied the most persistent theme. For if Cromwell had saved the nation from civil tyranny, so had he 'rescued the English race from popery.' Fierce applause greeted comparisons between his resistance to the 'persecuting sacerdotalism' of Archbishop Laud and the present-day struggle of 'imperilled Protestantism' against 'the threatened return of Romanism'.

The Cromwellianism of militant Nonconformity was confrontational and divisive. 'There are two Englands', the commemorators of the tercentenary in Cromwell's native town of Huntingdon were told, 'the England of Ethelred Unready, William Rufus, Bloody Mary and Charles II', and 'the England of Alfred, Harold, Good Queen Bess, and Oliver Cromwell. To which do you belong?' 'Ringing cheers answered, "Oliver's! Cromwell's!"' Nonconformist Cromwellians claimed to speak for 'the biggest half of the nation', for 'the great bulk of the people'. Hitherto, they observed, the 'biggest half' had been kept down, but now 'the boot is on the other leg'.

Not all Victorian Cromwellianism was militant or confrontational. There was a consensual Cromwellianism, which spoke not for 'two Englands' but for one, and which claimed Cromwell for the whole nation, not merely for an aggrieved part of it. As the great historian of the civil wars S. R. Gardiner declared in 1897, Cromwell had become 'the national hero of the nineteenth century'. Where militant Nonconformists wanted to see him as 'the typical free churchman', Gardiner judged him 'the greatest because the most typical Englishman of all time', a remark that would be incessantly quoted and echoed. Earlier in the century, emphases on Cromwell's 'Englishness' had betrayed an element of class hostility, which drew, usually at a subterranean level, on the tradition of complaint against the 'Norman yoke'. Cromwell had fought, it was intimated, in the cause of Saxon freedom against the foreign aristocracy which had subdued it in 1066. At the end of the century his 'Englishness', though it could still be a divisive theme, was more often a unifying one.

The same was true of his Puritanism. The nation's Puritan inheritance was not claimed solely by Nonconformists or by enemies to the establishment. Among a wider public it came to seem, in Gardiner's words, 'the most precious possession of the nation'. Certainly it was Nonconformists who had most to say about Cromwell's 'earnestness' and 'moral' sense, they who rejoiced most fulsomely in the thought that those had once been the virtues of an English ruler. Yet the same qualities spoke well beyond Nonconformity to the wider seriousness of the Victorian age. Upright virtues had been found in Cromwell before. His blameless private life, his habits of private devotion, his godliness on his deathbed, had sometimes been noticed, not without surprise, in the eighteenth century. Yet those merits had appeared hard

Cromwell in earnest. Augustus Leopold Egg, *The Night before Naseby*, detail (1859).

to square with the wickedness and duplicity of his public career. Now they seemed in character with his whole life. Cromwellians outside Nonconformity looked to a modernized Puritanism, which in countering the evils of this 'sensual and avaricious age' would retain the 'high seriousness' and 'moral earnestness' of its seventeenth-century predecessor while avoiding its 'narrowness'. Nonconformists were divided by the spread of consensual Cromwellianism. Some of them resented it. The more conciliatory figures among them, recognizing 'that they have no monopoly of the Lord Protector', found that they had more in common with Cromwellians outside the fold than within it. Many Nonconformists, stung by the charge of philistinism brought against their movement by Matthew Arnold, were eager to deny that the Puritan movement, past or present, was narrow. With other Victorians they emphasized Cromwell's 'largeness' of mind or heart and soul. They underlined – indeed overstated – his love of music and his interest in the arts.

Gardiner is a key figure in the consensual Cromwellianism of the later Victorian age, in what was called a 'moderating' approach to Cromwell. Prominent too was the Liberal Cabinet minister John Morley, whose biography of Cromwell appeared in 1900. Those men applauded Cromwell's ethical and religious aspirations. They also admired, even revered him as a man of action and courage and resolution. It was his sword, they agreed, that had saved England from political and spiritual tyranny. But while they could recognize the necessity of that achievement, unlike militant Nonconformists they could not take much pleasure in it. They took less pleasure still in the regicide. Gardiner believed, as Macaulay had done, that Cromwell had always preferred 'to walk in the ways of legality'. With Macaulay too he maintained that Cromwell's departures from those methods had been counter-productive when not disastrous. To Gardiner Cromwell's practical achievements, astounding and often indispensable as they were, were essentially negative and destructive. Many Cromwellians had insisted earlier in the century that the course of English history would have been far healthier if the protector had lived another ten years or been succeeded by an equal spirit, and if the calamity of the Restoration had thus been averted. The 'moderating' historians, by contrast, questioned the durability of the protectoral regime.

They also pointed to the presence, among its undoubted virtues, of moral weaknesses. Where radical Nonconformists steered memories away from the Restoration towards the glorious era of Puritan rule, Gardiner and Morley maintained that Puritanism had proved (in Gardiner's words of 1900) 'of better service' after 1660, 'when it was relegated from the exercise of power to the employment of influence'. Power, they thought, had given too much encouragement to the narrow and fanatical side of Puritanism. Cromwell's effort to impose a strenuousness of conduct beyond the nation's moral means, however edified in motive, had obliged him to rule without the concurrence of national feeling, that essential basis of lasting and improving statesmanship. Before the Restoration, Gardiner judged, Puritanism was only the creed of a party. After it, it permeated the moral sensibility of the nation at large, 'penetrating and informing its conquerors'. It was out of Restoration Puritanism that there had grown that earnestness of spirit which, when they were true to it, was Englishmen's finest quality. J. R. Green, in his *History of the English People* (1874), thought the same. In power, he judged, Puritanism had been marked by 'intolerance', 'doctrinal bigotry', 'narrowness'. In 1660, when it 'laid down the sword', it 'ceased from the long attempt to build up a kingdom of God by force and violence, and fell back on the truer work of building up a kingdom of righteousness in the hearts and consciences of men'. The reaction against the 'orgy' of depravity under Charles II, thought Green, 'left the mass of Englishmen what Puritanism had made them, serious, earnest, sober in life and conduct, firm in their love of Protestantism and of freedom'.

From that standpoint Cromwell's heroism in action was but one face of a seventeenth-century movement of the human spirit that had also had a number of other, gentler aspects. As the respect of the Victorians for the Puritan past became more ample and secure, so Puritanism came to seem to have had many parts, spiritual, literary, evangelical, theological, political, each making its own contribution to a movement of rich diversity. While many militant Cromwellians liked to think of him in lonely eminence, towering above his contemporaries, it gradually became commoner to place and assess him in the company of other Puritans, sometimes divines such as Thomas Goodwin and John Howe, sometimes the writers Milton and Bunyan.

What he shared with those men was the Puritan character, an attribute which was declared to have been of more durable and uplifting influence than his deeds. As Gardiner put it, 'the man – it is ever so with the noblest – was greater than his work'. With the broadening of Cromwellianism the wish of militant Nonconformists to keep him to themselves began to give offence. Why, it was asked, were the tercentenary commemorations, which ought to have been a 'national' event, made a 'sectarian' one? It was 'petty and pitiable', complained an Anglican clergyman, 'for an extreme section of the Protestant party to identify the memory of the great Cromwell with itself'.

There was one point, at least, on which Cromwellians of all stamps could agree. Cromwell had been tolerant in religion. His efforts to secure liberty of conscience and worship had looked forward to the great nineteenth-century movement of religious toleration. This was not the only subject where Victorian admirers of his domestic administration saw reflections of their own preoccupations and values. There is the approving attention given, by the age of Dickens, to the attempts made by the protector and his colleagues to reform the Court of Chancery and the laws governing imprisonment for debt. There is the somewhat strained conviction that he hastened the advance of modern communications by improving roads and the postal service. There is the equally questionable supposition that he was wedded to the ideal of free trade – though late in Victoria's reign, as politicians and the public came to terms with new ideas of state intervention, he was seen (in the words of the *Daily News* in 1900) as 'the first statesman who formed the concept of colonization as an organized effort by the state'. But it was in relation to religious liberty that he was most broadly recognizable as an enlightened figure by the century which emancipated Unitarians and Roman Catholics and Jews.

Admittedly Cromwell had not been tolerant enough. He had said much about freedom of conscience and done much for it, but the liberty he provided was confined to those with whose religion he could sympathize. His position, it was true, did differ commendably from that of orthodox Puritans, who regarded liberty of conscience as the path to the eternal damnation of erring souls and who had no inclination to tolerate error within Puritanism, let alone outside it. But it parted also from Victorian assumptions, which began with the right of all to worship freely. Even among Nonconformists, where anti-popery was so strong, many believed that he ought to have extended toleration to Roman Catholics, for among their altogether less friendly feelings towards English Catholicism the Dissenters recognized in it a fellow-victim both of the spirit of persecution and of the monopoly of the Anglican state Church. There was also some embarrassment among Cromwellians at the protector's proscription of Anglicanism. He had outlawed not only 'popery' but 'prelacy' (the practices of worship among those committed to the old order of bishops and the Prayer Book), even if the ban was only fitfully applied. Modern apologists for the Church of England, an institution whose own persecution of Dissent during the Restoration was repeatedly assailed by Nonconformist memory, found a useful counter-weapon in Cromwell's treatment of Anglicans. They used it to effect during the controversy between Church and Dissent in 1862, when Nonconformists observed the bicentenary of the 'Great Ejection' of the Dissenting clergy, that high moment of Anglican intolerance when Nonconformity had been defined.

If there were unsatisfactory restrictions on Cromwell's toleration, satisfactory arguments could be found to account for them or extenuate them. He had inevitably shared, it was decided, the limitations of his age. Or (it was more commonly said) he had been ahead of his age, an age that did not understand the principles of toleration or perceive the inevitable limits of doctrinal certainty. Victorians often judged Cromwell to have been in favour of universal toleration but to have been unable to carry the nation or his followers with him, or to have been thwarted by political pressures, or to have been provoked by the obstinate political disloyalty of worshippers outside Puritanism, who would have been allowed to worship as they wished had they not involved themselves in conspiracy against his rule.

Alongside the religious and ethical bases of Cromwellianism an older tradition of approval lived on. It was more interested in his might than in his motives, more impressed by his exploits of power than by his religion. When Gardiner called Cromwell 'the national hero of the nineteenth century' he feared that it was not the protector's faith or morality that had won him that status, but rather his achievements abroad. 'In recent years,' Gardiner was sorry to say, 'it has become customary to extol Cromwell's foreign policy at the expense of his domestic.' Gardiner did warm, with most Victorian commentators, to the ethical dimension of Cromwell's diplomacy, especially to the protector's intervention on behalf of the persecuted Protestants of Piedmont in 1655. That episode was widely held, as was the broader Protestant thrust of his foreign policy, to have represented 'the highest impulses of the nation'. Nonconformists took the lead, and 'moderating' Cromwellians largely concurred, in recommending his conduct during the Piedmont episode as an example of moral interventionism to be followed by the British government in response to the Turkish atrocities in Bulgaria in the 1870s and Armenia in the 1890s. But those who praised the ethical dimension of Cromwell's foreign policy were troubled when they detected an aggrandizing element in his diplomacy. Here, thought Gardiner, he had deceived himself into regarding his own motives, which were essentially material, as moral.

The aggrandizement, as Gardiner recognized, was an essential aspect of the protector's late Victorian appeal. If his religious tolerance was praised for anticipating nineteenth-century thoughts and practices of which he could have had no inkling, his foreign policy was hailed as the foundation of national aspirations still more distant from his mind. The 'national spirit' which, since his time, had 'carried the British flag to the four corners of the earth' was credited to his 'Imperial purpose' and 'colonial policy'. The conquest of Jamaica, at the time a burdensome acquisition for which the protector had settled after the fiasco on Hispaniola, was viewed, in later accounts, as the cornerstone of empire. So perhaps it was, but Victorians mistook inadvertent effects of Cromwell's policy for his intentions. Where the eighteenth century did not know about the apocalyptic internationalism which had coloured the approach of Algernon Sidney and Edmund Ludlow to diplomatic issues, the nineteenth century missed the same proclivity in Cromwell. Considerations of national stature and self-sufficiency, inseparable in his mind from a pan-European godly cause, were divorced from it in historical interpretation. 'Even those who refuse to waste a thought on his spiritual aims,' reflected Gardiner, 'remember with gratitude his constancy of effort to make England great by sea and land.' 'It would be well for them to be reminded', he added, 'of his no less constant efforts to make England worthy of greatness.'

Interest in and admiration for Cromwell the conqueror were heightened by the anxieties and enthusiasms generated by the international tensions of the 1890s. In John Morley's words, Cromwell became 'a name on the Imperialist flag'. His foreign triumphs, as often before, won support across party lines. 'There is scarcely a fossil Tory extant,' observed the *Daily News* in 1900 with pardonable exaggeration, 'who feels no pride in Cromwell, the soldier and statesman, whose patriotism was as deep as his religion.' The late Victorian military campaigns, especially those of the Boer War, produced a new degree of interest in Cromwell's military stature and tactics. To previous generations his campaigns, though notable for their leadership and bravery, had generally seemed too primitive or small-scale to merit extensive analysis. Now they received it. Nonconformists and other religious enthusiasts, eager for the moral and religious improvement of the British army, had their own reasons to commend the fighting qualities of his godly soldiers. Another late Victorian preoccupation recognized its counterpart in Cromwell's military and diplomatic achievements. His incorporation of Ireland and Scotland into a single British state touched the concerns of the age of Unionism. It was thanks to Cromwell, explained the historian C. H. Firth in 1900, that Britain had 'emerged from the chaos of the civil wars one strong state instead of three separate and hostile communities'.

The last years of the century, from 1895 to 1900, gave Cromwell what Morley called 'a fresh spell of vigorous popularity', which peaked at the tercentenary. Those were the years when Cromwell the Imperialist attracted most attention; they were the time when the consensual Cromwellianism of a Gardiner or a Morley won its widest influence; they were a period of renewed militancy and confidence within Nonconformity, though that flourish of the movement was to be its final one.

Another spirit was at work too. Morley noted that the 'fresh spell of vigorous popularity . . . fell in with some notions of the day about representative government, the beneficent activities of the state, the virtues of a Strong Man, and the Hero as Ruler'. This was the era of the National Efficiency movement, whose devotees fretted at the confinement of executive power, in both domestic and foreign policy, by outdated principles of parliamentary rule, of which Britain's neighbours and rivals were free. Such sentiments had precedents in the earlier and mid-Victorian age, when even liberals had learned to praise Cromwell's 'efficiency' alongside his zeal for 'liberty'. There often surfaced what seemed to some a troublingly 'German' yearning for a 'dictator', with the 'strong hand' and 'iron will' of a Cromwell. Military difficulties, especially during the Crimean War of the 1850s and the Boer War around the century's end, intensified it. So, in the 1890s, did the National Efficiency movement. Lord Rosebery, a prominent figure both in that movement and in the cult of Cromwell, hailed him as 'a mighty man of action' and remarked that 'we could find employment for a few Cromwells now'. Where Macaulay, early in the century, disliked Puritan fervour but deemed it to have been a necessary ally of 'liberty', Rosebery, no more attracted to the fervour, regarded it as an essential spur to 'action'.

Against that background Cromwell's celebrated coup of April 1653, the forcible expulsion of the Long Parliament, found new ground for favour. In many minds, it is true, it remained a blot on his reputation. The dissolution, noticed his approving biographer Frederic Harrison in 1899, was 'that which of all other things has weighed most heavily on his fame'. But the undercurrent of approval, which we noticed in nineteenth-century popular radicalism, drew in other allegiances too. In the minds of militant Nonconformists the episode became associated, and sometimes confused, with one closer to their hearts, which had occurred nine years earlier in Ely Cathedral. Again with troops at his back he had instructed an Anglican clergyman to 'come down' from the pulpit, a moment which reminded Cromwellians of the removal of the Speaker from his chair by one of Oliver's officers in April 1653. Lloyd George, using the tercentenary commemoration to tighten his Nonconformist following, delighted the audience in the City Temple by remarking that Cromwell would have 'dealt with Romish practices now' as summarily as he had dispatched 'the priest who babbled his Paternosters' in the cathedral. Oliver's 'virtues and principles', he added, were 'sadly needed today'.*

* Nonconformist admiration for the dissolution would endure. The historian John Walsh tells me that, when he used to visit his Methodist grandfather's terraced mill-town house in Lancashire between the wars, a Victorian print, 'Take Away that Bauble', 'hit the eye immediately as one came in through the front door'.

To men concerned not with popery but with the impotence of parliamentary government, the coup of 1653 had a different appeal. Members of the National Efficiency movement saw in it the termination of an unhealthy parliamentary monopoly of power. In one influential speech, Rosebery, who liked to be thought of as a Cromwellian figure, echoed Oliver's words at the dissolution. In 1900 Leo Maxe's *National Review*, speaking for National Efficiency feeling, remarked that

> never has parliament sunk so low; never have Englishmen been so able to apprehend the joy with which their forefathers saw the Commons bundled out of their seats by the strong hand of Cromwell. Even revolution may be preferable to the ruin of all national interests. The axe, after all, is better than decay.

John Morley mistrusted such sentiments. Yet when he took charge of the India Office in 1909 he came to grasp 'how impatience at the delays and cavillings and mistakings of very small points for very big ones at last drove Cromwell to send [the parliament] packing'.

We have traced the long-term developments which underlay Victorian Cromwellianism. Yet they do not, by themselves, explain its ardour or intensity or depth. The cult of Cromwell was not the product only of political and social and religious movements. It was the achievement of a book, which spoke to Victorians with extraordinary power. In 1845 there appeared by far the most revolutionary and influential biography of the man – for biography, in spite of its title, it effectively is – ever to have been published: Thomas Carlyle's edition of *Oliver Cromwell's Letters and Speeches*.

10

Carlyle's Cromwell

To Cromwell's admirers in the late nineteenth century, the standing he had acquired in the Victorian age had one principal cause. 'At a single stroke' Carlyle's edition of *Oliver Cromwell's Letters and Speeches* had 'completely reversed the verdict of history'. It had 'burst on the world as a kind of historic revelation'. To the less adulatory of the Cromwellians, it is true, Carlyle's worship of the man seemed, by the late Victorian age, overdone. Yet the emergence of a 'calmer' admiration for the Lord Protector was itself judged a measure of Carlyle's achievement, for 'we Oliverians', 'no longer battling for revision of an unjust sentence', no longer needed the argumentative extravagances that had been Carlyle's weapons of victory.

Such assessments, which echoed his own indications of the book's significance, involved some simplification and exaggeration. Yet even when we have qualified it we are confronted by an extraordinary historiographical coup: one little explored, historians having largely ceded the study of Carlyle to literary scholars and critics, among whose priorities neither the historical content of the *Letters and Speeches*, nor its impact on public opinion, has normally ranked high. The book, a best-seller read by high and low, stands beside the histories of Macaulay and J. R. Green among the Victorian works which stamped the modern image of the English past. Carlyle, as he watched the book 'silently making its way into the heart of the country', judged it 'probably the usefullest work I shall ever get to do'. He believed he had rescued Cromwell just in time, before Cromwell's beliefs and language, traduced for two centuries, had finally become unintelligible.

A century and a half later the idiosyncrasies of Carlyle's own prose and of his editorial procedures, and the extremity of his political

Thomas Carlyle. Photograph by Julia Margaret Cameron (1867).

incorrectitudes, can make his book as baffling as Carlyle judged Cromwell to have been. Carlyle saw that he could make Cromwell's life intelligible by explaining the convictions and purpose that had guided it. His study of him can be reclaimed on the same principle. It is worth the effort, for the *Letters and Speeches*, despite but also because of its peculiarities of manner and matter, is the one great book to have been written about Cromwell, even if it is easier to think of it as a great book than as a good one. In it a volcanic, untameable writer finds a volcanic, untameable subject, to which his gifts and convictions are eccentrically but uniquely suited.

The book was published shortly before Carlyle's fiftieth birthday, at the peak of his fame and influence, if a little beyond the peak of his powers. He had moved from his native Scotland to England in 1834, and had settled in the house in Cheyne Walk in Chelsea where he would live until his death in 1881. Two formative influences on Carlyle's thinking had been decisive. There was the devout Calvinism in which he was brought up in Dumfriesshire, and which left its imprint on his mind long after he had rejected its theology. And there was German Romanticism, the movement of Goethe and Schiller, to which much of his early writing was devoted. In a temperament as highly wrought as Carlyle's, the two ideals were an explosive combination. His uniquely individual and often lacerating prose acquired, in early Victorian England, a commanding appeal. Between 1838 and 1843 he published the series of books – *Sartor Resartus, The French Revolution, Of Heroes and Hero-Worship* (the work of 1841 which contained his first sketch of Cromwell's character), *Past and Present* – that made him the most powerful didactic writer of his time. The public disillusion with Whig parliamentary reform in the 1830s, the hard times and revolutionary prospects of the 1840s, and the awakening of moral and religious earnestness over those decades gave an urgent authority to a scourge and prophet who cried doom and preached regeneration. His insistence that, at that 'serious, grave epoch', 'the time for levity, insincerity and playacting is gone' spoke especially to the idealistic young, who found in his teaching a 'creed' and a 'religion'. Like his previous books, *Oliver Cromwell's Letters and Speeches* is a tract for the times. Like them it assails the values – liberal, utilitarian, rationalist, materialist – of early Victorian England: of a society turned from God to Mammon, from eternal verities of good and evil to the 'babblements' of rights and liberty and parliamentary enfranchisement.

The towering and enduring achievement of Carlyle's book, and the one that earned most Victorian gratitude, was his recovery of the thread of religious conviction that ran through Cromwell's life, and of the sincerity and intensity of those Puritan beliefs which earlier writers had condemned as hypocritical or absurd. His recognition of those qualities in Oliver came slowly. So did the means he found of expressing it. Even by Carlyle's standards of creative agony the composition of the book was a hideous ordeal. The chronological complexity of the civil wars, and the 'shoreless lakes' of unsorted documents they had bequeathed, induced tortured despair. He could not decide on a focus or a form. Was the book to be primarily about Cromwell himself, or was it to centre on the Puritan movement he had come to lead? Or should it rather be a general history of the earlier and mid-seventeenth century, in England and perhaps Scotland too? Eventually he settled on a biography – only to suspend and then abandon that ambition in favour of an edition of the letters and speeches, where Cromwell's words would be elucidated by Carlyle's commentary. Cromwell's words being many, Carlyle saw that the book would be long, perhaps unpublishably so. He therefore strove to keep his explanatory material to a minimum. Yet when the editing was complete, and even as the book was at the printer's, Carlyle (at whose very name compositors would groan) greatly expanded his commentary, introducing – or reintroducing from a mountain of abandoned drafts – passages that can seem arbitrarily selected or positioned. More than half the words of the book are Carlyle's rather than Cromwell's. The work is, he recognized, 'a kind of life of Oliver'.

More ambitiously than his earlier works, the *Letters and Speeches* looks to history for the remedy of present evils. Not, of course, to history as written by Carlyle's contemporaries, those 'cause-and-effect speculators' who supposed that the spiritual attainments of the past could be 'accounted for' by materialist explanation or subordinated to the ephemera of power-struggles and constitutional conflicts. For Carlyle history was a nation's bible, a record of God's government of its affairs; or else a Homeric epic, a witness to the divine capacity of heroes. The historian was a 'sacred poet', charged with identifying and singing the transcendent essence of the past. Yet there was a humbler role for him too. One of the few historical works Carlyle ever praised was an edition, published in 1840 by the recently formed Camden Society, of the chronicle of the twelfth-century monk Jocelin of Brakelond. From it he learned that competent editing can facilitate, even if in itself it does not constitute, insight into the historically divine. In *Past and Present*, published in 1843, the book of Carlyle with which the *Letters and Speeches* was most closely connected, Jocelin's narrative supplied the material for Carlyle's portrait of the divine hero Abbot Samson. Now, in the *Letters and Speeches*, his portrait of the divine hero Cromwell rested on his own, sometimes doggedly antiquarian labours.

Jocelin's chronicle showed Carlyle something else. The miraculous intimacies of recognition reachable through the 'chance crevices' of the archives could, he believed, prove to his own time, to an era imprisoned by present-mindedness, that the past never dies: that though its outward forms vanish irretrievably its soul is eternal. To him the progressive philosophy of his time, transfixed by the impermanent, was sundering the present from the past. The result was a creeping determinism, a proneness to see man as the product rather than the creator of his circumstances, a refusal to imagine the meeting of moral and spiritual challenges that earlier generations had been ready to confront. The more distant from the present, whether in time or in spirit, the documents recovered by an editor, the more profound their instructive scope. So the *Letters and Speeches* introduces the reader, across two centuries of unbelief, 'across the death-chasms, and howling figures of decay', to intimate documents of Puritan rule, of the nation's 'last glimpse of the godlike'. For if England were 'ever to struggle Godward again, instead of struggling Devilward', it was to 'new Cromwells' and 'new Puritans' that it must look.

Some Victorians chuckled at Carlyle's championship of seventeenth-century godliness: at the spectacle of 'sour, fanatical, strait-laced Puritanism' being 'fondled and poetized by one to whom Christianity is but the mythic expression of religion'. But if Carlyle had turned away from Calvinist theology, then morally and emotionally – even, in one part of his mind, intellectually – he remained unconquerably pledged to the Decalogue, to the Prophets and Psalms, to the terrors of hell, perhaps most of all to the operation of divine providence. Cromwell's own statement that 'all our histories' are enactments of God's providence, noticed Carlyle's disciple David Masson, 'expresses exactly one part of Carlyle's religion'.

Carlyle resolved to take his readers inside Cromwell's inner self and inspire them to emulate the 'living God-inspired soul' of that 'genuine king among men'. For whereas Carlyle's contemporaries sought political and economic solutions to England's sickness, for him – as for the Puritans themselves – reformation begins within the heart and soul, of whose evils the afflictions of society are merely an extension. The challenge of persuasion facing Carlyle seemed to him massive, not least because he judged the scriptural linguistic habits of the Puritans to have been turned, by the subsequent degeneration of Protestantism, into cant. If the printing of Cromwell's words were to overcome rather than confirm the prevailing impression of his character, the reader would need close guidance. Carlyle supplied it in those excited textual interpolations – reporting sometimes the expression on Cromwell's face as he addresses parliament ('elevating his brows; face assuming a look of irony'), sometimes the pitch of his voice (a 'sonorous bass', or 'risen somewhat into [alto] and rolling with a kind of rough music in the tones of it') – which now seem the most bizarre feature of the book, and at which even its Victorian admirers sometimes baulked.

An ominous figure stood in Carlyle's path. This was the imaginary historian whom he terms Dryasdust, and on whom, from first to last, he heaps abuse. Casual readers suppose Dryasdust to be a mere antiquarian. Yet it is his historical philosophy that is dry as dust. He is a Whig in politics and a sceptic in religion. For though Carlyle strenuously complained, as Whigs themselves did, of the baneful legacy of royalist and Tory accounts of the civil wars, of the damage wrought by Heath and Clarendon and Hume, his deeper quarrel is with the Whig and republican tradition which this book has traced. John Toland and his successors had stripped the civil wars of Puritanism and presented them as a struggle for civil liberty. They had created a pantheon of heroes who had mostly regarded Cromwell as the fatal betrayer not merely of the Roundhead cause but of all virtue and fidelity. Carlyle turned Toland's achievement on its head. The tradition of republican historiography begun by Toland reached its climax, and in effect its culmination, in William Godwin's *History of the Commonwealth* in the 1820s. Godwin was the first republican historian to find virtues in Cromwell, his account of whom has many superficial parallels with Carlyle's. Like Carlyle he admired Cromwell's 'earnestness' and (even though he did not think it lasted) his 'sincerity'. Yet where for Carlyle 'sincerity' is a mark of godliness, for Godwin it is a 'republican virtue', rooted in pagan and classical ideals. In Godwin's portrait the eighteenth-century image of Cromwell's hypocrisy persists: 'the language of pious enthusiasm never fell more consummate from the lips of a human being'. The 'enthusiasm' of the Puritans, retorted Carlyle, was 'not foolish but wise'.

Of course, Carlyle's reversion of Toland's historiographical achievement was unknowing. He could not be aware that Toland had rewritten Ludlow. He encountered Ludlow only as the author of the *Memoirs*, whose 'wooden' mind, he judged, was unequal to the recognition of Cromwell's spiritual splendour. If Ludlow's manuscript had come to light in Carlyle's time, Carlyle would surely have swooped delightedly on it. It is true that he would still have been troubled by Ludlow's hatred of Cromwell, which, though it takes a different form in the manuscript, is no less fierce there than in the *Memoirs*. It is true too that there are aspects of Ludlow's Calvinist theology to which Carlyle would not have taken. Yet in essential respects the radical Puritanism reflected in Ludlow's manuscript is the movement that Carlyle wished his present-day countrymen to emulate.

We have become so used to hearing the civil wars called 'the Puritan Revolution' – a concept that originates with Carlyle – that we may miss the radicalism of his decision to place Puritanism centre stage.* We may miss too the radicalism of his insistence, in an era when Whigs were writing so feelingly and influentially about the mid-seventeenth-century struggle for constitutional liberty, that that issue had been peripheral – or, even when it had not, ought to have been – to religious ones. Before he wrote, the nineteenth-century revival of respect for

* Carlyle's term was 'the Puritanic revolt'. His example soon spread. A writer of 1853, J. A. Langford, wrote of 'the great Puritanic Revolution'. The term 'the Puritan Revolution' was in use by 1878, when Peter Bayne, who had 'an almost reverential admiration' for the *Letters and Speeches*, published *The Chief Actors of the Puritan Revolution*. It would soon be given general currency by S. R. Gardiner.

Puritanism had made only limited progress. Nonconformist embarrassment at the violent and revolutionary measures of the 1640s persisted. If there was a single stimulus early in the century to the rise of sympathy for Puritanism it was the publication in 1806 of the *Memoirs* of Lucy Hutchinson. Their editor assured his readers that if only Lucy's husband, the regicide colonel at the centre of her narrative, had lived in modern times, when the struggle against civil and ecclesiastical tyranny had been largely won, he would have been unquestioningly loyal to Church and state.

Carlyle's account of the Puritan movement was quite different. In his hands its connection with revolutionary violence became not its curse but its virtue. The biblical fervour of the Puritans, their taste for Old Testament parallels (especially those reporting the scattering of God's enemies), their preoccupation with Antichrist, features of the movement which we encountered in intense forms in Edmund Ludlow's manuscript and which Whig and republican historians had always suppressed or disowned, gladdened his heart. He responded not, as Godwin and Macaulay had done, to the assistance lent by Puritanism to civil liberty but to its seizure of power and its imposition of godly rule. The Puritans, he rejoiced to observe, intended 'that England should all become a church', and that 'God's own law', 'the hard-stone tables, the God-given precepts and eternal penalties', should be brought 'into actual practice in men's affairs on the earth'. Under Cromwell Puritanism had stood 'erect, with its foot on the hydra Babylon, with its open Bible and drawn sword', chaining and punishing those evils which the laissez-faire philosophy of Carlyle's time was wantonly indulging. Now as then England needed rulers who would enforce the distinction between right and wrong: who would give the people, as Cromwell himself had put it, not what they want but what's good for them.

To Carlyle that was the function of heroes, whose divinity gives them a 'divine right' to exact obedience. Seeing into the eternal, heroes perceive what lesser mortals cannot glimpse and what no number of ballot-boxes will ever voice, the true will of a nation, its will towards good. Between 1839 and 1845, the years when his study of Cromwell was conceived and written, Carlyle's theory of hero-worship, which had always had its authoritarian streak, was taken over by it. In

Carlyle's early reflections on heroism, heroes are the true – because the best – representatives of the societies that produce them. By 1845 their bond with society has been broken. They have become not representatives but enforcers. Carlyle's two studies of heroes in 1843 (rival exercises, it must be said, in credulity), the one of Abbot Samson, who had sorted out the community of Brakelond, the other of the ruthless dictator Dr Francia, who had brought order and justice to modern Paraguay, reflect that development on a small scale. The *Letters and Speeches* reflects it on a large one. The book moved Carlyle towards the extreme position of the *Latter-Day Pamphlets*, the publication of 1850 that would burn his bridges with liberal England.

To heroize Cromwell, Carlyle needed to supplant the Whig heroes of the civil wars. Whigs, Carlyle complained, had 'as good as canonised' the parliamentary leaders of the late 1620s and early 1640s, Eliot and Hampden and Pym. The *Letters and Speeches* allows virtues to those men, but because of their Puritan zeal, not their commitment to civil liberty. Where Macaulay and others had distanced Hampden from fervent Puritanism, Carlyle detected Puritan beliefs, theocratic and providentialist, at his core. Even so he could not warm to Hampden or Pym as to Cromwell. They were, he concluded, 'smooth-shaven respectabilities', 'dreadfully dull'. It was the wild, rugged, ungainly Cromwell, the historiographical outcast, who had 'grappled like a giant, face to face, with the naked truth of things!' Carlyle, to whom a portrait could be much more instructive than a biography, was unable to forget Hampden's thin lips, as emblematic of narrowness of spirit as Cromwell's copious, tremulous ones were of greatness of soul. Sir Henry Vane, 'rather a thin man', paled beside Cromwell too. Dryasdust, notes Carlyle, is 'much taken' with Vane, finding 'endless virtues' in him, but for all his 'purity and elevation' Sir Henry was 'of light fibre'. He was not, as Cromwell was, 'a royal man'. Carlyle derided the 'thin patriotism' of 'unspotted' heroes, the 'marble-tablets' dedicated to 'incorruptible barren-figures' who had shunned the duties of power and action.

Since John Toland's time many Whig and republican historians had venerated the Long Parliament. Here as elsewhere Carlyle's thinking was changed by his study of Cromwell. His attacks on Whig history are an assault not merely on Dryasdust but on his own early beliefs, indeed on a side of himself that he could never quite suppress. In his youth (as he would not care to remember) he subscribed ardently to the historiographical enthusiasms – and to the ill view of Cromwell – bequeathed by eighteenth-century Whigs. Even in maturity he would intermittently voice sentiments, which can startle a reader acquainted with his assaults on Dryasdust, about the contribution of the constitutional conflicts of seventeenth-century England to modern liberty. His words on those occasions might have been uttered by Macaulay (whom Carlyle despised, as Macaulay did him). A part of Carlyle revered the Long Parliament, in conventional terms. In the eighteenth century there were patriot writers who wanted to show how superior the parliaments of the seventeenth century had been to present-day ones, and how, if only those earlier assemblies were imitated, present-day ones might now be transformed. Carlyle had a parallel ambition for nineteenth-century parliaments. Yet as he worked on Cromwell a different view became dominant in his mind. He saw that 'red tape', the 'official' mind, the taste for 'respectability', the paralysing instinct for 'constitutional logic' and for 'checks and balances', are innate to the institution of parliament. That was why the Long Parliament had had to be saved from itself by Cromwell's army at Pride's Purge and then forcibly expelled by it five years later. Thereafter, Carlyle approvingly reports, Cromwell's wrathful dissolutions 'conquered' the parliaments of the protectorate.

In the seventeenth century as in the nineteenth, Carlyle discovered, parliament was a mere 'talking-apparatus'. He repudiated the early nineteenth-century Whig cult of parliamentary oratory, whose devotees saw in Hampden, 'that exquisite orator', a precursor of modern rhetorical prowess. He had no time for Hampden's 'parliamentary eloquences', his 'measured euphemisms'. To Carlyle 'the art of speech', 'whereby a man speaks openly what he does *not* mean', was 'the falsest and most accursed affliction' of the nineteenth century, of an age so habituated to 'lying' that it had become blind to its own 'unveracity'. In the 'artless' speeches of Cromwell, who addressed his parliaments inarticulately but from the heart, he found the stick with which to beat the moderns. Cromwell was 'interesting to me by the very inadequacy of his speech'. The more deeply the protector's utterances stumble into incoherence, the more emphatically do Carlyle's editorial interjections applaud them. Even Cromwell's grammatical failings become witnesses to authenticity of soul, to depths far below the level of words. David Hume had written that a collection of the utterances of Cromwell, who had addressed his parliaments 'in a manner which a peasant of the most ordinary capacity would justly be ashamed of', 'might justly pass for one of the most nonsensical books in the world'. Carlyle turned that verdict on its head. When read attentively, with an eye to their spiritual import, the speeches 'glow with intelligibility', with 'the splendour of a genuine veracity'.

As Carlyle's admiration for the Long Parliament subsides, so his enthusiasm mounts for the 'armed soldiers of Christ' who first purged and then expelled it. The New Model army, that 'company of poor men' (a phrase of Cromwell that Carlyle made his own), had 'all the earnest . . . men of England in the rear of them'. Representing as it did England's 'serious minority', it was as rightly indifferent to parliamentary majorities as to parliamentary privilege. In Carlyle's commentary the vindication of Pride's Purge propounded in Edmund Ludlow's manuscript, as the triumph of a righteous sword, returns from the dead. The army's accomplishments, like the parliament's failings, had present-day relevance to Carlyle, who would soon be recommending the formation of drilled industrial regiments parallel in spirit to Cromwell's military ones. Carlyle, who thrilled to the invincible bravery and discipline of the New Model, laboured to reconstruct its military exploits on his visits to the sites of Cromwell's battles. But it is the army's revolutionary political deeds of 1649–53 that bring his narrative to fever pitch. The execution of Charles I was 'perhaps the most daring action' resolved on by 'any body of men to be met with in history': an action that trembled, as in its necessary extremities heroism always does, on the edge of madness. Above all it was a supreme act of justice. To Carlyle it is by justice, more even than by bread, that man lives.

A few months later, Carlyle explains, Cromwell's army carried justice to Ireland. Here too Oliver resolved to 'see God's judgements . . . exercised on this earth'. Carlyle despaired at the present condition of Ireland, its desperate hardship, its political incapacity, its mutinous protests. The blame, he maintained, lay not, as the Irish liked to tell themselves, with the legacy of Cromwell's conquest. On the contrary Cromwell had brought to that afflicted land the harsh Protestant truths which, if only his settlement had outlasted Puritan rule, might have saved it. The blame rested with lies: lies told both by the Irish themselves – by Catholic priests in the seventeenth century, by 'O'Connellism' now – and by those English governors who had undone Cromwell's work. Modern Ireland, Carlyle explained, would never be at peace with itself until it confronted the memory of the 'savage' massacre of English Protestants by Catholics in 1641 and repented of it. In that claim we hear again, nearly two centuries after its time, the voice from Ludlow's watch tower. When Carlyle turns to Cromwell's massacres of 1649, 'savage' becomes a term of praise. At Drogheda and Wexford, we read, Cromwell used the brute force that is hideous when practised by the wicked but has a dreadful beauty in the hands of the righteous. Like the regicide, it transpires, the killings at Drogheda and Wexford were acts of 'surgery'; and Cromwell, enthused Carlyle in a phrase that became famous or notorious, did not believe in 'the rose-water plan of surgery'. Alongside justice Cromwell brought to Ireland its equally implacable partner, 'veracity'. At Drogheda he 'promised', as Carlyle puts it, to sack the town if it refused quarter. Where politicians of Carlyle's time blithely break their word, Cromwell was faithful to his.

The divine anger which Cromwell visited on the Irish in 1649 was turned, four years later, on the Rump of the Long Parliament, in the coup which for republican historians had robbed the Roundhead cause of its moral purpose and warrant and sacrificed it to Cromwell's ambition. Again Carlyle turned conventional historiography upside down. The dissolution had had, as we saw, its earlier vindicators, who saw it as a necessary measure to prevent anarchy or who celebrated its assault on a parliamentary oligarchy. But no one since Cromwell's time had approved of the coup on Carlyle's ground, that it was the necessary preliminary to godly government. In its place came Barebone's Parliament, an assembly chosen, Carlyle was pleased to find, not by the electorate but by the godly leaders of the army. History had derided Barebone's, but for Carlyle it was 'the assembly with the notablest purpose' – the reign of God's law on earth – 'who have ever met in the modern world'. Unfortunately, since it made the mistake of adopting parliamentary procedures, it too became a 'speaking-apparatus'. Being thus ill-equipped to govern, it was thwarted by the 'shrieks of sham-Christianism', the protests of vested interests cloaked as religious orthodoxy, which its policies provoked. So Cromwell turned, as protector, to the laudable 'despotism' of the Major-Generals to impose godly rule.

Again, Carlyle was not the first historian to praise the protectorate. But the traditional grounds of approval – the vigour and ability and incorruptibility of its administration, the triumphs of its army and navy and diplomacy, its encouragement of trade – were not Carlyle's. He was not much drawn to the secular achievements of the regime. Unlike his predecessors he did not contrast them with the feeble or shameful deeds of England's hereditary rulers. Macaulay, who called Cromwell 'the most profound politician of that age', admired the 'legislative mind' behind the protectorate's policies: Carlyle, who despised 'politicians', took little interest in Cromwell's legislation. For Carlyle it was the 'perfect truth' of the protectorate, its spiritual aspiration, that made it the foremost government in the nation's history. He rejoiced in its godly mission: in its war on vice; its reform of the clergy; and, abroad, Cromwell's aim 'to unite the Protestant world of struggling light against the papist world of potent darkness'.

Even so Carlyle was not at ease with the protectorate. His account of it seems to have been hurriedly drawn together. For him the earlier Cromwell, the warrior-hero and agent of divine destruction, had transcended politics. As protector, charged not with destruction but with reconstruction, Oliver was obliged – as any ruler, heroic or not, would have been – to haggle with parliament. Sacred wrath had perforce yielded to a prudent readiness to conciliate and compromise. Carlyle acknowledges that Cromwell's godly policies were pursued 'with only partial, never with complete success'. The fault lay with the nation, which failed to rally to him. It was a damning omission, for 'the most significant feature in the history of an epoch' is 'the manner it has of welcoming a great man'. The nation's rejoicing on Charles II's return proved its unworthiness to sustain its godly mission – a point which Ludlow had made emphatically. Carlyle had earlier supposed that communities are drawn, as by a magnet, to the leadership of great souls. He found instead that they resist it. In Carlyle's narrative the protector becomes a worn-down figure, a subject for pathos and pity, bearing on his solitary shoulders a cause that will not survive him. Like other heroes of Carlyle he becomes more significant for what he was, for the ideals and qualities he represented, than for what he did.

Not only had the nation failed Cromwell. So had Puritanism. At first Carlyle, or at least a side of him, saw Cromwell merely as the most heroic embodiment of that heroic movement, which was representative – because it represented the best – of England. Yet Puritanism's 'mad suicide' after Cromwell's death – the disintegration of the godly cause in 1659 – showed that, like the Long Parliament which it had controlled, it was unequal to its divine task. Having held up 'the Puritanic age' for emulation, Carlyle acknowledged that it had had its shortcomings. They were those of the society from which it had emerged. Carlyle was never at home with the period between the later middle ages and the French Revolution. He knew about, and (mostly) liked, medieval feudalism. He acknowledged that the French Revolution had brought feudalism's final and inevitable destruction, and that democracy, for which he could not care, was inevitably replacing it. It was the non-feudal and non-democratic aspects of the intervening society that perplexed him. He had learned from the Scottish Enlightenment about the stages of social development. He recognized a divine impulse in the energy, industry and collective endeavour with which communities advance their social organization and economic resources. He accepted the view of his contemporaries that the civil wars had been in some way related to the rise of a commercial class. He took it that the 'fighting' of the high middle ages had 'given place to trading, ploughing, weaving and merchant adventuring', and that that change too was irreversible. Yet Carlyle, who rebuked historical nostalgia, succumbed to it. Hard as he tried to bring alive the texture of the society that had produced Puritanism, its starched ruffs and fringed breeches and pointed beards, his heart lay with the frugal spontaneity of an earlier age. He yearned for the time when kings were 'raised aloft on bucklers with clangour of sounding shields'. He wanted to think of the Puritan leaders as a continuation of the feudal ideal, as an 'earnest religious aristocracy', the last of England's ruling classes to combine rank with intellect. Yet intellect itself had assumed post-medieval forms which Carlyle found easier to admire than love. The age of the Renaissance had been sicklied o'er with the pale cast of thought, trusting too much to words, possessed by the self-consciousness of which truly heroic times are free.

If only Cromwell had been born in the middle ages! Carlyle's imagination links him to William the Conqueror, who sorted out the 'pot-bellied' natives; and behind him to the Norse kings commemorated in Icelandic sagas. Yet even the medieval age cannot contain Carlyle's Cromwell. He is a 'primeval' figure, his exploits decked in mythological and anthropological imagery, his place among the 'sanhedrim of the gods' announced by proto-Wagnerian outbreaks of thunder, lightning, fire. Carlyle, who had set out to heroize Puritan society, instead created a hero beyond society.

How did Carlyle's book, a work at once so hostile and eccentric to its age, come to be embraced by it? A part of the answer must lie in the central perception of his enterprise: that Cromwell's letters and speeches are indeed extraordinary documents; and that unlike the customary pronouncements of kings, which are couched in language intended to conceal the character within, they convey an authentic image of the inner man. Carlyle, himself indelibly marked by the Romantic movement, wrote for an age that retained its imprint. It liked to explore that subterranean landscape of past minds which the dry 'philosophic' historians of the eighteenth century were now reproached for having missed. The eighteenth century had put frames round its predecessors, had placed a distance of feeling between then and now. The nineteenth century, prompted by the fiction of Walter Scott (not least his novel of 1826, *Woodstock*, which is set in the civil wars), wanted to relive the past.* The *Letters and Speeches* answered to that appetite. Cromwell, unknowable from the jumbled and scattered versions in which his words had earlier been printed, now stood, enthused one reviewer of Carlyle's edition, 'in bodily and mental presence before us. We live, speak, correspond with him.' Twentieth-

* The tendency is demonstrated by the frequency and intensity of historical paintings, especially those of subjects from the civil wars. In his book *And When Did You Last See Your Father?*, Roy Strong reports that around 175 paintings of events of the mid-seventeenth century were displayed at the Royal Academy between 1820 and 1900, and that no other era of England's past attracted so much attention.

century scholarship warrantably emphasized Carlyle's weaknesses as an editor, his haphazard methods, his archival omissions and gullibilities, his dogmatically stated errors. Yet in its own age the book set new standards of editorial diligence and accomplishment. 'At one stroke,' declared another reviewer, Carlyle had 'placed himself at the head of our editors of documents.' There was special praise for the explanatory clarity of the passages of scene-setting that precede each document.

There was admiration too for the artful vividness of the book. Carlyle decried literary 'art' as another form of lying. At best it distracts writer and reader from the moral and instructive purpose that is writing's sole warrant. Yet no author is without it. As a feat of artistic reconstruction the *Letters and Speeches* is not the equal of Carlyle's *The French Revolution*. Perhaps no one could have sustained the level of imaginative intensity that inspired that earlier work again. Carlyle's growing tendency to separate his hero from society, and to focus on the first at the expense of the second, reduced his scope for the kind of social description that in the earlier work had given his imagination wing. There is more sense of the life of society in Carlyle's drafts of the *Letters and Speeches*, written when he intended its range of subject-matter to be broader, than in the final text. Besides, Carlyle's decision to produce an edition rather than a history or biography, while a stimulus to the ingenuity of his skills of narrative, also restricts them. None the less the *Letters and Speeches* bears the same genius as *The French Revolution* and the same hunger for its expression. Carlyle had been attracted to literary possibilities in Cromwell, in the 'wild image' of the man and his time, long before he saw didactic ones, indeed while he still held the view of him that the *Letters and Speeches* would defeat. The attraction persisted. While planning the *Letters and Speeches* he made a note to himself that the battle of Dunbar, perhaps the most remarkable of all Cromwell's victories, was one of Oliver's 'greatest scenes'. In the book it is immortally so. Together with the description of Cromwell's death the account of the battle became the passage of the book most often praised and anthologized.

The magnetic properties of the *Letters and Speeches* had another source too: the intimacy of the bond between author and hero. The book has an autobiographical subtext that recalls Carlyle's first literary triumph, *Sartor Resartus*. Carlyle could hardly have concealed, and the harshest critic of either Carlyle or Cromwell might not gainsay, the bond of courage, that indomitable and lonely force with which the two men take on the world and its conventions and stake their unremitting originality of character. Other resemblances owe more to literary or psychological contrivance. Time and again Carlyle's own memories and self-assessment determine or are reflected in the emphases of his narrative. There is the formation of impregnable, steadying values during Cromwell's long period of modest obscurity before his entry on the world's bustling stage – a period to which Carlyle devoted a degree of (largely frustrated) labour and imaginative energy far disproportionate to its documentary legacy. There is Oliver's devotion to his godly mother; his hypochondria (for Carlyle always a sign of grace); his rescue from agonies of despair through religious conversion. Well before he wrote on Cromwell Carlyle described the afflictions and progress of his own soul in language close to Oliver's. When Carlyle reaches Cromwell's maturity he links the solitary burden of his hero's decision-making with his own humbler but no less solitary responsibility of biographical resurrection. When he reaches Cromwell's last years he ties the protector's weary struggle towards rest with his own humbler but no less taxing labours of literary completion. We repeatedly learn that the words of both hero and author struggle to 'blaze' or to take 'fire'. Hero and author alike are enjoined to 'struggle', to 'take courage', to press 'forward'. Sometimes we can hardly tell, from Carlyle's personal pronouns, which of the two men is speaking.

Perhaps Carlyle himself hardly knew. Men who described the public lectures which he gave in London in 1838–40 reported the manner of his delivery – the struggle of an uncouth, clumsy speaker to give voice to earnestness and sincerity – in terms that strikingly anticipate Carlyle's own accounts of Cromwell's delivery. In the *Letters and Speeches* 'my friend Oliver' joins Carlyle against the hollow proprieties of classical structure and diction. The classical inheritance, enshrined in the eighteenth-century patriot pantheon, had in Carlyle's mind produced, in historical writing, the elevation of artificial, shallow, foreign values above natural, deep, native ones. The literary indecorum of the *Letters and Speeches*, its offences against grammar and syntax, its unevenness of pitch and proportion, its jump-starts and moments of spontaneous combustion, its very warts as it were, are vindicated by the features of Cromwell's character and speeches that they mirror.

Carlyle's emphasis on the early Cromwell aids his enterprise in one particular respect. He strives to form a bond not only between author and hero but between author and ideal reader. His aim is a triangular relationship that will unite the 'earnest' author, the 'earnest' hero, the 'earnest' reader. Like author and hero the reader is urged to take 'courage' and to work for good in the world. The early Cromwell, the 'Huntingdon farmer' who was 'content to plough the ground' and to 'read his Bible', but who 'threw down his ploughs' at the crisis of God's cause, is the earnest reader's model. That reader may be confined, like the young Cromwell, to provincial obscurity, silent and unsung, but he is 'the salt of the earth', who can do his bit for godliness and reform – for 'Is not every man, God be thanked, a potential hero?' More modest models are supplied by humble and inconspicuous devotees of Cromwell and of Puritanism who occasionally surface in the narrative, men of 'fervent faith, zeal and fearlessness'.

Yet readers, even hectored readers – even readers told, as Carlyle's insistently are, that their readiness to accept his estimate of Cromwell is a test of their salvation – are free agents. Many of Carlyle's readers, moved and mesmerized as they were by his books, felt able to applaud them only because they could pick and choose among his opinions. Can there be another instance in our literature of a writer speaking so profoundly to so many people who dissented so fundamentally from so many of his views? The absorption of Carlyle and his opinions into the society he scourged is perhaps as surprising a feature as any of high and late Victorian intellectual history. He reads like a Job or like Timon by his cave – and yet, as Thackeray said, had the best company in England ringing at his doorbell. Two overlapping characteristics of his writing assisted the process of assimilation. First, as we have noticed, not every side of him was committed to his most belligerent or iconoclastic statements. Inside Carlyle, amid all his anti-Whiggism, there is a thin Whig trying to get out, who is drawn to conventional positions which, Carlyle judges, have sufficient advocacy in the world to stand in no need of his own pleading. For all the wildness of his political unorthodoxies, readers could sense that his bark might be worse than his bite. Secondly there was his own indifference to conflicts of opinion, which, however fierce, he would not allow to impair his own warmth towards, or sympathy of spirit with, men whose views he judged misguided. Behind that quality there lay a generosity of spirit that rubbed off not only on his friends but on his readers. It has often been difficult, then or now, for Carlyle's less sympathetic readers, even for those repelled by his teaching or his language, to resist entirely his great crag of a heart.

The *Letters and Speeches* was particularly open to selective reception in the nineteenth century because its audience could, and sometimes did, simply read Cromwell's words and omit Carlyle's. Yet for the most part the process was more subtle. We saw how John Toland's editorial enterprises, which subtly commended a republican cause to a country-party audience, were assimilated by it. Carlyle had none of Toland's cunning. His readers were bludgeoned. Yet his writing, too, was absorbed into attitudes different from and less extreme than his own. Books, once published, have lives independent of their authors' intentions for them. We shall see how Carlyle, the great anti-Victorian, was Victorianized.

There would have been a Victorian following for Cromwell even if Carlyle had not written about him. The growth of interest, early in the century, in the civil wars, the taste for national heroes generated by the Napoleonic wars, and the emergence of sympathy for Puritanism, had ensured as much. A number of its readers related the success of the *Letters and Speeches* to the movement of opinion in Cromwell's favour over the previous quarter of a century. Others intimated (not all of them persuasively) that Carlyle had only told them truths about Cromwell that they already knew or suspected. The influence of Macaulay's and Godwin's characterizations in the 1820s, while generally far less potent than that of Carlyle's book, would mingle with it and occasionally even surpass it. Carlyle's own conversion to Cromwell, though he would never have admitted the fact, was a response to a succession of publications by lesser writers which had become conspicuous by the late 1830s, some years before the *Letters and Speeches* appeared. The most original contribution, the first study to accept Cromwell's faith and sincerity without qualification and to treat them as the thread of his life, was a review-essay by the occasional writer John Robertson in the *Westminster Review* in October 1839. Carlyle had expected to write the essay himself and was angry when the editor handed it to Robertson. Later Carlyle would claim that he had 'never read' Robertson's 'trash'. Yet the essay again and again anticipates Carlyle's work closely, in its sentiments and even its vocabulary. (It was eleven months after its publication that Carlyle described himself as having learned to revere Cromwell 'within the last twelvemonth'.) By 1845, the year the *Letters and Speeches* appeared, interest in Cromwell was seemingly ubiquitous. While the book was in the press a national controversy was provoked by a campaign, which would run through the century, for the erection of a statue of Cromwell at Westminster. The origins of that initiative, though owing something to the sketch of Oliver in Carlyle's *Of Heroes and Hero-Worship* in 1841, do not seem to have owed much. Carlyle liked to think of himself as a lone battler on his hero's behalf, the single-handed recoverer of Cromwell's nobility of soul. Yet in a letter of 1845 he let slip a different view: his book would, he hoped, end 'the controversy' about Cromwell's integrity.

If the *Letters and Speeches* did not begin the Cromwellian movement it rapidly took it over. It was one thing to commend Cromwell, as Robertson and others did, in the measured prose of literary periodicals, another to bring him vividly to life before a wide public. And it was one thing to assert Cromwell's sincerity, another to demonstrate it, the eloquent feat of Carlyle's editing and commentary. How widespread a movement Victorian Cromwellianism would have been without Carlyle we cannot say, but it was largely he who determined its character and gave it its power.

Perhaps the broadest and certainly the most enduring constituency won by the book was Nonconformity, a movement self-consciously the heir of seventeenth-century Puritanism. Its debt to the *Letters and Speeches* was frequently and handsomely acknowledged. Only after the publication of Carlyle's book did Nonconformists campaign conspicuously on behalf of Cromwell's memory. They played little part in the agitation for a statue in 1845, which seems to have caught them unawares. Cromwell's advocates in that campaign dwelt on his worldly deeds. Their arguments were largely republican or socialist rather than religious. They said little about the moral earnestness and the sincerity of belief which were Carlyle's theme and which would speak so directly to his Nonconformist readers. So quiet in 1845, Nonconformists took over the commemoration of 1899. When, during it, they told each other to 'awake' and 'work' they were consciously echoing the injunctions of Carlyle's book.

The enthusiasm of Nonconformists for Carlyle's writing was by no means confined to the *Letters and Speeches*. The breadth and depth of his appeal to them are initially startling, for it had to cross the enormous gap between their predominantly liberal political opinions and his illiberal ones. Men whose desire for social and economic independence was an article of political faith faced Carlyle's contempt for that ideal. Their views on, for example, slavery or capital punishment were often diametrically opposed to his. If there were massive differences of political perspective, so could there be of religious. Nonconformists had to endure, though sometimes under protest, Carlyle's disdain for their own faith, that empty shell, as he alleged, from which the heart and meaning of seventeenth-century Puritanism had long disappeared. He compounded the insult by mocking Nonconformist adherence to religious beliefs and practices for which, when he encountered them in the seventeenth century, he professed admiration.

Carlyle was only one of a number of nineteenth-century admirers of Cromwell who themselves came from Dissenting (or occasionally other) religious backgrounds and who in various ways had parted from the faith of their upbringing or youth. Others were William Godwin (divided as his feelings about Cromwell were), Cromwell's biographer (and Carlyle's friend) John Forster, the popular lecturer George Dawson, Frederic Harrison, W. F. Stead (that pioneer of investigative journalism, who produced an abridged version of the *Letters and Speeches* in 1899) and S. R. Gardiner. Then there were such Cromwellians as John Robertson who were linked or sympathetic to the Nonconformist movement but did not belong to it. It was the seriousness of Cromwell's religion, rather than its content, that appealed to those men. Nonconformists themselves could welcome seriousness in men who did not share their faith. They recognized, as did other religious groups, that Carlyle, whatever his own religion might or might not be, believed in belief. He was an ally against scepticism, who – as his critics complained – could make earnestness and sincerity sound like a system of belief, or at least a substitute for one. It was the achievement of Carlyle's 'gospel of earnestness' to appeal to people of all faiths and of none.

Uncomfortable as the point was for Nonconformists, it was the differences between seventeenth- and nineteenth-century Puritanism that made their appreciation of Carlyle possible. While no Nonconformist would have endorsed Carlyle's claims for the godlike capacity of heroic men, at least Dissent had largely shed that pessimistic assessment of human nature which had been sustained by their seventeenth-century Calvinist predecessors, to whom his philosophy of heroism, had they been able to understand it, would have seemed a blasphemous affront. Most Nonconformists had retreated, too, from the doctrinal rigidities of Calvinism. Though the experience of religious conversion was as fundamental to them as to their seventeenth-century forebears, their perception of it, like Carlyle's, was more emotional than theological. They could thus warm not only to the Calvinist conversion of Cromwell related in the *Letters and Speeches* but to the non-Calvinist, even non-Christian one of the hero of *Sartor Resartus*.

It was the militants within Nonconformity who responded most enthusiastically to his commentary on Cromwell. They welcomed Carlyle's emphasis on Puritanism's occupancy of power, that long overdue break, as they proclaimed, with the timid subservience of Dissenting to Whig historiography, and a no less overdue one from litanies of Nonconformist sufferings before and after the civil wars. Militants welcomed too Carlyle's observant pleasure in Cromwell's gory Old Testament allusions, from which staider Victorian readers averted their eyes.

There were, to simplify, two kinds of Cromwellianism in Victorian England, one hard, one soft. The hard version was the more miscellaneous, for it drew together men from opposite ends of the political spectrum, each of whom might be drawn to one aspect of Cromwell's career or personality but might not take to others. Militant Nonconformity belonged to the hard wing of Cromwellianism. So did the belligerent populism which recalled Cromwell's readiness to bring both Crown and parliament, those twin agencies, as they now seemed, of social oppression, to account. Here too there were fundamental differences of outlook between Carlyle and his admirers. Carlyle preached class harmony, not class conflict. Though he liked his heroes to be poor, as a stimulus to their spiritual earnestness and their appetite for struggle, he declined to join the voices commending Cromwell as an instrument of social liberation. Even so the pugilism of his accounts of the regicide, and of Cromwell's expulsion of the Long Parliament, boosted the protector's following among Chartists and socialists and populist republicans. So did his assumption that nobility of soul is 'better than all social rank'. The Chartist Thomas Cooper was one of many readers who, having earlier had doubts about Cromwell, were won over to him by Carlyle.

Other components of hard Cromwellianism took strength and courage from him. There was the businessman's Cromwell, who is represented by the Nonconformist entrepreneur Sir Richard Tangye, that devout collector of Cromwelliana. He is surely represented in fiction too: in *North and South*, the novel of 1855 by Carlyle's friend Elizabeth Gaskell. Her characterization of her protagonist Mr Thornton, that 'iron', 'rough' figure, 'no speech-maker', bent on 'justice' and a 'wise despotism', the 'resolution and power' of his features concealing an inner 'gentleness' and 'tenderness', time and again recalls Carlyle's Cromwell. For his country's salvation Carlyle looked to 'captains of industry' or 'silent industrial heroes'. Thornton is such a leader in the making. When he remarks on the inefficacy of 'rose-water surgery' in industrial relations, Mrs Gaskell expects her readers to recognize, as Thornton's interlocutor does, an allusion to Carlyle's statement that Cromwell, in crushing the resistance in Ireland in 1649, 'did not believe in the rose-water plan of surgery'. Carlyle's commendation of Cromwell's Irish deeds and policies became a component of hard Cromwellianism. Vindications of them had hitherto been rare and qualified. Now they were bolder and more frequent.

There were further components too. Carlyle's scorn for parliamentary sovereignty and procedures, and his preference for enlightened dictatorship, struck chords among those who wearied of the ineffectuality of Victorian parliaments and at the slow pace of their proceedings. People who disliked such sentiments blamed them on Carlyle. Yet once more there was a gap between him and the readers he swayed. For Carlyle it was Cromwell's divinity, not his efficiency, that qualified him for sovereign rule. Where parliamentary 'eloquence' is scorned by

Carlyle on account of its barrenness of soul, Lord Rosebery saw it as antipathetic to National Efficiency. Where Carlyle detested the eighteenth century for the godlessness it had bequeathed, Rosebery condemned that era's constitutional and administrative legacy, which he saw as a restraint on the dynamism and modernity of the state. There is a similar distance between Carlyle's Cromwellianism and that of the 'positivist' thinker Auguste Comte and his disciples. Carlyle thought 'Comtism', which described the gradual emancipation of humanity from religious and metaphysical conceptions, the 'ghastliest of algebraic spectralities'. Yet here too the divide of outlook was crossed. The biography of Cromwell by the Comtist Frederic Harrison for the most part followed reverently in Carlyle's wake.

A comparable process was at work in assessments of Cromwell's foreign policy. Dissenters and others did remember Carlyle's insistence on the moral and religious basis of Cromwell's diplomacy. With Carlyle they admired, and reproached worldly modern statesmen who failed to emulate, Cromwell's readiness to 'go to war for a creed' and his impatience, when God's cause stood in the balance, with considerations of 'policy' and 'protocol'. More commonly, however, Carlyle's account was absorbed by an older, less morally sensitive tradition which took pleasure, as Carlyle did not, in Cromwell's assertion of national might, and which now recruited that memory to the cause of Imperialist expansion.

Outside the Nonconformist fold, hard Cromwellianism did not share Carlyle's preoccupation with Cromwell's sincerity of belief. Here Carlyle's success lay rather among the practitioners of a gentler, kinder Cromwellianism. Where hard Cromwellianism was a miscellaneous coalition, the softer version belonged to the most conspicuous strand of Victorian moral thought.

Conventional morality was always in two minds about Carlyle. Should it emphasize the ground it shared with him or the differences between them? Many of his principles – work, duty, earnestness, sincerity – were archetypally Victorian in vocabulary. Yet they could be less so in content. Three virtues above all did win him conventional praise: his influence as a 'moral force' or 'moral teacher'; his 'earnestness'; his 'sincerity'. Yet Carlyle had grounds to mistrust such plaudits.

To him conventional invocations of 'morality' were cloaks for worldly advancement. He saw 'earnestness' as the enemy of 'respectability': convention was liable – so anyway its critics said – to yield the first to the second or conflate the two. To Carlyle 'sincerity' was the 'first characteristic' of a hero. Yet mainstream Victorians were troubled where not repelled by his doctrine of hero-worship, which, despite his denials, seemed to his readers, even some of the friendliest of them, to involve or imply the worship of force or to make might the judge of right. Even when the doctrine was remembered approvingly, as in those pious anthologies of Carlyle, with their whiff of the Sunday school, compiled around the end of the century, it was not for its vindication of divinely appointed leadership or of righteous force but as an antidote to levelling moral tendencies and as a spur to ethical uplift.

The sincerity of the Cromwell of the *Letters and Speeches* made many more friends than his heroism. Anthologists of Carlyle withdrew Cromwell from Carlyle's Valhalla, deleted the madness in him that in Carlyle's mind was inseparable from his greatness. The qualities that were conventionally commended in Carlyle – sincerity, earnestness, morality – were the ones which he ascribed to Cromwell, and which his readers were generally ready to recognize in Oliver. Again, however, Carlyle could mean, by those same words, different things. Victorians praised Carlyle for rescuing Cromwell's 'moral character'. Yet the nineteenth century's idea of character, like its notions of morality, seemed false to Carlyle. For conventional liberals Cromwell's morality, his commitment to the rule of principle, the high seriousness of his idealism, his courage and resolution on its behalf, were the essence of his greatness. Yet while those qualities made him widely attractive as an ethical model, the irregular aims and methods by which he had made force the arbiter of politics prompted dismay or unease in conventional minds.

On another front, too, conventional opinion assimilated Carlyle's Cromwell. Whig and liberal history, which the *Letters and Speeches* assailed, absorbed the work into its own philosophy. Whig historical writing had come far since the eighteenth century, mainly under the influence of Macaulay, who brought to it the perspective of political and social evolution that had been fashioned by the historians of the Scottish Enlightenment. No longer content to aim for the maintenance of present blessings of liberty or to lament the passage of past ones,

Whig historians now identified liberty's cause with new and dynamic ideals of social and constitutional progress, which answered to the growing confidence, optimism and prosperity of the period after about 1850. Carlyle saw around him not national progress but national degeneration. His influence, at its height in the bleak decade before the middle of the century, remained a mighty force thereafter, despite the growing extremism of his views. It none the less mingled with and was diluted by more emollient developments of opinion. The virtues which he had found in Cromwell and in Puritanism were judged to have blended with values Carlyle despised. In 1862 Peter Bayne, that devotee of the *Letters and Speeches*, declared the 'special glory' of the Puritans to have been that they 'combined all that is seen in them by Bentham' – the utilitarian thinker who was Carlyle's *bête noire* – 'with all that is seen in them by Carlyle'.

Whig history paid one tribute above all to Carlyle. It now placed Puritanism, as he had done, at the centre of the civil wars. Yet the Puritanism it celebrated, like the Cromwell it celebrated, was an ethical more than a political model. It had more in common with the peaceably and constitutionally inclined movement delineated by Dissenting historians of the early nineteenth century than with Carlyle's version. Only on the extreme wing of militant Nonconformity did Carlyle's identification of the best of Puritanism with military theocracy win a following. Carlyle thought that Puritanism spoke for England until it let Cromwell down: S. R. Gardiner, at the end of the century, thought that Puritanism spoke for the nation until Cromwell let it down, by attempting, through the rule of the Major-Generals, that dogmatic enforcement of biblical injunctions which for Carlyle was Puritanism's chief glory. It was as a sober, restrained, upright movement, not a zealous or dogmatic one, that Puritanism exercised its main Victorian appeal. Where Carlyle, overturning the judgement of two centuries, applauded Cromwell's 'enthusiasm', Victorians generally preferred (in the words of Oliver's biographer of 1847, Merle d'Aubigné) the 'moral' dimension of Puritanism to its 'enthusiastic or fanatical' one, which was held to have reflected or encouraged sectarian narrowness. David Hume had accused Puritanism of 'loosening all the ties of morality': to liberal Victorians Puritanism was above all a 'moral' force, which had represented the best of an unusually 'moral' age. The influence of

Macaulay, who liked Puritan morality (at least up to a point) but who disliked Puritan dogma, was again at work. Over the Victorian age Puritanism won that ethical high ground of seventeenth-century historiography which patriotism had occupied under the Hanoverians. Just as the nineteenth century made Cromwell, hitherto the enemy of liberty, its friend, so his Puritanism now made him the friend, where hitherto he had been the enemy, of morality. Some pre-Victorian writers had favourably compared the frugality and sobriety of his court with the decadent profligacy of Charles II's: Victorians, who brought a new high-mindedness to condemnations of Charles II's court, contrasted its conduct not merely with Cromwell's entourage but with the uprightness of Puritanism as a whole.

On no subject did Carlyle stand further from Victorian orthodoxy than religious toleration. Toleration was the proud achievement of nineteenth-century thought and legislation. It was the supreme ground of Nonconformist gratitude to Cromwell. For all the limits of the religious liberty that he had been able to secure, toleration was the aspiration and achievement of his that Victorian opinion was readiest to commend. Carlyle detested the 'babble of toleration' of his own time, which he attributed to religious 'doubt and indifference'. Cromwell, he thought, had rightly believed in 'toleration' only of 'the unessential' and in 'inexorable intolerance for the want of the essential'. 'On the whole', ruled Carlyle, men are placed on this earth not to 'tolerate' falsehoods but to 'extinguish' them. The eccentricity of Carlyle's stand to contemporary opinion can be glimpsed in his judgements on the prose works of Milton. Liberal Victorians were enraptured by Milton's *Areopagitica* (1644), that plea for freedom of faith and expression which so eloquently anticipated their own values. Carlyle much preferred Milton's assaults on popery in his anti-prelatical tracts of 1641–2, works whose 'dogmatic narrowness' dismayed other Victorian opinion.

As in religion, so in politics, Carlyle's Cromwell was assimilated. Gardiner portrayed the protector as the champion of 'liberty and peaceful progress' who from time to time had unfortunately lost sight of the constitutional principles he inherently favoured. Many Victorians judged that Cromwell wanted to rule constitutionally and were troubled when he was unable to do so: Carlyle thought it 'curious' that he so much as made the attempt. Before Carlyle, Cromwell was the villain who had destroyed the Whig aims of the parliamentary heroes: after him he was welcomed into Whig territory. In 1840 John Forster had published his *Statesmen of the Commonwealth*, an influential paean to Eliot, Pym, Hampden and Vane and to the constitutionalist cause criminally betrayed by Cromwell. Forster was one of those whom the *Letters and Speeches* instantly converted to Cromwell, of whom he now wrote an altogether more sympathetic account. Yet he soon returned to the Whiggish theme of the heroism of the leaders of the Long Parliament in its early stages, writing books on two critical moments in the history of constitutional liberty, the passage of the Grand Remonstrance in November 1641 and the attempted arrest of the five members in January 1642. Where, for Carlyle, the parliamentary leaders were Cromwell's inferior and disposable allies, in Forster's later writing their contribution to the defeat of Stuart tyranny is at least as substantial and edifying as his. Amid so much applause and respect for Carlyle, Macaulay's parliamentary and progressive perspective won through. Peter Bayne combined the reverence for Cromwell he had learned from Carlyle with a no less fulsome respect for the Long Parliament in 1640. Echoing Macaulay and many Whigs before him, Bayne called the parliament's first meeting 'a day memorable in the annals of the world'.

For to the later Victorians no less than to Macaulay, it was the thwarting of tyranny that was the enduring achievement of the civil wars. Carlyle, though he acknowledged that feat, took little interest in it. In conventional accounts the tyranny was held to have been at once political and ecclesiastical, the two being inseparably combined. The civil war had been a struggle for 'civil and religious liberty', a phrase which Whigs and republicans had insistently repeated since the seventeenth century and which in the Victorian era became a tireless term of tribute to Cromwell and to Puritanism. It was a phrase Carlyle liked to mock. What Carlyle was watching was the transformation of Cromwell into a Victorian liberal. Cromwell became an earlier Gladstone: an ironic development, for the Liberal leader seems on the whole to have had an unfavourable view of Cromwell, though not as low as Carlyle's of Gladstone.

*

Cromwell was not a Victorian liberal. Like Carlyle he cared much less for civil than for spiritual blessings. Like Carlyle's his conception of spiritual blessings was far removed from mainstream Victorian ones. Whenever Carlyle differs from other nineteenth-century, even from twentieth-century commentators about the inner springs of Cromwell's actions it is he who is right, or at least the more right. The deficiencies of his portrait are obvious enough. He found it easier to see the world through his hero's eyes than his hero through the world's. Disdaining political processes, he did not explore the practical goals and pressures of Cromwell's career very far. He was almost totally indifferent to the constitutional principles and arrangements of the protectorate. His study is distorted, too, sometimes to the point of an absurdity that he never feared to risk, both by his stereotype of the heroic character, which fits Cromwell's temperament into a preconceived pattern, and by Carlyle's German and Romantic frames of philosophical reference. Yet he grasped truths about his hero which succeeding generations have preferred not to confront. When S. R. Gardiner wrote about Cromwell, the Victorian religious revival, except on its extreme Nonconformist and ritualist wings, was in retreat. The new scepticism, which made it hard for writers to enter into the Puritan mentality, placed a veil over it. The veil was thinner than that in which John Toland had shrouded it, thinner too than that favoured by the eighteenth-century brand of scepticism denounced by Carlyle. Partly for that very reason, subsequent generations have barely noticed it.

Gardiner did not underestimate the religious element of the Puritan revolt. Religion, he judged, was the rock on which the nation split in 1642. But he could not grasp, as Carlyle so readily did, its consuming power. He could not get his mind inside Puritan providentialism, the force which we have encountered in Edmund Ludlow and which, despite the bitter differences between the two men, Cromwell shared with him. We can see the contrast between Carlyle and Gardiner in their accounts of Cromwell's great victory at Dunbar in September 1650. Both men visited the site and struggled to reconstruct that topographically complicated engagement, Carlyle walking the eighteen miles or so of scraggy coastal landscape from Edinburgh on an anniversary of the battle, Gardiner – if he followed his usual practice – travelling to the site on a bicycle. Never are Carlyle's Romantic sensibility, his gift for the description of landscape, his sense of historical drama more alive than on that visit. He imagines the beleaguered English army, hemmed in by the North Sea beneath the Scottish forces on the slopes above, waiting in an extremity of tension through the wet and wild night before the battle. He hears the bodeful moaning of the hoarse ocean as it swings against the whinstone bays, glimpses the harvest moon wading deep among clouds of sleet and hail. And then, at daybreak, Cromwell cries out in the words of the Psalmist, 'Let God arise, let his enemies be scattered!' Carlyle is at one with Cromwell's sense of the Lord's presence, which for both men gives the battle its meaning. Gardiner's dispassionate account, which concentrates on military strategy, touches on Cromwell's providentialism but is unequal to the imaginative re-creation of it.

It was Gardiner who led that revolution in seventeenth-century scholarship beside which Carlyle's archival labours seem innocent and his contextual settings thin. Yet Cromwell's deeds, and his impact on the world, are not properly intelligible without the story, which Carlyle tried to tell and which Gardiner evaded, of what Oliver called 'my inward man' (after II Corinthians 4.16: 'though our outward man perish, yet the inward man is renewed day by day'). Carlyle was alone among Victorian historians in grasping how low a priority in Cromwell's mind was 'civil' liberty, how deep was his indifference to constitutional forms when the cause of godly reformation was at stake. He also understood Cromwell's implacable commitment, so remote from the decent Victorian morality by which Gardiner lived, to the imposition of divine justice and divine vengeance. Carlyle's belief that 'there is no crime which the Supreme Powers do more terribly avenge' than 'the crime of being deaf to God's voice' attuned him to a facet of Cromwell's convictions of which later writers have missed the import. Cromwell knew that God's enemies, when they fail to acknowledge the evidence of divine disapproval and to repent their ways, must receive no mercy. As the only historian to have been comfortable with every manifestation of Cromwell's ferocity, Carlyle grasped that Oliver's conduct in Ireland, and his military coups in England, were consistent with his beliefs and conduct throughout his career, not, as the gentler Cromwellians of Victorian England preferred to suppose, troubling departures from his better feelings.

Carlyle is, too, the only historian to have grasped intuitively Cromwell's principle of liberty of conscience, and to have seen the difference between it and the Victorian sentiment that saw its own reflection in it. He realized at once that, for all the magnanimity and tenderness contained in Cromwell's personality, the toleration he had sought would have been confined to the godly, or at least to those in whom the protector saw the capacity for godliness; that it was intended to secure not, as liberal Victorians supposed, the rights of individuals but the advance of God's word, which persecution obstructs. For Cromwell it is the conscience, which God owns, that must be set free in his service. To the Victorians Cromwell's tolerance was illustrated by his attempt to secure the readmission of the Jews to England. He took that step not, as Victorians wanted to think, because he felt kindly towards Jews but because he knew from the Bible that only when the barrier between Jew and Gentile had been broken down would the world be ready for the Second Coming. Edmund Ludlow's approach to questions of freedom of conscience had its parallels to Cromwell's. John Toland, Ludlow's editor, was profoundly committed, as Ludlow was, to a large measure of religious toleration. Yet Toland's premises were fundamentally alien to Ludlow's. For Toland toleration was the necessary partner of civil liberty. Approaching Ludlow's text from that perspective he found nothing in it that he could convert into his own tolerationist sentiments. He would have had the same difficulty with Cromwell's letters and speeches. To Cromwell liberty of conscience was a means, alongside the preaching of the Gospel and the improvement of the ministry, to the Puritanizing of the land. In most twentieth-century accounts Cromwell's zeal for godly reformation, and his principle of liberty of conscience, are separate if not contradictory impulses. Carlyle knew their indivisibility.

Gardiner's partner in the professionalization of seventeenth-century studies was C. H. Firth, Ludlow's modern editor. Where Carlyle, had he known of the manuscript out of which Toland created the *Memoirs*, would have delighted in it, Firth would have been repelled by it. At a young age Firth imbibed Carlyle's doctrine of work, but for him that creed was a secular one. He described Puritan extremists, as eighteenth-century historians had done, as 'fanatics'. It was his distaste for Puritan zeal that, on that subject, restricted the imagination and thus impaired the judgement of so judicious a historian. Only by reference to that proclivity can we explain his decision, to which evidence before his eyes ran counter, that the *Memoirs* were authentic. If Carlyle wrote the one great book to have been written on Cromwell, Firth wrote the best good one, his biography of 1900. Yet a comparison of the prose of Carlyle, who as Leslie Stephen said believed that 'every sentence must be alive to its fingers' ends', with that of Firth is no advertisement for the efficacy of professional historical writing. Carlyle explained, histrionically no doubt but at least catching, and thus matching, the intensity of what he described, that Cromwell's Puritans 'knew in every fibre, and with heroic daring laid to heart, that an almighty justice does verily rule this world; that it is good to fight on God's side, and bad to fight on the Devil's side!' Here, on the same subject, is Firth: 'Briefly stated, Cromwell's argument was that the victories of the army, and the convictions of the godly, were internal and external evidences of God's will, to be obeyed as a duty.' At the end of the nineteenth century as of the seventeenth, the essence of Puritan fundamentalism slipped from historical view.

Gardiner and Firth wrote their lives of Cromwell when his posthumous standing was at its peak. In 1899 he at last achieved the recognition that his more ardent admirers had demanded for more than fifty years: the raising of a statue of him at Westminster. Behind that event there lies a story that illustrates in microcosm the passions and difficulties of the Cromwellianism of the century Carlyle addressed.

11

The Cromwell Statue

Outside the Houses of Parliament, opposite Westminster Abbey, there stand two imposing bronze statues of rulers of England. The first, of Richard Cœur de Lion, was erected by upper-class private subscription in the wake of the Great Exhibition of 1851. The second, a hundred yards away round Speaker's Corner, is Sir Hamo Thornycroft's monument to Oliver Cromwell of 1899. The two rulers seem surprising choices. Richard I may have answered to Victorian ideals of chivalry, but hardly of parliamentarianism, for he lived before parliaments were thought of. In Cromwell's life, of course, parliaments played a large part, as he in theirs. Yet a man whose troops four times used force on the House of Commons does not seem an obvious candidate for commemoration by the Mother of Parliaments.

Why is his statue there? To find the answer we need to go back to the planning of Barry's and Pugin's new Palace of Westminster, built in the decades following the fire that destroyed the old building in 1834. Here, decided parliament, was a major opportunity to depict and celebrate the nation's history. The enterprise would at the same time answer a public demand that parliament do more to encourage the fine arts. A parliamentary body, the Fine Arts Commission, was set up in 1841, under the active chairmanship of Prince Albert, to arrange for the building to accommodate a series of statues, paintings and stained-glass windows on national historical themes.

Of the problems facing the commission none was more delicate than the representation of the civil wars, which had divided the nation since their occurrence. The representation of the 'Glorious Revolution' of 1688 was easier. The old Jacobite hostility to the Revolution had all but evaporated, while the decline of patriot republicanism had all

OLIVER
CROMWELL
1599
1658

but healed the divisions about 1688 within the Whig camp. Yet if the later revolt was the less controversial of the two, we have seen that it was also, to an increasing number of people, the less inspiring of them. How were the claims of the two events to be represented and balanced? Two commissioners were especially influential in the choices of subject-matter for commemoration in (and on the exterior walls of) the new building. They were the pre-eminent Whig historians of the time, Henry Hallam and T. B. Macaulay. Hallam, the older man, was on the conservative wing of the Whig tradition. He revered the Glorious Revolution but was troubled by the Puritan one and appalled by its radicalization in the 1640s. Macaulay, in his younger years, had preferred the earlier revolt, though like many Whigs he believed it to have strayed into excess and folly at the regicide. Now his attention had settled on the later upheaval, around which he was writing his great *History*.

The commission by no means ignored the Puritan revolt. On the contrary it resolved to give equal weight to the two conflicts. They would be portrayed together as a single 'great contest' which had 'commenced with the meeting of the Long Parliament and terminated in 1689'. The principal results of that decision, which took many years to implement, are to be seen on the walls of the corridors that lead off Central Hall (or Central Lobby), where a series of paintings illustrates dramatic episodes both of the 1640s and of the 1680s. Yet between the representations of the two decades there is a difference. In the paintings the opponents of the absolutism of the later Stuarts speak for the nation. The Whig cause is the nation's cause. It is the tradition of establishment Whig history, which blossomed in the earlier nineteenth century, rather than its radical counterpart, which withered during it, that the pictures project. There is no room for Algernon Sidney, whom Hallam's and Macaulay's writings had helped to banish from public attention. In the late seventeenth century and for much of the eighteenth, Sidney's fellow-martyr William Lord Russell, a friend of limited monarchy where Sidney espoused republicanism, had been preferred to Sidney in the memory of establishment Whigs. During the earlier part of George III's reign that preference had been suspended. Now it had been revived. A painting was commissioned of Lady Russell's farewell to her husband, the ancestor of the current Whig leader Lord

John Russell, prime minister from 1846 to 1852, himself a member of the Fine Arts Commission, who assiduously fostered his forebear's reputation. In Macaulay's writings it is with Russell, not Sidney, that John Hampden is linked. At the time of the commission's deliberations there appeared Macaulay's essay 'The Earl of Chatham', which paid tribute to those who 'charged by the side of Hampden at Chalgrove' and 'exchanged the last embrace with Russell on the scaffold'. Another Whig martyr represented is Alice Lisle, the widow of Edmund Ludlow's fellow-exile, that victim of an assassin's bullet John Lisle. Alice, who had none of her husband's political radicalism, was infamously condemned to death by Judge Jeffreys merely for sheltering participants in Monmouth's rising of 1685, an injustice on which Macaulay's *History* waxes eloquent. The later Stuarts are by implication what they had seemed to an ever greater number of people since 1688: tyrants.

The depiction of the civil wars, by contrast, is even-handed. Roundhead and Cavalier loyalties are set beside each other within a national heritage that combines and balances them. Charles I raises his standard at Nottingham in 1642: the parliamentary trained bands set off from London for the relief of Gloucester in 1643. In those and the other pictures there is an even balance of sympathy. We see at work the principle invoked by Macaulay when he described Westminster Abbey as a 'great temple of reconciliation'. The commissioners achieved the same even-handedness in St Stephen's Hall nearby. There a succession of statues, erected between 1848 and 1858, salutes statesmen and orators across the centuries. Among them two royalist figures, Clarendon and Lord Falkland, stand opposite two parliamentarians, Hampden and John Selden. When the Roundheads and Cavaliers confronted each other in 1642, all four men shunned extremism. The nobility of spirit captured by their statues links them across the party lines.

In the late summer and autumn of 1845 the national and provincial presses were animated by a controversial suggestion. The commission had agreed that the statuary of the new building, though it would represent many aspects of the nation's past – political, military, intellectual, cultural – should give pride of place to England's monarchs down the ages. One ruler of England was conspicuously absent from the commissioners' plans: the Lord Protector, Oliver Cromwell. The question 'Should Cromwell Have a Statue?' was adopted in many parts of

Charles I raises his standard: the parliamentary trained bands set out.
Paintings by C. W. Cope for the Peers' Corridor (1861–5).

the country as a formula for debate and was widely and intensively discussed. Surfacing first in *Douglas Jerrold's Shilling Magazine*, it provoked debate in *The Times*, the *Morning Herald*, the *Standard*, *Punch*, the *Buckinghamshire Gazette*, the *Hampshire Telegraph*, the *Hampshire Advertiser*, the *Liverpool Mercury*, the *Lancaster Gazette*, the *Bradford Observer*. Though there was some strident opposition, which recycled the time-honoured charges against Cromwell's character, the supporters of the proposal believed they had public opinion on their side. Such a monument, they maintained, would offer a long-overdue recognition of the virtues and glories of his rule. It would also do something to repair the shame incurred by the nation when his body was barbarously treated at the Restoration.

The loudest voices behind the agitation were populist and republican (or semi-republican) ones. A number of writers used the controversy to mock the unworthy run of England's hereditary rulers, that 'profligate and imbecile' race, whom Cromwell put to shame. If Cromwell was a usurper, it was pointed out, so had many of England's monarchs been. Yet his admirers faced a dilemma. The majority position, which favoured his appearance among the royal statues, took him to have been a king in all but name, who was superior to many or most or even all of those who had held the kingly title. A vocal minority adopted an alternative stance, from which he was regarded not as the exception to the unsatisfactory run of kings but as the antithesis of them. Kings were motivated by aggrandisement, he by conscience. They rose from the aristocracy, he from the people. To 'put him amongst kings' would be less a tribute to his memory than an insult to it. It would be better to erect a monument to him in a separate place, 'by himself'.

The commission, for more conservative reasons, declined to yield to the public pressure to allow Cromwell a place among the royal niches. But there was a second possibility. The commission had suggested around 120 names of historic national figures, other than monarchs, who might be given statues in the Palace. It was unanimously in favour of about half of them, divided about the rest. Cromwell was in the second category. No statue of him followed, and he has never been formally commemorated within the building (though a figure who seems to be Cromwell does appear in C. W. Cope's painting in the Peers' Corridor of Charles I's attempt to arrest the five members; and late in the century a bust of Cromwell, privately donated, was placed in the Lower Waiting Hall of the Commons, where it remains). The failure of the commission – of the 'committee of taste', as its critics mockingly called it – to provide a monument to Cromwell, even in a non-regal capacity, was interpreted by devotees of Oliver as a 'new indignity'.* The contrast with the honouring of Hampden among the statues in St Stephen's Hall caused offence.

Greater offence was caused by the honouring of the royalist Falkland in the same place. A man devoted to moderation and decency, who like his friend Clarendon was among those won over to royalism as the war approached, Falkland owed his high reputation to the famous, loving account of him in Clarendon's *History of the Rebellion* and to the echo of it in that twin bane of Roundhead sympathizers, Hume's *History of England*. From the later eighteenth century, republican historians fought back. Catharine Macaulay, whose *History* was a reply to Hume's, derided Falkland's reputation for 'virtue'. Her case against him was essentially a country-party or patriot one: he had been upright enough while he held out against Charles's policies, but had sold out when he accepted the Secretaryship of State in 1642. In the nineteenth century that political objection to him yielded to a social one. His admirers customarily praised his 'chivalry'. From the age of Tom Paine onwards radicals turned on the ideal of chivalry, which they linked to the oppressive aristocratic mentality. Can it be an accident that in 1794 the republican historian of the Commonwealth William Godwin gave the name Falkland to the aristocratic and chivalrous figure unsympathetically portrayed in his novel *Caleb Williams*? In Victorian times Cromwell's militant supporters, who scorned the chivalry of the historical Falkland, were alleged to 'sneer' at that other source of his fame, the delicacy of his moral scruples. For in Falkland there lay, in a royalist guise, the 'thin incorruptible patriotism' which Carlyle and other champions of Cromwell now derided. Political and religious radicals who took up Cromwell's cause under Carlyle's

* Prince Albert made some amends as the energetic Chairman of the Royal Commission for the Great Exhibition. He was responsible for the naming of the thoroughfare 'Cromwell Road', which extends westwards from the Victoria and Albert Museum and on which work began in 1855.

Lord Falkland in St Stephen's Hall.

inspiration claimed that the protector's commitment to 'conscience' was a far deeper principle than those espoused by Falkland, or indeed by Hampden. Clarendon had noted the habitual 'neatness and industry' of Falkland's attire: Carlyle, who mocked Hampden's 'purest linen', laughed too at 'dainty little Falklands', a species with whom he contrasted the rough, coarse, ungainly Cromwell, a man thankfully 'not known to the man-milliner's species'. None the less Carlyle was torn over the agitation for a statue of Cromwell. Though he gave the proposal some encouragement, in his mind the recent surge of municipal statuary honouring unworthy figures, and the lists of potential honorands prepared by the 'committee of taste', testifed to his generation's barrenness of soul. One side of him wished to spare Cromwell inclusion in such company.

Defeated at Westminster, Cromwellians took their cause to the regions. There was a fresh burst of agitation in 1849–50, led from Birmingham, where Carlyle's disciple the Dissenting minister George Dawson drummed up support. Initiatives were now advanced for a statue in Cromwell's native Huntingdon or in nearby St Ives, or else at Naseby, the site of the victory which had smashed the divine-right cause and which, of all Cromwell's victories, gave most pleasure to the republican and populist component of Victorian Cromwellianism. An obelisk marking the battle was erected on the site in 1875, at a ceremony attended by 2,000 members of the National Agricultural Labourers' Union, but no statue of Cromwell himself was put up there. Meanwhile in 1858 an opportunity for renewed pressure for a statue at Westminster had been offered by the bicentenary of the protector's death. The moment passed, apparently because of some failure of coordination, but in the following year committees were reportedly at work in Liverpool, Manchester, Newcastle and elsewhere to redeem the omission. For it was in the north, especially in its swelling industrial cities and towns, that enthusiasm grew strongest, largely though not exclusively under the impact of Nonconformity. Agitation persisted elsewhere too. In 1859 there was a fresh proposal for a statue in Huntingdon, though it came to nothing. (It would fail again when revived in 1899, the tercentenary year. The weakness both of Nonconformity and of Cromwellianism in Cromwell's birthplace disheartened his admirers. It was in nearby St Ives, where Nonconformity was

The unveiling of the statue at St Ives (1901).

stronger, that the only statue of Cromwell to have been raised by public subscription was erected in 1901.)

It was Manchester that took the lead. Waterhouse's Assize Court, built in 1859–64, had a statue of Cromwell among a series of busts of England's monarchs. In the decades ahead, civic buildings or Nonconformist chapels elsewhere would represent him in statuary or stained glass: in Bradford, Cambridge, Fairhaven (Lytham St Annes), Faringdon (in London), Harrogate, Knutsford, Leeds, Oxford, Rochdale and Whitehaven. As in Manchester, so in Bradford, Leeds and Rochdale, Cromwell stood among hereditary rulers of England. Yet as Nonconformity, which had been almost silent on the subject of the statue in 1845, grew in size and confidence, so Puritan images of Cromwell came to vie with kingly ones. The tendency to place his life and character within a broad Puritan inheritance was stimulated by the bicentenary of the Great Ejection of 1662, an anniversary which produced much reflection on and celebration of Nonconformity's past. Some visual representations of Cromwell located him not among monarchs but alongside Puritan divines and poets and (though less often) other Puritan statesmen (Hampden particularly). It was in Puritan company that he was depicted in statuary at a Congregationalist hall in Faringdon in 1862 and on the exterior of a newly-built Congregationalist church at Harrogate the following year. He would again be flanked by fellow-Puritans in Edwardian stained glass in Nonconformist churches: in White Church in Fairhaven, in Emmanuel United Reformed Church in Cambridge and in the Congregationalist chapel of Mansfield College, Oxford. By now visual representations of Puritanism reflected something of the growing respectability – variously aldermanic or suburban or academic – of Nonconformity.

The more militant Cromwellians wanted something else. They pressed for a statue that would show him on his own, in towering eminence. Again Manchester was at the forefront. The statue of him among the kings in the Assize Court was judged an insufficient tribute. After a long delay caused by the cotton famine – and perhaps by a shift to the Right in Mancunian politics – the widow of a radical businessman funded a large statue of him that had been designed by Matthew Noble. It was raised in 1875. Before then, however, the plans for it had already come to the nation's attention, in an episode which

The Congregationalist chapel of Mansfield College, Oxford (1908). The stained glass of the building records the history of Nonconformity. Here Cromwell is flanked by Vane and Hampden. In the same window (unseen here), Milton, who stands immediately beneath Cromwell, is flanked by the Puritan divines William Twisse and Thomas Goodwin.

has been uncovered by Stephen Porter. It brought Cromwellianism in Manchester into collaboration with its counterpart in the capital. One morning in early August of 1871, MPs arriving at Westminster were surprised to find a grey plaster model of Noble's statue standing in flower-beds by the Houses of Parliament, the protector's face looking towards the members' entrance to the Commons. In 1867 a Liberal MP had attempted to revive the proposal for a statue at Westminster, to no avail. Now the idea had a fresh wind behind it. Its resurrection in 1867–71 was occasioned by the planning of statues of nineteenth-century statesmen at Westminster: of Canning, whose monument was built in 1867, and of Derby, Peel and Palmerston, the placing of whose statues was under discussion in 1871. The Commissioner of Works in 1871 was Acton Smee Ayrton, the abrasive MP for Tower Hamlets, a champion of Dissent and, in his own words, an 'extreme Liberal'. It was on the pretext of testing a site for the prime ministerial statues that he arranged for the erection of the Cromwell model. His real motive became evident when he told the Commons that another MP had handed him a subscription list, signed by twelve peers and 110 members of the Commons, to meet the cost of a permanent statue of Cromwell at Westminster. The correspondent of *The Times*, impressed by the grandeur and simplicity of the model, called it 'as fine a statue as any in London'. Pronouncing Cromwell to have been 'greater than' the prime ministers who were to be honoured, he called for a permanent monument to him at Westminster.

Like earlier initiatives of Cromwellianism, the move of 1871 drew on anti-establishment impulses. The model appeared only days after the leading republican Charles Bradlaugh had addressed a popular demonstration in London that marked a high point of nineteenth-century anti-monarchical feeling. Its appearance had an anti-parliamentary resonance too, for the model was interpreted as a reproach to the dilatoriness of the present parliament and as a reminder of the expulsion of its predecessor of April 1653.

The flurry of interest aroused by the episode ended during the summer parliamentary recess, when the model was returned to Noble's studio. It was in Manchester that, four years later, the statue appeared in its final form. Nine feet high, and weighing more than a ton, it was positioned by the cathedral, at the point where the first blood of the civil war was believed to have been shed (though in 1968 the monument would be removed to the outskirts of the city to make way for a one-way traffic system). According to its reviewer in *The Art Journal* in 1876 the statue possessed 'a boldness akin to audacity'. It made Noble's name. At the unveiling ceremony a Liberal MP proclaimed, before an enthusiastic crowd, 'this tardy act of justice' to the protector's memory. Five days later a 'great Conservative meeting' in the Corn Exchange, attended by the Chancellor of the Exchequer, answered back. The audience sang 'Rule Britannia' after cheering a Tory MP who attacked the decision to honour Cromwell and 'spoke of the time when the protector sent his soldiers to the House of Commons to expel the members'. The choice of song has a bearing on our larger story. Its words were from the patriot James Thomson's ode to Britannia in his masque *Alfred* of 1740. In eighteenth-century minds it was not only to foreigners, but to kings, that 'Britons never shall be slaves'. In the nineteenth century, when the term 'patriot' was more often used of defenders of the establishment than of challengers to it, the country-party resonance of the song faded.

Meanwhile the movement for a Westminster statue had gone quiet. It might never have been revived but for a political accident of 1894–5 which made the issue once more what it had been in the 1840s, a focus of national debate, and which brought success where previous agitation had failed.

The erection of the statue in 1899 was the achievement – the painful achievement – of Lord Rosebery, the Liberal Party leader. In Rosebery's mind Cromwell's greatness had nothing to do with the merits of the Roundhead cause, for which Rosebery had little sympathy, nothing to do with his Puritanism, everything with the effectiveness of his regime. Rosebery, who wrote admiringly about the energizing efficiency of Napoleonic rule, applauded Cromwell in the same spirit. It was not principally Rosebery's own Cromwellianism, however, that impelled him to favour the statue. He had a more pressing motive. A vital component of the Liberal Party's following was Nonconformity. Rosebery's problem was to win its affection. Nonconformists had been drawn to the moral earnestness and popular touch of Gladstone, who often reminded them of Cromwell, and whom Rosebery replaced as leader and Prime Minister in 1894. They were less taken with his rich, elegant, aristocratic successor. The whiff of sexual scandal surrounding him may not have spread far. A more serious problem, because of the Nonconformist hatred of gambling, was his ownership of racehorses and his membership of the Jockey Club. While an undergraduate at Christ Church, Oxford, that most aristocratic of colleges, Rosebery is said to have stated that he had two ambitions: to become prime minister and to win the Derby. In 1894 he achieved both goals, in that order, within a period of three months.* It was evidently in the hope of redeeming those worldly triumphs that his government resolved to commission and finance a statue of Cromwell, the Nonconformist hero, at Westminster.

In the short term the proposal turned, as Rosebery acknowledged, into a 'fiasco'. Its fate encapsulated the weaknesses of his fractious administration and heralded its collapse. One Cabinet meeting was mostly spent on a debate on the scheme. A minority, which included the future prime minister Sir Henry Campbell-Bannerman, thought there should be no statue at all. Others argued about the site and character of the monument. The old questions about the appropriate method of representing Cromwell resurfaced. Sir William Harcourt, the disaffected Chancellor of the Exchequer and leader of the government in the Commons, no advocate of the statue and no admirer of either Cromwell or Rosebery, argued that, if the protector were to be commemorated, he should stand between Charles I and Charles II in the row of busts which then stood in Westminster Hall. (The same suggestion had been made by the Liberal MP who was thwarted in 1867.) Rosebery was not willing to brave Queen Victoria with that suggestion. She had reportedly objected (though the evidence is ambiguous) to the honouring of Cromwell in Manchester,† and was said to be dismayed by Rosebery's own respect for Cromwell. Another thought, which recalls the episode of 1871, was to place Cromwell among the prime ministers in Parliament Square. Yet Cromwell, as

* He would win the Derby again the following year, when his premiership was disintegrating.

† Later, royal distaste for Cromwell was demonstrated by George V, who overruled a proposal of Winston Churchill, as First Lord of the Admiralty, to name a Dreadnought after the protector.

Rosebery lightly put it, was 'not a great parliamentarian in the strict sense'. Rosebery's own inclination was for Cromwell to stand in 'dignified isolation'. He got his way, though the only practical site, in a 'damp ditch', 'at the bottom of a hole', provoked some mockery in parliament.

Initially the government contemplated the commissioning of an equestrian statue, to match that of Richard I. (In 1871 Ayrton had at one point scouted the idea of an equestrian statue.) Instead the government settled for the less costly idea of a standing figure. When the statue had been built, *The Times* teased the more militant of the Nonconformists, who liked the violent streak in Cromwell, by suggesting that they 'would have preferred to see the protector in the act of hewing Agag in pieces'. The jest, though unfair, had a point. Thornycroft's representation of Cromwell is restrained. Rosebery himself would have liked it to be more aggressive. Oliver carries a sword in one hand and a Bible in the other. For Carlyle, and for the radical Nonconformists after him, those had been the '*real* emblems of Puritanism' and of Cromwell. But where militant Cromwellians remembered 'the bright flash of his sword', in the statue the point of the sword rests on the ground (while his Bible, which in Carlyle's image had been 'open', is closed). The plain, bare-headed figure is Puritan in spirit, but the Puritanism, being without belligerence or sectarianism, was of a kind to appeal beyond Nonconformity across that range of earnest Victorian opinion which had taken Cromwell up. The question whether Cromwell had been a legitimate sovereign was discreetly evaded, for the monument records only his name and the years of his birth and death, not his office of Lord Protector.

Unfortunately Rosebery, in attending to Nonconformist sensibilities, had omitted, not for the first time, to pay sufficient attention to Irish ones. The fate of the Cromwell statue became embroiled in Rosebery's unhappy relations with the Irish Nationalists, on whose votes the ministry's survival depended and whom the government, in proposing the statue, mistakenly believed it had squared. In June 1895, when the Commons was asked to vote money for the statue, John Redmond and his Nationalist colleagues reminded the House, in speeches of colourful recrimination, of Cromwell's massacres on Irish soil. John Morley, speaking for the government, had to withdraw the motion. That humiliating climbdown, which Nonconformists would shudder to recall in the years ahead, was greeted, Morley noticed, 'with anger and disgust from English Liberals; with thick-witted jibes from Unionists . . .; and with wild cries of aboriginal joy from our Irish friends'. Rosebery's administration, already demoralized, collapsed very soon afterwards following another Irish desertion.

Rosebery was none the less determined that the proposal should go ahead. Before leaving office he made a bargain with the incoming Tory government. The statue would still be built, but would be paid for by Rosebery himself (anonymously, but everyone knew who the donor was to be). The Tories' connivance in that arrangement indicates the extent to which, by the late nineteenth century, anti-Cromwellianism had lost its hold. In the subsequent debates on the statue the Tory leaders, Salisbury in the Lords and Balfour in the Commons, while distancing themselves from the scheme and gently mocking it, supported it when it counted. Earlier decades of the century, fearful of social revolution, had smelt danger in Cromwellianism. His name had seemed to its detractors a disturbing symbol of destruction, a reminder that civil war might come again. In the calmer social waters of the late Victorian period the cult of Cromwell no longer seemed a threat. One MP was reminded by the parliamentary debates over the statue of the proceedings of a youthful debating society. It was, he thought, 'a blessed thing that this country can now devote itself to these abstract questions'.

Cromwell had been accommodated within a politically ecumenical conspectus of the nation's past, which allowed for the honouring of 'great' men even when their goodness remained contested. In 1844, during the Fine Arts Commission's deliberations on the historical decoration of the new building, Henry Hallam had expressed the hope that the statues and paintings in the Palace would commemorate statesmen 'whose memory, now hallowed by time, we cherish with a more unanimous respect than contemporary passions always afford'. In the 1840s no such consensus could have been secured for the commemoration of Cromwell. The argument that even his adversaries should acknowledge his greatness fell on deaf ears. Yet in 1899 Balfour could successfully maintain that to reject the statue would be to 'carry ancient feuds very much too far'.

Thus it was that Cromwell, who had killed a king and destroyed monarchy and wrecked the parliamentary constitution, came to be honoured by parliament. When, in the twentieth century, Leo Amery and Michael Heseltine, the one at the fall of Neville Chamberlain, the other during the premiership of James Callaghan, drew on memories of Cromwell's expulsion of the Rump, their gestures were pro-parliamentary, not (as nineteenth-century invocations of it had been) anti-parliamentary. The two men were demanding that a government be called to parliamentary account. As a speaker who followed Amery in the debate pointed out, Cromwell had failed whereas the institution of parliament had survived him.

But if the establishment gradually learned to tolerate Cromwell, opinion outside it was not always so accommodating. Beside popular Cromwellianism popular anti-Cromwellianism lived on. The statement in the *Spectator* at the time of the tercentenary that 'all but a few fanatics' 'regard' Cromwell 'as a great and noble Englishman' was over-confident. So was Frederic Harrison's assertion that opposition to him had dwindled to 'the whining of a handful of Ritualists, Jew financiers and Jacobites'.* Despite the connivance of the Tory leadership in Rosebery's plan for a statue, there was enough opposition to make its implementation a delicate political operation. Resistance from the Tory backbenches in both houses was supported by an upsurge of resentment in a section of the public. Petitions against the building of the monument attracted thousands of signatures across the land. Obstructionist tactics in parliament prevented the raising of the statue in time for the tercentenary in April 1899, and then thwarted a substitute plan to unveil it on 3 September, 'Cromwell's day', the anniversary of his victories at Dunbar and Worcester and of his death.

Only on 14 November was the monument opened to public view. There was none of the excitement that had attended the unveiling of the Manchester statue a quarter of a century earlier. For fear of public disturbance the new statue was revealed, before a tiny huddle of spectators, at 7.30 a.m. There was no ceremony, though in the evening

* Not all Cromwellians would have welcomed that characterization. At the tercentenary Rosebery, who had married a Rothschild, made much of Cromwell's friendship to the Jews.

Rosebery did give an address in Queen's Hall which shamelessly invoked Cromwell's name in the cause of the Liberal leader's own current political concerns ('a piece of rotten politics', Morley called it). The furtiveness of the unveiling gave no pleasure to Cromwellians. But at least, and at last, the movement to honour their hero at Westminster had prevailed.

Cromwellianism, having peaked at the end of the century, thereafter entered a decline which, though uneven in pace and never complete, was soon conspicuous. In 1929 W. C. Abbott's *Bibliography of Oliver Cromwell* was conceived almost as an epitaph, so sharp, and seemingly so final, had been the recent decline of publications on Cromwell. Five years later principal writings on the Cromwellian era, Carlyle's *Letters and Speeches* among them, had reportedly gone out of print or become scarce. Modern parallels with Cromwell could still strike home, most notably in the age of the inter-war dictators. Cromwell, who had earlier reminded so many people of Napoleon, was now compared to Hitler and Stalin. Even so the passions of the past were rarely reignited.

The decline of Cromwellianism was matched by, and was intertwined with, that of Nonconformity. Nonconformist enthusiasm for Cromwell itself shrank, or at least learned to keep its head down, during the first decade of the twentieth century, as Dissent predominantly retreated from political engagement and resumed its earlier spiritual priorities. Though reverence for Cromwell within the movement would long persist, it became essentially a preservative, even a nostalgic impulse rather than a proselytizing or confrontational one. Even within the stridency and apparent confidence of the claims made for Cromwell by Nonconformity in and around the year of the tercentenary, there are already signs of change. By 1880 the battles for the emancipation of Dissent, for its freedom and equality in religion, politics, education, and society, had been mostly won. Thereafter Nonconformity began to lose something of its momentum and direction, even of its distinctive culture. There is a sense, as Nonconformist Cromwellians seek the attention of younger hearers and readers, that tomorrow's audience is being given yesterday's message. To the dismay of militants much of Nonconformity was being assimilated into conventional society. The Nonconformist commemorators of 1899 attacked enemies not only without but within. They condemned prosperous Nonconformist businessmen and politicians, 'milk-and-water men', who had distanced themselves from distinctively Nonconformist causes.

Another ground of unease is visible too. For all its fervour the commemoration in the City Temple was, as Nonconformists themselves noticed, 'too much a middle-class affair'. In the Cromwellianism of the nineteenth-century – most conspicuously perhaps in that of Edward Miall, who would have liked to merge the Nonconformist and Chartist movements – Dissenting aspirations had sometimes merged with egalitarian ones. By the century's end, for all the populist language of militant Nonconformity and despite the presence of a number of socialists in Nonconformist ranks, barriers of class and purpose were dividing the two movements. Cromwell, who had attracted many socialists earlier in Victoria's reign, attracted fewer at its end. During the centenary celebrations socialist organizations were conspicuous by their absence. They had found, in Cromwell's place, a new set of mid-seventeenth-century heroes: the Levellers, whom he had crushed.

12

The Levellers and the Left

Each year on Cromwell's day, 3 September, the Cromwell Association, the core of surviving Cromwellianism, gathers by the Westminster statue for a service of commemoration. Since 1975 there has been another annual attraction for mid-seventeenth-century loyalties, one promoted and attended by leading left-wing politicians and intellectuals. It is held, under the auspices of the Oxford Levellers Branch of the Workers' Educational Association, at Burford in Oxfordshire on a Saturday in May. It commemorates the Leveller movement, which met its conclusive defeat in the suppression of the army mutiny there in May 1649. After a swift court martial three soldiers were shot outside the church in which they had taken refuge. To the martyrs and victims of earlier times – the regicides executed in 1660–62; Algernon Sidney and the other Whig martyrs of Charles II's reign; Edmund Ludlow after his flights from England in 1660 and 1689 – the later twentieth century added the name of cornet William Thompson and those of corporals Church and Perkins, whose Christian names no contemporary had thought to preserve.

One Leveller acquired victim status much earlier: John Lilburne, who became a popular hero during his trials for treason, under threat of the death-sentence, in 1649 and 1653. His bravura defences of himself, and his acquittals by defiant juries, produced clamours of popular rejoicing, but later generations were struck less by the failure of the prosecution than by the fact that it occurred. Lilburne's main offence had been, not to conspire against Cromwell and the Commonwealth, but merely to publish criticisms of them (admittedly vitriolic ones). His tireless literary invective and his querulous self-dramatization were visited on all who affronted him. He was whipped and pilloried in 1638, and imprisoned for nearly three years, after printing and circulating attacks on the Laudian regime. In the civil war he enlisted for parliament and was soon captured by the royalists, who tried him for treasonably taking up arms against the king. Only the threat of reprisals from parliament saved him from death. He was released the following year, resumed his military service, fought bravely, rose to the rank of lieutenant-colonel. But by 1645 he was quarrelling with fellow-Roundheads and attacking parliament for its own offences against public liberty. He left the army in that year and was repeatedly under parliamentary imprisonment until 1649. By 1647 the principal target of his hatred was Cromwell, formerly his friend, whom he now saw, as so many radicals among the Roundheads came to do, as the betrayer of the cause.

Around Lilburne there gathered a group of allies and pamphleteers: above all Richard Overton, John Wildman, William Walwyn. Behind the group there lay enterprising printers and publishers, and perhaps – for the evidence is infirm – a network of organization through the city of London. The Levellers became masters of the polemical tract and the aggrieved petition. In 1647 their influence spread to the Cromwellian army. A system of representation grew up which enabled regiments to choose 'agents' or 'agitators' who would gather the grievances of the rank-and-file and submit them to the officers. Initially Cromwell cooperated with that development. By the autumn it had turned against him. At Putney, where the army was quartered, the agents and their friends in London assailed the officers' readiness to negotiate with the king. They drew up their own scheme of national settlement, an *Agreement of the People*, a far-reaching set of demands for political, social and religious reform which was submitted to the army's council.

There followed that series of animated discussions which the modern world knows as the Putney debates. Thanks to the shorthand skills of William Clarke, the army secretary, we have something like a full transcript of some of the debates. It was recovered in the new era of archival energy in the late nineteenth century and edited and published by C. H. Firth in 1891, three years before his edition of Ludlow's *Memoirs*. In this instance there is no problem of authenticity. The twentieth century, reading the Putney debates, marvelled at statements by the participants which seemed closer to its own concerns than to those normally encountered in the hierarchical society of the England of the civil wars. The debate on the parliamentary franchise, and in particular the claim that 'the poorest he that is in England' has the right to vote, exerted a power over many readers in the twentieth century reminiscent of that exerted by the transcript of Algernon Sidney's trial in the eighteenth century and Cromwell's letters and speeches in the nineteenth.

The radicals' demands at Putney were unavailing. Two regiments turned to mutiny, parading with copies of the *Agreement* stuck in their hats together with the motto 'England's Freedom! Soldiers' Rights!' The ringleaders were arrested and court-martialled, and one, Richard Arnold, was shot. The political representation of the regiments by 'agents' was ended. In 1648 the royalist revival and the second civil war restored army unity, which survived the strains placed on it by Pride's Purge and the regicide. Those events were a defeat for Lilburne and his London friends, who had wanted the army leaders to commit themselves to something like the *Agreement of the People* before striking against parliament and king. Instead, or so Lilburne afterwards judged, the officers occupied them in meaningless discussions in order 'to quiet and please us (like children with rattles)'. In his eyes the Commonwealth was a military tyranny, owing nothing to the consent of the people, from which all legitimate government derives.

Soon after the execution of the king Lilburne and his friends were in prison again, this time for inciting hostility to the new regime. Soon too there was fresh mutiny among the troops. It was crushed only after a lightning campaign in the spring by Cromwell and Fairfax, conducted from Wiltshire to Hampshire to the Cotswolds. The events at Burford fatally weakened, though they did not quite terminate, the military resistance. Lilburne could still animate public opinion, but the movement he had helped to lead was virtually over.

Posterity knows that movement as 'the Levellers', a term that it applies both to Lilburne's civilian following (mainly in London) and to the military agitation of 1647–9. But the term 'Leveller' – like 'republican' – began as a smear. It came into circulation just after the Putney debates, probably as a result of royalist propaganda, though Lilburne put the blame on the army officers. The men at whom the word was aimed were accused of intending to 'raise a parity and community in the kingdom', to destroy the nobility, to abolish property, and thus 'to make us all even, so that every Jack should vie with a gentleman and every gentleman be made a Jack'. Lilburne and his friends indignantly challenged those allegations, which were indeed unwarranted. It was, they protested, their desire 'that every man may with as much security as may be enjoy his propriety [= property]'. The claim 'that we would level all men's estates, that we would have no distinction of orders and dignities among men' was, they objected, a slander.

In April 1649, while the agitation that would lead to mutiny and to the prosecution of Lilburne was reaching its climax, another movement of protest arose. Unlike Lilburne and his associates, its adherents demanded the abolition of property and the holding of all things in common. Led by Gerrard Winstanley, an eloquent pamphleteer, they called themselves 'Diggers' or 'True Levellers'. The collapse of monarchy and the House of Lords, and the grave economic hardship of that year, combined to excite dreams of social and spiritual emancipation. Diggers, who regarded kingship as an act of theft from 'the people', saw property in the same light. Over the seventeenth and eighteenth centuries property was almost universally represented as the safeguard of liberty. To the Diggers it was its enemy. Landlords, in their eyes, were as oppressive and tyrannical and sinful as kings. The Diggers set up a propertyless colony on St George's Hill in Surrey. Army officers, ordered to suppress it, viewed it with more bewilderment than hostility and were slow to move. But an abusive local crowd soon gathered to dig up the new-sown seeds. The community lasted for a short while, and others that had followed its lead enjoyed a brief existence, but the larger aims of the Diggers were lost.

As a subject of historical scholarship and controversy the Levellers are a twentieth-century discovery. Over the past hundred years they have had a conspicuous, sometimes a revered position in writings on seventeenth-century England. Earlier accounts of them were much less ample and respectful. A mixture of interest and sympathy has replaced one of indifference and hostility. Some socialist and liberal historians of the twentieth century found the attitude of previous generations to the

Levellers wanting. In the 1960s an enterprise of collective research was conducted into nineteenth-century attitudes to Oliver Cromwell and the civil wars. It produced an invaluable archive which can now be read in the Bodleian Library. Though there was no uniformity of political outlook among the contributors, the venture was left-wing in inspiration. It was an offshoot of *History Workshop: A Journal of Socialist Historians*. In 1968 Tim Mason, the leader of the exercise, wrote a report on its preliminary conclusions in the historical journal *Past and Present*, which had been founded in 1952 as a Marxist publication and which retained something of that flavour. Mason was puzzled by one aspect of his and his colleagues' findings. Though they had found it easy to demonstrate the extent and intensity of nineteenth-century interest in Cromwell, they discovered much less evidence of nineteenth-century interest in the Levellers. In the eighteenth century, Mason noticed, the Levellers had attracted less attention still. Why, he asked, had a subject whose importance was self-evident to the modern age been so largely ignored earlier? The answer, he hinted, lay in a conspiracy of silence. He urged his colleagues 'to discover by what means the established order was able to blot out to so great an extent the memory of . . . the Levellers'.

That was a loaded injunction. We might equally well ask why the Levellers, whom few people before the twentieth century thought a worthy subject of historical investigation, came to be taken so seriously. That question is no less loaded. It is not easy, in tracing Leveller historiography, to unload our questions, so heavily have some of the preoccupations of the Levellers pressed on modern concerns. By reconstructing the framework of Leveller historiography since the Restoration, we shall see how profoundly the values of the twentieth century altered the perceptions of the Levellers bequeathed by earlier times. Liking about the Levellers what previous ages had disliked, the twentieth century did not so much cast aside the prejudices of earlier approaches as invert them.

From the late Victorian age the Levellers were thought of as friends of the future. A long succession of commentators – the socialists Henry Hyndman and J. Morrison Davidson in the 1890s, twentieth-century Marxists from D. W. Petegorsky to Christopher Hill and E. P. Thompson, but also a variety of liberal historians and thinkers over the same period – remarked that the Levellers 'anticipated' or 'looked forward to', or were 'forerunners of' or 'beforehand with', later developments of political thought and organization. They were 'far in advance of their age', 'a long way before their time'. They 'traced the thought patterns of three centuries of their successors' and 'had their feet on the main track to the democratic future'. Writer after writer remarked how 'modern' the Levellers were. Leveller ideas, or the practices of debate which they inspired, were deemed to have anticipated late eighteenth-century revolutionary thinking in France and America, the arguments of the Luddites and Chartists in Victorian England, the English trade union movement, the Workers' and Soldiers' Councils of the Russian Revolution. Leveller (and Digger) ideas and practices were given modern labels or interpreted with reference to them: 'socialist', 'communist', 'social democrat', 'anarchist'. From the late 1930s it was common for them to be described as 'the Left'.

Admittedly, within the Marxist perspective on the Levellers that became dominant in that decade, not everything about them seemed progressive. Their 'forward-looking proposals' had been combined with a 'backward-looking' regard for the disintegrating 'village community' and with a 'backward-looking' resistance to the centralization of power. But it was their forwardness that commanded most attention. Sometimes it offered an explanation of their failure: the world had not been ready for them. Sometimes too it afforded an explanation of the neglect of their memory over the two and a half centuries following their demise, when posterity had yet to catch up with them.

Once more, then, the present saw its reflection in the past. Yet the growth of interest in the Levellers was not merely a product of ideological sympathy. It was the result also of developments in historical scholarship. Enthusiasm for the Levellers emerged in the period when S. R. Gardiner and C. H. Firth were bringing new breadth, depth and rigour to accounts of the civil wars. The scholarship was mainly the achievement of historians unsympathetic to the Levellers or to socialism or to both. It was from a dialogue, sometimes amicable but sometimes not, between ideology and scholarship that modern perceptions of the Levellers emerged. In that respect the twentieth-century interpretative record differs from the eighteenth- and nineteenth-century ones traced in earlier chapters. If the passage of generations is one solvent of historical arguments, the research generated by historical controversy can be a quicker one. Except in its least sophisticated forms, the study of the Levellers has belonged to a process of scholarly inquiry, and been conditioned by a rapidity of scholarly discovery, which no didactic or partisan approach to the seventeenth century has survived for long. Modern approaches to the Levellers, as to everything else of their age, may be as vulnerable to the charge of present-mindedness as those of earlier eras, but they rest on a much larger and a more reliable base of information.

It was around 1885 that modern analysis of the civil wars was launched. The quarter of a century that begins with that date produced Gardiner's great narratives *History of the Great Civil War* (1886–91) and *History of the Commonwealth and Protectorate* (1894–1901), and Firth's *The Last Years of the Protectorate* (1909); Gardiner's edition of the *Constitutional Documents of the Puritan Revolution* (1889); Firth's edition of *The Clarke Papers* (1891–1901), which included in its opening volume the text of the Putney debates; the *Dictionary of National Biography* (1885–1900), the one aid on which all historians of Britain have become dependent; and G. K. Fortescue's catalogue of the Thomason Tracts (1908), the great collection of mid-seventeenth-century pamphlets which George III had presented to the British Museum but in which, until Fortescue's work, only the most acute or persistent historians had found their bearings. Before those publications, attitudes to the Levellers were formed in a world that lacked not only a broad interest in left-wing ideology but the bibliographical landmarks that the modern student takes for granted. Not everything that was said about the Levellers was unfriendly. Yet those who said friendly things, or who merely wanted to be fair or accurate, tended to lose themselves in the chronological complexities of the civil wars. When they turned to standard histories for guidance they encountered, and were easily misled by, basic errors of chronology.

Such errors permeated writings on the Levellers from the later seventeenth century. Few of the recollections of the civil wars that surfaced in Restoration England were exact and dispassionate. Most memories succumbed, as recollections of complex events easily do, to conflation. Accounts of the Levellers could not easily be checked, for very few pertinent documents were in print. With the passage of the generation that had participated in the civil wars, oral memory declined. The years around 1700 did, on the other hand, produce an expansion of the available printed evidence. The memoirs and histories published at that time, Ludlow's *Memoirs* and Clarendon's *History* at their fore, provided, for all their prejudices, a chronological shape for the years of Leveller influence. The *Memoirs* of Ludlow and Denzil Holles and Sir John Berkeley, put out by John Toland and John Darby in 1698–9, all contained fresh material on the army politics of the late 1640s, as did the autobiographical account by Major Robert Huntingdon republished in 1702, though in each case the Levellers played only a peripheral part in the narrative; the word Leveller barely appears in them. In 1701 the concluding volumes of the *Historical Collections* of John Rushworth, a prominent figure in the secretariat of the Cromwellian army, supplied a rudimentary account of the events of 1647. They also brought into print those key documents in the emergence of Leveller organization and thinking, the army remonstrances of June 1647 and the *Agreement of the People*.

None the less the great bulk of pamphlet material relating to the Levellers stood out of view. Over the eighteenth century it remained so. In the 1740s and 1750s, a productive era in the publication of historical documents, a few Leveller and Digger tracts were made newly available in the *Harleian Miscellany*, the *Somers Tracts* and the *Parliamentary or Constitutional History of England*. Yet over the remainder of the century only a handful of accounts of the Levellers drew on those collections. The Thomason Collection, though open to public inspection from the early 1760s, was used only by the most assiduous of historians and editors, and then sparingly. A pamphlet intimately connected to the *Agreement of the People*, which the Levellers published in October 1647 as *The Case of the Army Truly Stated*, appears not to have been cited until the 1820s, when that archival pioneer William Godwin turned to it. John Lilburne's *The Legal, Fundamental Liberties of the People of England* (1649), a tract essential to an understanding of Leveller conduct in the weeks and months before the regicide, was hardly ever referred to until Firth published an extract from it in *The Clarke Papers*. In spite of the great movement for parliamentary reform from the late eighteenth century, it was only with the publication of *The Clarke Papers* that the Levellers became associated with the issue of the franchise. Only one earlier commentator (J. T. Rutt in 1828) appears to have noticed their interest in the subject.

Until around 1890 the deficiencies of the available chronology and evidence excluded any sense of the Levellers as a continuous movement. In most accounts they popped up, seemingly from nowhere, in 1647. They popped up again in 1649. A handful of survivors from the protests of those years could be glimpsed plotting from time to time in the 1650s. But those various episodes were barely connected with each other by historians. Until the early twentieth century there was no interest in the intellectual origins or development of the movement. Essentially it was seen as a military organization, which had caused agitation and mutiny in Cromwell's army and had then, in 1649, threatened the new republic. Leveller ideas counted for less than Leveller actions. When the Levellers figured in narratives of 1647 it was primarily in relation to the rise of Cromwell in the spring and summer, when, it was widely agreed, he had egged on or manipulated or connived with the agitators for his own advancement.

For Cromwell had come to dominate the historiography of the years following the civil wars. A 'principal end' of *Biographia Britannica* in including a life of John Lilburne was 'to give a series of proofs, not commonly known, of the infinite guile and subtlety of Cromwell'. What interested historians about the Leveller mutinies of 1647 and 1649 (events which were sometimes confused with each other) was Cromwell's courage and dexterity in breaking them. On that theme as on many others the dearth of scholarly enterprise produced an interpretative paralysis. Time and again historians of the civil wars were content – as in their handling of other aspects of the conflict – to repeat the claims, even the words, of their predecessors. Cromwell's feat in breaking the Levellers was respected even by some royalist and Tory historians. Like the expulsions of the Rump and Barebone's it was held to have saved the country from anarchy. Besides, military insurrection was considered a black crime. The Leveller mutinies apart, the Cromwellian army was judged to have been impressively free of it, whatever its other misdeeds. Not for the first time we notice the coexistence of opposing perspectives on the civil wars, sometimes within individual minds. For in spite of the widespread association, which Ludlow's *Memoirs* had fostered, between that army and the evils of military rule, the army itself was often held in respectful memory, at least from the late eighteenth century. Even Edmund Burke, no friend to violent methods, commended it as a disciplined body, composed of sober and reflecting citizens, men of piety, morality, virtue and solid social position. If there were many historians who, following Ludlow's *Memoirs*, thought that Cromwell's ambition had corrupted the army, others blamed the Levellers for subverting it.

While Leveller actions were condemned, Leveller ideas, in so far as they were noticed, were generally caricatured. After the Restoration as before it, 'Leveller' was a smear. Memories of the Diggers, who unlike Lilburne and his friends had called themselves Levellers, barely survived. The term 'Leveller' remained fixed to the group that had disowned it. Not every writer on the civil wars in Restoration England endorsed that usage. Lucy Hutchinson, widow of the regicide Colonel Hutchinson, wrote of the 'honest' and 'sober' men who 'were nick-named Levellers' (though her words would not be printed until the early nineteenth century). She denied, as the Levellers themselves had done, the charge that they 'endeavoured the levelling of all estates and qualities'. The Puritan divine Richard Baxter, echoing a complaint by Lilburne himself, wrote in his autobiography, published posthumously in 1696, that Cromwell had termed Lilburne and his friends Levellers in order 'to make them odious, as if they intended to level all men of qualities and degrees'.

Royalist writers were mainly less discriminating. The royalist historian of Charles II's reign James Heath, in his *A Chronicle of the Late Intestine War*, described the 'devilish intention' of the Levellers 'by a wild parity to lay all things in common'. The long-term victory of that view can be principally attributed to Clarendon's *History of the Rebellion*. Clarendon explained that in 1647 'a new faction' in the army 'were, either by their own denomination or with their own consent, called Levellers'. They 'declared that all degrees of men should be levelled, and an equality should be established, both in titles and estates, throughout the kingdom'. Clarendon's account would be often echoed, sometimes repeated verbatim. Hume followed it, explaining that the soldiers of 1647 had agreed that 'all ranks of men must be levelled, and an universal equality of property, as well as of power, be introduced'. Even thereafter, it is true, we find occasional voices ready to acknowledge or protest against the distortion and misrepresentation wrought by the word Leveller. For the most part, however, it was supposed through the eighteenth and nineteenth centuries that the men described as Levellers had sought social parity and that the term therefore suited them.

Smears can work only if there is a public ready to welcome them. Yet, at least once the seventeenth century is past, it is hard to explain the success of the imputation of social levelling in terms of those anxieties that are sometimes held to have gripped the ruling class or to have shaped its ideology. Uses of the term 'Leveller' by eighteenth-century historians reveal contempt for Lilburne and the army agitators, but also something close to amusement. What Tim Mason called 'the established order' did not live in fear that the Levellers might return. Rather the Levellers seem mostly to have been thought of as faintly ridiculous, even faintly exotic products of broken times. They were deemed worthy of mention when they affected national political events, or in illustration of the folly of the turbulent period they had inhabited, but there seemed no reason to accord them much prominence in narratives of those congested years, when more influential groups had competed for power.

If there was no dread that the Levellers might come again, there was, it is true, plenty of anxiety lest the civil wars might come again. The fear was most often voiced during the exclusion crisis of 1679–81, but it would sometimes be audible well beyond it, even in the later eighteenth and earlier nineteenth centuries. Yet that anxiety was focused not on social levelling but on constitutional conflict and religious Dissent. Under Charles II, indeed through the eighteenth century and beyond it, it was in relation to the struggles over monarchical absolutism and ecclesiastical conformity that the civil wars offered a mirror to the present and commanded its attention. When the Levellers were mentioned it was normally in connection with those issues. They were regarded as fringe manifestations of the two evil tendencies with which the civil wars were normally associated and which royalist and Tory historians held to have infected much, perhaps all, of the Roundhead cause: 'fanaticism' or 'enthusiasm'; and 'republicanism', a term hurled not merely at the handful of men who had wanted an end to monarchy but at the much larger number who had welcomed the execution of the king. That picture of the Levellers was based, not on evidence – though evidence could have been found for it – but on stock images of mid-seventeenth-century radicalism. Again Clarendon was an influential voice. He shaped subsequent thinking in two ways: first by referring to 'Lilburne, Overton, and other anabaptists and fanatics'; secondly by indicating that the Levellers' hostility to rank and property was of a piece with their 'great malice . . . against the king'. The charge of anti-monarchism proved if anything more effective than that of fanaticism. In 1725 Cromwell's biographer Isaac Kimber described the Levellers as the 'chief actors in the King's death', though they had in fact kept clear of the episode. From the Restoration until the end of the nineteenth century the Levellers were almost universally associated with antipathy to kingship. Their social programme – their demand for an end to trading monopolies and tithes and for the rectification of the legal and electoral systems – attracted far less attention, though it had been of more consistent concern to them.

In the Restoration period, when former Levellers remained alive, it was easy for upholders of the new regime to allege that Leveller ideas persisted too. The government, vigilant against conspiracy and ready to scare the public by exaggerating it, knew that its enemies included a number of men who had had connections with the Leveller movement. We might therefore expect pro-government polemicists to have referred frequently to the Levellers' continuing existence. In fact they used the term only rarely, and far less often than they mentioned the persistence of the republicanism and fanaticism of the civil wars. The remains of the Leveller movement were in truth not much of a threat. Claims made by modern historians for the influence of Leveller ideas in the radical Whig pamphlets of Charles II's reign are hard to sustain.

During the conflict of 1688–9 we do find a moment when the demands and language of the *Agreement of the People* were revived, probably by the ex-Leveller John Wildman, who was now to be found among the radical Whigs. In the ensuing century, too, some concerns of the Levellers would resurface. One of them was the abuse of social privilege by the nobility, an evil disliked by Toland and his associates in the late seventeenth century and by a different generation of radicals in the late eighteenth. Another was the need, felt as keenly by eighteenth-century patriots as by the Levellers before them, to make members of parliament responsible to their electors and to curb the legislature's powers over them. In the 1640s the huge expansion of the functions, powers and patronage of parliament to meet the demands of civil war had provoked its own hostility. Lilburne and his allies were as appalled by parliamentary tyranny, and as suspicious of executive power, as eighteenth-century patriots would be; and in eighteenth-century memory the Levellers occasionally acquired a patriot face. In 1734 the establishment Whig Lord John Hervey's pamphlet *Ancient and Modern Liberty Compared*, deriding modern patriots, observed that the Levellers had anticipated some of their demands. Mischievously Hervey claimed that the country-party journal *The Craftsman* was basing its programme on the 'Levelling texts' of the 1640s. In October 1739 the patriot publication *Common Sense* published an extract from Richard Overton's tract of 1646, *A Remonstrance of Many Thousand Citizens*, attacking the abuse by the corrupt Long Parliament of the power vested in it by the electorate. But *Common Sense* did not present the tract as a Leveller document, and did not mention the egalitarian strain in Overton's thinking.

There are few other eighteenth-century sightings of Leveller documents. When reformers turned to the seventeenth century for support for their positions, it was not the Levellers whose views they normally noticed and repeated but two writers in the Darby–Toland canon: James Harrington (on the subject of noble privilege) and Algernon Sidney (on parliamentary accountability). Harrington was hostile to Leveller thinking, and Sidney's writings do not mention it. Since their lifetimes, in any case, the current of reforming thinking had in one important respect flown in a direction opposite to that of Leveller idealism. If Toland and his allies were hostile to aristocratic oppression, it was a very different aspect of their social teaching that struck chords among their contemporaries and eighteenth-century successors. Where the Levellers – or at least many of them – had seen the extension of the franchise as a means to expand the social basis of politics, reformers after 1688, fearing that only men of economic substance would resist corruption by the executive, argued for a restriction of the social basis of the electorate and of the membership of the Commons. It was apparently John Wildman himself who in 1689 urged the narrowing of the franchise from the existing qualification, the ownership of land yielding produce worth forty shillings a year, to one of forty pounds. The Levellers had hit at 'rich' men, but Toland and other reformers of the 1690s urged the election of 'rich' MPs.

Over the first eight decades or so of the eighteenth century the Levellers almost vanished from public discussion. They appeared, of course, however briefly, in histories of the civil wars, but were rarely mentioned elsewhere. So remote were they from the centre of political consciousness that, outside the history books, the terms 'leveller' and 'levelling', though they remained as pejorative labels, only occasionally brought the Levellers of the 1640s to mind. A pamphlet of 1703 called *The Levellers* was about a proposal to abolish marriage settlements and arranged marriages. The mid-seventeenth-century Levellers are nowhere near its author's thinking. 'Leveller' and 'levelling' normally referred to a principle or proclivity, far less often to particular historical people or circumstances. They described an impulse towards parity, whether constitutional or social or economic or some indeterminate mixture of the three. Or 'Leveller' described a person – as Jeremy Collier had put it in 1689 in a passage quoted in the entry on the word in Dr Johnson's *Dictionary* – who 'won't allow any encouragement to extraordinary industry and merit'. It was in that last vein that the republican Catharine Macaulay (who herself sought to rescue Lilburne and his allies from the slurs of other historians) complained of 'that general spirit of levelling which pervades modern society'. She judged it 'a new circumstance among us' and blamed it for Sir John Dalrymple's attack on her hero Algernon Sidney. She was in turn associated by Dr Johnson, on the famous occasion when he mocked her social views by proposing that her footman be invited to dine with them, with 'the levelling doctrine', with the wish to 'level down'. For radicals other than Macaulay, too, 'leveller' and 'levelling' were pejorative terms. John Wilkes condemned 'levelling principles'. John Thelwall equated 'levelling' with 'plunder'. The elasticity of the vocabulary of levelling is demonstrated by its application both to Edmund Burke ('the first complete leveller I ever met with', taunted Thelwall) and to Burke's antagonist Tom Paine (who heard his *The Rights of Man* called 'a levelling system').

So remote had the memory of the mid-seventeenth-century Levellers become that historians found it hard to know how to introduce them to readers who, they recognized, could not be presumed to have heard of them, and whose credulity might be strained by descriptions of so outlandish a phenomenon. Rapin, the leading Whig historian of the early eighteenth century, set a pattern by finding it 'incumbent on me to explain' that there had been a party in the army 'called Levellers'. In 1763 the index to the *Parliamentary or Constitutional History* carried an entry: 'Levellers, who meant by them'.

John Lilburne, it is true, was known about (far more so than any of the other Levellers, to whom the history books gave at most walk-on parts). Yet it was not as a Leveller leader or an exponent of Leveller ideas that he was famed. He owed his celebrity rather to the legal issues raised by his trials of 1649 and 1653, to his spirited and colourful performances at them, and to the popular clamour they aroused. Like Algernon Sidney he had been a victim of an unjust treason law. The text of Lilburne's trial of 1649, which had been printed in that year, was reprinted in William Winstanley's *England's Worthies* in 1660 (where Lilburne made his surprising appearance 'not as a Worthy, but as a Wonder'). It was printed again in 1710, and again in successive editions of the *State Trials* from 1719. As an enemy of the executive, Lilburne acquired a patriot face, though one only fleetingly glimpsed. In January 1741 James Ralph's patriot paper *The Champion* placed the name 'Lilburne' under an article praising Cato and Marcus Brutus. Interest in Lilburne's afflictions grew in the age of Wilkes, whose sufferings were compared with his as with Sidney's. It was strengthened by late eighteenth- and early nineteenth-century concerns about the rights of trial by jury, a cause in which, again, Sidney's name was also invoked.

Yet even the emergence of parliamentary and popular radicalism in the later eighteenth century brought no wave of interest in the Levellers of the 1640s. Catharine Macaulay, it is true, wrote plaintively on behalf of the group which had been 'in derision called Levellers', and which she placed within an essentially country-party perspective. They had, she judged, been 'honest to the principles of equal and general freedom'. The version of the *Agreement of the People* of January 1649, hammered out by Levellers and army officers, was 'a better model than any which had yet been offered to the public', providing as it did for 'the reformation of all the grievances which the people of England then laboured under and which to this very day they do at equal rate sustain'. Yet hers was an isolated voice. The Society for Constitutional Information, aiming to educate the nation in the principle, which had been dear to the Levellers, that parliament is responsible to the electorate, introduced its readers to a wealth of seventeenth-century writings but did not mention the Levellers, whose pamphlets could have offered eloquent support for the Society's programme. E. P. Thompson, in his *The Making of the English Working Class* (1963), was struck by the resemblances of the radicalism of the 1640s to that of the 1790s, but detected no influence of the first on the second. Christopher Hill, in his classic essay 'The Norman Yoke', first published in 1954, noted the parallels between the Leveller view of the Norman Conquest and the populist perception of it which surfaced in the 1790s. Yet the advocates of the latter sentiment do not seem to have known that the Levellers had anticipated them.

If there was no cult of the Levellers in the late eighteenth century, the words 'leveller' and 'levelling' probably had a wider circulation at that time, and as fierce a pejorative slant, as in any period of English history since the civil wars. Advocates of the rights of man, it was generally alleged, intended to 'level' monarch and subject, rich and poor, the propertied and unpropertied. Yet even now the memory of the mid-seventeenth-century Levellers, to whom so many historians had attributed the same ambition, did not surface in political discussion. In 1792 John Reeve set up the Association for Preserving Liberty and Property against Republicans and Levellers. Its extensive publications, which include a narrative of Puritan rule, contain only one reference to the Levellers of the 1640s (a passing one, in a quotation).

In the early nineteenth century the growth of populist radicalism did produce some voices sympathetic to the Levellers. Lilburne came to be thought of as 'the Cobbett of the seventeenth century'. In 1828 J. T. Rutt surmised that the men 'so unjustly described Levellers' had 'probably been misrepresented and unjustly censured' and were 'probably the only consistent republicans of their time'. Yet, as Rutt's words indicate, while the term 'republican', for so long one solely of contumely, could now be one of approbation, 'Leveller' remained beyond the pale. In 1846, when the word was directed at the Chartists, a Chartist newspaper repudiated it. Chartists and Victorian republicans seem to have been little interested in the Levellers. Instead we find in their writings two different traditions of seventeenth-century enthusiasm. The first, now at the end of its life, revered Algernon Sidney and the incorruptible Whig patriots. The second tradition, mounting in volume and confidence, applauded Oliver Cromwell. In 1850, admittedly, the republican Joseph Barker regretted Cromwell's suppression of the Levellers at Burford. Yet Barker concluded that Cromwell had only been doing his duty. Here he was following Carlyle, whose narrative shed a passing tear for the Levellers but endorsed Oliver's suppression of them. Cromwell's Victorian admirers generally held the Levellers to have got in his way. In 1846 Edmund Clarke informed the Manchester Mechanics Institute that Cromwell had been a 'dauntless and inflexible opposer of oppression and arrogance . . . under any name, whether it were of king or priest, peer or commoner, respectable presbyterian burgher or enthusiastic military leveller'.

For Clarke, Cromwell's main feat was to have defeated the aristocracy. By the 1880s socialist thinking had identified the bourgeoisie, rather than the aristocracy, as the people's principal enemy. Cromwell's populist credentials were reassessed accordingly and found wanting. He became the people's bourgeois antagonist, a man devoid of 'sympathy with democracy and freedom', against whom, as Joseph Conrad's colourful socialist friend Cunningham Grahame wrote in *The People's Paper* in 1890, 'honest John Lilburne' had led 'the poor' in revolt. In the later 1890s the Levellers' standing rose as a result of the accounts of them in Henry Hyndman's *The Historical Basis of English Socialism* and John Morrison Davidson's book, aimed at a popular readership, *Annals of Toil*. Those and other socialists of the late nineteenth century derided men who 'take as their hero the bourgeois and narrow-minded Cromwell', that political instrument of the 'powerful, profiteering class'. Cromwell, whom Carlyle had commended as a 'solid farmer', was now deemed to have been a 'capitalist farmer'. Nonconformist commemorators of 1899 reasserted the claim that Cromwell had defended 'the rights of the people', but they could not carry many socialists with them. Socialist hostility to Cromwell was hostility to Nonconformity too. The 'pious, prayerful Cromwell', socialists alleged, had represented at once 'the chapel' and 'the till', those twin bases of Nonconformist power and sanctimony. He had stood for 'the Nonconformist conscience', for 'highly respectable' and 'hypocritically ascetic Puritans'. He had pulled down maypoles, an initiative offensive to socialists critical of the 'municipal Puritanism' that was suppressing popular pleasures in their own time. He had introduced the wretched 'British Sunday', an institution which, in their speeches and articles during the tercentenary celebrations, Nonconformists defended from its decadent assailants.

Morrison Davidson, who promoted the Levellers, also saluted the Diggers, on whom he produced a pamphlet in 1904. Barely mentioned by history for two and a half centuries, the Diggers were seemingly now everywhere. The international socialist Eduard Bernstein published pioneering studies of them in 1895 and 1908. G. P. Gooch wrote about them in 1898 (calling them 'the communists'). The socialist L. A. Berens's book *Gerrard Winstanley and the Diggers* appeared in 1906. Amid those works, as in later writings on the Levellers and Diggers, we glimpse the varieties of English socialist thought, especially the divide between the native, sentimental tradition and the imported, theoretical one. Davidson, resolutely empirical in his discussion, was averse to the Continental dogmas of Marxism. He seems to have been unaware of Bernstein's work. Yet it was to Bernstein, as Gooch acknowledged, that 'the honour of discovering Winstanley belongs'. Though Bernstein worked in England he seems to have had no contact with the British scholarly community until the publication of his book of 1908. Then he received a heartening letter from C. H. Firth, that ubiquitous encourager of research into the civil wars, who sought to have an English translation of the book made. By that time, however, the flurry of interest in the Diggers had evidently subsided. Only in 1930 would Bernstein's study become available in English. Even then it had to be given a misleading title, *Cromwell and Communism*, to catch a readership. In 1940 D. W. Petegorsky's *Left-Wing Democracy in the English Civil Wars* did give extensive coverage to Winstanley.

None the less the Diggers never quite found the place in twentieth-century affections that was given to Lilburne and his allies.

Firth did as much as anyone to make the modern study of the Levellers possible. Yet he was no unstinting admirer of them. Like S. R. Gardiner he thought the Levellers – let alone the Diggers – unrealistic. His interest in them faded once he had edited the Putney debates. Gardiner saw the conflict over the franchise at Putney, which the twentieth century would take to its heart, as a 'side issue'. Neither he nor Firth was much interested in the development or composition of the Leveller party. A reader whose knowledge of the 1640s was confined to Gardiner's *History of the Great Civil Wars* would not know of the existence of Lilburne's leading associate Richard Overton.

For the modern picture of the Levellers to emerge, another stage of historical investigation was necessary. Only when historians took the Levellers as a subject by itself, and were willing to trace Leveller ideas systematically through the pamphlet material, would the Levellers be credited with a continuous or evolving programme. That breakthrough was achieved in two publications, both of which seem to have reached a wide audience. The first was G. P. Gooch's *History of English Democratic Ideas in the Seventeenth Century*, published in 1898, where a chapter is devoted to the political opinions of the army. Gooch was no socialist. He regarded the Levellers' commitment to natural rights as essentially anarchic, and he regretted that they had failed to see the need for a political aristocracy. The second, more ambitious approach was T. C. Pease's *The Leveller Movement*, published in 1916. Though he declared a 'prepossession in favour of the Levellers', Pease was no socialist either. Writing in America, he found liberal rather than socialist virtues in Leveller teaching. He made no mention of the Diggers except in his Bibliography, which described Bernstein as 'an avowed socialist' who 'distorts his account of the Leveller movement to make it serve as a mere prelude to communism'. To Pease the significance of the Levellers was that they sought 'the establishment in England of democratic government limited and bounded by law'. They were the party of constitutional and legal rights.

Pease saw that guiding principle as a virtue. To the Marxist historian

D. W. Petegorsky a quarter of a century later, the Levellers' preoccupation with 'constitutional mechanisms' was their limitation. Around 1900 socialist historians had tended to regard the Levellers as their ancestors. By the late 1930s they were viewing them with warier eyes. From then until around the 1960s there is a tension in left-wing approaches to the Levellers, emotional approval contending with intellectual disappointment. What the Levellers lacked, Petegorsky judged in 1940, was realistic social and historical analysis. 'Law, they failed to recognize, is but the reflection and crystallization of the social relationships it is intended to regulate, a result rather than a cause.' It was the achievement but also the shortcoming of the Levellers, he maintained, that they pointed ahead to 'radical liberalism' and 'liberal democracy'. Petegorsky's study, a Left Book Club choice, appeared in the same year as the long pamphlet by Christopher Hill, *The English Revolution 1640*, that would soon be reprinted in the Marxist Textbook series. In Hill's analysis, to which Petegorsky's is close, the Levellers represented 'the petty bourgeosie', a class doomed to division and impotence, being squeezed as it was between 'the big bourgeoisie' on the one hand and the landless proletariat on the other. Hill noted the absence of any 'organized working-class movement' to lead 'a frontal attack on the power of big capital'.

Alongside the Marxist and socialist interpretations of the Levellers that caught headlines of twentieth-century writing on the civil wars, there ran, less conspicuously, the liberal tradition favoured by Pease. It has been stronger in the United States than in Britain. Its origins are British none the less. It can be said to begin with Gardiner's distinction, on which others would soon build, between the 'political' Levellers – Lilburne and his friends – whose aim was liberty and democracy, and the 'social' ones, the Diggers, who wanted equality and socialism. Since the Restoration, historians had generally been content to regard the political and the social levelling of the civil wars as inseparable urges of destruction. Now the two were prised apart. Whatever Lilburne's failings, Gardiner reflected, at least he had not been a socialist. In Gardiner's mind the distinction between political and social levelling worked to the Levellers' advantage and the Diggers' disadvantage. In time Marxist history, catching up with the distinction, would use it to reverse that preference.

In the liberal tradition, particularly in the United States, two features of the Leveller programme proved especially influential. The first was the principle, which was announced in the *Agreement of the People* and which subsequently reappeared in the American Constitution, that the people have rights which they must keep to themselves and out of the hands of their representatives. The second was the demand for the abolition of monopolies, an evil which the Levellers saw as an instrument of social oppression but which in modern America has seemed a block on free enterprise. To Petegorsky, by contrast, the Levellers' complaints about monopolies revealed the limits of their social sympathies, for monopolies were 'irrelevant to the situation' of the 'propertyless classes'. In 1962 another Canadian, the Marxist C. B. Macpherson, in a study hailed by Hill as seminal, interpreted the 'individualism' of the Levellers as evidence of a bourgeois mentality, which placed them in the company of that classic exponent of the identification of liberty with property, John Locke.

The distance between the socialist and liberal traditions of interpretation need not be exaggerated. On both sides there was a recognition that the 'individualism' of the Levellers was combined with a sense of communal responsibility. None the less Leveller individualism was discussed more indulgently by writers of liberal than of socialist outlook. In 1944 liberal sentiments on the Levellers' behalf were voiced in two collections of Leveller tracts, published in the United States, which made a sizeable body of Leveller literature available for the first time since the civil wars. William Haller, introducing one of them, judged that Lilburne had looked to 'free enterprise' as the means 'to satisfy every need that nature plants in the human breast'. The other, edited by D. M. Wolfe, was introduced by Charles Beard, the eminent historian of America, who claimed that the Levellers' manifestos, anticipating as they did much that would be said by Locke and Jefferson, 'deserve a permanent place as a fundamental exhibit in the history of constitutional government and liberty in England, the United States, indeed the whole English-speaking world'. In 1955 another American study of the Levellers, by Joseph Frank, written under the shadow of McCarthyism, described the establishment of constitutional and individual rights as their 'central purpose'. 'The battle for an *Agreement of the People*,' Frank noted, 'is still being waged.' In the contention between the liberal and socialist interpretations of the Levellers we see, in microcosm, the enduring twentieth-century debate about the relationship between liberty and equality. It is fitting that the 350th anniversary of the Putney debates in 1997 was commemorated by conferences held in two places: in Putney church, with speeches by Christopher Hill and Tony Benn, representatives of the socialist tradition; and at the Folger Library in Washington, the 'capital of the free world'.

A century or so ago the rise of socialism allied with historical scholarship, not always harmoniously, to elevate the Levellers. In recent decades historical scholarship and the decline of socialism have combined, with less sense of strain, to reassess them. The approval given to the Levellers for anticipating socialism, and the reproaches cast on them for not anticipating it more fully, have begun to look as debilitatingly anachronistic as the eighteenth century's habit of singling out patriot attitudes in Sidney and the nineteenth's of weighing Cromwell's liberalism. In each case commentators, in selecting their material, extracted it from a complex structure, remote from their own experience, of thought and feeling and language.

In relation to the Levellers the Marxist vocabulary of class conflict, especially the term 'bourgeois', lost its public hold at the very time when historians were demonstrating its inapplicability to the social and economic conditions of seventeenth-century England. The realization that some leading Levellers came from gentle backgrounds, albeit modest ones, made it harder to think of the movement's conflicts with parliament as a class struggle. There are clear enough indications of the close sympathy of 'Levelling Ludlow', that MP from an eminent gentle family, with the army agitators and of his cooperation with the Leveller leaders against Cromwell. When MPs sympathetic to the Levellers did quarrel with them, it may have been at least as much because those members sat in and respected the parliament which Leveller pamphlets abused as because of any divergence of social origin or attitude. The term 'Leveller', which as a smear appealed so readily and misleadingly to seventeenth-century antipathies, misled the twentieth century by appealing so readily to its sympathies.

The preoccupation of historians with the debate over the franchise at Putney is another victory of twentieth-century priorities over seventeenth-century ones. The franchise was very low on the Levellers' agenda. They cared much more about another aspect of parliamentary reform, the radical redistribution of parliamentary constituencies, a principle on which they and the army officers were heartily agreed and which would be endorsed by the Commonwealth and implemented by Cromwell. Gardiner was right to describe the debate on the franchise at Putney as a 'side-issue'. The Levellers did not include it among the subjects they asked to have discussed there. It was raised by Cromwell's son-in-law Henry Ireton, in an attempt, which caught the soldiers' representatives off their guard, to expose the irresponsibility of their intentions. At the time of Putney the Levellers were more immediately concerned with a political issue: the fate of the king and of the monarchy. Their statements on that subject, then as at other times, were inconsistent and sometimes evasive. Yet when Cromwell and Ireton moved against Charles I in late 1648 and early 1649 they were finally accepting the position which the Levellers had urged on them in the autumn of 1647 – even though, from mistrust of the army officers' intentions, Lilburne and his allies had now retreated from it. Twentieth-century historians of the Levellers, predominantly more interested in social issues than in constitutional ones, scarcely noticed the Leveller contribution to the rise of anti-monarchical feeling. If we ask, not how far the Levellers anticipated the values of modern times, but what impact they made on events, then those earlier historians who dwelt on the Levellers' hostility to the king were closer to the mark than many of their modern successors. Whatever the gains of the expansion of historical research over the past century or so may have been, the easy assumption that we know better than our predecessors is not among them.

Epilogue

Sometimes, in their approaches to the seventeenth century, the twentieth-century Marxist and liberal historians who figured in the last chapter look no different from their Whig and Tory and patriot predecessors. That is as true of those of them, the majority, who have worked within universities as of those outside them. For historians do not cease to be citizens of their time when they become professionals. Academic history has its own determining environment, one far from immune to present-centredness. The influence of developments in a wider world on current academic writing about the history of class or race or gender is obvious enough. So is the debt to recent social and political change of the demand for 'history from below' and for the study of the 'marginalized' and 'oppressed'; of the new interest in the past's habits of leisure and consumption and in its private lives; of the decline in the appeal of diplomatic and military and constitutional history; of the faltering of Marxist interpretation. At the same time the self-absorption of the academic world is reflected in the growing preoccupation, in the study of the humanities, with words rather than things. No doubt it is reflected too in the growing interest of historians in historiography.

With respect to seventeenth-century England the principal founder of professional history is Gardiner. His exertions left him little time for anything else. There were full-time historians before him, but most of the influential judgements on the civil wars had been passed by men with other strings to their bow. Clarendon, the greatest contemporary historian of the wars, was one of the leading statesmen of his age. Ludlow's editor John Toland was famous for his writing not on history but on religion. Eighteenth-century historians of the wars had a variety of interests and occupations. There were the poet John Oldmixon, the novelists Oliver Goldsmith and Tobias Smollett, the philosopher David Hume. The four most influential students of the civil wars in the first half of the nineteenth century were the philosopher and novelist William Godwin, the politician Macaulay, the essayist and author of *Sartor Resartus* Thomas Carlyle, the statesman François Guizot. When in 1867 William Stubbs, whose impact on medieval history was akin to Gardiner's on the later period, became Regius Professor at Oxford he announced a new order. He came, he said, 'not as a philosopher, not as a politician, but as a worker at history'.

Behind the English movement of later nineteenth-century scholarship there lay the German one led by Leopold von Ranke, 'the father of modern historical research' as Gardiner called him. It was Ranke who argued for 'scientific' history, for an objectivity that would transcend the perspectives of the present. Marxist history, from a different angle, had the same aspiration. Its English flagship, the journal *Past and Present*, was christened 'a journal of scientific history'. In both cases objectivity proved a chimera. Gardiner strove for it. He saw earlier writing on the civil wars as the mere fodder of party controversy. Whig and Tory history, with their 'partisan rancour' and 'constant avowed or unavowed comparisons of the past with the present', were 'altogether destructive of real historical knowledge'. Scholarship, he insisted, rises above partisanship. Although, as our look at eighteenth-century patriotism has shown, he was by no means the first commentator on the civil wars to wish to stand back from the contest of parties, he innovated in linking that aspiration to a historical method. Yet his hostility to parties, like many of the adjectival judgements, moral and political, that run through his work, now looks transparently of its age.

No less than the historical traditions that it renounced, Gardiner's writing had a present aim. In common with other late Victorians, he hoped for a consensual England with a consensual understanding of its past. Party feeling, he thought, impaired national identity. Properly 'the achievement of nationality is but the stepping-stone to a still wider development of the social feelings of humanity', but 'English national feeling' was 'too often the mother of much narrowness of view'. He wanted a nation that would bring Cavalier and Roundhead virtues

S. R. Gardiner.

together, that would blend chivalry with earnestness, aristocratic idealism and self-sacrifice with middle-class sobriety and energy. Partisanship, to his mind, led not merely to bad history but to bad government. The scientific deployment of the intellect would produce not only better history but better government: government in the interests not of a section of the nation but of the whole. Elsewhere, too, what Gardiner thought of as his scholarly detachment had its inspiration in contemporary developments. As we saw when we compared his approach to Carlyle's, his handling of seventeenth-century Puritanism was coloured by Victorian moral concerns and by the waning of the Victorian religious revival. That background helps to explain Gardiner's and then Firth's acceptance of the authenticity of Ludlow's *Memoirs*, which we might expect their scholarly instincts to have queried.

None the less, and in spite of every criticism about twentieth-century historical writing that might be made, the landscape has changed. Since Ranke and Stubbs and Gardiner, something of their spirit has informed most historical investigation of a serious kind. The change is reflected in an increasingly disciplined approach to sources. If the *Memoirs of Edmund Ludlow* took historians in for most of the twentieth century, it is also true that, since Gardiner, that text has been less often relied on. The deepening immersion of scholars in, and their more exacting uses of, documents written at the time of the civil wars have reduced the authority of such retrospective sources as the *Memoirs*. (The standing of the Tory rival to the *Memoirs*, Clarendon's *History*, has diminished for the same reason.) Ironically Firth's edition of the *Memoirs*, which made them much more accessible and much easier to use, also produced, through his exposure of their factual inaccuracies, a newly critical attitude to the narrative they supply, even if not to its language.

There has been a literary price to pay for the changes which Gardiner began. Victorians, who found his prose 'bare and poverty-stricken', would scarcely have taken to some of its academic successors. Yet there have also been intellectual gains – or at least what will seem gains to anyone working within the determining scholarly environment that Gardiner helped to create. The vigilance of scholars against the misuse of evidence, and their insistence on contextual and chronological complexity, have made the drawing of simple or tendentious lessons from the past subject to ever speedier embarrassment – and have made the efforts of politicians to appropriate it ever more vulnerable. The documentary foundation of Marxist and liberal treatments of the Levellers soon came under critical scrutiny. In response came revision, modification, fresh exploration. Patriot readings of the civil wars in the eighteenth century, and the cult of Cromwell in the nineteenth, had experienced no comparable challenge. The intensity of historical labour has generated a momentum of discovery before which certainties fast dissolve. Historical scholarship did not begin with the late Victorians, but the revolution they accomplished has altered the balance of power between it and society's expectations of the past. It has not killed the kind of controversy explored by this book, but it has muted and refined it.

That is one reason why our survey has dwelt less long on the twentieth century, especially its later part, than on its predecessors. Another is that, in historiography as in everything else, recent times are more resistant to historical perspective than distant ones. There is a third reason too. It lies in a development for which the rise of professional history may bear some responsibility but of which it can hardly be the sole cause. Over the twentieth century the past lost not (or not always) its interest, but much of its authority. We have become, whether in the short term or the long, less backward-looking. Never has public life been less historically conscious or informed. The Victorian controversy over the demand for a statue for Oliver Cromwell lasted half a century. The monument can still, it seems, arouse antagonism. At the time I write the Shadow Home Secretary has recently declared, in language of a kind that might have been heard from Victorian backbenchers but not frontbenchers, that the sight of the Westminster statue of Cromwell 'causes me a quick grinding of the teeth. He was a bigot, a regicide and a deeply oppressive ruler.' Beside that atavistic exclamation, however, we must set the desire of the present Mayor of London to have two statues of Victorian generals removed from Trafalgar Square, not because he objects to their deeds or opinions but, he says, because he has no idea who they are.

What should they know of the present who only the present know? Yet the story traced by this book poses a no less troubling question.

What do they know of the past who are content to project the present's concerns on to it? We may be tempted by what we have seen of the treatment, by successive generations, of Puritans and republicans, of Cromwell and the Levellers, to despair at the mutability of historical understanding, at the fickleness of Clio its muse. So we should, were it not for the past's capacity to answer back: to yield discoveries to which – at least within a liberal and pluralist polity – our preconceptions have to adjust. We should not hope too much from that process, or expect to see the past other than through a glass darkly. Yet if our limitations are inevitable, scholarship can at least make them less narrow. By itself it does not make us thinkers. When it becomes an end in itself it may do the opposite. Yet as anyone who has worked for long in archives knows, immersion in the evidence not only gives unexpected answers to the questions our preconceptions have brought to it. It alters the questions themselves.

It does something else. Through it there lies our surest route into the differentness of the past, into foreign ways, however imperfectly we apprehend them, of thinking and feeling. Carlyle, who discovered in the scholarly labours of the editor of Jocelin of Brakelond those 'chance crevices' through which we can move outside our own era into the soul of another, put the point in half-Romantic, half-mystical terms. We may make it more prosaically by saying that an entry into values peculiar to another time will teach us how ephemeral may be those dominant in our own. Our story has shown how the certainties of one age, in historical interpretation as in other walks of life, become follies to the next. Without scholarship there is no history, only fashion.

Bibliographical Survey

What follows is principally intended as a guide to further reading. It has two other purposes. First it acknowledges the permission of the publishers of a number of essays of mine to reproduce material from them (for the greater part in very different forms). The essays are marked by asterisks (*). Secondly it points the reader towards the sources on which my arguments have been based. The asterisks serve that aim too, for full documentation of a majority of my statements can be found in the same essays. I shall here indicate, where my main text has not already done so and where the specialist reader might otherwise not find them easy to locate, the origins of the remainder. In cases where particular difficulty might arise I give chapter and verse. The indexes may help the reader using this survey.

PROLOGUE

R. C. Richardson, *The Debate on the English Revolution: Revised* (Routledge, 1988) traces the historiography from the seventeenth century onwards (though its main concern is modern writing). Interpretations of the civil wars during the later seventeenth century are analysed by Royce MacGillivray, *Restoration Historians and the English Civil War* (Marynus Nijhoff, The Hague, 1974); see also, on a narrower front, my 'The "Diary" of Bulstrode Whitelocke', *English Historical Review*, 1993. The caricaturing of Roundheads and Cavaliers can be approached through Peter W. Thomas, *Sir John Berkenhead 1617–1689* (Oxford U[niversity] P[ress], 1969); see too John Gillingham, *Cromwell. Portrait of a Soldier* (Weidenfeld & Nicolson, 1976), ch. 2,

Thomas Corns, *Uncloistered Virtue* (Oxford UP, 1992), Introduction, and F. T. R. Edgar, *Sir Ralph Hopton* (Oxford UP, 1968), p. 41. The scale of the civil wars and their effect on the population are studied in Charles Carlton, *Going to the Wars* (Routledge, 1992) and Stephen Porter, *Destruction in the English Civil Wars* (Alan Sutton, 1994). On the statute enjoining the commemoration of 30 January and 29 May see John Spurr, *The Restoration Church of England* (Yale UP, 1991). The persistence of the divisions of the wars is traced by Helen Randall, 'The Rise and Fall of a Mythology: Sermons on Charles I', *Huntington Library Quarterly*, 1946; J. P. Kenyon, *Revolution Principles. The Politics of Party* (Cambridge UP, 1977); George Watson, 'The Augustan Civil War', *Review of English Studies*, 1985; Françoise Deconinck-Brossard, 'Sermons commémorant la mort de Charles Ier', *Confluences*, Université de Paris X Nanterre, 2000; also C. H. Firth, *Cromwell's Army* (Methuen, 1962 edn.), pp. 230–31. The reputation of 1688 over the succeeding century is outlined in H. T. Dickinson, 'The Eighteenth-Century Debate on the "Glorious Revolution"', *History*, 1976. On Victorian paintings of subjects from the civil wars see Roy Strong, *And When Did You Last See Your Father?* (Thames & Hudson, 1978).

The Whig historical tradition is discussed in Hugh Trevor-Roper's Introduction to the Penguin English Library edition of Lord Macaulay's *The History of England* (1979); Trevor-Roper's 'Our First Whig Historian: Paul de Rapin-Thoyras', in his collection of essays *From Counter-Reformation to Glorious Revolution* (Secker & Warburg, 1992); John Burrow, *A Liberal Descent. Victorian Historians and the English Past* (Cambridge UP, 1992); J. G. A. Pocock, 'The Varieties of Whiggism from Exclusion to Reform', in Pocock's *Virtue, Commerce and History* (Cambridge UP, 1985); and, from a literary perspective, David Womersley (ed.), *Augustan Critical Writing* (Penguin, 1997). A different view of Laurence Echard from the one I have presented can be found in Deborah Stephan, 'Laurence Echard – Whig Historian', *Historical Journal*, 1989.

CHAPTERS 1–4

The best account of Edmund Ludlow's career is C. H. Firth's Introduction to his edition of *The Memoirs of Edmund Ludlow* (2 vols., 1894). The Bodleian manuscript is MS. Eng. hist. c. 487. On the editing of the *Memoirs* see my edition of *Edmund Ludlow, *A Voyce from the Watch Tower 1660–1662* (Royal Historical Society, 1978), and my *'Whig History and Puritan Politics: the *Memoirs of Edmund Ludlow* Revisited', *Historical Research*, 2002; between them the two pieces cover much technical ground, and some points of detail relating to the editing of the *Memoirs*, which I have passed over in this book. The parliamentary career of Sir Henry Ludlow can be traced in: *Journal of the House of Commons; Historical Manuscripts Commission Report* v. 147, 178; W. H. Coates (ed.), *The Journal of Sir Simonds D'Ewes* (Yale UP, 1942); Anthony Fletcher, *The Outbreak of the English Civil War* (Edward Arnold, 1981); Conrad Russell, *The Fall of the British Monarchies* (Oxford UP, 1991); Vernon F. Snow and Anne Steele Young (eds.), *The Private Journals of the Long Parliament* (Yale UP, 1992). The background to Edmund Ludlow's stay in Ireland in 1659 is supplied by Aidan Clarke, *Prelude to Restoration in Ireland* (Cambridge UP, 1999).

For luminous accounts of the interaction of politics and religion in the seventeenth century, as well as of the relationship of English or British and Continental developments, see Hugh Trevor-Roper, *Religion, The Reformation and Social Change* (Macmillan, 1967) and his *Catholics, Anglicans and Puritans* (Secker & Warburg, 1987). The massive recent literature on the civil wars is best approached through John Morrill, *The Nature of the English Revolution* (Longman, 1993). An illustrated introduction to the period can be found in Blair Worden (ed.), *Stuart England* (Phaidon, 1986). Parallels between Ludlow's and Milton's responses to the Restoration are explored in my 'Milton, *Samson Agonistes* and the Restoration', in Gerald MacLean (ed.), *Culture and Society in the Stuart Restoration* (Cambridge UP, 1995).

The apocalyptic streak of Puritan thought is analysed in William Lamont's seminal study *Godly Rule* (Macmillan, 1969). Letters of Ludlow during the civil wars are printed in the appendices to volume 1 of Firth's edition of the *Memoirs*. For Miles Corbet's autobiographical fragment see Sotheby's sale catalogue, 24 July 1978 (cf. Clive Holmes, *The Eastern Association* (Cambridge UP, 1974), p. 9). For Ludlow's speeches in 1659 (pp. 60–61) see J. T. Rutt (ed.), *Diary of Thomas Burton* (4 vols., 1828), and John F. Hughes, 'The Commonwealthmen Divided: Edmund Ludlowe, Sir Henry Vane and the Good Old Cause 1653–1659', *The Seventeenth Century*, 1990. The colours and motto of Ludlow's regiment (p. 61) are described in Ian Gentles, 'The Iconography of Revolution: England 1642–1649', in Gentles, John Morrill and Blair Worden (eds.), *Soldiers, Writers and Statesmen in the English Revolution* (Cambridge UP, 1998). I have discussed the Puritanism of Cromwell and his circle in *'Oliver Cromwell and the Sin of Achan', in Derek Beales and Geoffrey Best (eds.), *History, Society and the Churches* (Cambridge UP, 1985) and 'Providence and Politics in Cromwellian England', *Past and Present*, 1985; and I have sketched problems relating to 'The Question of Secularisation' in the later seventeenth century in Alan Craig Houston and Steven Pincus (eds.), *A Nation Transformed* (Cambridge UP, 2001), on which subject see too Steven Zwicker, 'England, Israel and the Triumph of Roman Virtue', in Richard Popkin (ed.), *Millenarianism and Messianism in English Literature and Thought* (E. J. Brill, 1988). The experiences and conspiracies of radical Nonconformists under the Restoration are described in Richard L. Greaves's trilogy: *Deliver Us From Evil* (Oxford UP, 1986); *Enemies Under His Feet* (Stanford UP, 1990); *Secrets of the Kingdom* (Stanford UP, 1992).

On Milton and the Whigs of the 1690s see Helen Darbishire (ed.), *The Early Lives of Milton* (Constable, 1932); George F. Sensabaugh, *That Grand Whig, Milton* (Stanford UP, 1992); Nicholas von Maltzahn, 'The Whig Milton', in David Armitage, Armand Himy and Quentin Skinner (eds.), *Milton and Republicanism* (Cambridge UP, 1995); also William Kolbrener, '"Commonwealth Fictions" and "Inspiration Fraud": Milton and the *Eikon Basilike* after 1689', *Milton Studies*, 1999. On the editing of Richard Baxter: William Lamont, *Richard Baxter and the Millennium* (Croom Helm, 1979).

An admirable introduction to the politics of William III's reign is Craig Rose, *England in the 1690s* (Blackwell, 1999), while David Ogg's *England in the Reigns of James II and William III* (Oxford UP,

1955) retains its value. For the origins of hostility to placemen see Gerald Aylmer, 'Place Bills and the Separation of Powers: Some Seventeenth-Century Origins of the "Non-Political" Civil Service', *Transactions of the Royal Historical Society*, 1965, and David Underdown, *Pride's Purge* (Oxford UP, 1971), ch. 3. The country sentiment of the 1690s, and the reforming, pious and providentialist instincts of the decade, are described and analysed in D. W. Hayton, 'Moral Reform and Country Politics in the Late Seventeenth Century', *Past and Present*, 1990, and Tony Claydon, *William III and the Godly Revolution* (Cambridge UP, 1996). Pertinent to those themes too are J. A. Downie, *Robert Harley and the Press* (Cambridge UP, 1979); Colin Brooks, 'The Country Persuasion and Political Responsibility in England in the 1690s', *Parliaments, Estates and Representations*, 1984; John Spurr, '"Virtue, Religion and Government": The Anglican Uses of Providence', in Tim Harris *et al.* (eds.), *The Politics of Religion in Restoration England* (Blackwell, 1989); and John Brewer, *The Sinews of Power* (Unwin Hyman, 1989), ch. 5.

For radical Whig thought see Mark Goldie, 'The Roots of True Whiggism', *History of Political Thought*, 1980; Goldie's 'The Revolution of 1689 and the Structure of Political Argument', *Bulletin of Research in the Humanities*, 1983; and Melinda Zook, *Radical Whigs and Conspiratorial Politics in Late Stuart England* (Pennsylvania State UP, 1999). On the standing army controversy: Lois Schwoerer, *'No Standing Armies': The Antiarmy Ideology in Seventeenth-Century England* (Johns Hopkins UP, 1974). For the third Earl of Shaftesbury see Lawrence Klein, *Shaftesbury and the Culture of Politeness* (Cambridge UP, 1994); also Robert Voitle, *The Third Earl of Shaftesbury* (Louisiana UP, 1984). On Sir Richard Cocks: D. W. Hayton (ed.), *The Parliamentary Diary of Sir Richard Cocks* (Oxford UP, 1996); on Henry Neville and Walter Moyle: Caroline Robbins (ed.), *Two English Republican Tracts* (Cambridge UP, 1969).

For the case before the Court of Chancery in 1696 (p. 89) see Public Record Office, C10/245/13. On John Toland see Robert E. Sullivan, *John Toland and the Deist Controversy* (Harvard UP, 1982), and Justin Champion's edition of Toland's *Nazarenus* (Voltaire Foundation, Oxford, 1999). Toland's letter to Shaftesbury in 1705 (p. 117) is in the Public Record Office, PRO 30/24/20 (ii), no. 105.

CHAPTERS 5–7

Our knowledge of Algernon Sidney's career has been transformed by Jonathan Scott's two volumes, *Algernon Sidney and the English Republic* and *Algernon Sidney and the Restoration Crisis, 1677–1683* (Cambridge UP, 1988, 1991). Sidney's *Court Maxims* have been edited by H. W. Blom, Eco Haitsma Mulier and Ronald Janse (Cambridge UP, 1996), and his *Discourses concerning Government* by Thomas G. West (published by The Liberty Fund, Indianapolis, 1990); the life of Sir Henry Vane is printed in Violet Rowe, *Sir Henry Vane the Younger* (Athlone Press, 1970). I have written on Sidney in my *'The Commonwealth Kidney of Algernon Sidney', *Journal of British Studies* (University of Chicago Press), 1985. The radicalism of Algernon's great uncle Philip is explored in my *The Sound of Virtue. Philip Sidney's 'Arcadia' and Elizabethan Politics* (Yale UP, 1996); on the family's thought see too my 'Classical Republicanism and the Puritan Revolution', in Hugh Lloyd-Jones *et al.* (eds.), *History and Imagination* (Duckworth, 1981). 'Algernon Sidney and the Motto of the Commonwealth of Massachusetts' (p. 127) are discussed by Chester N. Greenough in *Proceedings of the Massachusetts Historical Society*, 1917–18. I have placed Sidney (and James Harrington and John Toland and others) within the movement of seventeenth-century republicanism in my four essays in David Wootton (ed.), *Republicanism, Liberty, and Commercial Society* (Stanford UP, 1994). For the intellectual background to the republican movement see J. G. A. Pocock, *The Ancient Constitution and the Feudal Law* (Cambridge UP, 1957); Pocock's *The Machiavellian Moment* (Princeton UP, 1975); and Gordon Schochet, *Patriarchalism in Political Thought* (Blackwell, 1975). *The Political Works of James Harrington* have been edited by Pocock (Cambridge UP, 1977). John Wildman's observation that Rome was not built in a day (p. 140) is reported in William Baron, *The Dutch Way of Toleration* (1703).

Peter Karsten, *Patriot-Heroes in England and America* (University of Wisconsin Press, 1978), which deserves to be better known and to which I am much indebted, is an invaluable guide to the posthumous reputation of Sidney – as well as those of John Hampden and others. Eighteenth-century interpretations of Sidney are assessed, predominantly from an American perspective, by Caroline Robbins, 'Algernon Sidney's *Discourses Concerning Government*: Textbook of Revolution', in Barbara Taft (ed.), *Absolute Liberty. A Selection from the Articles and Papers of Caroline Robbins* (Archon Books, 1982); Alan Craig Houston, *Algernon Sidney and the Republican Heritage in England and America* (Princeton UP, 1991); and Bernard Bailyn, *The Ideological Origins of the American Revolution* (Harvard UP, 1967). My 'Commonwealth Kidney of Algernon Sidney' (above) looks at his posthumous reputation in England, on which see also Zook, *Radical Whigs* (above), and Roger North, *Examen* (1740), p. 410. Caroline Robbins's *The Eighteenth-Century Commonwealthman* (Harvard UP, 1959) remains the standard survey of its subject.

For Thomas Hollis see Francis Blackburne, *Memoirs of Thomas Hollis* (1780); Caroline Robbins, 'The Strenuous Whig, Thomas Hollis of Lincoln's Inn', in Taft, *Absolute Liberty* (above); W. H. Bond, *Thomas Hollis of Lincoln's Inn: A Whig and his Books* (Cambridge UP, 1990). Charles James Fox can be approached through Leslie Mitchell, *Charles James Fox* (Oxford UP, 1992); Catharine Macaulay through Bridget Hill, *The Republican Virago. The Life and Times of Catharine Macaulay* (Oxford UP, 1982); Sylas Neville through Basil Cozens-Hardy (ed.), *The Diary of Sylas Neville 1767–1788* (Oxford UP, 1950); John Wilkes through John Almon (ed.), *The Correspondence of the Late John Wilkes* (5 vols., 1805), especially v. 158ff., and Peter D. G. Thomas, *John Wilkes. A Friend to Liberty* (Oxford UP, 1996).

For Walter Moyle on Sidney and Sparta (p. 148) see *The Whole Works of Walter Moyle* (1727), pp. 56–7. C. H. Firth's remark about Ludlow's and the Earl of Leicester's accounts of the dissolution of the Rump (p. 149) is in his 'The Expulsion of the Long Parliament (continued)', *History*, 1918. *Cato's Letters* have been edited by Ronald Hamowy (2 vols., Liberty Fund, 1995). On Pitt and Cicero (p. 157) see *The Trial of England's Cicero* (1767). F. G. Stephens, *Catalogue of Prints and Drawings in the British Museum* (4 vols., 1870–83), has been my main source for eighteenth-century visual satire. On Ludlow and the motto '*omne solum forti patris*' (p. 161) see *Notes and Queries*, 25 November 1939, and Ovid, *Fasti*, i. 493.

There are some excellent studies of eighteenth-century patriotism and of subjects related to it, though there is much more to discover. Christine Gerrard, *The Patriot Opposition to Walpole* (Oxford UP, 1994), is the most searching study, but other important assessments are Quentin Skinner, 'The Principles and Practice of Opposition: The Case of Bolingbroke', in Neil McKendrick (ed.), *Historical Perspectives* (Cambridge UP, 1974); Marie Peters, 'The "Monitor" on the Constitution, 1755–1765', *English Historical Review*, 1971, and Peters's *Pitt and Popularity* (Oxford UP, 1980); John Brewer, *Party Ideology and Popular Politics at the Accession of George III* (Cambridge UP, 1976), ch. 6; Robert Harris, *A Patriot Press. National Politics and the London Press in the 1740s* (Oxford UP, 1993). Pertinent too are Marie-Sophie Róstvig, *The Happy Man: Studies in the Metamorphoses of a Classical Ideal* (Norwegian UP, 1962); Maurice Goldsmith, 'Faction Detected. Ideological Consequences of Robert Walpole's Decline and Fall', *History*, 1979; Bertram Goldgar, *Walpole and the Wits* (University of Nebraska Press, 1976); Linda Colley, 'Eighteenth-Century English Radicalism before Wilkes', *Transactions of the Royal Historical Society*, 1981; Reed Browning, *Political and Constitutional Ideas of the Court Whigs* (Louisiana State UP, 1982); Shelley Burtt, *Virtue Transformed. Political Argument in England, 1688–1740* (Cambridge UP, 1992); Paul Langford, 'Politics and Manners from Sir Robert Walpole to Sir Robert Peel', *Proceedings of the British Academy*, 1997; Philip Woodfine, *Britannia's Glories. The Walpole Ministry and the 1739 War against Spain* (Boydell & Brewer, 1998).

On the production of the 1747–66 edition of *Biographia Britannica*, and on its successors, see Isabel Rivers, 'Biographical Dictionaries and their Uses from Bayle to Chalmers', in Rivers (ed.), *Books and their Readers in Eighteenth-Century England* (Leicester UP, 2001). There are glimpses of the emergence of *Biographia Britannica* in *The Castrated Letter of Sir Thomas Hanmer in the Sixth Volume of Biographia Britannica* (1763) and in various advertisements for the dictionary in the comprehensively indexed *Gentleman's Magazine*, a work on which my account of eighteenth-century historiography often draws.

For eighteenth-century Whig and patriot admiration for seventeenth-century figures other than Sidney see Elizabeth Story Donno (ed.), *Andrew Marvell. The Critical Heritage* (Routledge & Kegan Paul, 1978); John Dunn, 'The Politics of Locke in England and America in the Eighteenth Century', in J. W. Yolton (ed.), *John Locke: Problems and Perspectives* (Cambridge UP, 1969); Mark Goldie (ed.), *The Reception of Locke's Politics: From the 1690s to the 1830s* (5 vols., Pickering and Chatto, 1999); H. F. Russell Smith, *Harrington and his Oceana* (Archon Books reprint, 1971); Nicholas von Maltzahn, 'Acts of Kind Service. Milton and the Patriot Literature of Empire', in Balachandra Rajan and Elizabeth Sauer (eds.), *Milton and the Imperial Vision* (Duquesne UP, 1999). Glimpses of Robert Blake's reputation, in and after the eighteenth century, are visible in *Lives, English and Foreign* (2 vols., 1704); Dr Johnson's account in *The Gentleman's Magazine*, June 1740; *Oliver Cromwell's Ghost* (n.d. [1750s]: Bodleian Library pamphlets, Firth b. 18); Gerrard, *Patriot Opposition to Walpole* (above); Henry N. Shore, 'Robert Blake, "General at Sea" of the Commonwealth', *Navy League Journal*, 1904. For Sidney and resistance in America (p. 174) see John Sainsbury, *Disaffected Patriots* (McGill–Queen's UP, 1987). For the royalist engravings of 1746 and 1757 (p. 182) see *King Charles I and the Heads of the Noble Lords, and Others, Who Suffered for their Loyalty*, published in those years. William Warburton's remarks on Milton and Toland (pp. 189, 194) are in British Library, Additional MS. 4320, fos. 118–19. The proposed reproduction of Ludlow's 'Letters' and *Memoirs*, and Sidney's *Discourses*, in 1761 (p. 192) is advertised in the reprint in that year (in a single volume) of John Toland's *The Life of John Milton* and *Amyntor*.

Adjustments to the patriot ideal from the late eighteenth century, and the decline of its earlier forms, are assessed in the essays by Linda Colley, Peter Furtardo and Hugh Cunningham in volume I of Ralph Samuel (ed.), *Patriotism. The Making and Unmaking of British National Identity* (3 vols., Routledge, 1989); Colley's *Britons: Forging the Nation, 1787–1837* (Yale UP, 1992); my *'The Revolution of 1688 and the English Republican Tradition', in Jonathan Israel (ed.), *The Anglo-Dutch Moment* (Cambridge UP, 1991); and my 'Commonwealth Kidney of Algernon Sidney' (above). On the use of Sidney's name in 1803 (p. 204) see Frank J. Klingberg and Sigurd B. Hustvedt, *The Warning Drum. The British Home Front Faces Napoleon* (University of California Press, 1944).

For the emergence of popular radicalism see John Dinwiddy, *Radicalism and Reform in Britain, 1780–1850* (Hambledon, 1992). Henry

Yorke can be met in his tract *These Are The Times* (1795), and John Thelwall in Gregory Claeys (ed.), *The Politics of English Jacobinism. Writings of John Thelwall* (Pennsylvania State UP, 1995); for Thelwall's alterations to the text of Walter Moyle's *An Essay upon the . . . Roman Government* (p. 209) see Robbins, *Two English Republican Tracts* (above); for J. T. Rutt see his edition of the *Diary of Thomas Burton* (above). T. B. Macaulay's early views on the civil wars can be approached through his essays on 'Milton' (1825), 'Hallam's History' (1828), and 'John Hampden' (1831), while his essays on 'William Pitt, Earl of Chatham' (1834) and 'The Earl of Chatham' (1844) reveal his attitude to eighteenth-century patriotism. All those essays are in the Everyman edition of *Critical and Historical Essays by Thomas Babington Macaulay* (2 vols., 1907); and see T. B. Macaulay, *A History of England in the Eighteenth Century*, ed. Peter Rowland (Folio Society, 1982).

CHAPTERS 8–11

Some fine work has been done on nineteenth-century attitudes to Cromwell and to the civil wars. Karsten, *Patriot-Heroes* (above), has valuable material on Cromwell, and R. C. Richardson (ed.) *Images of Oliver Cromwell. Essays for and by Roger Howell, Jr.* (Manchester UP, 1993) – which proceeds from the late seventeenth century to the twentieth – is a most useful collection. The rich essay by Ralph Samuel, 'The Discovery of Puritanism, 1820–1900: A Preliminary Sketch', in Jane Garnett and Colin Matthew (eds.), *Revival and Religion* (London, 1993), and Timothy Lang's excellent book *The Victorians and the Stuart Heritage* (Cambridge UP, 1995), are indispensable. I have made extensive use of the 'Nineteenth-Century Cromwell' archive now in the Bodleian Library, MS Eng. c. 6759. The contributions by Clyde Binfield, Brian Harrison, Colin Matthew, K. R. M. Short and Ralph Samuel have been especially helpful. The archive has most to say about attitudes towards Cromwell among the labouring classes and their sympathizers, but it illuminates much else too.

W. C. Abbott, *A Bibliography of Oliver Cromwell* (Harvard UP, 1929) is an invaluable handbook. Maurice Ashley (ed.), *Great Lives*

Observed: Cromwell (Prentice-Hall, 1969) contains a brief anthology of assessments of Cromwell from his time onwards. Perceptions of Cromwell by his contemporaries are ably studied in Laura Lunger Knoppers, *Contrasting Cromwell. Ceremony, Portrait and Print, 1645–1661* (Cambridge UP, 2000). Alan Smith informatively surveys 'The Image of Cromwell in Folklore and Tradition', *Folk-Lore*, 1968, and there is a valuable essay by J. P. D. Dunbabin on 'Oliver Cromwell's Popular Image in Nineteenth-Century England', in J. S. Bromley and E. Kossmann (eds.), *Britain and the Netherlands* (1975). I have written *'The Victorians and Oliver Cromwell', in Stefan Collini, Richard Whatmore and Brian Young (eds.), *History, Religion and Culture. British Intellectual History* (Cambridge UP, 2000). J. C. Davis, *Oliver Cromwell*, in Blackwell's 'Reputations' series (2001), appeared after my book was finished.

For George Crabbe see the edition of his *Complete Poetical Works* edited by Norma Dalrymple Champneys (3 vols., Oxford UP, 1988), ii. 86–7, 703; for Lord Shelburne: Lord Fitzmaurice, *Life of William Shelburne* (2 vols., 1912 edn.); for J. W. Croker: William Thomas, *The Quarrel of Macaulay and Croker* (Oxford UP, 2000); for Benjamin West: Timothy Clayton, *The English Print 1688–1802* (Yale UP, 1997).

Symptoms of nineteenth-century changes in attitudes towards the relationship between Cromwell and Milton will be found in: Benjamin Brook, *The History of Religious Liberty in England* (2 vols., n.d., *c.* 1820), i. 513; George Brodie, *A History of the British Empire* (4 vols., 1822), iv. 322; Daniel Wilson, *Oliver Cromwell and the Protectorate* (1848), pp. 171, 238; *Banbury Advertiser*, 2 April 1857; Milton, *Paradise Lost*, ed. Robert Vaughan (London, 1866), p. liii; John Tulloch, *English Puritanism and its Leaders* (1861), pp. 236–7; Thomas Lathbury, *Oliver Cromwell or the Old and New Dissenters* (London, 1862), pp. 6–7; George Gilfillan, *Modern Christian Heroes* (London, 1869), pp. 76–7; Peter Bayne, *Chief Actors of the Puritan Revolution* (1878), p. 331; George Dawson, *Biographical Lectures* (1886), pp. 73, 87; S. R. Gardiner, *Cromwell's Place in History* (London, 1897), p. 109; F. W. Aveling, *Cromwell and Puritans* (London, 1899), p. 44; C. S. Horne, *A Popular History of the Free Churches* (London, 1903), pp. 128–9, 146; *Notes and Queries*, 13 July

1907; Hilaire Belloc, *Oliver Cromwell* (1927), p. 20; and (on the paintings), John Milton French, *Life Records of John Milton* (5 vols., Rutgers UP, 1949–58), iii. 69–70, iv. 30. I have written 'John Milton and Oliver Cromwell', in Gentles *et al.*, *Soldiers, Writers and Statesmen* (above). On Sir Henry Vane's reputation after 1800 see *Westminster Review*, 1837, pp. 262–3, and Bulwer Lytton, *Richelieu; or, The Conspiracy* (1839), pp. 124–32; Peter Bayne, 'The Younger Vane', *Contemporary Review*, 1873; Bayne's *The Chief Actors of the Puritan Revolution* (1878); James Hosmer, *The Life of the Young Sir Henry Vane* (1888). On his finances: Rowe, *Sir Henry Vane the Younger* (above); also *The Life and Death of Sir Henry Vane, Kt.* (1662), pp. 97–8.

On Victorian Nonconformity and politics see G. I. T. Machin, *Politics and the Churches in Great Britain from 1832 to 1868* (Oxford UP, 1977); Michael Watts, *The Dissenters* (Oxford UP, 1978–); Richard Helmstadter, 'The Nonconformist Conscience', in Peter Marsh (ed.), *The Conscience of the Victorian State* (Harvester, 1979); D. W. Bebbington, *The Nonconformist Conscience. Chapel and Politics, 1870–1914* (Allen & Unwin, 1982). J. R. Green's views on Puritanism are discussed in Julia Stapleton, 'Political Thought and National Identity in Britain, 1850–1950', in Collini, *History, Religion and Culture* (above).

There is a large literature on Carlyle, which might be best approached through the succinct and perceptive introduction to him by Lawrence Le Quesne, *Thomas Carlyle* (Oxford UP, 1982). For biographies see Fred Kaplan, *Thomas Carlyle. A Biography* (Cambridge UP, 1983) and Simon Heffer, *Moral Desperado* (Weidenfeld & Nicolson, 1995). Carlyle's approach to history is studied by John D. Rosenberg, *Carlyle and the Burden of History* (Oxford UP, 1985). There is a monumental edition of Carlyle's letters: Charles R. Sanders and Kenneth J. Fielding (eds.), *The Collected Letters of Thomas and Jane Welsh Carlyle* (Duke UP, 1970–). The composition of the *Letters and Speeches* is explored in C. H. Firth's Introduction to the revised edition by S. C. Lomas (3 vols., 1904) and, in close-up, by Dale Trela's very useful *A History of Carlyle's 'Oliver Cromwell's Letters and Speeches'* (Lewiston, New York, 1992). I have written *'Thomas Carlyle and Oliver Cromwell', *Proceedings of the British Academy*, vol. 105 (1999). For a glimpse of early nineteenth-century Romantic Cromwellianism (p. 278) see M. Sharples, 'The Fawkes-Turner Connection and the Art Collection at Farnley Hall, Otley, 1792–1937', *Northern History*, 1990. For Frederic Harrison see Martha S. Vogeler, *Frederic Harrison. The Vocations of a Positivist* (Oxford UP, 1984). I have assessed Cromwell's approach to religious liberty in 'Toleration and the Cromwellian Protectorate' in *Studies in Church History*, 1984.

The deliberations of the Fine Arts Commission, which was responsible for the historical statuary and decoration of the new Houses of Parliament, can be followed in its reports in the House of Lords Sessional Papers in the House of Lords Record Office; see too Janet McLean, 'Prince Albert and the Fine Arts Commission', in *The Houses of Parliament, History, Art, Architecture* (Merrell, 2000). Newspaper coverage of the statue controversy of the 1840s can be found in the 'Nineteenth-Century Cromwell' archive in the Bodleian Library (above); see too Dawson, *Biographical Lectures* (above). Reactions to the busts of Hampden and Falkland at Westminster are glimpsed in Wilson, *Oliver Cromwell* (above), preface, and Goldwin Smith, *Three English Statesmen* (1867), p. 82; cf. S. R. Gardiner, *History of England from . . . James I to the . . . Civil War* (10 vols., 1883–4, x. 78–9, 127, 146). On Cromwell Road (p. 302n.) see Ben Weinrob and Christopher Hibbert (eds.), *The London Encyclopaedia* (Macmillan, 1983), p. 219. On the demand for a statue between the 1840s and the 1890s: Alessandro Gavazi, *Justice for Oliver Cromwell* (London, 1859); *The Times*, 10 August 1871 (Westminster) and 29 November, 2 and 7 December 1875 (on Manchester); Benedict Read, *Victorian Sculpture* (Yale UP, 1982) (on Manchester); Pamela Horn, 'Nineteenth-Century Farm Workers', *Northamptonshire Past and Present*, 1972 (on Naseby: cf. Andrew Halliday (ed.), *The Savage Club Papers* (1867); Clements Markham, *A Life of the Great Lord Fairfax* (1870), p. 230; S. R. Gardiner, *History of the Great Civil War*, (4 vols., 1898 edn.), i. 218); Roland Quinault, 'Westminster and the Victorian Constitution', *Transactions of the Royal Historical Society*, 1992, pp. 86–7 (Westminster); C. P. Petty, *History of Trinity Church Huntingdon in the Nineteenth Century* (Huntingdon, n.d., *c.* 1958). For the episode of 1871 see Stephen Porter, 'A Political Sculpture? The first appearance of Matthew Noble's "Oliver Cromwell"', *Cromwelliana*, 2001, and the sources cited there.

For representations of Cromwell in and on Nonconformist ecclesiastical buildings: *The Observer*, 28 July 1968 (on Faringdon) ; *Congre-*

gational Year Book 1863, pp. 299–302, and Valentine Cunningham, *Everywhere Spoken Against. Dissent in the Victorian Novel* (Oxford UP, 1975) (on Harrogate); Clyde Binfield, *So Down to Prayers. Studies in English Nonconformity 1780–1920* (Dent, 1977) (on Knutsford); *The Times*, 2 December 1875 (on Rochdale); Samuel, 'Discovery of Puritanism' (above) (on Leeds and Manchester). Photographs of many visual representations of Cromwell were displayed in an exhibition organized by John Goldsmith at the Cromwell Museum in Huntingdon in the early months of 1999.

The 1890s phase of the statue controversy can be studied in: *Hansard* (through its indexes); Lord Rosebery, *Oliver Cromwell. An Eulogy and an Appreciation* (London, n.d., 1899 or 1900); John Morley, *Reminiscences* (2 vols., 1917), and Morley's remarks in *The Critic*, 1900; *Proposed Statue to Oliver Cromwell* (1899: annotated copy in the Bodleian, Godwin Pamph. 2975 (see too Q. D. East, *Last Days of Great Men* (1903)); Robert Rhodes James, *Rosebery* (Weidenfeld & Nicolson, 1963); David Brooks, *The Destruction of Lord Rosebery* (Historians' Press, 1986); F. S. L. Lyons, *The Irish Parliamentary Party 1890–1914* (Faber and Faber, 1951); Paul Nevett, *Marking the Tercentenary* (Cromwell Museum, Huntingdon, 1999). On the government's discussions see Cabinet Papers, Rosebery Papers vols. 96 and 97; British Library, Additional MS. 45,968, fos. 25–31; and (for the Cabinet meeting) Bodleian Library, MS Harcourt dep. 418, fo. 73.

CHAPTER 12 AND EPILOGUE

A good introduction to the Levellers is Gerald Aylmer (ed.), *The Levellers in the English Revolution* (Thames & Hudson, 1975). A recent collection of essays is Michael Mendle (ed.), *The Putney Debates of 1647* (Cambridge UP, 2001). It includes my *'The Levellers in History and Memory, c. 1660–1960'. Keith Thomas, 'The Levellers and the Franchise', in Gerald Aylmer (ed.), *The Interregnum. The Quest for Settlement* (1972) remains the best account of its subject, while Austin Woolrych, *Soldiers and Statesmen* (Oxford UP, 1987) is the authoritative account of the army politics of 1647. Christopher

Hill's essay 'The Norman Yoke' can be found in his *Puritanism and Liberty* (Secker & Warburg, 1958). On the Diggers see Gerrard Winstanley, *The Law of Freedom, and Other Writings*, ed. Christopher Hill (Cambridge UP, 1983) and Andrew Bradstock (ed.), *Winstanley and the Diggers* (Frank Cass, 2000).

There are helpful accounts of Gardiner and Firth in the *Dictionary of National Biography*; for Gardiner see too Nicholas Tyacke, 'An Unnoticed Work of Samuel Rawson Gardiner', *Bulletin of the Institute of Historical Research*, 1974, and J. S. A. Adamson, 'Eminent Victorians: S. R. Gardiner and the Liberal as Hero', *Historical Journal*, 1990. Marxist interpretations of the civil wars are assessed by Alastair MacLachlan, *The Rise and Fall of Revolutionary England* (Macmillan, 1996). A little-known pamphlet is Henry Holorenshaw, *The Levellers and the English Revolution* (Left Book Club, 1939).

General Index

Adams, John, his republican thinking 157, 210
Addison, Joseph, his play *Cato* 155, 184
Agreements of the People (1647–9) 317, 318, 323, 327, 331, 336
Albert, Prince-Consort 296, 302n, 357
Alfred, patriot king 152, 171, 204, 211n, 254, 309
America
  Revolution in 121, 174, 227, 351, 353
  political thought in 210, 335
  English republicans assessed in 32, 121, 350–51
  Levellers assessed in 334, 335, 336
  see also Massachusetts, State of
Amery, Leo, at fall of Chamberlain 244, 313
anabaptists *see* Baptists
Anglicanism *see* Church of England
Anne, Queen, her reign xi, 4, 8, 65, 169, 183
  her ecclesiastical adviser 108
Annual Register (1767) 246
Armenia, massacres in 260
army
  Victorian 261
  see also New Model Army
Arnold, Matthew, on Puritans 256
The Art Journal (1876) 309
Association for Preserving Liberty and Property (1792) 331
Athens *see* Greece
Australian Federal Conference (1891) 244
Ayrton, Acton Smee, Commissioner of Works 308, 311

balance or mixture, constitutional 112–13, 137, 138, 141, 148, 153, 163, 164, 169, 173, 197, 210–11, 273
Baldwin, Anne (Abigail), bookseller 87, 100, 108, 114, 118
Baldwin, Richard, bookseller 86–7, 89, 90, 92, 99, 100, 118
Balfour, A. J., on Cromwell statue 312
Bamford, Samuel, weaver-poet 246
Banbury, an election in 238
Banks, John, biographer of Cromwell 196, 216, 224
Baptists, anabaptists, baptism 45, 47, 251, 252, 327
Barebone, Praisegod 30
  Barebone's Parliament (1653) 30, 56, 78, 275–6, 324
Barillon, Paul, French ambassador 129, 164, 178, 179, 187, 212
Barker, Joseph, republican 332
Barkstead, John, regicide 50, 53–4, 159
Baron, Richard, editor 122, 191–2, 202
Baron, William, polemicist 39, 86, 88–9, 108, 350

Barry, Sir Charles, architect 296
Bastwick, John, Puritan 195
Bate, George, royalist writer 221
Baxter, Richard, Puritan divine 63, 325, 348
Bayle, Pierre, his *Dictionary* anglicized 15, 95, 96
Bayne, Peter, Victorian writer 270n, 289, 291
Beckett, Gilbert, his *Comic History* 244
Beckford, Richard, his patriot journal *The Monitor* 163, 179, 352
  on 17th century 177, 178, 195, 216, 227
  on elder Pitt 170, 173
Bell, Andrew, bookseller 87, 89
Belloc, Hilaire, on Cromwell 238
Benn, Tony, on Levellers 337
Bentham, Jeremy 289
Berens, L. A., on Diggers 333
Berkeley, Sir John, his *Memoirs* 39, 87
Bernstein, Eduard, on Diggers 333, 334
Bethel, Slingsby
  and exclusion crisis 69, 129
  and Ludlow pamphlets 89, 97
  and Ludlow's *Memoirs* 88–92, 99, 101n, 108, 118, 119
  The World's Mistake (1668) 89, 195, 220, 221, 231
  The Providences of God (1691) 89, 90
Bickham, George, on Stowe 170
Bill of Rights (1689), shortcomings of 66, 112, 226, 227
Biographia Britannica (1744–66) 181–97, 222, 225, 234, 240, 242n, 324, 352
Birmingham, Cromwellianism in 304
Bisset, Alfred, republican historian 232–3
Black Prince *see* Edward, Prince of Wales
Blackburne, Francis, and Hollis 174, 177, 351
Blake, Admiral Robert 185, 186, 197, 198, 236, 241, 353
bloodguilt 50–51, 128, 144, 145, 159
Boer War, and Cromwellianism 261, 262
Bolingbroke, Henry St John, 2nd Viscount 165, 166, 211n, 352
  his patriot writings 169
Book of Common Prayer 1, 24, 229, 259
Boswell, James 179
Bradford (Yorks.)
  Cromwellianism in 306
  Bradford Observer (1845) 248, 301
Bradlaugh, Charles, republican 308
Bradshaw, John, regicide 193
British Library, manuscripts in 353, 358
British Museum, and Thomason Tracts 322
British Quarterly Review (1846) 235
Brutus, Lucius Junius 172
Brutus, Marcus, model virtue of 130–31, 154, 156–7, 210, 330
Buckinghamshire Gazette (1845) 301
Buckley, Samuel, scholar-printer 93–4
Bulgaria, atrocities in 238, 260
Bunyan, John 257
Burford (Oxon.), and Levellers 316, 318, 332
Burgh, James, radical writer 204, 225
Burke, Edmund 325, 330–31
Burnet, Gilbert, Whig historian 9, 56
  on Sidney 124, 130, 143, 151, 156
  on Cromwell 196
Bute, John Stuart, 3rd Earl of 173, 174
Byron, Lord, on Sidney 207

Caesar, Julius 155, 222, 233
  slain 154, 210
Caesar, Octavius, no patriot 154, 157, 222
Calamy, Edmund, Puritan divine 183
Caligula, Emperor, Cromwell compared to 218
Callaghan, James 313
Calves Head Club 88

Calvinism
and Ludlow 47, 48, 82, 142, 270
in late 17th century 64
in 19th century 285
and Carlyle 266, 268, 270
Cambridge, Cromwellianism in 306
Camden Society 268
Campbell-Bannerman, Sir Henry, on Cromwell 310
Canning, George, statue of 308
Capel, Arthur Lord, royalist 182, 183
Cardiff, Sidney and 125
Carlile, Richard, radical writer 208–9
Carlyle, Thomas
life and career 266, 280, 281, 340, 356
his mother 280
and Cromwell 11, 14–15, 244, 248, 263–95, 302, 311, 332, 336
on proposed Cromwell statue 304
and Dryasdust 269, 272, 273
and historical philosophy 267–8, 269, 277–8, 280, 344, 356
and parliaments 244, 272–4, 286–7
and patriotism 14–15, 272
and religion 14, 266–77, 280, 283–5, 286–7, 289–90
The French Revolution 266, 279
Latter-Day Pamphlets 272
Of Heroes and Hero-Worship 266, 283
Oliver Cromwell's Letters and Speeches: composition 267, 274, 282–3, 356; editorial procedures 264–6, 267, 269, 274, 278–9, 280, 283; reception and influence 14, 16, 264, 270–71, 278–91, 314; reviews of 278, 279; abridged 284
Past and Present 266, 268, 272, 344
Sartor Resartus 266, 279, 285, 340
anthologized 288
see also heroism, conceptions of; Whigs, Whiggism
Carte, Thomas, Jacobite historian 182
Cartwright, Major John 204
The Case of the Army Truly Stated (1647) 323
Cassius, Marcus, Sidney compared to 131, 152
Catholicism *see* Roman Catholicism
Cato the Censor 155
Cato the Younger, model virtues of 81, 155–7, 169, 170, 173, 180, 192–3, 194, 222, 234, 330
see also Addison, Joseph
Cato's Letters 151–6, 164, 180, 183–4, 196–7, 204, 351
Cavaliers, origin of term 2
Chalgrove, Hampden's death at 176, 299
Chamberlain, Neville, fall of 244, 313
Chancery, Court of 89–91, 258, 349, 358
Charles I
rule and character of 1, 23–8, 98, 136, 173, 184: historical accounts of them 6, 9, 34, 36, 44, 55, 76, 98, 108, 169, 177, 228, 229, 230, 234, 235, 299, 300
trial and execution 1, 11, 12, 28, 30, 33, 51, 52–3, 125, 127, 133, 145–6, 193, 338: commemorated 5, 35, 108, 177, 218, 230, 346; vindicated or praised (1660–1800) 10, 35–6, 56, 65, 83–4, 98, 153, 175, 177, 182, 217; condemnation of (1660–1800) 9, 10, 35, 83, 85, 145, 182, 189, 192, 193, 194, 215, 217, 223, 327; 19th-century views on 215, 228n, 230, 231, 246, 250, 274, 275, 285–6, 298
statue of 310
Charles II 32
his restoration to throne 31–2, 49, 111, 256, 257, 276
restoration commemorated 5, 207, 346
reign of 1, 3, 127, 129, 148, 163, 176, 178, 185, 217, 220–21, 327:

Charles II – *cont.*
its immorality 140, 143, 178, 257, 290; ecclesiastical policy in 3, 48–9, 183, 259
judgements on reign 10; in 1690s 34, 134; by Ludlow 49–52, 124, 272; in Ludlow's *Memoirs* 50, 55, 76, 79–80; by Sidney 124, 127, 128, 129, 140, 143, 148; in 18th century 178, 182; in 19th century 254
statue of 310
see also exclusion crisis; Popish Plot
Chartists 209, 248, 286, 315
and Levellers 321, 332
English Chartist Circular 209
Chatham, Earl of *see* Pitt, William
Chesterfield, Philip Stanhope, 4th Earl of 175, 176, 177
chivalry, ideal of 2, 7, 229, 247, 296, 302, 342
Christie, W. D., on Ludlow's *Memoirs* 41
Church, Corporal, shot 316
Church of England
in Charles I's reign 1, 5, 23, 45, 46, 182, 262
in Interregnum 3, 30, 45, 46, 183, 259
restored 3, 49, 259; *see also* Charles II: reign of, ecclesiastical policy in
high churchmen in 1690s 33–4
Victorian and Edwardian Anglicanism 7, 229, 235, 253, 258, 259; *see also* Puseyism
see also episcopacy
Churchill, Awnsham, Whig bookseller 89–92, 99, 101n, 108, 117, 118
Churchill, Winston, and Cromwell 310n
Cicero, Marcus Tullius
preferred to Bible 61
Sidney compared to 122, 151
on action 156
18th-century views of him 154, 156–7, 222, 351
Cincinnatus, patriot 170
Cinque Ports, elections in 77
civil liberty, civil liberties 7, 45, 55, 57, 60, 62, 63, 143, 251, 271, 272, 291, 293, 294
Civil Service, examinations for 248–9
Clarendon, Edward Hyde, 1st Earl of 25, 202, 299, 302, 339
his *History* 1: published 39; on Cromwell 216, 219, 224, 236; on other Roundheads 23, 25, 198, 234, 235, 236; on Levellers 325–6, 327; on Falkland 302, 304; readership and influence of 21–3, 182, 194, 202, 269, 323, 342
Clarke, Edmund, Manchester lecturer 210, 247, 332
Clarke, William, army secretary 317, 322, 323–4
clergy, views on 45, 116, 251, 262
Cobbett, William 247, 331
Cobden, Richard 247
Cobham, Richard Temple Viscount, patriot 170, 184
Cocks, Sir Richard, country-party MP 84–5, 349
Coleridge, Samuel Taylor
on Cromwell 236
on Sidney 207, 208
on Milton 208, 236
Collier, Jeremy, defines levelling 329
colonialism, colonization 258, 260
Comic History of England see Beckett, Gilbert
Common Sense, patriot journal (1730s) 5, 328
Commonwealth (1649–53)
rule of 1, 9, 28–9, 125–6, 136, 137, 176, 197, 327
single-chamber government 137, 138
reputation and assessments of: in later 17th century 29, 56, 76, 77, 85, 113, 126, 153, 194–5, 211, 221, 222–3, 231; in 18th century 5–6, 153, 182, 190, 192, 194–5,

206, 211, 217, 222, 223, 231, 232, 244, 272; in 19th century 223, 231, 272–4, 291
as anarchy/anarchical legacy of 153, 213, 224, 232, 275, 324
its Council of State 28, 31, 125, 193
its fall *see* parliaments: Long Parliament, dissolution of
restored (1659) 9, 31, 126, 233; falls again 31, 277
see also electoral reform: redistribution of constituencies
commonwealthmen
in 1650s 31, 69, 73, 103, 113, 143, 167, 189, 193, 223, 348
in 1660s 33
in 1680s 33, 69
in 1690s 73, 113
in 18th century 216, 351
Comte, Auguste, positivist 287
Congregationalism, Independency 143&n, 144, 251, 252, 306
Congregational Union 253
The Congregationalist 252
Conrad, Joseph 332
Conservative Party *see* Tories
Conventicle Act (1664) 48
Convention *see under* parliaments
Cook, John, regicide 32, 192
Cooke, Thomas, editor of Marvell 187
Cooper, Thomas, Chartist 209, 286
Cope, C. W., painter 300, 301
Copenhagen, Sidney in 126, 127, 157
Corbet, Miles, regicide 50, 52–3, 348
corruption, political
corruption and incorruptibility in civil wars 75–7, 84, 109–10, 130, 200, 221, 223
Roundhead corruption and incorruptibility: assessed under William III 75–7, 84–5, 109–10, 113, 147–50, 151, 163, 168, 200, 223; assessed in 18th century 147, 157, 164, 178, 180, 185–7, 189, 211n, 221, 222, 223, 232, 248, 328
preoccupation with corruption: under William III 67, 76, 109–10, 113, 162, 163, 202; in 18th century 13–14, 15, 16, 150, 154, 157, 162, 163, 164, 168, 169, 170, 173, 177, 181, 192, 203, 204, 211n, 218, 226
Macaulay on 213
country party, country philosophy 66–70, 71, 75, 80–81, 83, 84, 106, 109, 110, 114–15, 121, 124–5, 142, 148, 149, 150, 152, 154–6, 166, 167, 168, 172, 175, 190, 191, 198, 200, 203, 205, 213, 221, 222, 223, 226, 231, 232, 282, 302, 309, 328, 330, 349
see also independent country gentleman, ideal of; patriotism
courts, monarchical, antipathy to 66, 68, 69, 70, 75–7, 109–10, 111, 112, 115, 147–8, 149, 156, 157, 168, 172, 179, 184, 187, 192, 204, 205, 221, 222, 223, 231, 290
Crabbe, George, poet 217–18, 246, 355
The Craftsman 150, 328
cricket 7
Crimean War 262
Croker, J. W., on Cromwell 234, 355
Cromwell, Oliver
social origins 224, 247, 248–9, 286, 301, 332–3
his mother 280
early life 280, 281
private life 254–6
career 1640–53: 26, 27–9, 62, 75, 78
and Levellers 315, 316, 317, 318, 324, 332, 337
in Ireland (1649–50) 28–9, 62, 224, 274–5, 286, 293, 311–12
in Scotland (1650–51) 29, 224
dissolves Long Parliament (1653) *see* parliaments: Long Parliament, dissolution of

Cromwell, Oliver – *cont.*
Lord Protector (1653–8) 9, 30–31, 185: refuses Crown 30–31, 250; regime praised 215, 216, 217, 220–25, 231–2, 233, 235–8, 241, 248, 250, 251, 252, 256, 258, 259, 259–61, 276–7, 294, 300–301, 309; as usurper and tyrant 15, 31, 51, 55, 56, 58–9, 74, 75, 78, 89, 111, 124, 126, 150, 198, 200–201, 216, 219, 220, 225, 231, 235, 236, 269, 301; *see also* Instrument of Government; Humble Petition and Advice
foreign policy, estimates of 58–9, 89, 192, 195, 220–21, 222, 223, 224–5, 236, 238, 258, 259–61, 276, 287
his religion 15, 60, 62–3, 196, 197, 215–16, 222, 250–60, 267–71, 274–7, 281, 287, 289–90, 292–5, 348
his speeches 273–4, 278, 280
and music and arts 256
death (1658) 254, 256, 279
and Ludlow 15, 31, 51, 56, 58, 62–3, 124, 126, 219, 270
in Ludlow's *Memoirs* 45, 56, 58–9, 62, 62–3, 73, 74, 75, 76, 78, 83, 85, 89, 125, 190–91, 192, 193, 216, 219, 220, 221, 236, 270, 325
biographical accounts of 196, 215, 216, 218, 221, 224, 225, 263, 267, 289, 295, 325, 327
pre-Victorian retrospective attitudes to 6, 15, 21, 192, 214, 215–26, 231–7, 240–46, 247–8, 250–51, 256, 261, 270, 273, 282, 312, 320, 324, 332, 344, 354–5
Victorian attitudes to 14, 15–16, 21, 214, 215, 216, 218, 218–19, 230, 233–315, 320, 324, 332–3, 337, 343, 344, 354–6
20th-century attitudes to 218–19, 237, 263, 292, 294, 313, 314, 316
bicentenary of death (1858) 304
tercentenary of birth (1899) 15, 215, 226, 252–3, 253–4, 258, 261, 284, 304, 314–15, 333, 358
'Cromwell's day' (3 September) 316
Modest Vindication of (1698) 224
Bibliography of 314, 354
Cromwell Association 316
Cromwell Museum 358
Cromwelliana (1810) 225
'Nineteenth-Century Cromwell' project xii, 320, 354, 357
see also liberty of conscience; Ludlow, Edmund; statuary
Cromwell, Richard, Lord Protector (1658–9) 31, 32, 76–7
Cuffe, Henry, Elizabethan conspirator 201
Cyclopaedia of English Literature (1844) 185

Daily News (1900) 258, 261
Dalrymple, Sir John, exposes Sidney 178–80, 207, 213, 329
Danby, Osborne Sir Thomas, 1st Earl of, courts Marvell 187
The Danger of Mercenary Parliaments (1698) 76, 107, 109–10, 114
Darby, John (sr), printer 86–9, 94, 99–100, 104, 105, 106, 116, 117, 125, 202, 203, 207, 214, 323, 332
his children 86, 87
d'Aubigné, Merle, on Cromwell 289
Davidson, John Morrison, socialist historian 332, 333
Dawson, George, lecturer 237, 249, 284, 304
A Defence of the Parliament of 1640 (1698) 98
Defoe, Daniel 87
Denmark, 107, 163
Derby, Edward Stanley, 14th Earl of, statue of 308
The Derby 310
A Dialogue between Whig and Tory (1692) 65

Dickens, Charles 258
Child's History of England 244
Dictionary of National Biography 322
Diggers 319, 359
their tracts published 323
memories and assessments of 321, 325, 333–4, 335
Diodati, Charles, friend of Milton 103
Diodati, John, minister 103–4
Dissent, Dissenters *see* Nonconformity
Domitian, Emperor, Cromwell compared to 218
Douglas, John, on Ludlow's *Memoirs* 93
Douglas Jerrold's Shilling Magazine (1845) 301
Drake, Sir Francis, 18th-century admiration for 171, 185
Dryden, John, his *Absalom and Achitophel* 89
Dublin *see* Ireland
Dunbar, battle of (1650) 62, 279, 292–3, 313
Dunton, John, on book trade 93, 94
Dutch *see* United Provinces

Echard, Laurence, Tory historian 5, 189–90, 202, 346
Edgehill, battle of (1642) 26
Edinburgh Review (1808) 207–8
Education Bill (1902) 253
Edward III 152
Edward, Prince of Wales ('Black Prince') 171
Egg, Augustus Leopold, painter 255
electoral reform, calls for and enactment of
accountability of MPs 69–70, 205, 327, 328, 331, 336
franchise 203, 205, 318, 324, 328–9, 334, 337–8, 358
frequency of elections 66, 110, 162, 167
redistribution of constituencies 1653: 76, 85, 111, 113, 221, 222–3, 232, 338
later calls for 111, 203
Great Reform Bill (1832) 244
Eliot, Sir John, MP 231, 272, 291
Elizabeth I, her memory venerated 152, 171, 204, 254
Ely Cathedral, Cromwell in 262
Enlightenment 12, 143, 277, 288
enthusiasm, and fanaticism, judged reprehensible 12, 14, 17, 64, 82, 116–17, 143, 146, 195–7, 201, 206, 215–16, 250, 270, 289, 294, 326–7
episcopacy 46
prelacy 259, 290
Essex, Arthur Capel, Earl of 205
Essex, Robert Devereux, 3rd Earl of 26
Ethelred the Unready 254
Evelyn, John, on Sidney 130
exclusion crisis (1679–81) 4, 35, 69, 89, 128, 135–6, 178, 191, 326

Fairfax, Thomas, Lord General 26, 29, 318
his *Memorials* 39, 63
his posthumous reputation 184, 242n
Fairhaven (Lancs.), Cromwellianism in 306
Falkland, Lucius Cary 2nd Viscount, reputation and honouring of 299, 302–4, 357
Farnley Hall, Otley (Yorks.), Cromwellianism in 356–7
Fielding, Henry 6
Fénelon, François de Salignac, his *Télémache* 93, 94–5
Ferguson, Robert, radical Whig 73
Fifth Monarchy Men 60, 143
Filmer, Robert, patriarchalist 101, 132–3
Fine Arts Commission (from 1841) 296, 299, 301–2, 312, 357
Firth, C. H., historian 16, 261, 321, 333, 351, 359

Firth, C. H – *cont.*
and Ludlow's *Memoirs* 11, 41–2, 149, 294–5, 317, 342, 347
and Cromwell 294–5
and *Clarke Papers* 317, 322
and Levellers 333, 334
five members, attempted arrest of (1642) 24, 25, 243–4, 291, 301
Five Mile Act (1665) 48
Folger Library, Washington 192, 337
Foot, Isaac, on the civil war 7
Forster, John, historian 228, 229, 234, 241, 284, 291
Fortescue, G. K., catalogues Thomason Tracts 322
Fox, Charles James 134, 174, 175, 209, 252, 351
on 17th century 135, 161, 177, 193, 205
Foxe, John, *Acts and Monuments* 48
France 32, 128, 137, 159, 163, 178
England's relations and wars with 32, 67, 77, 159, 162, 174, 178, 204, 207, 208, 211, 221, 227, 228, 229, 233; *see also* Ryswick, Peace of; Seven Years' War
influence of English republicanism in 121, 158, 207
French Revolution 121, 174, 207–8, 227, 277; *see also* Carlyle, *The French Revolution*; Girondins
see also Louis XIV
franchise *see under* electoral reform
Francia, Dr Jose, dictator of Paraguay 272
Frederick, Prince of Wales, patriot prince 152, 173, 184
Free Briton (1732) 165
free enterprise, free trade 258, 336
see also monopolies

Gardiner, S. R., historian 16–17, 18, 233n, 294, 321, 339–42, 359
his publications 322
on Cromwell 254, 256–7, 258, 259–60, 289, 290, 292–3, 295
on Puritanism 254, 257, 270n, 284, 289, 292–3
on Levellers 334, 335
Gaskell, Elizabeth, *North and South* 286
Gentleman's Magazine 5, 183n, 352, 353
George I, reign of 8, 135, 151–2, 173, 226–7
George II, reign of 8, 93, 135, 151–2, 173, 181
George III, reign of 135, 153, 173–55, 179, 206, 211, 223, 298
benefactor 322
George V, anti-Cromwellian move of 310n
Germany 137
Anglo-German ideological and intellectual relations 206–7, 262, 266, 292
see also Thirty Years' War
Gibbon, Edward, on Littlebury 95
Girondins, and Wordsworth 207
Gladstone, W. E. 309–10
on Cromwell 291
Gloucester, relief of 299, 300
Glover, Richard, poet 236
Godwin, William 210, 234, 340
on civil wars 194, 230, 231, 240, 270, 323
on Cromwell 225–6, 231–2, 282
on Puritanism 251, 271
Caleb Williams 302
Godwyn, Francis, Oxford don 95–6
Goethe, Johann 266
Goldsmith, Oliver 340
Gooch, Graham, cricketer 7
Gooch, G. P., on Levellers 333, 334
good old cause 36, 39, 73, 88, 89, 146, 212, 240
Goodwin, Thomas, Puritan divine 257, 307
Gordon, Thomas, his writings 151, 154, 155, 196–7, 201
Gower, David, cricketer 7
Gracchi, and popular rights 206

Grahame, Cunningham, on Levellers 332
Grand Remonstrance (1641) 24, 229, 291
Granger, John, biographical dictionary of 193–4, 235
Gray, Thomas, 'Elegy' by 222, 234
Great Ejection (1662) 259
  bicentenary 259, 306
Great Exhibition (1851) 296, 302n
Great Reform Bill, passage of (1832) 244
Greece, ancient, political lessons of 70, 138, 161, 210
  Athenian constitution 161
  Spartan constitution 140, 148, 161, 351
Green, J. R., *History of the English People* 228, 257, 264, 356
Grey, Charles 2nd Earl of 252
Guizot, François, on English republicans 45, 213, 346
Guthrie, William, historian 194

habeas corpus 206, 212
Hallam, Henry, Whig historian 212, 213, 298, 312, 354
Hampden, John
  and ship money 24, 175–6, 229, 235
  death 176, 299
  and religion 251–2, 272
  reputation of 21, 133, 350: in 18th century 171, 175–6, 177, 180, 183, 187, 206, 207, 211n, 222, 234–5, 238; in 19th century 180, 204, 207, 209, 229, 231, 234–5, 238, 272, 273, 291, 299, 304, 306–7, 354
  linked to Sidney 175–6, 177, 187, 204, 206, 207, 208, 209, 212, 222, 238
  statue of 299, 302, 357
  grandson of 133
  Hampden clubs 231
Hampshire 302, 318
Hampshire Telegraph (1845) 301
Harcourt, Sir William, on Cromwell 310
  Harcourt papers 358
Harleian Miscellany 323
Harley, Robert 68, 70, 170, 349
  and Toland 106, 110, 111, 112
Harney, George, his *The Red Republican* 248
Harold, King 254
Harrington, James, republican writer
  thought of 61, 114, 136–8, 140, 148, 152, 161, 328, 350
  and religion 142, 143, 159, 198
  his works published (1700) 11, 87, 96, 100, 100–101, 106, 107, 111, 115–16, 121, 141 198; republished 202, 350
  his posthumous reputation and influence 11, 114, 148, 152, 164, 177, 198, 207, 211n, 213, 328, 353
Harris, William, biographer of Cromwell 224
Harrison, Frederic 357
  on Cromwell 244, 284, 287, 313
Harrison, Major-General Thomas 126, 244
Harrogate, Cromwellianism in 306, 358
Hayley, William, on Milton 193, 236
Heads of the Proposals (1647) 232
Heath, James, royalist historian 218, 219, 269, 325
Hebden Bridge (Yorks.), a Cromwellian debate in 250
Henrietta Maria, Queen 24
Henry V 152
Henry VIII, and Reformation 46–7, 137
Herbert, Sir Thomas, his *Memoirs* 39
Herodotus, translated 93, 94–5
heroism, conceptions of 13, 14–15, 16, 17, 214, 233, 234, 242n, 254, 259, 269, 282, 290, 291, 350
  Carlyle's 14–15, 271–2, 277, 278, 279, 285, 288, 292
Hertfordshire Record Office 200

Heseltine, Michael, seizes mace 244, 313
Hesilrige, Sir Arthur 168
Hetherington, Henry, his *Poor Man's Journal* 247
Hervey, Lord John, on 17th century 194, 328
High Commission, Court of 9
Hispaniola, military fiasco on 58–9, 79, 260
History Workshop 320
Hitler, Adolf, Cromwell compared to 314
Holland *see* United Provinces
Holles, Denzil Lord
 his *Memoirs* 39, 102–3, 107, 323
 his great-nephew 102
Hollis, Thomas 172, 173, 174, 177, 351
 on Cromwell 223
 and Ludlow 93, 94, 100
 and Milton 188, 237
 and Sidney 100, 122, 146, 160, 174, 177, 181, 188
 on regicide 153, 175
 and iconography 172, 182
Horatian ideal 155, 156
Hornby, Charles, Tory pamphleteer 87
House of Lords 112
 abolished (1649) 1, 28, 30, 137, 319
 role of 2, 148, 173
 papers of 357
Howard of Escrick, Edward Lord 76, 130
Howe, John, Puritan divine 257
Humble Petition and Advice (1657) 30, 232
Hume, David 269, 340
 on Blake 185
 on Cromwell 219, 274
 on Falkland 302
 on Milton 189
 on Sidney 166, 179
 on Levellers 326
 on Puritans 289
Huntingdon, Major Robert 323
Huntingdon, Cromwell's place of upbringing 254, 281, 304, 357, 358
Hutchinson, Lucy
 her *Memoirs* 271, 325
 her husband 271, 325
Hyde *see* Clarendon, 1st Earl of
Hyndman, Henry, socialist historian 320, 332

Icelandic sagas, Carlyle on 278
Imperialism 260, 261, 287
 literature of empire 353
independent country gentleman, ideal of 13, 68, 71, 84, 115, 154, 172
The Independent Whig (1721) 154
Industrial Revolution 209, 233
Inns of Court 26, 53
 Lincoln's Inn 53
 Middle Temple 26
Instrument of Government (1653) 30
Ireland xi, 32, 33
 rebellion in 24, 28, 275
 and civil wars 28, 29, 347
 Cromwellian conquest of 28–9, 62, 126, 224, 274–5, 286, 293, 311
 incorporated 29, 261
 Dublin militia 78–9
 Toland and 97, 99, 107
 and 19th century 274–5, 311–12, 358
Ireton, Henry 338
Italy 70, 127, 137, 140–41, 155, 203

Jacobites 34, 66, 73, 74, 110, 162, 169
 and civil wars 8, 41, 182, 228, 296
 on Cromwell 73, 225, 313
 risings of 65, 134, 167
Jamaica, Cromwellian conquest of 260
James I, reign of 173
James II
 as Duke of York 4, 135, 140, 165

reign of 4, 10, 34, 37–8
fall of 4, 10, 35–6, 65–6, 70, 74, 80, 227, 228n, 230
Jefferson, Thomas 336
Jeffrey, Francis, Whig writer 207–8
Jeffreys, Judge George 36, 66, 86, 122, 129, 130, 141, 145, 205, 299
Jews 89, 95, 258, 294, 313&n
Jocelin of Brakelond, chronicler 268, 344
Jockey Club 310
Johnson, Dr Samuel 5, 169
on Blake 185, 353
on Milton 188, 236
on Sidney 179
on levelling 329
on Long Parliament 244
The Idler 244
Dictionary 329
Jones, John, regicide 54
Jones, William, Nonconformist historian 251

Keats, John, and Sidney 207
Kennett, Bishop White, Whig historian 9, 151
Kimber, Isaac, biographer of Cromwell 224, 327
King Charles I no such Saint . . . (1698) 98
Knutsford (Cheshire), Cromwellianism in 306, 358

Lambert, John, Cromwellian commander 30
Lancaster Gazette (1845) 301
Langford, J. A., on Puritanism 270n
Langport, battle of (1645) 26
Laud, Archbishop William, regime of 7, 23, 45, 46, 49, 195, 253, 317
law
dissatisfaction with legal system 30, 76, 111, 327
Cromwellian reforms 221, 258
law and society 335
Leeds, Cromwellianism in 306, 358
Left Book Club 335, 359
Leicester, Robert Sidney, 2nd (17th-century) Earl of 124, 149, 351
Lenthall, William, Speaker of Commons 243–4, 262
Letters of Junius 221
Levellers 315–38, 344, 358–9
uses of term 318, 319, 325–6, 329–30
and king and kingship 318, 327, 338
and franchise 318, 324, 338
and property 319, 336
social programme of 327, 328
The Levellers (1703) 329
liberalism
and civil wars 16, 17
and Cromwell 17, 262, 291
and Milton 290
and Carlyle 266, 284, 288–9
and Levellers 318–19, 319–20, 335, 336–7, 339, 343
Liberals, Liberal Party 253, 309–12
and civil wars 6, 7, 256, 308, 309
see also Gladstone, W. E.; Rosebery, 5th Earl of
liberty of conscience 45, 46, 240, 252
Cromwell and 217, 251, 258–9, 260, 294, 357
Licensing Act, lapse of (1695) 90
Lilburne, John
career 316–17, 318
trials of 316, 319, 330
and king 318, 338
and parliament 328
and property 319
Legal, Fundamental Liberties 323
historical reputation 324, 325, 327, 329, 330, 331, 334, 335
Lisle, Alice, Whig martyr 299
Lisle, John, regicide 32, 299
Littlebury, Isaac, radical Whig 93–5, 97, 100, 105, 118
Liverpool, Cromwellianism in 304
Liverpool Mercury (1845) 301

Lives, English and Foreign (1704) 185
Livingstone, Ken, Mayor of London, his historical views 343
Livy 48, 172
Lloyd George, David, on Cromwell 262
Locke, John
  and Ludlow's manuscript 41, 44, 107
  and property 336
  and religion 64, 97
  and resistance/conspiracy 135, 182
  18th-century reputation of 135, 164, 171, 182, 204, 352–3
London (and Westminster), 167, 182
  and civil wars 2, 24, 28, 299, 300, 317, 318
  and Restoration politics 89, 129, 157
  Toland in 97, 99
  18th-century youths in 6
  Victorian School Board 235
  a modern mayor 343
  Bartholomew Close 86
  Cheyne Walk (Chelsea) 266
  City Temple (Holborn) 215, 253, 262, 315
  Cromwell Road 302
  Farringdon 306, 357
  Guildhall 157
  Lambeth Palace 41
  Queen's Hall 314
  Tower 205
  Tower Hamlets 308
  Trafalgar Square 343
  Tyburn 218
  Westminster Abbey 218, 296, 299
London Gazette (in William III's reign) 94
London Journal (1720s) 150–51
Louis XIV of France 128, 159
Louis XVI of France 207
Lowery, Robert, radical writer 246
The Loyal Martyrology (1665) 218
Luddites, Levellers compared to 321
Ludlow, Edmund 21–121
  family 23, 202
  his wife (Elizabeth *née* Thomas) 32, 89, 90, 91, 119
  life and career 26–33, 347
  letters by 57, 347–8
  and religion 11–12, 44–64, 77, 81–2, 92, 102, 115–17, 124, 142, 143n, 144, 146, 158–9, 195, 197, 217, 260, 270, 271, 275, 292, 294
  in civil war 26, 61, 82–3, 168, 348
  in parliament 27, 28, 60–61, 69, 103, 189, 202
  and levelling 202, 337
  and regicide 50–51, 83, 189
  and Ireland 29, 31, 32, 33, 275
  during protectorate 31, 57, 60–61, 190–91, 348
  hides in 1660: 32, 347
  flees abroad 32, 46, 101, 316
  view of Restoration 48–9, 51–2, 276
  in Switzerland 32–3, 42, 47, 57, 59, 89, 127, 161, 299, 351
  and executions of regicides 32, 51–4, 83, 127, 146, 190
  visits England in 1689: 33, 143n, 316
  relations with Sidney 125, 127–8
  and Vane 127, 198–200, 238
  on the sword in politics 55–6, 60, 111, 274
  'A Voice from the Watch Tower': manuscript of 42–3, 347; composition of 43–4, 46, 59, 87; prose of 80; sources of 59; concluding note of 89–90, 92, 119, 120
  'Letters' (1691–3 pamphlets) 33–4, 35–6, 56, 71, 83, 86, 89, 97–9, 147, 159, 192, 227, 353
  Memoirs: edited (1690s) 11, 11–12, 39, 41, 42–4, 83–4, 85–121, 339, 347, 351; published 11, 13, 21, 39, 86–7, 102; republished in 18th century 41, 93, 100, 122, 164, 191–2, 202; planned republication (1761) 192, 353; republished 1894: *see* Firth;

translated 158; prefaces to 1st edition 54, 55, 71, 72, 74, 78, 80–81, 83, 99, 102, 103, 115–16, 202; preface to 1751 edition 93, 94, 164, 191–2; prose of 80, 96, 97, 115; opening passage 73, 101, 131; as source 15, 193n, 316, 342; annotated 192; reception of 1st edition 39–41, 64, 71, 78, 84–5, 87, 88, 224; longer-term influence and reputation 11, 14, 15, 16, 21–3, 71, 155–6, 161, 164, 170, 176, 189–95, 201, 216, 219–20, 222–3, 225, 233, 236, 240, 316, 325, 342; decline of status 15, 200, 213, 235–6, 241, 270, 342
see also Cromwell, Oliver; Nonconformity; standing armies, opposition to
Ludlow, Sir Henry, Edmund's father 23, 25–6, 53, 61, 168, 347
Ludlow, Henry, Edmund's nephew 91, 92
Ludlow, Nathaniel, Edmund's brother 91, 92
Lutheranism 47
Luttrell, Narcissus, diarist 94
luxury, evil of 13
Lytham St Annes *see* Fairhaven
Lyttelton, George Lord, patriot writer 156–7, 223
Lytton, Edward Bulwer, dramatic dialogue by 240

McCarthyism 336
Macaulay, Catharine, republican historian 153, 226, 302, 329, 351
and Cromwell 225
and Ludlow 193, 194
and Milton 188
and Sidney 180, 188, 194, 240, 329
and Levellers 330–31
and Long Parliament 194, 231
and 1688 226
Macaulay, Thomas Babington 70, 234, 264, 288, 298, 299, 340, 346
on civil wars 228, 229, 273, 298, 354
on Long Parliament 230–31, 244
on regicide and Commonwealth 230, 231
on Puritanism 251–2, 262, 271, 272, 289–90
on Cromwell 216–17, 225, 233, 248, 256, 276, 282, 291
on Hampden 234–5, 251–2, 272, 299, 354
on Milton 237, 252, 354
Machiavelli, Niccolò
and Sidney 155, 157
and Cromwell 218
Mackintosh, James, Whig writer 210
Magna Carta 210
Maiden Bradley (Wilts.) 23
Major-Generals, regime of 30, 78, 111, 276, 289
Manchester
in civil war 308–9
radicalism in 208, 210, 247, 332
Cromwellianism in 304, 306–8, 308–9, 310, 313, 357, 358
Mann, Charles, Nonconformist historian 251
Mansfield, Lord Chief Justice James 174
Marlborough, John Churchill, 1st Duke of 175, 204
Markham, Clements, biographer of Fairfax 242n
marriage settlements 329
Marston Moor, battle of (1644) 2, 7, 26, 125, 249
Marten, Henry, regicide 26, 61, 143
Marvell, Andrew
and religion 144, 159
posthumous reputation 185–7, 209, 211n, 222, 352
Account of the Growth of Popery 86

Marxist history and historians 17, 18, 320, 320–21, 333, 334–5, 337, 339, 340, 343, 359
Mary I, reign of 59, 254
Mary II xi, 33
Maseres, Francis, Whig writer 227
Massachusetts, State of, its motto 127, 350
Masson, David, on Carlyle 269
Maxe, Leo, his *National Review* 263
Mayer, John, editor 60n
maypoles, pulled down 333
Meadley, G. W., biographer of Sidney 180, 208
Mechanics Institutes 210, 247, 250, 332
Medici family 140–41
Miall, Edward, egalitarian Nonconformist 315
middle ages 137, 138, 139, 210, 211, 213, 277–8
Middlesex Grand Jury (1690s) 99
Milton, John
  at Restoration 37
  and religion 63, 115–16, 142–3, 187–8, 198, 252
  and Cromwell 189, 236–8, 242, 257, 355–6
  and Vane 238
  poems: sonnets 198, 238; *Paradise Lost* 37, 142, 188, 188–9; *Samson Agonistes* 52, 188, 347
  prose 187: anti-prelatical tracts 115, 290; *Areopagitica* 290; defences of regicide and of English people 37, 133, 188, 236; at approach of Restoration 153; *History of Britain* 189
  works and reputation promoted in 1690s 11, 36–7, 63, 87–8, 96, 97, 98, 100, 101, 103–4, 108, 115–17, 121, 348
  18th-century reputation 153, 170, 171, 177, 180, 187–9, 193, 194, 211n, 222, 236, 353
  19th-century reputation 180, 207, 208, 212, 213, 236–8, 242, 257, 290, 354, 355–6
  20th-century reputation 237, 307
  Life Records 356
Molesworth, Robert Viscount 211n
  his *Account of Denmark* 107, 163
The Monitor see Beckford, Richard
Monk, George, and Restoration 111
Monmouth rebellion 33, 133, 175, 299
monopolies 327, 336
Montagu, Charles, Whig statesman 67
morality, preoccupations with 68–9, 82, 84, 179–80, 257, 287–90, 293, 349
  see also Charles II: reign of, its immorality
Morley, John, Victorian statesman-writer
  on Cromwell 232, 256, 261, 263
  and Cromwell statue 311–12, 314, 358
Morning Herald (1845) 301
Moyle, Walter
  on Harrington 152
  on Sidney 135
  on classical republics 148, 209, 351, 354
  on armies 105, 114, 135, 148, 151, 183
  posthumously praised 183
municipal Puritanism 333
Mutual Improvement Societies 250

Napoleon Bonaparte, Cromwell compared to 233, 233–4, 309, 314
Naseby, battle of (1645) 26, 62, 249
  commemorated 255, 304, 357
National Agricultural Labourers' Union 304
National Council of Evangelical Free Churches 253
National Efficiency movement 261–2, 263, 287
National Review see Maxe, Leo

National Unity Recommended (patriot journal, 1742) 176
navy
  in 1650s 29, 77, 113, 185, 194, 197, 198–200, 238, 276
  in 1690s 77
  under George V 310n
Nayler, James, Quaker 195–6
Neal, Daniel, historian of Puritanism 9, 220, 224
Nelson, Horatio Viscount 204, 233
Nero, Emperor, Cromwell compared to 218
Neville, Henry, 17th-century republican
  and religion 61, 143, 144
  his *Plato Redivivus* 11, 100, 121, 144, 349
Neville, Sylas, 18th-century republican 153, 177, 351
Newcastle, John Holles, Duke of 102
Newcastle-on-Tyne, Cromwellianism in 304
New Model Army 346
  as fighting force 26, 28–9, 62
  as political force 27, 28, 30, 31, 78, 273; *see also* Levellers; parliaments: Long Parliament
  mutinies in 27, 316, 318, 324
  religion in 47
  decline and fall 79, 104–5, 200–201
  admired by Burke 325; by Carlyle 274
newspapers, Victorian local 248, 250, 301
A New Test of the Church of England's Loyalty (1702) 4
Newton, Isaac 171
Newton, Thomas, on Milton 236, 237
Nickolls, John, editor 60n
Nineteen Propositions (1642) 109, 232
Noble, Matthew, sculptor 306, 308, 308–9, 357
Nonconformity 3
  heir of Puritanism 14, 116, 217, 251, 252–7, 259, 283–5, 306
  under later Stuarts 48–50, 143, 144–5, 183, 217, 252, 259, 326, 348
  relations with Ludlow 32–3, 48–50, 57, 59, 143n
  under William III 8, 63–4, 97, 116, 117–18, 217 , 252
  in 18th century 217–18, 246, 251
  in 19th 6, 7, 14, 17, 240, 250, 292, 309–10, 314–15, 356, 357–8
  in decline 14, 314–15
  and Cromwell 18, 215, 217, 220, 250–61, 283–7, 290, 304–8, 310, 311, 312, 314, 331–2
  and Whig party 4, 12, 252
  and Carlyle 283–5, 287
  and socialism 315, 333
  see also Congregationalism, Independency; Unitarians
'Norman Yoke' 254, 331, 359
Norse kings, Carlyle on 278
North, Frederick Lord 179
North, Roger, Tory writer 193n, 351
Northern Tribune (1854) 248
Northumberland, Henry Percy, 9th Earl of 124
Nottingham, Charles I at 25, 299, 300

Okey, John, regicide 50
The Old Whig (1737) 177
Oldmixon, John, Whig historian 4–5, 9, 151, 169, 189, 190, 201, 202, 251, 340
order, achieved by Cromwell 233
Orme, William, Nonconformist historian 251
Overton, Richard, Leveller 317, 327, 334
  his *Remonstrance* 328
Ovid 161, 351
Oxford
  in civil war 26
  parliament at (1681) 69, 129
  Oxford Levellers Branch *see* Workers' Educational Association

Oxford University
  Ludlow at 26
  historians at 16, 340
  a Victorian don 235
  University Extension Lecture 250
  Bodleian Library 42, 95, 97, 98, 320, 347, 354, 358
  Balliol College 95
  Christ Church 310
  Mansfield College 306, 307

Paine, Thomas 210, 330
  his *Rights of Man* 226–7
paintings *see* visual representations
Palmerston, Henry Temple, 3rd Viscount, statue of 308
Paraguay, Carlyle and 272
Parker, Joseph, Nonconformist preacher 253
Parliamentary or Constitutional History of England 323, 330
parliaments
  1625–9: 24, 231
  Short Parliament (1640) 24
  Long Parliament (1640–53, 1659–60) 24–7, 31, 191, 337: its opening day extolled 98–9, 230, 291; elections to 25, 27, 125, 202; purged by Col. Pride (1648) 28, 56, 103, 189, 191, 193, 241, 273, 274, 318, 349; dissolution of (1653) 29, 56, 126, 150, 198; (coup assessed by posterity) 78, 85, 220, 231, 243–7, 248, 262–3, 273, 275, 286, 293, 308, 309, 313, 351; the parliament's historical reputation 29, 34, 56, 75, 161, 175, 177, 182, 191, 195, 197, 227, 228, 230–31, 247–8, 272–5, 277, 291, 328; *see also* Commonwealth; five members, attempted arrest of; Grand Remonstrance; Nineteen Propositions
  Barebone's Parliament *see* Barebone, Praisegod
  1654–5: 30
  1656–8: 30, 114; *see also* Humble Petition and Advice
  1659 (Richard Cromwell's) 31, 60–61, 69, 76–7
  Convention (1660) 31–2
  of later Stuarts 37–8, 69, 129
  of William III 33, 66–70, 71, 77, 84, 108, 130
  of George III 179
  see also electoral reform; House of Lords; placemen, place bills; statuary
Past and Present (historical journal) 320, 340
The Patriot (1740) 189
The Patriot (1753) 184
The Patriot (1792) 165, 177, 211&n, 227
patriotism
  18th-century 13, 163, 168–73, 175, 180, 184, 206, 222, 226, 227, 231, 232, 236, 243, 248, 273, 280, 309, 339, 350, 351–3: and Commonwealth 194, 195, 222, 231; and Cromwell 222–3, 232; and Sidney 159–61, 165, 172, 175, 178, 180, 205, 206, 209, 211, 213, 235, 332, 337; and Levellers 328, 330; and Ludlow 54, 158–61, 235; and 17th-century history and figures 175, 183, 184, 187, 191, 194, 197, 211n, 236, 302, 343, 352–3; and *Biographia Britannica* 182–91
  later 18th- and earlier 19th-century 203–4, 205, 206, 207, 209, 211n
  decline and change of ideal 14–15, 203–4, 211, 213, 214, 234, 242n, 243, 247–8, 272, 296–8, 302, 309, 332, 353, 354
  see also Beckford, Richard; *Common Sense*; country party, country philosophy; *National Unity Recommended*; Ralph, James: *The Champion*

Pease, T. C., historian of Levellers 334
Peel, Sir Robert, statue of 308
Penshurst (Kent), Sidney's home 124, 158
People's Paper (1854) 209
People's Paper (1890) 332
Pepys, Samuel, on Cromwell 221
Percy, Dorothy, Sidney's mother 124
Perkins, Corporal, shot 316
Persians, tyranny over 194
Phelips, Sir Robert, MP 23
  niece of 23
Phillips, John, nephew of Milton 97
Piedmont, persecution in 58, 238, 260
Pitt, William (the elder), 1st Earl of Chatham 173, 299, 354
  and Cicero 157, 351
  and patriotism 161, 170–71, 180, 184, 222, 231, 352
  and 17th century 161, 170, 222
placemen, place bills 67, 68, 70, 71, 75, 83, 84, 154, 168, 213, 248, 349
Plague, Great (1665) 52
Plato, Platonism 143
plays and dramatic dialogues 218, 240
  see also Addison, Joseph; Shakespeare, William
Political Penny Magazine (1836) 246
Polybius 48
Pope, Alexander
  and patriotism 169–70, 171, 193n
  on Cromwell 224
  Essay on Man 194, 224
popery *see* Roman Catholicism
Popish Plot (1678) 128, 129
popular/populist radicalism 133, 203–6, 208–11, 212, 216, 226–7, 243, 246–50, 253–4, 285–6, 315, 330–32, 353–4
  see also socialism
Portugal 137
positivism 287, 357
postal service 258
postmodernism 19
Powell, Frederic York, historian 16
Prayer Book *see* Book of Common Prayer
predestination, doctrine of 48, 116, 142
prelacy *see* episcopacy
Preston, John, Puritan divine 53
Price, Thomas, Nonconformist historian 251
Pride's Purge *see* Parliaments: Long Parliament
protectorate *see* Cromwell, Oliver; Cromwell, Richard
providentialism 144, 272, 348
  Ludlow's 45–6, 49, 52, 57–8, 60, 61–2, 81
  in 1690s 63–4, 349
  18th-century views on 196–7
  Carlyle and Cromwell's 268–9, 292–3, 293, 295
Pugin, Augustus Charles 296
Pulteney, Sir William, and patriotism 170, 180
Punch (1845) 301
Puritan Revolution, origin of term 270&n
Puritanism 7, 30, 39–64, 102, 124, 142, 143, 145, 344, 348
  assessments and treatments of in 1690s 12, 44–64, 80, 81–2, 115–16, 117–18, 119–21, 159, 190, 198, 201
  18th-century views on 185, 195–8, 201, 215–16, 223, 238–40, 289
  19th-century views on 14, 16, 215–16, 229, 240, 250–58, 282, 289–90, 292–5, 306, 309, 311
  Carlyle and 14, 16, 267–72, 277, 278, 281, 289–90, 295, 311
  see also Calvinism; Nonconformity; predestination, doctrine of; providentialism
Puseyism, ritualism 253, 292, 313
Putney debates (1647) 317–18, 318, 322, 334, 337–8, 358
  anniversary of 337

Pym, John, his historical reputation 206, 231, 235, 272, 291

Quakers 47, 195
Quarterly Review (1821) 223

Raleigh, Sir Walter, 18th-century admiration for 171, 185
Ralph, James, patriot writer
on Sidney 151, 164, 172, 193
The Champion (patriot journal) 330
History of England 151
The Use and Abuse of Parliaments 67
Ranke, Leopold von 340
Rapin Thoyras, Paul de, Whig historian 9, 56, 151, 330, 346
Rawlinson, Richard, antiquary 41
The Reasoner (1860) 236
Redmond, John, and Cromwell 311
Reeve, John, his association 331
Reformation 23, 46–7
see also Lutheranism; Calvinism
regicides, punishment of (1660–62) 32, 50–51, 51–4, 83–4, 127, 145, 146, 190, 200
Renaissance 107–8
courts of 68, 156, 231
political thought of 70, 71, 158, 201, 203
Carlyle and 277–8
republicanism
before 1688 18, 26, 76, 89, 113, 136–8, 152, 153, 193, 210, 318, 350
Sidney and 14, 124, 135–41, 151, 154, 177, 189, 193–4, 203, 212, 298
under William III 9–10, 13, 17, 18, 76, 94, 152, 183, 350
Toland's 95, 98, 112–13, 139–40, 152–3, 269, 272, 282
and Ludlow 13, 14, 75–6, 112–13, 190, 271
and Cromwell 15, 18, 248, 301
18th century and 9, 13, 14, 17, 18, 76, 151–2, 185, 188, 189, 190, 192–3, 210, 231, 331
19th century and 18, 210, 212, 213, 231, 248, 283, 296–8, 301, 331–2
English republican historiography 9–10, 13, 122, 269–70, 271, 272, 275, 282, 291, 296–8, 332, 344
Tory and royalist historians and 8–9, 326–7
see also United Provinces
resistance, principle of 128, 129, 133–5, 165–6, 174–5, 189, 206, 208, 212, 227, 253
Restoration *see* Charles II
Revolution of 1688 109, 141, 162, 165–6, 190, 346
relationship to civil wars 4, 8, 10, 17–18, 28, 35–6, 226, 227–8, 249, 296–9
assessments of 35–7, 65–9, 73–4, 110, 112, 134, 151, 162–4, 165, 166, 169, 174, 177, 207–8, 208, 211, 212, 213, 226–8
centenary of 215, 226
bicentenary of 228
Revolutions of 1848 229
Richard I, statue of 296
roads, improved 258
Robertson, John, on Cromwell 282–3, 284
Rochester, John Wilmot, 2nd Earl of 147, 149&n
Roman Catholicism 24, 258, 259
anti-popery 8, 24, 34, 47, 97, 253, 258–9, 262–3, 275, 276
Roman history, parallels with and lessons of 13, 61, 70, 71, 81, 84–5, 130–31, 138, 139, 140–41, 150, 154–5, 156, 161, 170, 172, 173, 198, 204, 206, 209–10, 214, 218, 222, 233, 236
see also under individual Romans
Romanticism
and civil wars 6, 240, 356

Carlyle and 266, 278, 292–3, 344
see also Sidney, Algernon: Romantics on
Rosebery, Archibald Primrose, 5th Earl of, and Cromwell 262, 263, 287, 309–12, 313, 314, 358
Rothschild family 313n
Roundhead, origin of term 2
Royal Academy 278n
royalists 73, 74, 219
18th-century views on 182–3, 353
royalist historiography 4–6, 17, 218, 219, 221–2, 229, 249, 269, 324, 326–7
Rump, abusive term 6; for Rump Parliament *see* Commonwealth; parliaments: Long Parliament, dissolution of
Rushworth, John, his *Historical Collections* 323
Russell, Lord John, on 17th century 208–9, 298–9
Russell, William Lord, Whig martyr 86, 141, 174, 175, 181–2, 206, 208, 209, 212, 222, 298–9
his wife Rachel 298–9
Russia 230
Russian Revolution 321, 337
Rutt, J. T., republican 210, 241, 324, 331–2, 348, 354
Rye House Plot (1683) 129, 133, 202
Ryswick, Peace of (1697) 37, 70, 73

St George's Hill (Surrey) 319
St Ives (Hunts./Cambs.) 304–6
Salisbury, Robert, 3rd Marquis of, and Cromwell 312
Sallust 150
Salmon, Nathaniel, Tory writer 165–6
Sancroft, Archbishop William 190
Savage, Richard, on historians 5
Saxons, freedom of 254
Schiller, Friedrich von 266
Scipio Africanus, model Roman 81
Scotland xi, 129, 178
and civil wars 24, 26, 26–7, 28, 229, 267
conquered and incorporated 29, 76, 126, 224, 261
Toland in 97
Enlightenment in 277, 288
Dumfriesshire 266
Edinburgh 97, 158, 212, 292
Glasgow 97
see also Dunbar
Scott, Sir Walter, his *Woodstock* 278
Scrope, Adrian, regicide 54
second civil war (1648) 27–8, 62
Seditious Meetings Act (1795) 206
Selden, John, statue of 299
Self-Denying Ordinance (1645) 247–8
Sellar, W. C., and R. J. Yeatman, *1066 And All That* 229
'sentimental revolution' (18th-century) 240
Seven Years' War 170, 220
Seymour, Sir Edward, Tory MP 69–70
Shaftesbury, Anthony Ashley Cooper, 1st Earl of
and Ludlow 41, 44, 107
and exclusion crisis 135–6
an 18th-century view of him 194
Shaftesbury, Anthony Ashley Cooper, 3rd Earl of 121, 349
and Toland 99, 106–10, 117, 349
Characteristics 109
Inquiry concerning Virtue 107, 108
see also Danger of Mercenary Parliaments
Shakespeare, William 171
his plays alluded to 226, 281
Sharp, John, Archbishop of York 108
Shelburne, Sir William Petty, 1st Marquis of, on Cromwell 223–4, 355
Shelley, Percy Bysshe, and Sidney 207
ship money 24, 175–6, 212, 229, 235
A Short State of our Condition (1693) 66

Sidney, Algernon 122–80
  life and career 13, 102, 124–9, 350, 351
  family 124
  character 13, 122–4, 125, 156, 176, 179–80, 202
  in civil war 125, 159
  and Commonwealth 126, 211
  and Cromwell 15, 124, 125, 126
  and Ludlow 125, 127–8
  and Vane 197, 200, 238
  in exile (1660–77) 127–8, 140–41, 157
  back in England (from 1677) 83, 128–9, 157, 164–5, 185–7
  takes French money 178–80, 187, 212
  trial, death and martyrdom (1683) 66, 86, 122, 125, 129–30, 131, 133, 134, 145, 174, 205, 206, 209, 212, 212–13, 240, 316, 318, 330
  body exhumed 207
  on parliaments and electorate 205, 328
  and religion 115–16, 142–6, 198, 200, 206, 217, 240, 260
  and republicanism 13, 14, 124, 135–41, 151, 154, 161, 189, 203, 211, 212, 213, 298
  and resistance 133–5, 165–6, 174–5, 182, 206, 208, 212
  social values 202–3, 208
  his posthumous reputation 11, 12–14, 15, 16, 36–7, 122–5, 130–31, 133, 134–5, 141–3, 146, 147–81, 185–7, 188, 189, 193, 193–4, 210–11, 213, 222, 238, 329, 350–51; its decline 15, 200, 203, 207–11, 213, 235–6, 238, 298–9, 332
  popular radical admiration for 203–9, 211, 332
  Romantics on 207, 208, 240
  perceptions of him overseas 121, 157, 206–7, 350–51
  as educational pattern 179–80
  his *Court Maxims* 128, 131, 144, 145, 147–8, 164, 200, 201, 350
  his *Discourses*: composed 129, 130, 158; prose of 132, 147, 208; opening passage 101, 131, 157–8; passages seized (1683) 129–30, 131; edited 100–101, 115–16, 119, 131–2, 144; publication 11, 13, 87, 101, 121, 122, 128; republished 94, 100, 122, 181, 188, 192, 204–5, 350; planned republication 192, 353; translated 158; annotated 95, 207; revered 122, 170, 188, 206
  'Letter' of (1697) 147–9, 180, 181, 200
  Sidney Redivivus (1689) 36, 133
  Sidney's Exhortation (1775) 174
  see also Hampden
Sidney, Sir Philip 124, 350
Sidney, Robert *see* Leicester, 1st Earl of
slavery, views on 210, 284
Smiles, Samuel, and self-help 248
Smith, Goldwin, on 17th century 214, 234, 249
Smollett, Tobias 340
social interpretations of civil wars 6–7, 114, 137, 217, 243, 247–50, 253–4, 285–6, 312, 332–7
socialists, on civil wars 17–18, 248, 283, 286, 315, 316, 319–20, 332–7
Society for Constitutional Information, publications of 204, 331
Socinianism 48, 116
  see also Unitarians
Somers, John Lord 37, 67, 121, 213, 252
Sotheby's 42, 348
South Sea Bubble (1720) 153
Southey, Robert, poet, on 17th century 6, 21, 207, 223

Spain 137, 185, 221, 230
Spanish Inquisition 130
Sparta *see* Greece
Spectator (1899) 313
Stafford, William 1st Viscount, alleged plotter 129
Stalin, Joseph, Cromwell compared to 314
Stamp Act crisis (1775–6) 174
Standard (1845) 301
standing armies, opposition to
under later Stuarts 37–8
1697–9: 37–8, 70–71, 77, 114, 168, 349
pamphlet debates 1697–9: 70, 71, 78, 87, 94, 105, 118, 148; *see also* Toland: *The Militia Reformed*
and Ludlow's *Memoirs* 71, 77–80, 82, 84, 85, 104–5, 111, 219, 233, 325
18th-century 85, 154, 161, 168, 204, 223, 227, 233, 325
19th-century 209, 325
decline 233
see also Toland, John
Star Chamber, Court of 9, 235
State Trials 330
statuary
18th-century 170, 171, 187, 222
19th-century 306, 343
and Houses of Parliament 296, 299, 301–2, 303, 304, 308, 310, 311, 312, 357–8
of Cromwell 15, 222, 283, 295, 296–314, 316, 343, 357–8
Stead, W. F., Cromwellian 284
Stephen, Leslie, on Carlyle 295
Stephens, William, radical Whig 65, 108–9, 114, 118, 152
Stoicism 81, 114, 155, 157, 178, 200, 233, 234
Stone, Andrew, Hanoverian politician 93–4
Stowe, Temple of British Worthies at 170, 171, 187, 222
Strafford, Thomas Wentworth, 1st Earl of 24, 184
Stubbs, William, historian 340
Sweden 137
Swift, Jonathan, on Ludlow 193n
Switzerland
religion in 47, 59, 104
Ludlow in 32, 33, 47, 59, 89, 272
Sidney in 127
Bern 32, 47
Geneva 32, 104, 127
Lausanne 32
Vevey 32, 33, 86, 161
see also Tell, William
Sykes, George, biographer of Vane 199

Tacitus 81, 141, 150, 156, 201
Tangye, Sir Richard, Cromwellian entrepreneur 286
Tell, William 59
Tenison, Archbishop Thomas 89
Tennyson, Alfred Lord 207, 228n
Thackeray, William Makepeace, on Carlyle 281
Thelwall, John, radical 204, 205–6, 209, 216, 225, 329–30, 354
his sons 206
Thirty Years' War 23–4
Thomas, Elizabeth *see* Ludlow, Edmund
Thomason Tracts 322, 323
Thompson, Flora, her *Lark Rise* 218
Thompson, George, Chartist 248
Thompson, William, mutineer 316
Thomson, James, patriot poet 152, 169, 178, 197, 222, 309
Thornycroft, Sir Hamo, sculptor 296, 311
Thurloe, John, Secretary of State 236
Tiberius, Emperor, Cromwell compared to 236
The Times, and Cromwell statue 301, 308, 311, 357, 358
tithes, and clerical maintenance 45, 327

Toland, John
life and career 97–100, 107, 349
patrons of 97, 106–10, 116
character 97–8, 106, 107–8, 110, 117
canonical achievement of 118, 125, 166–7, 202, 203, 207, 214, 231, 243, 269–70, 272, 282, 332
on civil wars 226
on Cromwell 111, 243
and Harrington 96, 100, 100–101, 102, 106, 111, 115–16, 141, 152, 198
and Holles 102–3, 107, 323
and Ludlow's *Memoirs* 95–121, 131–2, 155, 189, 190, 191, 192, 194, 219–20, 231, 270, 294, 323, 339
and Ludlow pamphlets 97, 98
and Milton 87, 96, 97, 98, 100, 101, 102, 103–4, 108, 115–17, 188, 194, 198, 353
and Sidney 100–102, 115–16, 131–2, 139–40, 141, 149, 152–3, 155, 194, 198, 231
and Vane 198, 201
political thought of 95, 98, 103, 110–15, 139–40, 140, 141, 149, 152–3, 269
and religion 95, 97–8, 99, 108, 115–18, 142–3, 269, 292, 294, 339
social views 111, 114, 202, 328, 329
and standing armies 104–5, 111, 155, 168, 204
Anglia Libera (1702) 102
Art of Governing by Parties (1701) 106, 148
Christianity not Mysterious (1695–6) 97–8, 99, 116, 117–18
The Militia Reformed (1698) 99–100, 104–5, 107, 114, 155
A Memorial of the State of England (1705) 117
Two Essays 99
and anonymous tracts 98–9, 105, 148; *see also Danger of Mercenary Parliaments*
toleration *see* liberty of conscience
Toleration Act (1689) 252
Tolpuddle martyrs 246
Tooke, Horne, radical 204, 205, 206, 225
Tories
on civil wars 4–5, 8–9, 9, 14, 35, 64, 133–4, 183, 185, 228–9, 249, 269, 312, 324, 326–7, 339, 340
Tory party and its followers: before 1714: 4, 6, 34, 68, 69, 70, 74, 118, 121, 190; 1714–1800: 6, 93, 165–6, 169, 170, 172–3, 174, 175, 176, 179, 194; 19th-century 211, 229, 261, 309, 312
Towers, Joseph, his biographical dictionary 193
treason trials 66, 129–30, 205, 206, 330; *see also*: regicides, punishment of; Sidney, Algernon: trial, death and martyrdom
Treasonable Practices Act (1795) 206
Trenchard, John
under William III 105, 108–9, 118, 183
under George I 151, 154, 155; *see also under Cato's Letters*
and religion 196–7
Trinity, Holy *see* Socinianism; Unitarians
True Levellers *see* Diggers
Tudor rule 133, 249
see also individual monarchs
Turks, and oppression 194, 238, 260
Twisse, William, Puritan divine 307
Tyers, Thomas 175, 238
on Ludlow 93, 164, 192–3
Tyler, Wat, pseudonym 246
Tyrrell, James, his *General History* 103

Unionism 261
Unitarians 240, 258
United Provinces

internal politics 51, 137
England's wars with: 1652–4: 29, 76, 126, 128, 185; 1664–7: 33, 50, 52, 127–8, 129, 220
and English conspirators and radicals 33, 50–51, 86, 89, 107, 127–8, 158, 159
bloodguilt 50–51, 159
republicanism in 33, 113, 127–8, 139, 153, 158
Ludlow's *Memoirs* and Sidney translated in 158
Toland in 97, 98, 107
Toland on 113, 139, 153
Dutch favourites of William III 66
Cato's Letters on 153
Leiden 97
Utrecht 97
Zutphen 124
United States *see* America

Vane, Sir Henry (the younger) 350, 356
naval reformer 77, 197
his finances 200, 356
his religion 77, 146, 198–201, 240
contemporary devotees of 146, 197, 198, 200
historical reputation 197–200, 238–41, 272, 291, 307, 356
Vaughan Robert, Nonconformist historian 251
Venice, its republic admired 137, 140
Victoria, Queen 215, 244, 310
Victoria and Albert Museum 302n
Vincent, Henry, Victorian radical 248
visual representations
pre-19th-century portraits, engravings, medals, cartoons 22, 102, 122, 170, 172, 182, 188, 217, 222, 244, 351
19th-century pictures 2, 229, 238, 250, 262n., 278n; in new Houses of Parliament 296, 298–9, 300, 301–2, 312
Carlyle on portraits 272
see also statuary

Walker, John, on Anglican clergy 183
Walpole, Horace 6, 93, 172, 175
Walpole, Sir Robert, regime of 153–4, 156, 166, 167, 168, 169, 170, 172, 184, 189, 203–4, 220, 244, 252, 352
Walwyn, William, Leveller 317
Warburton, William, on 17th-century 189, 194, 353
Wardour Castle, siege of 26
Warwick, Sir Philip, his *Memoirs* 39
Warwick Castle, manuscripts from 42, 128
Waterhouse, Alfred, architect 306
Watlington (Oxon.), a debate in 250
Wentworth *see* Strafford, 1st Earl of
West, Benjamin, painter 244, 245, 355
West, Gilbert, patriot poet 184
Westminster Abbey *see* London
Westminster Review 216, 233, 240, 282
Whigs, Whiggism
Whig party and following: pre-1714 4, 7–8, 8, 10, 34–7, 68, 69, 71, 73, 74, 121, 129, 183, 203, 327; 1714–1800 6, 7–8, 8, 93–4, 151, 153–4, 170, 172–6, 179, 203, 211, 231; 19th-century 7–8, 208–9, 211, 231; and Nonconformity 4, 12, 252
Whig historiography: pre-1800 4–5, 7–8, 8–9, 11, 14, 17, 35–7, 69, 71, 73, 122, 151, 161, 172, 174, 175, 176, 179, 185, 194, 211, 218, 219, 228n, 230, 231, 248, 269, 271, 272, 273, 291, 327, 332, 339, 340, 346, 348, 351, 352–3; post-1800 7–8, 17, 208–9, 211, 212–13, 219, 228, 228–9, 229, 230, 231, 249, 270, 271, 272, 273, 288–9, 291, 298, 332, 339, 340, 346
Carlyle and Whig history 269, 272, 272–3, 273, 288–9
Whig political thought 140, 141, 151, 165, 201–2, 213, 349, 352; *see also* republicanism

White, R., engraver 22, 102
Whitehaven, Cromwellianism in 306
Whitelocke, Bulstrode, MP and memorialist 29, 44, 124, 191, 345
Widdecombe, Ann, politician, her opinion of Cromwell 343
Wildman, John, Leveller and commonwealthman 140, 143, 317, 327, 329, 350
Wilkes, John 153, 351
his afflictions 174, 188, 246, 330
his thinking 163, 203, 204, 209, 329
William I
Carlyle on 278
see also 'Norman Yoke'
William II 254
William III
reign of 4, 8, 33, 34–7, 38, 74, 77, 121, 173, 177, 183
contemporary perceptions of him 33, 51, 66, 73, 74, 76, 77, 85, 152, 158, 162, 164–5
retrospective assessments 152, 171, 175, 195 , 204, 224, 226–7
Williams, Daniel, Nonconformist divine 97
Winstanley, Gerrard, Digger 319, 333, 359
Winstanley, William, his *England's Worthies* 330
Wiltshire 318
and Ludlow family 23, 25, 26, 82, 114, 202
Witt, John and Cornelis de, Dutch statesmen, murdered 51
Wood, Anthony, his *Athenae Oxonienses* 183
Worcester, battle of (1651) 29, 78, 85, 220, 313
Wordsworth, William 207, 237, 238, 242
Workers' Educational Association 316

Yeames, W. F., painter 229
Yorke, Henry, radical writer 188, 206, 210, 211, 225, 353–4

Index of Modern Historians and Editors

For historians who wrote before 1918, see the General Index

Abbott, W. C. 314, 354
Adamson, J. S. A. 359
Armitage, David 348
Ashley, Maurice 354–5
Aylmer, Gerald 349, 358

Bailyn, Bernard 121, 351
Bebbington, D. W. 356
Beales, Derek 348
Beard, Charles 336
Best, Geoffrey 348
Binfield, Clyde 354, 358
Blom, H. W. 350
Bond, W. H. 351
Bradstock, Andrew 359
Brewer, John 349, 352
Bromley, J. S. 355
Brooks, Colin 349
Brooks, David 358
Browning, Reed 352
Burrow, John 346
Burtt, Shelley 352

Carlton, Charles 346
Champion, Justin 97, 349
Champneys, Norma Dalrymple 355
Claeys, Gregory 354
Clarke, Aidan 347
Claydon, Tony 349
Clayton, Timothy 355
Coates, W. H. 347
Colley, Linda 352, 353
Collini, Stefan 355, 356
Corns, Thomas 346
Cozens-Hardy, Basil 351
Cunningham, Hugh 353
Cunningham, Valentine 358

Davis, J. C. 355
Darbishire, Helen 348
Deconinck-Brossard, Françoise 346
Dickinson, H. T. 346
Dinwiddy, John 353
Donno, Elizabeth Story 352
Downie, J. A. 349
Dunbabin, J. P. D. 355
Dunn, John 352–3

Edgar, F. T. R. 346
Fielding, Kenneth J. 356
Fletcher, Anthony 347
Frank, Joseph 336
French, John Milton 356
Furtardo, Peter 353

Garnett, Jane 354
Gentles, Ian 348, 356
Gerrard, Christine 352, 353
Gillingham, John 345
Goldgar, Bertram 352

Goldie, Mark 349, 353
Goldsmith, John 358
Goldsmith, Maurice 352
Greaves, Richard L. 348

Haller, William 336
Hamowy, Ronald 351
Harris, Robert 352
Harris, Tim 349
Harrison, Brian 354
Hayton, D. W. 84, 349
Heffer, Simon 356
Helmstadter, Richard 356
Hibbert, Christopher 357
Hill, Bridget 351
Hill, Christopher 18, 320, 331, 335, 336, 337, 358–9
Himy, Armand 348
Holmes, Clive 348
Holorenshaw, Henry 359
Horn, Pamela 357
Houston, Alan Craig 348, 351
Hughes, John F. 348
Hustvedt, Sigurd B. 353

Israel, Jonathan 353

James, Robert Rhodes 358
Janse, Ronald 350

Kaplan, Fred 356
Karsten, Peter 235, 350, 354
Kenyon, J. P. 346
Klein, Lawrence 349
Klingberg, Frank J. 353
Knoppers, Laura Lunger 355
Kolbrener, William 348
Kossmann, E. 355

Lamont, William 347, 348
Lang, Timothy 354
Langford, Paul 352
Le Quesne, Lawrence 356
Lloyd-Jones, Hugh 350
Lyons, F. S. L. 358

MacGillivray, Royce 345
Machin, G. I. T. 356
McKendrick, Neil 352
MacLachlan, Alastair 359
MacLean, Gerald 347
McLean, Janet 357
Macpherson, C. B. 336
Maltzahn, Nicholas von 348, 353
Marsh, Peter 356
Mason, Tim 320, 326
Matthew, Colin 354
Mendle, Michael 358
Mitchell, Leslie 351
Morrill, John 347, 348
Mulier, Eco Haitsma 350

Nevett, Paul 358

Ogg, David 348–9

Petegorsky, D. W. 320, 333, 334, 335, 336
Peters, Marie 352
Petty, C. P. 357
Pincus, Steven 348
Pocock, J. G. A. 346, 350
Popkin, Richard 348
Porter, Stephen 308, 346, 357

Quinault, Roland 357

Rajan, Balachandra 353
Randall, Helen 346
Read, Benedict 357
Richardson, R. C. 345, 354
Rivers, Isabel 352
Robbins, Caroline 87, 349, 351, 354
Rose, Craig 348
Rosenberg, John D. 356
Røstvig, Marie-Sophie 352
Rowe, Violet A. 200, 350, 356
Rowland, Peter 54
Russell, Conrad 347
Russell Smith, H. R. 353

Samuel, Ralph 354, 358
Sainsbury, John 353
Sauer, Elizabeth 353
Saunders, Charles R. 356
Schochet, Gordon 350
Schwoerer, Lois 349
Scott, Jonathan 158, 350
Sensabaugh, George F. 348
Sharples, M. 356
Short, K. R. M. 354
Skinner, Quentin 348, 352
Smith, Alan 355
Snow, Vernon 347
Spurr, John 346, 349
Stapleton, Julia 356
Stephan, Deborah 346
Strong, Roy 278n., 346
Sullivan, Robert 117, 349

Taft, Barbara 351
Thomas, Keith 358
Thomas, Peter D. G. 351
Thomas, Peter W. 345
Thomas, William 355
Thompson, E. P. 320, 331
Trela, Dale 356
Trevelyan, G. M. 18
Trevor-Roper, Hugh 346, 347
Tyacke, Nicholas 359

Underdown, David 349

Vogeler, Martha S. 357
Voitle, Robert 349

Walsh, John 262n
Watson, George 346
Watts, Michael 356
Weinrob, Ben 357
West, Thomas G. 350
Whatmore, Richard 355
Wolfe, D. M. 336
Womersley, David 346
Woodfine, Philip 352
Woolrych, Austin 358
Wootton, David 350

Yolton, J. W. 353
Young, Anne Steele 347
Young, Brian 355

Zook, Melinda 349, 351
Zwicker, Steven 348